DB2 9 System Administration
for z/OS
Certification Study Guide

DB2 9
System Administration
for z/OS
Certification Study Guide

Judy H. Nall

MC Press Online, LP
Lewisville, TX 75077

DB2 9 System Administration for z/OS: Certification Study Guide
Judy H. Nall

First Edition
First Printing—July 2010

Every attempt has been made to provide correct information. However, the publisher and the author do not guarantee the accuracy of the book and do not assume responsibility for information included in or omitted from it.

The following terms are trademarks or registered trademarks of International Business Machines Corporation in the United States, other countries, or both: DB2, Lotus, Tivoli, WebSphere, Rational, IBM, the IBM logo, and IBM Press. Java and all Java-based trademarks are trademarks of Sun Microsystems, Inc. in the United States, other countries, or both. Microsoft, Windows, Windows NT, and the Windows logo are trademarks of the Microsoft Corporation in the United States, other countries, or both. Linux is a registered trademark of Linus Torvalds. Intel, Intel Inside (logo), MMX, and Pentium are trademarks of Intel Corporation in the United States, other countries, or both. OSF/1 and UNIX are registered trademarks and The Open Group is a trademark of the The Open Group in the United States and other countries. Other company, product, or service names mentioned herein may be trademarks or service marks their respective owners.

MC Press offers excellent discounts on this book when ordered in quantity for bulk purchases or special sales, which may include custom covers and content particular to your business, training goals, marketing focus, and branding interest.

For information regarding permissions or special orders, please contact:
> MC Press
> Corporate Offices
> 125 N. Woodland Trail
> Lewisville, TX 75077 USA

For information regarding sales and/or customer service, please contact:
> MC Press
> P.O. Box 4300
> Big Sandy, TX 75755-4300 USA

ISBN: 978-158347-096-1

Acknowledgments

There are many people who have helped me over the course of my career
and in writing this book. I would like to thank them all and
apologize to anyone I forget to list; you know I love you.

First, I want to thank my Uncle Billy.
Without his generosity, there would be no book and a lot of other things.

To my brother and sister-in-law, David and Kathy Hobson,
for standing by me when things got really bad.

To my parents, whom I miss every single day; love you.

I would like to thank Richard Nall,
for twenty-five years of support in all my endeavors.
I wish him health and happiness.

To Gary Joehlin of Pikes Peak Software.
You are a true friend and a great DB2er.
Thank you for all your time and effort in editing the book,
making suggestions, and keeping me straight.
I really don't know what I would have done without you.

Roger E. Sanders, author and DB2 expert.
You were so helpful in getting me started in writing
and so generous in your time and expertise. Thank you.

Merrikay Lee, my publisher at MC Press,
who has the patience and fortitude to keep dealing with me.
You are a gem; thank you for this opportunity.

Katie Tipton, the best editor in the entire world.
You made things so easy. Thanks.

Roger Miller at IBM,
who has been a guiding light throughout all my DB2 years.
Thank you for all your help with the book and your dedication to DB2.

Susan Visser, Publishing Program Manager,
Information Management, IBM Software Group, IBM Canada,
who always believed in me. What an inspiration you are!
Thank you so much for everything you have done for me.

Susan Dykman, IM WW Certification Delivery Program Manager, IBM,
who gave me an opportunity to work on the 737 certification exam.
Your support and help is so much appreciated.

Judy Ruby-Brown at IBM.
I told you once you were my hero, and I wasn't kidding.
Rock on, girl.

Teressa Jimenez, IBM DB2 Gold Team Program Leader
and IBM Analyst Relations, System z Pricing and Licensing, IBM.
Thank you for supporting our group, helping me, and putting up with us all.

The IBM DB2 Gold Team members,
especially my friends Marie Buretta and Gerald Hodge,
who are always ready to jump in and help.
Marie, you are something else, girl; thanks for the support.
Gerald, you have been so helpful in so many ways; thank you.

John Morbach, someone who gave me a chance to work with DB2
when it was first released. What would I have done if you
had not given me that opportunity?

Thanks to all my friends, who listened and supported me,
especially Larry Long and Holly Nelson.
Also the LA (Lower Alabama) girls: Cindy, Mona, and Angie.

Last, but not least, my best friends: Maggie, Minnie, and Willie.
You have listened to DB2 for months.
I deem you all DB2 9 for z/OS System Administrator Certified #737 Dogs —
big kisses to you all.

May all who take the time to read this book
benefit and have a happy DB2 experience.

Contents

Introduction to DB2 9 for z/OS

This chapter addresses the job responsibilities of the DB2 system administrator, describes what to expect on the IBM DB2 9 System Administrator for z/OS Exam (Test 000-737), and reviews the basic prerequisites assumed for the reader of this book.

Purpose of the Book

As the certification study guide for Test 737, this book guides you through the responsibilities, tasks, and methods used by a DB2 9 for z/OS system administrator. It covers all the objectives of the exam and provides sample exam questions and answers to test your knowledge.

The book provides a broad understanding of the responsibilities of a DB2 for z/OS system administrator, gives examples of day-to-day work requirements, describes techniques to assist you in your work, and provide details about how to develop your skill sets.

Test 737: DB2 9 System Administrator for z/OS

The system administrator exam certifies that the candidate has the skills, knowledge, and abilities to describe the architecture and administer the processes required to plan, install, manage, and tune secure DB2 for z/OS environments. To obtain this certification, you must pass two tests:

- *Test 730*: DB2 9 Family Fundamentals

- *Test 737*: DB2 9 System Administrator for z/OS

Test 737 is 90 minutes in duration and consists of 60 questions. The passing score is 62 percent. The exam consists of six sections, each of which includes questions and some scenarios for you to evaluate:

- *Section 1: Installation and Migration* (15 percent of the test) — Tests your knowledge of the installation and migration planning process, how to execute an installation/migration plan, and how to evaluate appropriate subsystem parameter (DSNZPARM) configuration settings (Chapter 3)

- *Section 2: Security and Auditing* (7 percent) — Assesses your understanding of how to protect DB2 resources, auditing techniques, and role-based security (Chapter 4)

- *Section 3: System Operation and Maintenance* (21.5 percent) — Deals with the management of DB2 components, commands, monitoring, and threads (Chapter 7)

- *Section 4: Backup and Recovery* (20 percent) — Tests your knowledge of the procedures for system-level backup, recovery from system failures, and disaster recovery processes (Chapter 5)

- *Section 5: Performance and Tuning* (21.5 percent) — Presents scenarios and asks you to analyze the performance; tests your knowledge of buffer pools, DSNZPARMs, statistics, traces and tools, efficient use of memory, and DB2 workload manager settings (Chapter 6)

- *Section 6: Troubleshooting* (15 percent) — Tests your problem-solving abilities, including your knowledge of operator commands and traces, how to identify contention problems, diagnostics in dealing with utilities, and resolving and identifying data sharing problems (Chapter 7)

Certification Web Site

The IBM Professional Certification Program Web site, *http://www.ibm.com/certify*, provides information that can help you prepare for the exam, including a sample test, a list of training resources to help you prepare for the exam, and information about testing centers worldwide. Take the time to visit this site and become familiar with the information it offers.

The sample assessment test is a good place to start. You can practice taking the exam and see how well you score on each section to evaluate your strengths and weaknesses. Remember, though, that passing the sample test does not result in credentials. For instructions about how to access the Web-based assessment test delivery tool, including registration and payment procedures, see the information page for Test 737.

DB2 System Administration Requirements

To work as a DB2 9 for z/OS system administrator, you need a strong background in DB2 for z/OS. For example, if you are currently a database administrator with a couple years of experience, or if you have several years as a DB2 advanced programming lead under your belt, you have the baseline to start working on your system administration skill set and certification.

Your understanding and background should include familiarity with the DB2 and System z architectures.

Knowledge of DB2

Your DB2 experience should include the following:

- DB2 catalog tables, DB2 directory, bootstrap data sets (BSDSs)
- DB2 active and archive logging
- DB2 virtual buffer pools (VBPs)
- SQL query writing, **EXPLAIN**, and troubleshooting
- Data Definition Language (DDL) and physical structures in DB2
- DB2 IBM administration tools and the Optimization Service Center (OSC)
- IBM or other vendor DB2 utilities (e.g., **COPY**, **LOAD**, **RUNSTATS**)

System z Architecture

Your z/OS skill set should include the following:

- How to write Job Control Language (JCL) to execute a job in z/OS

- How to use the Interactive System Productivity Facility (ISPF) and Program Development Facility (PDF) to display data set lists or define a data set

- How to use the System Display and Search Facility (SDSF) and/or the Interactive Output Facility (IOF) to find job execution information

- Familiarity with the System Modification Program/Extended (SMP/E) tool and its basic functions

- Knowledge of Workload Manager (WLM) and its basic functions

Familiarity with other software products, such as Customer Information Control System (CICS), WebSphere, and non-IBM vendor offerings is a plus. We will build on your DB2, z/OS, and product skills throughout this book.

To obtain more information about DB2 9 for z/OS, visit IBM's DB2 for z/OS Web site, *http://www-01.ibm.com/software/data/db2/zos*, where you will find downloads, product support, product documentation, and more.

CHAPTER 2

DB2 for z/OS Overview

This chapter reviews the tasks, services, structure, architecture, and components of DB2 9 for z/OS that constitute required knowledge for a DB2 system administrator.

CSECTs and Subcomponents

Let's begin with a short overview of how the DB2 code is structured internally:

- In DB2, each object module contains a single control section (CSECT).

- A CSECT typically performs one function, and the object module and CSECT have the same name.

- Member **DSNWMODS** in library **SDSNSAMP** contains the readable data set associated with a CSECT for DB2.

- CSECT names and message identifiers begin with the letters "DSN" in DB2.

- The fourth character of a DB2 CSECT name identifies a subcomponent. For example, the prefix **DSNJ** indicates the recovery log manager subcomponent, and these letters are used for the module and message prefixes related to that facility.

DB2 subcomponents are groups of closely related DB2 for z/OS modules that work together to provide a general function. There are three groups of subcomponents in DB2:

- System services

- Database services

- Distributed Data Facility (DDF) services

DB2 Resource Managers

The software that comprises the DB2 resource managers is usually responsible for managing a specific resource. The resource being managed can be physical or logical. DB2 usually has one subcomponent per resource manager, but exceptions exist. For example, the precompiler is not a resource manager, and the instrumentation facilities subcomponent contains two resource managers.

A resource manager identifier (RMID) identifies a resource manager. The RMID indicates the source of diagnostic output in your dumps. For your reference, the appendix at the end of this book provides a list of subcomponents and identifiers.

Address Spaces

In DB2, there are four major address spaces, some of which are known by several different acronyms:

- The main address space (**DSN1MSTR**), also known as the system services address space (SSAS) or the Data Systems Control Facility (DSCF)

- The data manager address space (**DSN1DBM1**), also known as the database services address space (DBAS or DSAS) or the Advanced Database Management Facility (ADMF)

- The Distributed Data Facility address space (**DSN1DIST**)

- The Internal Resource Lock Manager address space (**IRLMPROC**)

System Services

System services manage logs, agent services, and more by executing various subcomponents in the system services address space. This address space is also called the Data Systems Control Facility space.

Here are a few of the subcomponents that execute in the SSAS:

- System parameter manager
- Recovery manager
- Recovery log manager
- Group manager
- Distributed transaction manager
- Storage manager
- Agent services manager
- Message generator
- Initialization procedures
- Instrumentation facilities
- General command processor
- Subsystem support

Database Services

Database services use system services and z/OS to handle the actual database structures. The database services address space consists of three main components:

- Buffer manager
- Data manager (DM)
- Relational data system

The function of the DBAS is to manage the physical structures and data, execute SQL, and manage the buffers. Even though these are independent components, they work together to make a proper subsystem of z/OS. The database services address space is also referred to as the Advanced Database Management Facility address space.

Subcomponents of interest that execute in the DBAS are:

- LOB manager

- Service controller

- Stored procedures manager

- Data space manager

- Utilities (these work with associated code in an allied address space)

Distributed Data Facility Services

Running as an additional address space in DB2, the DDF services consist of one subcomponent called the Distributed Data Facility. DDF controls the connecting of distributed applications to DB2 for z/OS. The naming convention for this subsystem is *xxx*DIST.

Four resource managers are associated with DDF:

- Data Communications Resource Manager

- Distributed Data Interchange Services

- Distributed Relational Data System Manager

- Distributed Transaction Manager

These subcomponents execute in the DDF address space.

DB2 Distributed Relational Data Architecture (DRDA) subsystems and other relational databases can communicate with DDF by using Transmission Control Protocol/Internet Protocol (TCP/IP) or Virtual Telecommunications Access Method (VTAM) on the same network. DDF supports two network protocols, Systems Network Architecture (SNA) and TCP/IP, as well as the DRDA database communications protocol.

DRDA is set of database protocols that describe the architecture that allows connection and access to distributed relational data in multiple database systems. DRDA defines what must be exchanged and how it must be exchanged and then coordinates the communications between systems. Three components make up DRDA:

- Application requestor

- Application server

- Database server

Internal Resource Lock Manager

DB2 also requires the address space subsystem services of the Internal Resource Lock Manager (IRLM), which resides in its own address space. (Note that this "IRLM" is different from the Information Management System, or IMS, Resource Lock Manager.) The lock manager works with DB2 to serialize access to data. DB2 requests locks from IRLM to ensure data integrity when applications, utilities, and commands all attempt to access the same data.

In DB2 9, you must continue to specify the IRLM-related subsystem parameters **PC** and **MAXCSA**, but their values are no longer used. IBM has retained these parameters for compatibility reasons. Specific system site specifications now determine the amount of available storage for IRLM private control blocks, including locks. All IRLM locks are in the IRLM private address space; locks are no longer placed in the extended common service area (ECSA). IRLM control block structures are estimated at 540 bytes per lock and reside above the 2 GB bar. **DXB**, not **DSN**, is the prefix for IRLM.

Other Address Spaces

DB2 communicates with other address spaces, known as *allied address spaces*, in the z/OS environment. DB2 communicates with these "allied agents" to facilitate requests. Here is a list of allied agents with which DB2 communicates:

- Time Sharing Option (TSO) attachment facility

- Subsystem support

- Message generator, stand-alone only (**DSN1SDMP**)

- IMS attachment facility

- Call attachment facility

- Customer Information Control System (CICS) attachment facility

- Resource Recovery Services (RRF) attachment facility

- Utilities

Connections or threads to these allied agents are controlled through the subsystem parameter **CTHREAD** (which defaults to **200**, has a maximum value of **2000**, and is updatable online). The **CTHREAD** setting defines the number of concurrently allocated threads for local connections. If you find that you are waiting for a connection to access the DB2 subsystem, you might need to increase the number of allied connections specified through **CTHREAD**.

The **CTHREAD** setting, along with the **MAXDBAT** DSNZPARM, protects the virtual storage allocation. Be careful not to overcommit your virtual storage resources. If the number of remote threads is queued with work waiting, you might need to increase the **MAXDBAT** value.

Utilities use parallelism, so you will have one thread for each utility and an additional thread for each subtask. Thus, a single utility may be using many threads. You need to make sure to specify a **CTHREAD** value that will accommodate utility parallelism.

Non-allied address spaces do not communicate with DB2. Several subcomponents execute in non-allied address spaces:

- DB2 does not communicate with the DB2 precompiler (PRE), but the precompiler may require an allied address space, depending on the precompiler options you have selected.

- The full message generator for DB2 resides in the system services address space. The message generator can also run stand-alone in allied or non-allied address spaces.

- Portions of the instrumentation subcomponent run in a non-allied address space.

- DB2 stand-alone utilities run in non-allied address spaces.

Work Requests in DB2

DB2 tasks and agents are subcomponents that run in an allied address space. Each DB2 work request is represented by an agent. Several classes of agents exist: system agents, allied agents, and database access agents. DB2 tracks the agent (the work) using an agent control element (ACE). Each ACE is associated with one or more execution blocks (EBs).

A one-to-one relationship exists between a z/OS execution unit and an execution block. An EB is used to describe each unique unit of dispatch work, which can be dispatched in either task control block (TCB) or service request block (SRB) mode in z/OS. All allied agents to which the primary EB is related point to the user's home address TCB.

In the DB2 address space, when execution units are created in TCB mode, they are known as *service tasks*. Resource managers in DB2 can dynamically delete and create service tasks. When you initialize DB2, service tasks are created, and these usually exist until DB2 is stopped. The service tasks remain idle until their services are needed in DB2.

Examples of permanent service tasks include the following:

- System service tasks
- Log manager
- Recovery manager
- Database services tasks
- Buffer manager
- Data manager
- DDF tasks
- Distributed transaction manager

DB2 9 System Structure Basics

Figure 2.1 provides an overview of the DB2 subsystems.

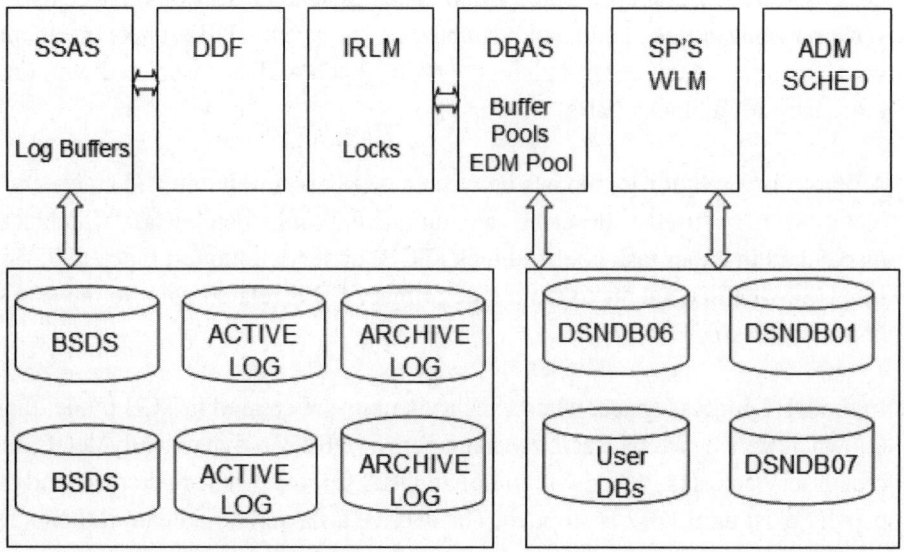

Figure 2.1: Subsystem overview

DB2 uses several types of private address spaces, each requiring storage:

- DB2 system services address space (**DSN1MSTR**)

- DB2 database services address space (**DSN1DBM1**)

- DB2 DDF address space (**DSN1DIST**)

- IRLM address space (**IRLMPROC**)

- DB2 allied agent address spaces

- DB2 stored procedures address spaces (established by the Workload Manager, or WLM)

- DB2 administrative scheduler address space

When you start your DB2 subsystems, there is a recommended dispatching priority for these address spaces in z/OS: Without locking to protect your resources, you cannot begin, so IRLM is started first. Next, you start the DB2 performance monitors, then the **DBM1** address space, and then the **MSTR** address space.

Attachment Facilities

An *attachment facility* provides the interface between DB2 and another environment, such as TSO. In TSO and your batch environments, you can use the TSO, call, and Resource Recovery Services (RRS) attachment facilities to access DB2. Other attachment facilities, including those for CICS and IMS, are DB2 subcomponents that run in the user's address space.

Figure 2.2 depicts how the various attachment facilities interact with DB2.

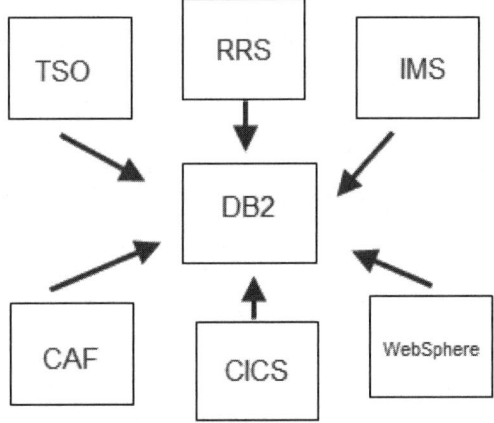

Figure 2.2: Attachment facilities

Call Attachment Facility

For TSO and batch applications that require tight control over their session environment, DB2 provides the Call Attachment Facility (CAF) as an option for connection. Programs can explicitly control the state of their connections to DB2 by using connection functions supplied by CAF.

First, make available the CAF load module, **DSNALI**. Once this language interface module is available, your program can use CAF to connect to DB2 by including

SQL statements or Instrumentation Facility Interface (IFI) calls in your program. You can also access CAF by writing explicit **CALL DSNALI** statements.

Resource Recovery Services

DB2 supports Resource Recovery Services, which is a newer implementation of an attachment capability. This z/OS system feature coordinates the two-phase commit processing of recoverable resources.

RRS runs in its own address space and can be started and stopped independently of DB2. Once z/OS RRS is started, you can run the Resource Recovery Services Attachment Facility (RRSAF) application. RRS needs to be at an equal or higher priority than the dispatching priority of DB2.

After RRS is started, you can start or restart an RRSAF connection. The RRSAF language interface load module, **DSNRLI**, must be available. Your program can then use RRSAF to connect to DB2 by using SQL statements or IFI calls in the program or by using a **CALL DSNRLI** statement to invoke RRSAF connection functions to establish a connection between DB2 and RRS and allocate DB2 resources.

Stored procedures running in a WLM address space require the RRS attachment facility. Resources such as SQL tables, Data Language/I (DL/I) databases, MQSeries message programs running in batch or TSO, and recoverable Virtual Storage Access Method (VSAM) files within a single transaction scope can use the RRS attachment facility. Keep in mind that the DB2 command **DISPLAY THREAD** will include the RRS unit of recovery (UR) IDs for DB2 threads.

Threads

When a thread is allocated, the storage used by that thread is held until de-allocation. The **CONTSTOR** parameter in macro **DSN6SPRM** controls each active thread's working storage area. The default value for **CONTSTOR** is **NO**. If you are experiencing a high private virtual storage usage in **DBM1**, setting **CONTSTOR** to **YES** may reduce the unused storage. This setting enables DB2 to periodically check the thread storage that is unused from a committing process and return that storage to the operating system. You can set the **CONTSTOR** parameter dynamically using the DB2 **SET SYSPARM** command.

DB2 will examine the thread use of the storage pool, and if the thread has used more than 2 MB or if there are more than 50 commits, the storage blocks that have been used and are no longer in use are freed and returned to the operating system. This procedure can reduce the amount of virtual storage used in **DBM1**, especially for long-running threads. However, you incur associated CPU overhead from **GETMAIN** and **FREEMAIN** requests to the operating system, so you need to carefully consider the benefits.

One other thing to keep in mind: Use of the **RELEASE(DEALLOCATE)** parameter on the **BIND** command requires more virtual storage due to the increase in the size of the package or plan that occurs with this parameter. Specifying **RELEASE(DEALLOCATE)** nullifies the process of using **CONTSTOR YES**, and no storage contraction will take place. That is because a **COMMIT** does not trigger the **CONTSTOR YES** processing. Until the thread is actually deallocated, it just keeps getting bigger.

Storage

DB2 allocates different subpools for storage. Storage pool 229 (**SP229**) is storage acquired by a **GETMAIN** request and released by a **FREEMAIN** request in **DBM1**. Allied and database access threads are users of this storage.

The z/OS Resource Measurement Facility (RMF) tracks how much virtual storage you are using and reports this information in the Virtual Storage Private Area Report (VSTOR) in System Management Facility (SMF) type 78-2 records. To get an idea of the total virtual storage consumption, you can set the option **REPORTS(VSTOR(D, *xxxx*DBM1))**. In DB2, you can use Instrumentation Facility Component Identifiers (IFCIDs) 217 and 225 to view the consumption of virtual storage in **DBM1**.

Real and Auxiliary Storage

DB2 uses the extended common service area of z/OS virtual storage and the z/OS Shared Memory Facility. In z/OS, the 64-bit address space includes a virtual line at the 16 MB address and a virtual line called "the bar" that marks the 2 GB address. Storage below the 2 GB address is referred to as "below the bar," and storage above this address is "above the bar." The area above the bar is intended for data, and no programs run above the bar. Figure 2.3 depicts the memory areas of z/OS.

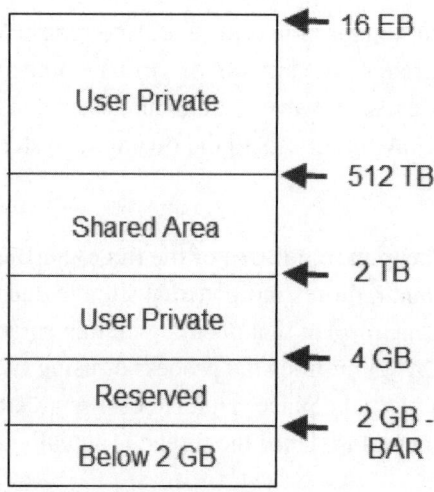

Figure 2.3: z/OS memory

There is no area above the bar that is common to all address spaces, and no system control blocks exist above the bar. There is also an IBM reserve area of storage above the bar for special uses.

You can set a limit on how much virtual storage above the bar each address space can use. This limit is represented by the **MEMLIMIT** keyword on the **JOB** and **EXEC** statements. The **MEMLIMIT** setting limits the total amount of usable virtual storage above the bar for a single user:

- If you do not set a **MEMLIMIT**, the system default is **0**, meaning that no address space can use virtual storage above the bar.

- If you want to use virtual storage above the bar, you must set a **MEMLIMIT** explicitly. You can set an installation default **MEMLIMIT** through SMF member **SMFPRM***xx* in **PARMLIB**.

- You can also set a **MEMLIMIT** for a specific address space either in the JCL that creates the address space or by using SMF exit **IEFUSI**.

- The default takes effect if a job does not specify **MEMLIMIT** on the JCL **JOB** or **EXEC** statement or set **REGION=0** in the JCL.

- The **MEMLIMIT** specified in an **IEFUSI** exit routine overrides all other **MEMLIMIT** settings.

- If **REGION=0** is specified in the JCL and the **IEFUSI** exit limits the **REGION** size but does not set **MEMLIMIT**, **MEMLIMIT** defaults to the **REGION** size above 16 MB.

Distributed Data Facility

The DDF address space is started as part of the startup procedure in the **DSN1DIST** address space. The DB2 9 improvements for DDF are available in all modes, and DDF now uses 64-bit storage.

Processing Flow

DDF reduces the CPU processing time by using service request blocks rather than task control blocks. Tasks can request that an SRB be scheduled that requests a service to take place. The SRB can be in the same address space or a different one. The data that is shared by the task and the service must reside in common storage.

Enclave

An *enclave* is an independent, dispatchable unit of work that can span multiple address spaces and can include multiple SRBs and TCBs. The enclave is an anchor for accumulating the resources consumed by a transaction regardless of where it may be executing. It provides a way to account for resources consumed by multiple work units, even across multiple address spaces. The MVS System Resource Manager (SRM) manages enclaves separately according to their goals or priorities.

DB2 owns all the enclaves coming into the system through DDF, and they are created by DDF on the incoming connection when the first SQL statement starts to execute:

1. A connection request comes to **DDF**, associated with a DBAT.

2. At the first SQL statement, **DDF** calls WLM to create the enclave.

   » The enclave is the basis for assigning resources to the DDF transaction.

- You assign performance goals to enclave transactions.

   » The enclave is the basis of reporting thread performance.

3. WLM manages the enclave based on assigned workload characteristics.

Deletion of an enclave depends on whether the DBAT can become pooled:

- If the DBAT becomes pooled, the enclave is deleted.

- If the DBAT cannot become pooled; the enclave is deleted only at thread termination time.

- If the DBAT becomes type 1 inactive (private protocol connection), the enclave is deleted.

When a request comes in over TCP/IP using DRDA, DB2 schedules an SRB. DB2 then creates an enclave for each transaction and classifies the request. When queries access DB2 via DRDA over TCP/IP, connections are dispatched within z/OS as enclave SRBs. A portion of each enclave SRB work can be directed to a z/System Integrated Information Processor (zIIP) engine. Only DRDA work coming from TCP/IP is zIIP engine eligible. DB2 notifies the WLM that an enclave is eligible to direct a portion of the work to a zIIP processor. WLM, along with the z/OS dispatcher, dispatches the work to a zIIP or to a general processor.

Management of the work to DDF is done with the use of MVS enclaves to exchange data across address spaces and the WLM. Running in DDF, these processes can access the database address space by using cross memory services (CMS). Through CMS, the data and programs can be synchronously accessed in different address spaces.

The **DDF**, **DBM1**, and **IRLM** address spaces allocate control blocks above the 2 GB bar in 64-bit addressing mode.

Other DDF Information

Native stored procedures invoked from DRDA over TCP/IP, or queries that access DB2 via DRDA over TCP/IP, are dispatched in z/OS as enclave SRBs, and a portion of their work can be directed to the zIIP engine.

If DRDA work is requested via SNA, it will not be zIIP-eligible. Some batch and non-native SQL stored procedures are not implemented in SRB mode or in enclave SRBs that would not be eligible for zIIP processing.

In DB2 9, you can also still communicate using private protocol from DB2 to DB2, although this method is not recommended. You should take a look at the tools provided in DB2 9 to help you migrate away from private protocol. One of those tools is the private to DRDA protocol REXX tool, **DSNTP2DP**. During migration, the customized **DSNTIJPD** job invokes the **DSNTP2DP** tool. You can no longer **BIND** plans and packages for private protocol because **DSN6SYSP.DBPROTCL** in the DSNZPARMs has been eliminated. To help with the migration task, the generic collection ID **DSNCOLLID** is defined to maintain collections of remote packages.

DDF and z/OS Shared Virtual Memory

DB2 9 for z/OS supports 64-bit addressability in DDF using z/OS *shared virtual memory (SVM)*. SVM is a new virtual storage type that permits multiple address spaces to share storage. The shared memory exists only once in z/OS instead of in each address space. SVM is available to address spaces that are registered with z/OS as being able to share this storage.

Before DB2 9, when DDF invoked DB2 to process a request, the data was copied from the **DDF** address space to the **DBM1** address space and then copied back to **DDF** at the completion of the request using cross-memory (XM) moves. Virtual storage in the **DBM1** address space below the 2 GB bar is reduced in DB2 9 by running DDF in 64-bit mode and accessing the SVM areas. This new virtual storage type lets multiple address spaces share storage, is always addressable, avoids access register (AR) and XM moves between **DDF** and **DBM1**, reduces data formatting and data movement, and improves performance.

The database services address space creates a new virtual shared object (VSO) in shared virtual memory at DB2 initialization time. As the **DBM1**, **MSTR**, and **DIST** address spaces go through their local storage initialization, they are registered to use this VSO.

DB2 startup requires 128 GB of 64-bit shared private storage for each DB2 subsystem above the 2 GB bar for shared memory objects. The default size is 2 TB; DB2 requires a minimum of 128 GB.

All DB2 address spaces for the subsystem are registered with z/OS to access the virtual shared object. The address spaces are registered with z/OS to be able to share this storage and also have visibility to this storage.

A memory object in SVM is a contiguous range of virtual addresses:

- These pages are allocated by programs as a number of application pages.

- The pages are in 1 MB multiples on a 1 MB boundary.

- They exist once for each address space.

At the time each address space is terminated during shutdown, it requests that its interest in the VSO be deleted. At DB2 termination, the shared memory object is freed. It is interesting to note that almost all the control blocks for DDF have moved from ECSA to shared memory.

The DB2 utilities **CHECK INDEX**, **LOAD**, **REBUILD**, **REORG**, and **RUNSTATS** also take advantage of the DB2 VSO. The use of shared memory objects avoids the movement of rows between the batch and **DBM1** address spaces and reduces CPU usage. The environmental descriptor manager (EDM) pool also takes advantage of VSO.

Shared Memory Objects

The size of the shared memory addressing area is between 2 TB and 512 TB. To use this memory, an address space must be registered; there is no automatic addressability or access to it. The macro **IARV64** in z/OS provides virtual storage services for DB2. The z/OS parameter **HVSHARE** in member **IEASYS*xx*** in library **PARMLIB** registers and controls the address spaces.

In the **IARV64** macro, parameter **HVSHARE** governs how much virtual storage can be shared and permits multiple address spaces to share virtual storage above 2 GB. Be sure to define a high enough value for **HVSHARE** to satisfy all component requests for shared memory within your z/OS image.

To see the current defined storage and how much total storage is currently allocated, you can issue this z/OS command:

```
DISPLAY VIRTSTOR,HVSHARE
```

Two **IARV64** macro parameters allocate and allow access to data in a shared memory object:

- **IARV64 GETSHARED**

    » The shared memory object is allocated by the **GETSHARED** service.

    » This service creates a memory object that can be shared across multiple address spaces.

- **IARV64 SHAREMEMOBJ**

    » Parameters define the program request to the **SHAREMEMOBJ** service to get access to the shared memory object.

    » An address space can issue more than one **SHAREMEMOBJ** request for the same memory object.

    » You separate each request for the same memory object by specifying a different user token.

IFCIDs 217 and 225 track the space usage in DDF. In both 217 and 225, fields have been added to record the amount of virtual shared storage used by the ***ssnm*DBM1** address space. In 225, the trace records are changed from SMF type 102 to SMF type 100 subtype 4. To obtain this information, you need to make sure that statistics class 6 is activated. For each DB2 subsystem above the 2 GB bar, DB2 requires 128 GB of 64-bit shared private storage.

Shared Memory Storage Requirements Restriction

When using shared memory, you should see a decrease in overall storage allocation to **DSN1DIST**. Note that shared memory is not charged against the **MEMLIMIT** of an address space.

The shared memory storage enhancement requires

- z/Architecture, z/OS 1.7 or later

- Enablement of 64-bit virtual shared storage

- Sufficient shared private storage configured to allow all shared storage exploiters on the logical partition (LPAR) to allocate their shared objects

Figure 2.4 depicts multiple address spaces sharing storage. This configuration reduces data movement and data formatting and decreases virtual storage because the data exists only once. The data in the shared area can be shared across address spaces X, Y, and Z.

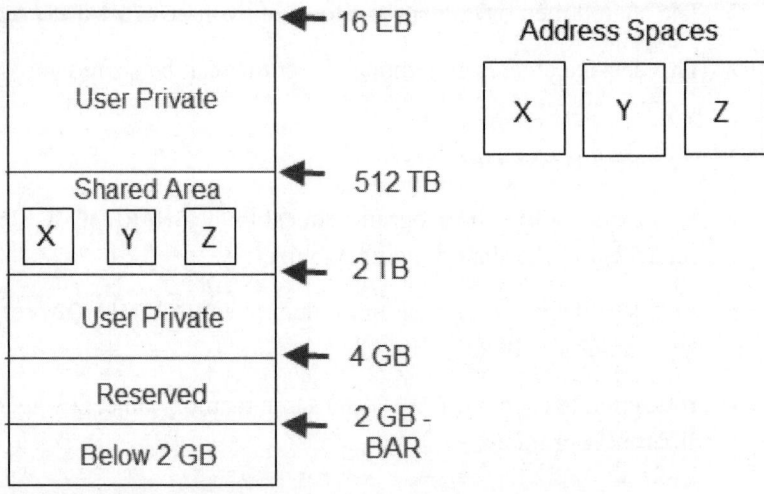

Figure 2.4: Data shared area

Informational APAR II14203 describes the TCP/IP and z/OS prerequisite APARs that are required to enable the shared memory enhancement. To take advantage of this functionality, make sure TCP/IP and z/OS have the required maintenance before migrating to DB2 9 for z/OS. Shared virtual memory resides above the 2 GB bar in z/OS and is organized as a virtual shared object that programs create.

Distributed Thread Processing

Database access threads in the **DBM1** address space are distributed thread connections. DB2 for z/OS supports thread pooling, which is actually inactive connections waiting for more work and associated with a remote requester.

An *inactive DBAT* (formerly called a type 1 inactive thread) has the same characteristics as the inactive threads that were available in releases before DB2 9. Inactive DBATs require a large number of threads to support a large number of connections. We refer to inactive type 1 DBATs as "real DBATs." These threads are idle between units of work. They use private protocol and the old style of inactive processing.

The **MAXTYPE1** parameter in macro **DSN6FAC** defines the number of inactive DBATs permitted by DB2. Be careful when setting this parameter because over-allocation can adversely affect system performance.

An *inactive connection* (previously called a type 2 inactive thread) uses less storage than an inactive DBAT and as such is preferred, but not all threads can be inactive connections. These connections are disassociated from the thread.

Threads that are not currently processing a unit of work are called *pooled threads*. Pooled threads can be reused for other connections, either new or inactive. Pooled threads typically represent a small number of threads that can be used to service a large number of connections and provide better resource utilization.

These DDF threads are defined in macro **DSN6FAC** by parameter **CMTSTAT**. To see the inactive type 2 DBATs in your system, use this **DISPLAY THREAD** command:

```
-DISPLAY THREAD TYPE(INACTIVE)
```

The purpose of a DBAT is to reuse an existing connection in **DBM1**. Without this pooling, each new connection request would create a new thread (DBAT) in **DBM1** each time. A pool of DBATs is created and maintained dynamically for use by any inbound DRDA connection. When work is committed, the DBAT is released back to the pool. With or without connection pooling, DDF creates a new connection when an application or agent request is made to DDF in DB2.

There is a separation of connections in DDF from the DBATs in **DBM1**. This separation results in no repeated creation and destruction of DBATs, which saves CPU time and reduces the memory requirements for DBATs and virtual storage. See PK75626 for this reference; PK77228 provides further information.

DSNZPARM Values to Control Threads

Several subsystem parameters work in conjunction with parameter **MAXTYPE1** to handle distributed thread processing support:

- **CMSTAT**: The **CMSTAT** parameter (field **DDF THREADS** on installation panel **DSNTIPR**) specifies the status a thread should take after a commit or rollback or when it no longer holds cursors against resources. The default value is **ACTIVE**. Change this setting to **INACTIVE** to enable DBAT pooling for DRDA access and more effective WLM classification per unit of work.

- **POOLINAC**: The **POOLINAC** parameter (field **POOL THREAD TIMEOUT** on installation panel **DSNTIP5**) sets a timeout value for the automatic termination of idle DBATs. The default setting is **120** (seconds).

- **MAXDBAT**: The **MAXDBAT** parameter (field **MAX REMOTE ACTIVE** on installation panel **DSNTIPE**) specifies the maximum number of concurrently active DBATs. As you find threads queued for remote work, this value should increase. The default value is **200**, and the setting cannot exceed **2000**. If you raise or lower the **MAXDBAT** value, you also raise or lower the storage requirements below the 2 GB bar in **DBM1**.

- **CONDBAT**: The **CONDBAT** parameter (field **MAX REMOTE CONNECTED** on installation panel **DSNTIPE**) sets a limit on the total number of inbound DDF connections. It is highly recommended that the setting for **MAXDBAT** be less than that for **CONDBAT**.

A rule of thumb is to set **CMTSTAT** to **INACTIVE**, adjust **CONDBAT** to the maximum number of connected DBATs that provide good performance, and set **MAXDBAT** to the maximum acceptable number of active DBATs.

To determine the total number of threads that can access data in DB2, add the values of **MAXDBAT** and **CTHREAD**. IFCID 225 provides details for major consumers. If you overextend the number of threads, you can potentially overextend virtual storage and cause DB2 to abend with abend code 878 (no storage available).

To help you monitor these situations and choose values for **MAXDBAT** and **CTHREAD**, IBM provides a no-cost program that writes to a comma-delimited trace output data set from IFCID 225 (SMF 102) for analysis. You can obtain this utility by going to *http://www-03.ibm.com/support/techdocs/ atsmastr.nsf/WebIndex/PRS3431* (document ID PRS3431 by Judy Ruby-Brown at IBM).

Depending on the communications protocol used, each DDF connection consumes approximately 7.5 KB of memory inside the **DIST** address space. In addition, each active DBAT consumes about 200 KB of memory at a minimum, depending on the type of SQL activity requested.

Private Protocol Access

We know that private protocol is going away in a future DB2 release. In your efforts to move away from it, you need to determine which applications use private protocol access and which sites those applications access. To obtain this information, run the following performance trace for IFCIDs 157 and 168:

```
-START TRACE(PERFM) CLASS(30) IFCID(157,168) DEST(GTF)
```

The trace report will show:

- SQL statements that reference aliases before they have been resolved

- Whether the package or plan that the statement is running under was bound with **DBPROTOCOL(PRIVATE)**

- The aliases that are referenced in the statement

To display additional details about the DDF environment, enter this command:

```
-DISPLAY DDF DETAIL
```

Native Stored Procedures in DB2 9

Native stored procedures — that is, those whose bodies are written entirely in SQL — are eligible for zIIP engine processing if they are invoked from DRDA TCP/IP connections. SQL queries that access DB2 via DRDA over TCP/IP connections are dispatched within z/OS as enclave SRBs, and z/OS directs a portion of this work to the zIIP. DRDA work that is requested via SNA is not zIIP-eligible. Native stored procedures are stored in the DB2 directory.

Database Management

The DB2 catalog is a database called **DSNDB06** that contains table spaces that reflect your objects, security, and access packages and plans. Most DB2 system table spaces use the naming convention **SYSIBM.SYS***xxxxxx* — for example, **SYSIBM.SYSTABLESPACE**.

You can have the catalog and user-defined databases, table spaces, and index spaces start automatically when DB2 is started. To specify this, use the **RESTART** option and the object definition **ALL** on the **DSNTIPS** installation panel.

Indexes on the DB2 catalog or directory tables are no different from indexes on any other tables created in DB2. DB2 catalog data can be accessed via indexes and links; there are no hashes in the catalog.

Before migration to DB2 9 for z/OS, a **REORG** of your catalog is recommended. You should increase the size of the underlying VSAM clusters/linear data sets for the catalog and directory before migrating.

In DD2 9, you can define up to 500 indexes against DB2 catalog tables. Each release of DB2 increases the number of table spaces, tables, and indexes in the **DSNDB06** database, so you always need to keep in mind the new space requirements for these additional objects.

Sizing of the catalog has also increased. The default sizes for an installation are specified in megabytes and range from a small-site size of 199 MB to 747 MB for an extra-large site.

Even though the **ALTER** statement has become a powerful tool for online schema changes, you cannot alter any column of the DB2 catalog.

Because of object changes in DB2 9 (e.g., the maximum number of partitions supported in a table space), IBM has made adjustments to the catalog tables. For example, catalog tables have been changed to reflect the **MAXPARTITIONS** setting in **SYSIBM.SYSTABLESPACE**, which is the value you specified in the **CREATE** or **ALTER** statement. Be careful, because this setting does not reflect the physical number of existing partitions. You can find the allocated number of partitions in the **PARTITION** column; for example, you would look for a **G** for partition-by-growth table spaces.

Regardless of the number used for the **MAXPARTITIONS** parameter, only one row is added to **SYSIBM.SYSTABLEPART** when you create the table space. Additional rows are added to this catalog table as your table grows, and additional partitions are allocated if the amount of data exceeds the associated data set size (**DSSIZE**).

Three new **SYSIBM.SYSSTOGROUP** columns — **DATACLAS**, **MGMTCLAS**, and **STORCLAS** — contain the storage management subsystem (SMS) classes used on the **CREATE STOGROUP** or **ALTER STOGROUP** statement. If these new parameters are not defined, DB2 uses the management class and storage class assigned to the corresponding automatic class section (ACS) routine.

DB2 9 Catalog Tables

Table 2.1 describes the catalog tables that are new in DB2 9 for z/OS.

Table 2.1: New catalog tables in DB2 9 for z/OS	
Table	**Description**
SYSIBM.SYSCONTEXT	Contains one row for each trusted context.
SYSIBM.SYSCONTEXTAUTHIDS	Contains one row for each authorization ID with which the trusted context can be used.

2.1: New catalog tables in DB2 9 for z/OS (continued)	
Table	Description
SYSIBM.SYSCTXTTRUSTATTRS	Contains one row for each list of attributes for a given trusted context.
SYSIBM.SYSDEPENDENCIES	Records dependencies between objects.
SYSIBM.SYSENVIRONMENT	Records environment variables when an object is created.
SYSIBM.SYSINDEXSPACESTATS	Contains realtime statistics for index spaces.
SYSIBM.SYSJAVAPATHS	Records the complete Java archive (JAR) class resolution path and the dependencies that one JAR has on the JARs in its Java path.
SYSIBM.SYSKEYTARGETS	Contains one row for each key-target that is participating in an extended index definition.
SYSIBM.SYSKEYTARGETSTATS	Contains partition statistics for selected key-targets. For each key-target, a row exists for each partition in the table. Rows are inserted when the **RUNSTATS** utility collects indexed key statistics or non-indexed key statistics for a partitioned table space. No row is inserted if the table space is non-partitioned.
SYSIBM.SYSKEYTARGETS_HIST	Contains rows from the **SYSKEYTARGETS** table. When rows are added or changed in **SYSKEYTARGETS**, the rows are also written to this table.
SYSIBM.SYSKEYTGTDIST	Contains one or more rows for the first key-target of an extended index key.
SYSIBM.SYSKEYTGTDISTSTATS	Contains zero or more rows per partition for the first key-target of a data-partitioned secondary index. Rows are inserted when **RUNSTATS** scans a data-partitioned secondary index. No row is inserted if the index is a secondary index.
SYSIBM.SYSKEYTGTDIST_HIST	Contains rows from the **SYSKEYTGTDIST** table; whenever rows are added or changed in **SYSKEYTGTDIST**, the rows are also written to this table.
SYSIBM.SYSOBJROLEDEP	Lists the dependent objects for each role.
SYSIBM.SYSROLES	Contains one row for each role.
SYSIBM.SYSROUTINESTEXT	Serves as an auxiliary table for the **TEXT** column of **SYSIBM. SYSROUTINES** and is required to hold the large object (LOB) data.
SYSIBM.SYSTABLESPACESTATS	Contains realtime statistics for table spaces.
SYSIBM.SYSXMLRELS	Contains one row for each XML table that is created for an XML column.
SYSIBM.SYSXMLSTRINGS	Contains rows that each hold a single string and its unique ID that together are used to condense XML data. The string can be an element name, attribute name, name space prefix, or namespace uniform resource identifier (URI).
SYSIBM.XSRCOMPONENT	Serves as an auxiliary table for the binary large object (BLOB) column **COMPONENT** in **SYSIBM.SYSXSROBJECTCOMPONENTS**. It is located in LOB table space **SYSXSRA3**.

2.1: New catalog tables in DB2 9 for z/OS (continued)	
Table	**Description**
SYSIBM.XSROBJECTS	Contains one row for each registered XML schema. Rows can be changed only using static SQL statements issued by the DB2-supplied XML schema repository (XSR) stored procedures.
SYSIBM. XSROBJECTCOMPONENTS	Contains one row for each component (document) in an XML schema. Rows in this table can be changed only using static SQL statements issued by the DB2-supplied XSR stored procedures.
SYSIBM.XSROBJECTGRAMMAR	Serves as an auxiliary table for the BLOB column **GRAMMAR** in **SYSIBM.SYSXSROBJECTS**. It is located in LOB table space **SYSXSRA1**.
SYSIBM. XSROBJECTHIERARCHIES	Contains one row for each component (document) in an XML schema to record the XML schema document hierarchy relationship. Rows in this table can be changed only using static SQL statements issued by the DB2-supplied XSR stored procedures.
SYSIBM.XSROBJECTPROPERTY	Serves as an auxiliary table for the BLOB column **PROPERTIES** in **SYSIBM.SYSXSROBJECTS**. It is located In LOB table space **SYSXSRA2**.
SYSIBM.XSRPROPERTY	Serves as an auxiliary table for the BLOB column **COMPONENT** in **SYSIBM.SYSXSROBJECTCOMPONENTS**. It is located in LOB table space **SYSXSRA3**.

Realtime Statistics Tables in DB2 9

During DB2 enable-new-function (ENF) mode processing, job **DSNTIJEN** moves the realtime statistics data from your user-defined tables to the catalog tables **SYSIBM.SYSTABLESPACESTATS** and **SYSIBM.SYSINDEXSPACESTATS**. After the job moves the data to the catalog tables, you can drop the user-defined tables.

In conversion mode (CM), the realtime statistics data remains in the user-defined tables. If you revert to conversion* (CM*) mode, DB2 keeps the realtime statistics data in the catalog tables and does not use the user-defined tables.

Object Management in the Catalog

In DB2, the data manager handles the manipulation of the system catalog tables. The DM relies on database descriptors (DBDs) to manage data. Each DBD corresponds to a single database and contains subdescriptors called object descriptors (OBDs). The internal structure of a DBD is a complicated hierarchical network of OBDs that are chained together. Each OBD has a unique identifier called an object identifier (OBID). The chain pointers that are used are the actual OBIDs, and DB2 employs an algorithm to locate an OBD within a DBD.

Management of the Catalog

In the day-to-day administration of the catalog, various utilities and jobs help you manage the physical structure and organization of the catalog.

To improve query performance, you should reorganize the indexes on the catalog tables to reduce table size and improve performance. You generally do not reorganize the entire set of catalog tables unless you are migrating to a new release of DB2. You might reorganize your catalog tables once a year, if that often. If you do decide to reorganize the catalog tables, keep in mind that there may be associated directory table spaces that also should be reorganized.

Table 2.2 lists the catalog table spaces and the corresponding directory table spaces that would require reorganization. For example, if you reorganize the **SYSPLAN** catalog table space, you would also reorganize the directory table space **SCT02**.

Table 2.2: Catalog and directory table spaces	
Catalog table space (DSNDB06.*xxxx*)	Directory table space (DSNDB01.*xxxx*)
SYSDBASE	DBD01
SYSPLAN	SCT02
SYSPKAGE	SPT01

CAUTION

Remember to always take a full image copy before and after you reorganize catalog or directory objects. In addition, if you should need to recover the catalog or directory objects, you must do so in a particular order. All table spaces associated with the directory and the catalog must be recovered to the same point in time.

Some utilities that support the catalog, such as **COPY**, **LOAD**, **REBUILD INDEX**, **RECOVER**, **REORG**, and **TABLESPACE** have been updated to reflect changes in

DB2 9, such as the new partition-by-growth table space structure. The following utilities and installation jobs have also undergone changes:

- **DSN1COPY**: You can now use the **DSN1COPY** DB2 stand-alone utility to copy VSAM data sets. Remember that the row format (RRF or BRF) must be the same for the data set from which or into which you are copying. Using the utility's **CHECK** option, you can check each page of a data set.

- **DSNTIJID**: The **DSNTIJID** installation job initializes the system data sets associated with the bootstrap data set (BSDS), catalog, directory, and active logs.

- **DSNTIJTC**: Installation job **DSNTIJTC** invokes the **CATMAINT** utility to tailor your catalog. **CATMAINT** updates the catalog during the migration or installation of a new release of DB2. **DSNTIJTC** contains jobs that perform tailoring of the catalog. It also creates and updates indexes on catalog tables.

- **DSNTIJIC**: The **DSNTIJIC** job also provides an image copy of the catalog and directory for backup, enabling recovery of the catalog and directory. In DB2 9, the job has been modified to copy to disk instead of to tape, but it is limited to two disk volumes. You will have to make modifications to the job to change the number of disk volumes.

- **DSN1CHKR**: The **DSN1CHKR** stand-alone utility is a service aid used for verifying the integrity of the DB2 catalog and directory table spaces for potential data inconsistencies. It checks for broken links, or chains and records that are not part of any chain or link. The utility executes outside the control of DB2. Its use requires a detailed knowledge of DB2 data structures.

- **DSNTIJEN**: In ENFM* or ENFM, job **DSNTIJEN** invokes the **CATENFM** utility to update the catalog for the new release. If this job does not complete successfully, job **DSNTIJNF**, which is used to put DB2 into NFM, will return an error. After **DSNTIJEN** finishes, the catalog conversion is complete. See PK7728 for command list (CLIST) changes to job **DSNTIJEN**.

DB2 Directory

DSNDB01 is the name of the DB2 directory database. This underlying VSAM data set should be in your primary Integrated Catalog Facility (ICF) catalog. You cannot access the information in the directory using SQL. No descriptions of these structures are provided in the catalog for you to see.

The **DSNDB01** database consists of the five table spaces **DBD01**, **SCT02**, **SPT01**, **SYSLGRNX**, and **SYSUTILX**. Each table space is contained in a VSAM linear data set. An example of the naming convention is **DSNDB01.DBD01**. The size of the EDM pool (both above and below the bar) that supports the **DBD01**, **SCT02**, and **SPT01** table spaces is calculated during the installation process and displayed on the **DSNTIPC** panel. The general recommendation is to make the EDM pool 10 times the size of the largest DBD or plan, whichever is greater.

EDM Pool

The EDM pool is a system buffer pool that minimizes I/O against the catalog and the directory. It contains the database descriptor, the cursor table (CT), the package table (PT), the skeleton cursor table (SKCT), the skeleton package table (SKPT), the plan and package authorization cache, and a dynamic SQL skeleton for dynamic SQL caching. These are separate areas of storage, not part of one contiguous EDM pool. CTs and SKCTs result from a static **BIND** of a **PLAN**. PTs and SKPTs result from a static **BIND** of a **PACKAGE** (use of **ACQUIRE(USE)** is implied).

DB2 9 introduces some changes to the storage in the **DBM1** address space. A portion of the CTs and PTs are now above the 2 GB bar, along with a new component above the bar for SKPTs and SKCTs, called the EDM skeleton pool. This skeleton pool is set by a new parameter on installation panel **DSNTIPB**.

In DB2 9, **DBM1** below-the-bar storage relief for heavy package and plan activity is significant. To take advantage of all the improvements, you must perform a DB2 9 rebind. An average estimated reduction is from 20 percent to 90 percent. During the monitoring of your EDM pool pages in use, if this statistic is steadily less than 50 percent, your EDM pool size is probably too large. In general, EDM pool utilization should be around 80 percent.

In DB2 9 new-function mode, native SQL procedures are converted to a representation that is stored in the database directory as other SQL statements are. The stored procedure parameter list options are stored in the database catalog tables as in previous DB2 releases.

When you call a native SQL procedure in DB2 9, the procedure is loaded from the DB2 directory, and the DB2 engine then runs the procedure. Several additional functions and extensions in DB2 9 provide consistency with the SQL standards and the rest of the IBM DB2 family.

In DB2 9, the DB2 catalog and directory use buffer pool **BP0**. If the structure to process a statement is not already present, it is read into database buffer pool **BP0** in 4 KB pages and copied from there into the EDM pool areas. Where the sections are placed in the EDM pool depends on whether a package (SKPT, PT) or a plan (SKCT, CT) is being processed, as Figure 2.5 illustrates.

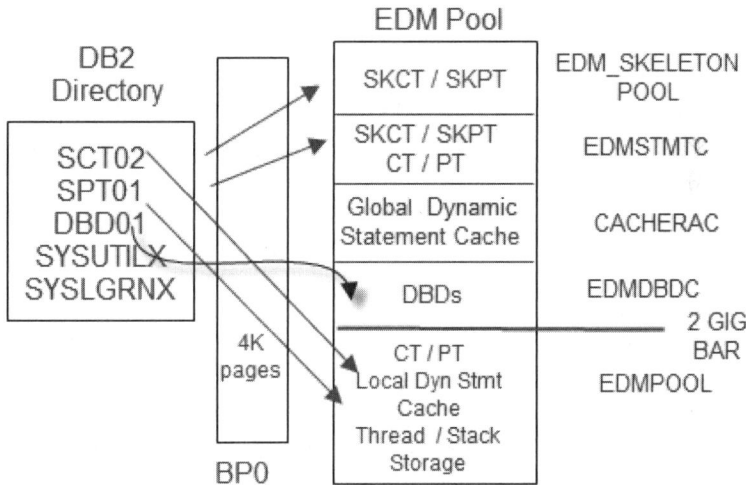

Figure 2.5: EDM pool

SKCTs and SKPTs are now above the 2 GB bar. The static SQL sections (CT/PT) are split between above and below the 2 GB bar. Distributed applications and some storage acquired for dynamic SQL statement execution (which includes the parse trees and a portion of runtime blocks) has also moved above the 2 GB bar. Tables, object blocks, and mapping blocks that are associated with the EDM fixed storage pools have moved above the bar. Fixed storage pools contain the larger object identifying control blocks and the small mapping control blocks that map each block of EDM storage above or below the bar.

EDM Statement Cache

The EDM global dynamic (SQL) statement cache resides above the 2 GB bar in the EDM pool. It consists of a pool of pages used for prepared (**PREPARE**) SQL statements in the **DBM1** address space and contains either the prepared SQL statement (called a short prepare) or a full prepare.

The global dynamic statement cache includes a statement cache table, **DSN_ STATEMENT_CACHE_TABLE**, that is used by the **EXPLAIN STMTCACHE ALL** statement that was introduced in DB2 8 for z/OS. The contents of the cache table are nearly identical to IFCID 316 and 317 statistics. The **EXPLAIN STMTCACHE ALL** statement extracts all the statements from the global cache and inserts one row into the table for each entry. You can also extract a single statement from the global dynamic statement cache by using the **EXPLAIN STMTCACHE STMT_ID** statement.

DB2 9 provides four caching options:

- Local dynamic statement caching
- Global dynamic statement caching
- Full caching
- No caching

Caching of dynamic SQL statements and statement text typically reduces the **PREPARE** operations required for those statements. You control the local and dynamic cache using DSNZPARMs, **BIND** options, and application constructs.

To enable local statement caching, use the **KEEPDYNAMIC(YES)** option of the **BIND** command, which will keep a copy of the prepared statement and the statement string. The **MAXKEEPD** DSNZPARM controls the maximum number of prepared statements to keep past a commit point. The statement text is always kept. The implicit **PREPARE** eliminates the need for an application to execute multiple **PREPARE**s for the same statement.

To enable global statement caching, set the **CACHEDYN** DSNZPARM to **YES**. Global statement caching permits the reuse of prepared statements across units of work within the program and across program executions. The prepared statements, called skeleton dynamic statements (SKDSs), are cached in the global dynamic statement cache. These statements can be copied into local storage when possible; such statements, known as short prepare statements, are dynamic statements in the global cache. You can monitor the global statement cache using IFCID 316 and IFCID 317.

Full caching is a combination of local and global statement caching that provides the ability to avoid prepare operations completely (a feature known as prepare avoidance). Statements kept in local thread storage are not invalidated across commits. To enable full caching, set **CACHEDYN=YES**, **KEEPDYNAMIC(YES)**, and **MAXKEEPD>0**.

SCT02: Skeleton Cursor Table

When you bind a plan, DB2 creates a structure called a *skeleton cursor table* in the **SCT02** table space. The SKCT contains the internal form of the SQL statements that are in your application program. As a plan is executed, DB2 uses this information to access the data it needs. In DB2 9, the SKCTs move above the 2 GB bar in the EDM pool.

SKCTs are stored as a sequence of SKCT sections because a single SKCT can be longer than the maximum record length supported by DB2. These sections begin with a skeleton cursor table parent record (SCTR), which contains as much of the SKCT section as the record can fit. The SKCT section is stored in this record if it fits; if it does not fit, it is stored in one or more SCTRs. Each SCTR is identified by a unique section/sequence number.

SPT01: Skeleton Package Table

A *skeleton package table* is created when you **BIND** a package. It contains the internal form of the SQL statements in your application program. In DB2 9, these structures move above the 2 GB bar in the EDM pool. When initially loaded to execute, they are copied to buffer pool **BP0** and then into the EDM pool in sections.

These sections can include a header and other sections that are the SQL statements to execute.

Parameter **EDM_SKELETON_POOL** (field **EDM SKELTON POOL SIZE** on installation panel **DSNTIPC**) determines the minimum size of the EDM skeleton pool.

Table space **SPT01** is used to store SKPTs. These tables store the access paths to DB2 data. DB2 uses this information to access the data it needs when a package is executed.

Because a single SKPT can be longer than the maximum DB2-supported record length, SKPTs are stored as a sequence of SKPT sections. The skeleton package table parent record (SPTR) contains as much of the SKPT section as the record can fit. It is possible that the entire SKPT section can be stored in this single record. If the record cannot hold the entire SKPT section, the rest of the SKPT is stored in one or more SPTRs records. Each SPTR is identified by a unique section or sequence number.

APAR PK80375 enables compression of the **SPT01** table space. As you use plan stability and increase the space requirements, this capability will help you manage storage consumption. Be aware that the 64 GB limit can be a constraint if you enable plan stability.

DBD01: Database Descriptors

Database descriptors uniquely represent databases within DB2, including user databases, **DSNDB06**, and **DSNDB07**. A one-to-one relationship exists between the database structures and a DBD. The descriptors of objects such as files, page sets, fan sets, and records are contained in each DBD format.

The DBD contains object identifiers (OBIDs) that define the objects within the database to DB2. Each **CREATE** statement for databases, table spaces, and tables is given a unique internal number, or OBID.

In DB2 9, the DBDs are above the 2 GB bar. This area is used for the definitions of objects located in user databases, starting with the database, table space, tables, and so on. The OBIDs are strung together in a hierarchical list of dependencies that identifies each database. For each database, you will have a construct to describe the objects based on the OBIDs. The CLIST calculates the DBD cache size; the default size is 11,700 KB.

Services are available to maintain the DBDs as well as to access these internal objects within DB2. These services provide the following functions and services:

- Retrieve, insert, replace, and delete the internal objects in **DSNDB01**
- Retrieve and update data stored in the system directory
- Maintain DBDs
- Maintain and retrieve SKCT blocks and SKPT blocks
- DM data manipulation services
- DM database descriptor management
- Many other DM services for access to DBDs
- Services used by the service controller subcomponent

DBDs do not require contiguous storage, but they do require 34 KB pieces. The data manager environmental descriptor manager function provides services, such as access and management, to the internal objects. DBDs are stored in the **DBD01** page set in chained records. A parent, called a DBDR, is connected via a link to a child records, called DBDSs.

DBDs can have many sections. A DBD is a contiguous block of information representing a database that contains OBDs for various DM objects within the database. Each object's object identifier represents the name of the object that was defined with Data Definition Language (DDL) statements.

To reclaim the storage in the DBD, you can use the **MODIFY RECOVERY** utility.

Fact Summary About Pages in the EDM Pool

EDM Relational Data Server (RDS) pool (CT and PT sections reside above and below the bar):

- Each executing user application must have a CT or a PT with access paths to execute.
- Each user has a working copy (CT or PT) of the SKCT or SKPT that is executing. The CT or PT does not have to have contiguous storage. These are sections of copies of the SKCT or SKPT that are chained together.
- CT pages (cursor tables in use):
  - » Stored in sections
  - » Contain a working copy of an SKCT
- PT pages (package table sections in use):
  - » Can already be in the EDM pool, no I/O
  - » Stored in sections
  - » Contain a working copy of an SKPT
- The authorization cache is in the RDS pool.

EDM skeleton pool (both completely above 2 GB):

- The EDM skeleton pool is new in DB2 9. It is defined in the DSNZPARMs as **EDM_SKELETON_POOL**. This parameter, which specifies the size of the EDM skeleton pool, defaults to 5,120 KB in size at install time.
- The pool space is not automatically increased or decreased. To override the current value, use the **SET SYSPARM** command.
- The EDM skeleton pool is used for skeleton cursor tables (SKCTs) and skeleton package tables (SKPTs). It also has control blocks used for fixed pools, mapping blocks, object blocks and hash tables.
- SKCT pages (skeleton cursor table):
  - » Shared by users
  - » Created in **SCT02** when you bind a plan

» Describes the structure of the SQL statements in application plans and consists of executable SQL and RDS control structures related to access paths

■ As each SQL call is made, the required sections are loaded into the pool. They remain there until a **BIND REPLACE**, **FREE**, or **REBIND** command is executed or until least-recently-used (LRU) replacement takes place.

» Stored in a sequence of SKCT sections that are loaded for execution

■ The first section, called an SCTR, is a parent record. If additional space is required to store the sections, one or more SCTRs, each identified by a unique section or sequence number, are chained.

● SKPT pages (skeleton package table):

» Created in **SPT01** when you **BIND** a package

» Applies to packages, which are shared among the plans that reference them

» Describes a collection of packages grouped by a **BIND PACKAGE** with a collection ID

» Contains a directory, header, and one or more sections of SQL

EDM database descriptor pool (above the bar) in DBD01:

● The EDM database descriptor pool contains the database descriptor (DBD) pages.

● A DBD is created whenever the **CREATE DATABASE** statement is executed.

● Database structures are cached here.

● Each DBD describes a database and all its objects and contains access information.

● DB2 uses an algorithm to locate an object descriptor (OBD) within a DBD. There are two descriptions for a database. One is in the catalog, and the other is the internal representation of the data in the DBD in the directory. This is a one-to-one relationship.

- The OBD has subdescriptors of all the objects contained in the database, including table spaces, tables, indexes, constraints, and relationships with the LOB columns.

- Internally, there are six types of OBDs: file, page set, record type, fan set, check constraint, and auxiliary relationship. The OBDs contain information about how the records are organized, stored, and accessed and represent the internal representation of the objects.

- You can find object identifiers in the DB2 catalog under the object table definitions. Columns in them will have **DBID**, **PSID**, **OBID**, and **ISOBID** for database, table spaces, tables, and indexes.

- A DBD starts as a single block. As it grows due to objects being defined with **CREATE**, additional blocks can be added. It is read from DASD as a chain of blocks into storage.

- If you use the **DROP** statement to remove an object from the database, the object identifier is not automatically removed from the DBD hash chain.

SYSUTILX

For every utility job running in DB2, a row is placed in table space **SYSUTILX** in the DB2 directory. This row is used if you have to restart the utility. When the utility finishes running, the row is removed. Information for a copy of **SYSUTILX** is located in the log.

Keep in mind the following points related to **SYSUTILX**:

- You cannot **REORG** the **SYSUTILX** table space.

- The **SYSUTILX** table is a dependent of the **SYSUTIL** table.

- Rows in **SYSUTILX** are uniquely identified by a utility identifier and sequence number.

- When information in the parent record exceeds the record size of table **SYSUTIL**, a record is created in the **SYSUTILX** table.

The **SYSUTIL** table stores the status of DB2 utilities that are stopped or started. Each record in the table is uniquely identified by a utility identifier. Each row contains the information for one utility execution step. When a utility finishes running, the corresponding entries in the **SYSUTIL** table are deleted.

SYSLGRNX

The DB2 **MODIFY** utility checks user authorization, issues appropriate messages, deletes specified records, and updates the **SYSIBM.SYSLGRNX** table in the DB2 directory. **SYSLGRNX** is a log range table space that tracks the opening and closing of table spaces, partitions, and indexes. DB2 tracks the information by the relative byte address (RBA) that is written in the log after the most recent copy, reducing the amount of time required to recover an object.

The directory table spaces and associated indexes do not have entries in **SYSIBM. SYSLGRNX**, even if they were defined with **COPY YES**.

The size of the directory depends on the number of user databases, packages, plans, and tables in DB2. At installation, the **DSNTINST** CLIST calculates the sizes of the EDM pools (above and below the 2 GB bar), the EDM statement cache, the EDM database descriptor cache, and the EDM skeleton pool. Look at your calculated sizes on the **DSNTIPC** installation panel.

When a table space is open for updates, or when an index is defined with **COPY YES**, DB2 records the recovery log range times in **SYSLGRNX**. This information provides an efficient way for DB2 to access the appropriate log records for recovery, without having to scan every record in the recovery log for a specific table.

Catalog/Directory Access Methods

The DB2 directory uses links that exist between the DBD parent record for a given DBD and the database child record records.

Another access path to data in the DB2 catalog or directory is called a link. A link consists of a record identifier and a hash, which are, respectively, a page number and an offset to an anchor point. A link is a parent/child relationship between two tables or records. There are links that exist between rows of tables in the DB2 catalog.

Hashing Algorithms

The method of hashing is used to access data only in the DB2 directory and in the **DBD01** page set. A database descriptor is created when you issue the **CREATE DATABASE** statement. The DB2 data manager allocates 4 KB of storage initially and formats a DBD.

- The hash key for **DBD01** is the database identifier (DBID).

- Index **DSNSCT02** is used to access data in the **SCT02** DB2 directory page set.

- Indexes **DSNSPT01** and **DSNSPT02** are used to access data in the **SPT01** page set.

- Table space **SYSUTILX** uses indexes **DSNLUX01** and **DSNLUX02** to access data.

- Table space **SYSLGRNX** uses indexes **DSNLLX01** and **DSNLLX02** to access data.

DSNZPARMs for the EDM Pool

The following table provides a simple key to relate the various terms involved with the EDM pool to the subsystem parameters associated with the pools in the EDM pool:

Term	Related DSNZPARM
RDS pool	EDMPOOL
DBD pool	EDMDBDC
Statement pool	EDMSTMTC
Skeleton pool	EDM_SKELETON_POOL

You also have subsystem parameter **EDMBFIT**; specify **NO** (the default) to optimize performance or **YES** to optimize storage utilization. Parameter **EDMBFIT** controls how space is freed for EDM pools that are greater than 40 MB. **YES** specifies a better-fit algorithm to handle **EDMPOOL** full conditions for these large pool sizes. **NO** specifies a first-fit algorithm, usually for smaller **EDMPOOL**s, and is set when class latch 24 contention starts to exceed 500 contentions per second. Latches are used to serialize access to many memory resources. The object of a latch is a page in DB2. Latch class 24 is used for the EDM pool least-recently-used (LRU) chain and the buffer manager page unlatch and prefetch. You can find the description of each class in the **DSNDQVLS** macro in **SDSNMACS**.

Storage Above and Below the Bar

Virtual Storage Constraint Relief (VSCR) below the bar in the **DBM1** address space is achieved by moving the plan and package skeletons completely above the bar into their separate EDM pools. In DB2 9, the EDM fixed storage pools (FSPs) are moved above the bar; they include all the hash tables, mapping blocks, and object blocks. This area contains small mapping control blocks that map each block of EDM storage both above and below the bar and the larger object identifying control blocks. By moving these control blocks above the bar, scaling of the number of EDM objects can occur without affecting below-the-bar storage usage.

The last control block in DB2 9 that is associated with each dynamic SQL statement is moved above the bar. The EDM statement cache pool can expand above the bar without increase to any statement cache control blocks below the bar.

Dynamic SQL statements now have a larger portion split above the bar than for static SQL in DB2 9 plans or packages. This split has to do with the extra storage required in dynamic statement storage for **DESCRIBE** column information and **PREPARE** options. These options, of course, do not exist as part of the statement storage for static statements. The **DESCRIBE** and **PREPARE** storage is now all above the bar. Individual statement storage is generally larger for dynamic SQL than for static SQL.

The moving of some short-term control blocks above the bar has reduced peak storage usage for **BIND** dynamic **PREPARE**. This short-term storage (called parse tree storage), which is held during a full prepare of SQL statements, has decreased significantly. Some estimates of peak storage usage for full prepares have been reduced by 10 percent.

Other items that have moved above the bar are some tracing storage and mini-plan storage. Stack storage, system thread storage, and user thread storage usage has remained about the same, but some of the savings may be offset by increases in other areas.

To reduce the EDM latch class 24 serializations, the below-the-bar EDM pool cache now has no LRU objects. You must size the below-the-bar EDM pool for peak usage. No automatic expansion of this storage pool occurs, and the possibility of an EDM pool full condition exists. You modify this setting via a DSNZPARM change and activate the change using the **SET SYSPARM LOAD** statement. Parameter **EDMPOOL** in **DSN6SPRM** is the value associated with below-the-bar 2 GB bar storage.

You should carefully size the below-the-bar EDM pool to accommodate peak usage plus a cushion for fragmentation. Best practices dictate that the size of the EDM pool storage below the bar be between 110 percent and 130 percent of peak usage. This sizing will take into account any pool fragmentation and the need to allocate contiguous storage for any section.

If you do experience EDM pool full situations, IFCID 31 will identify the object type, size, and requestor. If this IFCID is active, it produces trace records only when the EDM pool full situation occurs.

In addition, IFCID 02 collects EDM statistics. Take a look at member **DSNWMSGS** in library **SDSNSAMP** for field definitions of this and other trace records. **DSNDQISE** and **DSNDQWS1** contain the field definitions for this trace record.

It is a good idea to add 10 percent to 30 percent to your initial estimate, just to have a cushion of storage in case you need it. The number of dynamic statements that are active below the bar can cause this critical shortage. The only way to increase this area is by using the **SET SYSPARM** statement.

A new DB2 9 subsystem parameter, **CACHEDYN_FREELOCAL** in macro **DSN6SPRM**, can free cached dynamic statements to relieve the shortage below the bar. This setting applies only if you have activated the **BIND** option **KEEPDYNAMIC(YES)**.

The **CACHEDYN_FREELOCAL** parameter is changeable online via the **SET SYSPARM RELOAD** statement. Changing the value of this parameter changes the triggering level at which DB2 9 tries to free local SQL cache storage below the bar.

The values **0** (zero, the default in DB2 8) through **3** are available to represent the trigger levels DB2 uses to reclaim local SQL cache below-the-bar storage. Specifying **1** (one), the default in DB2 9, causes DB2 to free some cached dynamic statements if the storage usage is high. If you specify **0**, no cached dynamic statements are freed. The built-in **DBM1** storage monitor writes information to the console to let you know how much storage is currently consumed as limits are met. The IFCID 225 trace record also collects information about the cache storage.

If you size the EDM storage pools too small, you could see increased I/O on the **DBD01**, **SPT01**, and **SCT02** directories, along with increased response times and a smaller number of threads running concurrently because of lack of storage.

To achieve the above- and below-the-bar storage for PTs and CTs, you must rebind your plans and packages in DB2 9 to move the relevant sections of these objects to 64-bit storage addressing.

Storage Pools

Dynamic SQL execution storage can be extensive and can be one of the largest factors driving **DBM1** below-the-bar virtual storage constraints. Two new IFCIDs, 217 and 225, collect information about storage above and below the bar. Statistics about the storage manager pools are produced at the interval specified by parameter **STATIME** in the DSNZPARMs.

DB2 8 introduced 30 global variable-length storage pools that contain the dynamic SQL statement storage used for statement execution in below-the-bar storage. In DB2 9, the individual statement storage is split between above-the-bar and below-the-bar portions. We use these values instead of pool totals to understand how peaks in the cached SQL statements drive the total storage use in **DBM1**.

To collect IFCID 217 and IFCID 225 records, you must activate the DB2 **STATIME** interval. This parameter specifies the number of minutes between statistics collections. The default interval for **STATIME** is now five minutes (**5**).

IFCID 225 provides a summary report of the storage being used in the **DBM1** address space, and IFCID 217 produces a detail report of activity. IFCID 225 records collect data on the first failure.

IFCID 217 produces SMF type 102 storage detail data records. IFCID 225 is added to **STATISTICS** trace class 1, and its statistics are written as SMF type 100 with a subtype of 4 records. DB2 keeps an internal cache of IFCID 225 records so that storage changes over time can be evaluated during dump analysis. No separate instrumentation fields for the accumulated size of the 30 statement cache pools are kept.

You can activate collection of these statistics using the following command:

```
-START TRACE(GLOBAL) IFCID(217)
```

MAXKEEPD

You use the **MAXKEEPD** subsystem parameter to limit the number of dynamic statements that are held in the cache after a commit point. These locally cached statements can consume large quantities of **DBM1** virtual storage. This setting applies to full caching only. If a large number of **PREPARE** operations are occurring on a system and application logic is not committing frequently, **MAXKEEPD** can be exceeded before the release of the cached statements can occur.

Stored Procedures

Native and external SQL procedures can be called in DB2 9 in new-function mode.

- The PL/SQL native logic for the SQL is stored in the DB2 directory.

- Native SQL procedures are executed entirely in the DB2 **DBM1** engine and should outperform external SQL procedures.

- Native SQL procedures can be created starting in DB2 9 NFM:

» You use the **CREATE PROCEDURE** statement to create a native SQL procedure.

» The **FENCED** or **EXTERNAL** keyword cannot be used.

» Above-the-bar storage is used for native stored procedures.

External SQL procedures will continue to work in DB2 9 either in conversion mode or NFM.

- You use the **CREATE PROCEDURE** statement to create an external SQL procedure.

- The **FENCED** or **EXTERNAL** keyword is required.

External SQL procedures from prior releases are executed in the WLM environment. **DSNTPSMP** is an SQL procedure processor you can use to prepare the external procedure. **DSNTPSMP** requires DB2 for z/OS REXX language support and WLM stored procedure address space (SPAS) with the setting **NUMTCB=1**. This procedure can be invoked only by an SQL call from an application program or from IBM DB2 Data Studio Developer.

DSN1CHKR

If you suspect that data inconsistencies exist in the link or hash chains in the pages of the DB2 catalog or directory, you can run the **DSN1CHKR** stand-alone utility to validate one or more data pages in question in the DB2 catalog or directory.

BINDNV DSNZPARM

The new DSNZPARM **BINDNV** controls the authority needed to add a new package in DB2. When **BINDNV** is set to **BIND**, the creation of a new package requires only the **BIND** privilege. With this privilege, if a user has **BIND** authority on a package, he or she can create a new **VERSION** of a package. If you set the **BINDNV** parameter to **BINDADD**, only users with **BINDADD** authorization can add a new **VERSION**.

RID Pools

The row identifier (RID) pool is an area of local storage reserved for sort processing of record identifiers from an index or indexes (multiple index processing). A RID is made up of a page number and a row identifier that defines the row in the data page of the table for that key value. In general, there are multiple **LEAF PAGE**s in the index structure containing multiple entries of RIDs for each row in a table.

RIDs are stored in leaf index pages and identify the records stored in data pages. A RID can be a four- or five-byte page number followed by a one-byte page ID map. Five-byte RIDs are associated with large table spaces that are defined with a **DSSIZE** that is 4 GB or larger or with LOBs (auxiliary tables). Four-byte RIDs are associated with all other table space definitions; these identifiers consist of a three-byte page number and a one-byte ID pointer.

Each RID describes a page number and an ID that points to a row in the table space. Figure 2.6 shows the relationship between the RID and the row of data in the table.

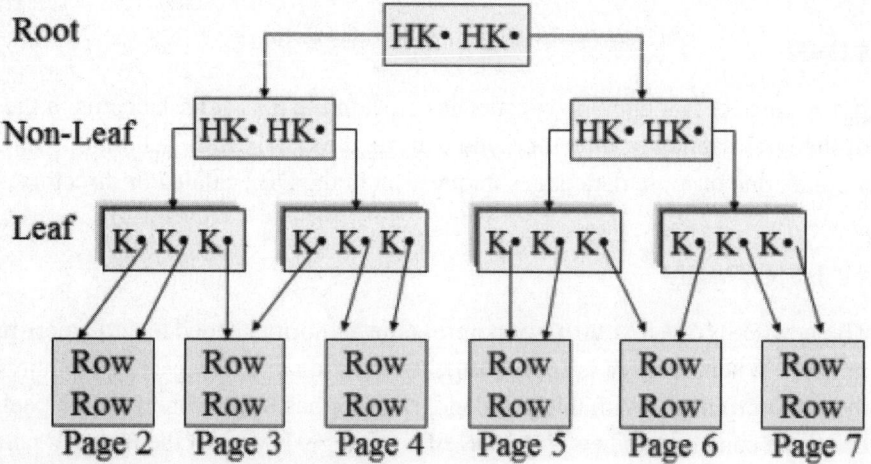

Figure 2.6: Relationship between RID and data row

The **MAXRBLK** subsystem parameter in macro **DSN6SPRM** defines the number of RID blocks allocated for the RID pool storage. **MAXRBLK** is stored internally as a number that is divided by 32 because DB2 allocates RID blocks in 32 KB chunks.

The **DSNTIPC** migration panel displays the **RID POOL SIZE** field, whose default is 8,000 KB. Acceptable values are 0 KB or a setting between 128 KB and 10,000,000 KB. A single RID list maximum size would be approximately 26 million RIDs.

During processing, the index RIDs are selected and sorted in the RID pool according to page number within RID. This list of RIDs, in page number order, provides access to the data pages within the table space in order. DB2 uses this sorted list to access the table rows by reading 32 pages per I/O operation and trying to read ahead one block of 32 pages as well.

The RID pool is split into two parts. The area below the 2 GB bar (approximately 25 percent) stores the RID maps, and the area above the 2 GB bar (approximately 75 percent) contains the RID list. No space is actually allocated in the pool until RID storage space is needed. At that point, the space is allocated in 32 KB RID blocks as needed. Each new agent requesting RID pool usage is given two 32 KB blocks, one for the RID list and one for the RID map, for a total of 64 KB per agent.

The RID pool is used in hybrid joins, multiple index processing, list prefetching, and the enforcement of unique keys during row updates. If the RID pool runs out of space, the SQL statement reverts to sequential processing at the point of failure. The more common RID pool failures can also be caused by not running **RUNSTATS**. When enabling list prefetch, the optimizer sets a threshold of 25 percent of the number of rows in the table. If the RIDs exceed this number, processing reverts to sequential processing.

RID sorts occur totally in memory. You can track RID list processing with IFCID 003 and IFCID 002. You can also determine whether list prefetch has ended if more than 25 percent of the rows in table are accessed with IFCID 125 in a performance trace.

Optimistic locking also uses the RIDs and a change token to ensure integrity of the data being read.

DB2 9 uses dynamic prefetch more frequently, and the formula for tracking pages now tracks the cluster ratio with prefetch quantity and buffer pool size considerations. The algorithm has been enhanced to count each RID in the **CLUSTERRATIO** formula rather than just the distinct key values. In addition, a new column in **SYSINDEXES** called **DATAREPEATFACTOR** tracks whether rows are found on a page other than the current one. This information, along with the **CLUSTERRATIO**, can distinguish between dense and sequential rows.

The DB2 9 enhancement of star join group or pair-wise join depends on the resources of the RID pool. Using this join method requires a one-column index on a fact table that supports each dimension table join column. Don't forget that list prefetch is disabled on a **VOLATILE** table. Also, **OPTIMIZE FOR 1 ROW** will avoid RID processing. **RID** is also a new built-in function that returns the RID of a row.

Although there is no RID list in the **EXPLAIN** tables, a column **PREFETCH** type of **L** indicates that RIDs are being processed to read data pages.

Physical Rows and Pages for Table Spaces

The physical structure of a table space consists of 4 KB pages. Each table space type has a specific structure. Figure 2.7 shows the basic format of the table space pages. In DB2 8, the table space structure added a system page to support online schema versioning.

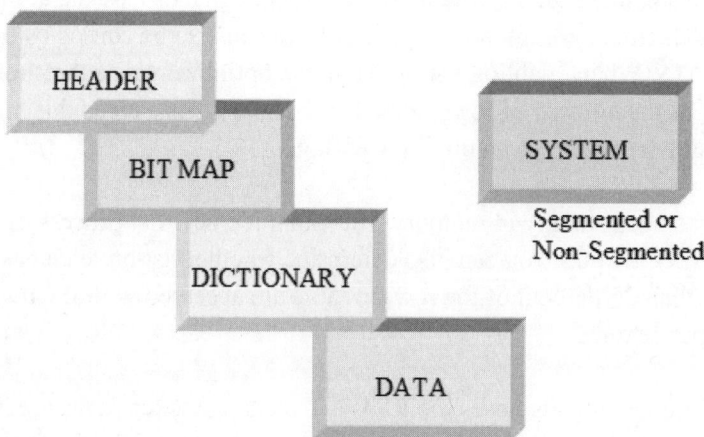

Figure 2.7: Table space pages

Header Page

The first page in any table space type or index is a header page. All header pages have the format shown in Figure 2.8.

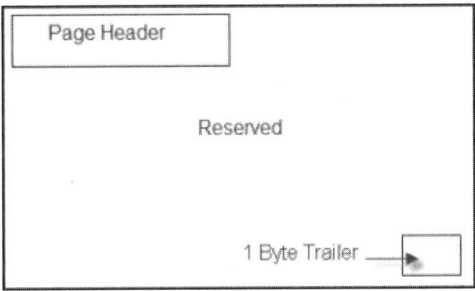

Figure 2.8: Header page format

Bit Maps or Space Maps

There are actually six space maps, or bit map formats, but we will look at only two here. The two types of bit maps inside the structure of a table space are one map type for segmented table spaces and one for nonsegmented table spaces. The bit map page distinguishes which data pages have free space to accommodate additional row inserts. Each space or bit map covers a specific range of pages, based on the page size and whether the table space is a segmented or a nonsegmented table space.

Figure 2.9 depicts the structure of the segmented bit map.

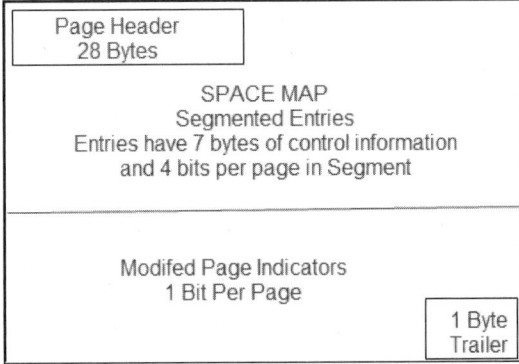

Figure 2.9: Segmented bit map

In the segmented bit map, each four-bit entry indicates the amount of free space remaining in the corresponding data page. Table 2.3 describes the binary values in the four-bit entries.

Table 2.3: Binary values for segmented bit map	
Binary entry	**Meaning**
B'0000'	Page is empty — not formatted.
B'0001'	Page is empty — caused by a mass delete statement.
B'0010'	Page is empty — typically caused by normal delete functions.
B'0010'	Page has free space greater than or equal to the maximum record size.
B'0100–B'1010'"	These bit settings are for variable-length records.
B'1011'	Space is less than, greater than, or equal to minimum size of record.
B'1111'	Page is full.

Space or bit maps associated with nonsegmented table spaces have a different layout. The nonsegmented, or partitioned, space map (Figure 2.10) covers a fixed number of pages. Each two-bit entry corresponds to a page within the range that the space map covers.

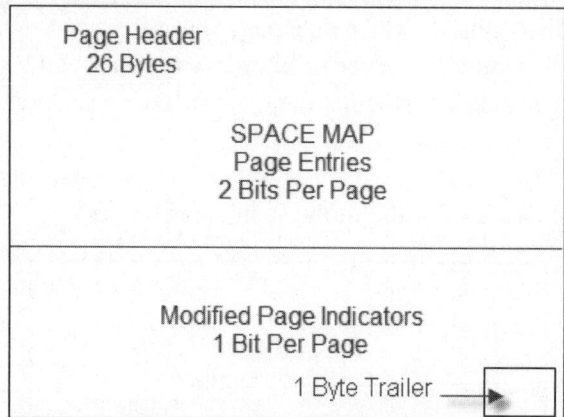

Page Header
26 Bytes

SPACE MAP
Page Entries
2 Bits Per Page

Modified Page Indicators
1 Bit Per Page

1 Byte Trailer

Figure 2.10: Nonsegmented bit map

So, as an example, the number of pages per space map would be as follows:

- A 4 KB page size for any type or partition would cover 10,764 pages.

- An 8 KB page size for any type or partition would cover 21,680 pages.

- A 16 KB page size for any type or partition would cover 43,528 pages.

- A 32 KB page size and number of pages would depend on the number of partitions and whether a table space is associated with a member cluster.

You can find more information about sizing in the *DB2 Diagnosis Guide and Reference* (LY37-3201).

The two bits describe how much free space is left in the corresponding data page. Table 2.4 lists the four possible values.

Table 2.4: Binary values for nonsegmented bit map	
Binary value	**Meaning**
B'00'	Free space is greater or equal to maximum record size.
B'01'	Free space is greater or equal to average record size.
B'10'	Free space is greater or equal to the minimum record size.
B'11'	Free space is less than the minimum — full page.

The modified page indicators in the second part of the nonsegmented or partitioned space map indicate whether the page has changed since the last time the **COPY** utility was run. Interestingly enough, this information is available only if the table space was created or altered with the **TRACKMOD YES** option. Whenever a full image **COPY** is run or an incremental copy is made, the bits are reset to **0**.

Large objects have two types of space maps, and index spaces have a space map entries page, but in an index space map there are two differences: First, there is one bit to each corresponding page, and second, there are no modified page indicators.

Dictionary Pages

If you have compression set on in your table space, you will have dictionary pages. The dictionary pages will come after the first space map and before the data pages. There can be up to sixteen 4 KB pages in your table space structure to form the dictionary pages. These dictionary pages are created with the **LOAD** or **REORG** utility, using the proper settings, to build new dictionary pages or to keep the already-built dictionary pages built for compression. When the table space is accessed, the compression dictionaries are stored above the 2 GB bar.

The SQL statement to turn on compression is **CREATE** (or **ALTER**) **TABLESPACE ... COMPRESS YES**.

Remember that you can run the DB2 stand-alone utility **DSN1COMP** to estimate the amount of compression. The unit of compression in ESA is a table row. This type of compression is not used in work files, the catalog, the directory, LOB table spaces, or table indexes.

Data Pages

The data pages (Figure 2.11) all start with one page header followed by rows with a row header and then the row data. One byte in the row header supports the "version" of the row.

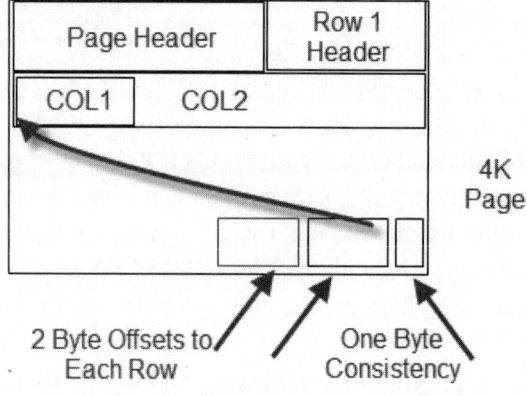

Figure 2.11: Data page

System Page

A system page helps with the management of online **ALTER** schema changes or versions of the object. The system page tracks format changes to the rows in a table space. System pages are inserted in the table space as you make versioning changes. The **COPY** utility gives you a choice of whether to copy these pages or not; the default is **YES**.

SYSIBM.SYSOBDS in **DSNDB06** contains one row for each table space or index that can be recovered to an image copy that was made before the first version was generated (version 0, unaltered objects). The **SYSODBS** table contains the information listed in Table 2.5.

Table 2.5: SYSIBM.SYSODBS table space	
Column name	**Definition**
CREATOR	Authorization ID
NAME	Object name
DBID	Internal database ID
PSID	Internal table space or index space ID
OBID	Internal table/index ID
OBDTYPE	Object type
VERSION	Version when altered
CREATDTS	Timestamp
OBD (varchar 30000)	OBDREC
IBMREQD	IBM flag

If you look in **SYSIBM.SYSTABLESPACE**, you can also find entries for the DBID, OBID, and PSID for identification of the internal definition of your databases, tables, and index spaces.

Base and Clone Tables

DB2 9 provides support for fast replacement of tables. You generate a copy of the base table by building a *clone*. You can insert or load data into the clone table and use the SQL **EXCHANGE** statement to perform a fast replacement of the original data. Interestingly, the table space name is the same for both the base and the clone table. The **RUNSTATS** utility does not collect statistics on clone tables.

SYSIBM.SYSCOPY will reflect the **CREATE** of a clone with the new **ICTYPE** of **C**. Revisions to columns in the DB2 catalog include new column descriptions and values and changed data types, column lengths, or both.

In DB2 9, a new column of interest is the **INSTANCE** column, which always has a value of **1** or **2**. This column has been added to some DB2 catalog tables to reflect the base versus the clone data sets.

Universal Table Spaces

DB2 9 features new table spaces to provide key functions of both segmented and partitioned table spaces. This combination of features is called a universal table space (UTS). There are two types of UTSs:

- *Partition by growth (PBG)*: These table spaces allow segmented tables to be partitioned as they grow without the need for key ranges.

- *Partition by range (PBR)*: These table spaces are just like the existing partition table spaces but are segmented.

Partition-by-Growth Table Spaces

Partition-by-growth is now the default table space type in DB2 9. A partition-by-growth table space is very useful for table spaces whose tables lack a suitable partitioning key but are expected to exceed the 64 GB limit. You do not define a partitioning key with PBG. Each PBG table space holds a single table.

If you plan to make changes to **DSSIZE** and **SEGSIZE**, you will need to do a **DROP** to change your table space; there is no **ALTER** option. A partition-by-growth table space can grow up to 128 TB; the **MAXPARTITIONS**, **DSSIZE**, and page size values determine the maximum size.

The following restrictions apply when using PBG:

- The **LOAD** utility does not allow the **LOAD PART** option for partition-by-growth table spaces.

- Only non-partitioning indexes are allowed with PBG, and the table spaces must be storage-group–controlled.

- The **REORG** utility does not delete the existing partitions, even if they are no longer needed.

- A PBG table space is incompatible with the **ADD PARTITION** and **ROTATE PARTITION** options of the **ALTER TABLE** statement.

Partition-by-Range Table Spaces

Segmented table spaces that are approaching the 64 GB limit can be converted to partition-by-range universal table spaces that support up to 128 TB. You can choose your **DSSIZE** parameter value. If you specify **LARGE**, the size is limited to 64 partitions. To move above this range, you will need **DSSIZE**. Parameter **DSSIZE**, the page size, and the number of partitions determine the maximum size of the table.

PBRs offer better space management and improved delete performance due to the segmentation bit map structure that was originally used in segmented table spaces. To specify a PBR, you use the parameters **NUMPARTS** and **SEGSIZE** in one **CREATE TABLESPACE** statement. These types of table spaces still require a partitioning column.

Index Structure

Tables support multiple indexes in DB2, and each index has a format consisting of a B-tree structure. The data row diagram that we looked at previously (reproduced in Figure 2.12) depicts a clustering index.

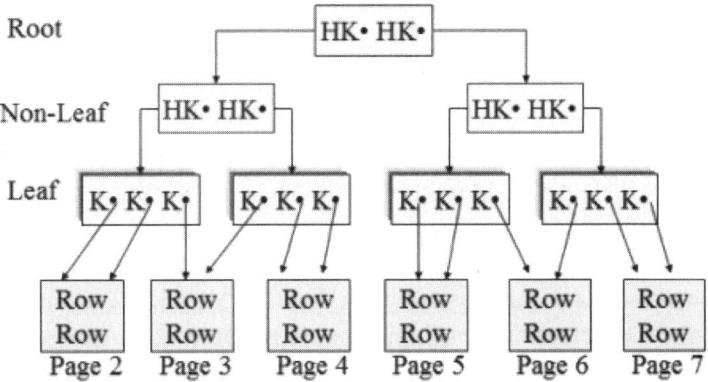

Figure 2.12: Index structure

In this clustering index structure, each block represents a 4 KB page. The first, or highest, level is the root, followed by multiple non-leaf pages, and then the leaf pages, which contain the key and row ID that point to the data in the table.

The contents of the root and non-leaf pages are the highest key and a pointer to the next level. The contents of the leaf pages are the full key and the address location of the associated row in the table space (RID).

DB2 supports clustering indexes, unique indexes, non-unique indexes, partitioning indexes, partitioned indexes, and no indexes at all on tables.

BRF and RRF Formats and Logging

Up to now, table row formats in DB2 have been what we call *basic row format (BRF)*. DB2 9 introduces a new row format, called *reordered row format (RRF)*, for user data. In DB2 9, the catalog and directory tables remain in basic row format.

If you are in NFM and your table space does not use an **EDITPROC** or **VALIDPROC** routine and you use either the **REORG** or **LOAD REPLACE** utility, the row format will be changed from BRF to RRF.

During migration from DB2 8 to DB2 9, DB2 by default ignores the **KEEPDICTIONARY** parameter of the **LOAD** and **REORG** utilities when converting tables from BRF to RRF. If you want the **KEEPDICTIONARY** parameter to be honored, you must set the subsystem parameter **HONOR_KEEPDICTIONARY** to **YES**.

In RRF, if a table contains any varying-length columns (with or without nulls), all fixed-length columns are placed at the beginning of the row, followed by the offsets to the varying-length columns, followed by the values of the varying-length columns.

ROWID and indicator columns are treated like varying-length columns. Row IDs are **VARCHAR(17)**. A LOB indicator column is **VARCHAR(4)**, and an XML indicator column is **VARCHAR(6)**. The LOB indicator column is stored in a base table in place of a LOB or XML column and indicates whether the LOB or XML value for the column is null or zero in length.

You use the **DSN1COPY** stand-alone utility to populate one table space to another table space. Be aware that the row formats of the two table spaces must match. If they do not, the utility will fail, or unpredictable results may cause integrity problems. Use the following SQL statement to check the row format of your table space before executing **DSN1COPY**:

```
SELECT DBNAME, TSNAME, PARTITION, FORMAT FROM SYSIBM.SYSTABLEPART ...
```

If the **FORMAT** column in the **SYSTABLEPART** catalog table has a value of **R**, the table space or partition is in RRF. If the **FORMAT** column contains a blank value, the table space or partition is in BRF.

Figure 2.13 illustrates the two row formats in DB2.

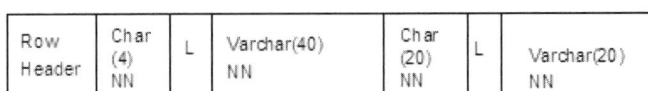

Basic Row Format (BRF)

Row Header	Char (4) NN	L	Varchar(40) NN	Char (20) NN	L	Varchar(20) NN

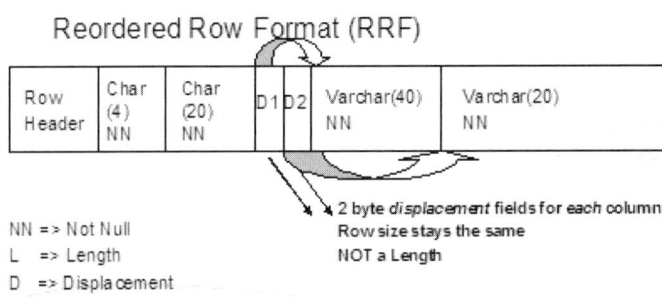

Reordered Row Format (RRF)

Row Header	Char (4) NN	Char (20) NN	D1	D2	Varchar(40) NN	Varchar(20) NN

NN => Not Null
L => Length
D => Displacement

2 byte *displacement* fields for each column
Row size stays the same
NOT a Length

Figure 2.13: Row formats

Index Compression

DB2 9 provides index compression, but this compression does not use a dictionary. Index compression occurs at the page level via software compression, but only for the leaf level in the index structure. The pages are compressed at write time and are decompressed during reading. This technique to compress the index keys and RIDs is called *prefix compression*.

The index keys are composed of two parts: the key of the index and associated page number and an offset to the data. The key map, associated with each entry on the leaf, is not compressed. This information is actually rebuilt at the time of decompression.

To work with compression, DB2 transparently manages an I/O work area that is separate from the buffer pool. DB2's deferred write engine asynchronously compresses a leaf page from a buffer into an I/O work area and then writes the page to disk. Compression begins immediately on the contents of the index if you use the following statement:

```
ALTER INDEX COMPRESSION YES
```

This compression cannot be activated at the partition level; it is for the whole index. The compression occurs, not key by key, but by the leaf page level. There is no ability to randomly find a key in the index and decompress that key. A random probe of the index requires a B-tree search. There are no compression dictionaries; this is compression done on-the-fly at the page level.

The index page size must be larger than 4 KB, and the index data is compressed "down" to 4 KB size on disk.

You can have 32 KB, 16 KB, or 8 KB index page sizes for indexes in NFM of DB2 9. Turning on compression can save you up to eight times the disk space and reduce the frequency of index page splits. IBM's estimates for compression savings run from 25 percent to 75 percent disk savings. To see whether you should compress your indexes, run **DSN1COMP**; this utility has been enhanced in DB2 9 to provide information about possible page sizes.

Note that an **IMAGE COPY** of a compressed index creates an uncompressed output file. In addition, the log records for the index keys are not compressed.

Asymmetrical Split on Index Pages

Support for asymmetrical splitting of index pages is a new feature in DB2 9. In earlier releases, when all the RID space of an index leaf page is consumed during inserts, page split processing takes places, and DB2 allocates a new page in the index, moving half of the entries from the old page to the new index page. If you are performing sequential inserts and adding index keys in ascending order, the freed space in the old page of the index will never be reused.

With this enhancement, DB2 detects various insert patterns in an index and chooses an algorithm from several available to DB2 to use for page splitting. These asymmetrical algorithms are available in NFM of DB2 9. Asymmetric page splitting, along with an increase in the index page size from 4 KB to 8 KB, 16 KB, or 32 KB, provides better space use and also reduces contention in the index.

Active Logs

DB2 uses dual logging for the active log, archive log, and bootstrap data sets. When the active log is offloaded to the archive log, the first information that goes to tape or disk is a copy of the BSDS.

The primary function of the dual active logs is to provide recoverability by recording the changes to your data within the system. DB2 uses automatic offloading of these logs to the archive logs to establish a baseline for user data recoverability.

Once DB2 is started, the logs remain allocated exclusively to DB2 until DB2 terminates. The active logs are defined in the BSDS and are allocated dynamically for use. You define the number and size of the log data sets on installation panel **DSNTIPL**. A DB2-provided offline utility, **DSNJU003** (change log inventory), lets you add new logs or replace an active log. To use this utility, you must stop DB2, make your changes, and then restart the DB2 subsystem.

To minimize the filling and "spilling" of logs to archive logs, make sure the active log data sets are large enough to avoid frequent offloading. In addition, be sure to set the **OUTBUFF** DSNZPARM value large enough so that log buffers can avoid the need to wait for a buffer to become available. **OUTBUFF** specifies the output buffer size used in writing active log data sets.

The BSDS should be converted in DB2 9, so you will have 93 active logs available. These are VSAM linear data sets stored as dual sets for log recoverability. The **DSNTIPL** installation panel's **NUMBER OF LOGS** field permits a maximum entry of **31**, the traditional number supported in the BSDS. Check APAR PK77228 in

DB2 9 for a fix that updates this maximum to **93** to match the new BSDS format required by DB2 9.

Records in the dual active log show the activity for updates, deletes, and inserts to table spaces, index spaces, and system events. When log records are written, they are broken into segments. Records are first written sequentially into the output log buffers located in the system services address space before they are written into the active logs. These records are VSAM-formatted control intervals (CIs), which have been assigned an ever-increasing RBA or, in a data-sharing environment, a log sequence number (LRSN) that is written to the active log.

Output log buffers collect the activity against data and system events. When these buffers become full, or when DB2 forces them at commit time, they are written to the active log set. You could thus have log records written several times. The system services address space handles the log buffers, and they are defined with the installation CLIST.

As the dual active log sets fill, they automatically spill or roll off to the assigned archive log sets in a process called offloading. The next set of active logs continues to record system information while this offloading occurs. Active logs are "wrap-around," provided the first log has been archived. DB2 does support striped active log data sets.

Log Definition

Entries on the **DSNTIPL** installation panel describe the logging environment. Macros **DSN6LOGP** and **DSN6ARVP** contain the parameters that control logging.

The system uses the **UPDATE RATE** and **ARCHIVE LOG FREQ** fields of the installation CLIST to calculate the data set size of each active log data set. Your management of the logs and the archives is used in system recoverability.

A log record is identified by an RBA in the first byte of its header. This number uniquely identifies this record.

The log print record is split into four parts: summary information, log record header, log record sub-header, and logged data. To understand more about the formats of the logs, look at the mapping information in member **DSNDQJ00** in the **SDSNMACS** library. Log records include undo/redo records, in-place updates that represent both the before and after images, and partial image records.

Each log record has a header that indicates its type and the DB2 subcomponent that made the record. Log records can contain compressed data if a table contains compressed data. Reading compressed data requires access to the data dictionary.

When a change is made to a database, DB2 writes a unit of recovery log record that describes the change. These rows, which are logged in the active log, are called undo/redo records. Also written is a Begin UR (begin a unit of recovery) record, which records the first request to change a database. If a unit of work is committed or rolled back, you will see also an End Phase 2 record to reflect that the work has been completed. Exception records can also be written. These are registered as database exception table (DBET) log records to record database exception states when any database table space, index space, or partition is in an exception state.

Checkpoint log records are written when the checkpoint frequency specified by the **CHECKPOINT FREQ** field on panel **DSNTIPL** is reached. Many records can be written for a single checkpoint. The checkpoint will log the current status of DB2 and register the log RBA of the checkpoint in the bootstrap data set.

Log Data Capture

DB2 log data is available for recovery purposes in real time through the log capture exit routine. This online exit captures the data that DB2 writes to the active log, but it does not return data or enter data to DB2.

It is better to use the Instrumentation Facility Interface rather than the log capture exit to read data from the log. You can also read the records with IFI while DB2 is running. Doing so requires a program that uses the IFI commands **READA** and **READS** to capture the log information into a buffer. (You can return the records directly to the program.) To gather the information, you would first run a **START TRACE** command, using IFCID 126 to accumulate active log records into a buffer. This will cause records to be recorded into the buffer as well as to the active log in DB2. Use the following command to start the performance trace to collect the records:

```
-START TRACE(P) CLASS(30) IFCID(126) DEST(OPX)
```

If you set the **DATA CAPTURE CHANGES** option on a **CREATE TABLE** or an **ALTER TABLE** statement, you can retrieve the log information using programs such as Remote Recovery Data Facility (RRDF) or DB2 DataPropagator.

Recovery Log Manager

Within DB2, the recovery log manager (RLM) maintains the DB2 recovery log by writing log records and retrieving log information in response to resource manager requests. RLM maintains the DB2 BSDS that contains linkage information pointing to all the DB2 log data sets, and it controls the movement of full active log data sets to the archive log. It supports other DB2 resource managers by reading and writing data on the DB2 recovery log. RLM also copies active log data sets to archive log data sets when they become full.

Log records are assigned ascending RBAs and are mapped into physical data sets as described in the BSDS. DB2 data-sharing log records are read from the data-sharing group (or from selected members of the data-sharing group) in merged LRSN sequence.

The recovery log manager provides:

- The **RECOVER BSDS** command.

- The **ARCHIVE LOG** command (the change log inventory utility job that updates the BSDS).

- Print log map utility: Produces a listing showing the log RBAs and LRSNs contained in each log data set. All active and archive data sets that contain log data are included in the listing, as well as all active log data sets that are available for use, all conditional restart control records, the subsystem checkpoint queue, and the DDF communications record.

- DB2 stand-alone log services: Provide an assembler language macro capability that enables user-written application programs to read the DB2 log from a z/OS job environment.

- Log format utility: Pre-formats new active log data sets.

Log I/O Enhancements

DB2 9 for z/OS provides the following enhancements for log I/O:

- The number of active log input buffers is increased from 15 to 120.

- Archive log files are now read using Basic Sequential Access Method (BSAM) instead of Basic Direct Access Method (BDAM).

- Archive log files can use Data Facility Storage Management Subsystem (DFSMS) striping and compression.

- Archive log files input buffers are increased from 1 to N, where N is proportional to the number of stripes. For each stripe, DB2 uses 10 tracks' worth of buffers, regardless of the block size.

- Archive log buffer processing is converted from **AMODE(24)** to **AMODE(31)**, so DB2 can now move these buffers above the 16 MB line, enabling them to be much larger.

- By exploiting z/OS 1.7 **DSNTYPE=LARGE** disk data set support, installations can have 4 GB DASD archive logs. Active logs no longer require multi-volume allocations.

Installation Panel DSNTIPL

The system services address space in DB2 uses two log buffer areas: one for input and one for output to the active log. You define these log buffer areas, along with other key components, on installation panel **DSNTIPL**. In DB2 9, the panel provides the following fields associated with logging:

OUTPUT BUFFER

The **OUTPUT BUFFER** field specifies the size of the output buffer that is to be used for writing active log data sets. Acceptable values range from 40 KB to 400,000 KB.

Log writes can be synchronous and asynchronous. The logs are written synchronously at commit time. If you reach the write threshold specified in **OUTBUFF** for the log buffer, the flushing is asynchronous. If your performance traces report log buffer write failures greater than zero, set **OUTBUFF** higher; it is not large enough. This setting is updatable using subsystem parameter **OUTBUFF** in macro **DSN6LOGP**.

NUMBER OF LOGS

This field defines the number of data sets to be established for each copy of the active log. If you have converted the BSDS, the number of logs can be defined from **2** to **93**.

ARCHIVE LOG FREQ

This field sets the interval (number of hours) to be used in offloading the active log. The default is **24**, which ensures that the log is offloaded at least once each day.

UPDATE RATE

The default **UPDATE RATE** setting assumes that 400 bytes of data will be logged for each update, insert, or delete. When the CLIST is run, this field and the **ARCHIVE LOG FREQ** field together determine the size of the logs.

LOG APPLY STORAGE

This field sets the maximum amount of **DBM1** storage used by the fast log apply process. During restart, this process is always enabled. This setting is updatable using subsystem parameter **LOGAPSTG** in macro **DSN6SYSP**.

CHECKPOINT FREQ

This field specifies the interval (in minutes or in number of log records) that will start a new checkpoint in DB2. The default setting for the **CHKFREQ** subsystem parameter in macro **DSN6SYSP** is 500,000 records. Use the **SET LOG** command to change the time or number of records between checkpoints in DB2.

FREQUENCY TYPE

This field indicates whether the units specified for checkpoint frequency represent a number of log records (**LOGRECS**) or time (**MINUTES**).

UR CHECK FREQ

This field specifies the number of checkpoint cycles DB2 goes through before issuing a warning message to the console. The value of your checkpoint interval divided by your limit for issuing commits is the best value to use for the system. This setting is updatable using subsystem parameter **URCHKTH** in macro **DSN6SYSP**.

UR LOG WRITE CHECK

This field indicates how many log records are to be written by an uncommitted unit of recovery before a warning message is issued, providing a good indicator of long-running URs. This setting is updatable using subsystem parameter **URLGWTH** in macro **DSN6SYSP**.

LIMIT BACKOUT

This field indicates whether to postpone backward log processing. Possible values are **AUTO** (the default), **YES**, and **NO**. This setting is updatable using subsystem parameter **LBACKOUT** in macro **DSN6SYSP**.

BACKOUT DURATION

This field defines how much log to process for back-out when the **LIMIT BACKOUT** field is set to **YES** or **AUTO**.

RO SWITCH CHKPTS

This field defines the number of consecutive checkpoints permitted after a partition or page set is updated. When this threshold is reached, DB2 will convert the partition or page set to read-only status. Table spaces for which **NOT LOGGED** has been specified are always converted to read-only after one checkpoint. The default **RO SWITCH CHKPTS** value is **5** (five checkpoints). This setting is updatable using subsystem parameter **PCLOSEN** in macro **DSN6SYSP**.

RO SWITCH TIME

Specified in minutes, this field's value works with that of the **RO SWITCH CHKPTS** field to change the partition or page set from read-write to read-only status. For infrequently used table spaces, this setting can reduce the recovery and logging process. The default value is **10** (minutes). For **NOT LOGGED** table spaces, DB2 converts the partition or page set after one minute, regardless of this field's value. The **RO SWITCH TIME** setting is updatable using subsystem parameter **PCLOSET** in macro **DSN6SYSP**.

LEVELID UPDATE FREQ

This field controls how often (in number of checkpoints) the level ID of a table space set or partition is updated. It also controls how often the value that the **RECOVER LOGONLY** utility uses as a starting point for log apply is updated. The default is **5** (checkpoints). This setting is updatable using subsystem parameter **DLDFREQ** in macro **DSN6SYSP**.

Notes on Logs

Some additional points to note related to the active logs:

- DB2 must pre-format a VSAM control area before writing the active log records the first time. Use the **DSNJLOGF** stand-alone utility to pre-format the active log data sets before they are used by DB2.

- If you compress your data, the log information about that data is also compressed. However, any indexes you compress are not logged as compressed records.

- Logging rates have improved in DB2 9, and striping is supported for archive logs.

- The DB2 **ARCHIVE LOG** command truncates the current active log data sets. This operation runs an asynchronous offload and updates the BSDS with a record of the offload.

- The **SET LOG** command flushes only the log buffers.

- The **STOP DATABASE** command makes certain the active log is not allocated to DB2. You can then use the **DSN1LOGP** utility to read the active log.

- Choices in DB 9 include **LOG YES** or **LOG NO** for logging attributes on the **CREATE TABLESPACE** and **ALTER TABLESPACE** statements. You can have different logging attributes for partition table spaces. Specifying **LOG NO** for a segmented table space that contains multiple tables affects all the tables in that segmented table space. You can find the setting in the catalog in the **SYSIBM.SYSTABLESPACE LOG** column. *Use the **LOG NO** option with caution.*

It is no surprise that **SYSLGRNX** (system log range) records are not kept for **NOT LOGGED** table spaces. Note in **SYSCOPY** that the column **LRSN** indicates the point in the log where the logging attribute was changed. A new column, **LOGGED**, has been added to the **SYSCOPY**. The value **Y** indicates logging, **N** is for no logging, and a blank indicates the row was built before DB2 9.

The Log Itself

The VSAM control interval holds 4,089 bytes of DB2 log information. This is what is referred to as the physical record. When information is written, this is the logical record, and its length depends on the space available in the CI.

All logical records have a header, called a log record header (LRH), that contains control information. A suffix, called the log control interval definition (LCID), describes how the record segments are placed into the physical control interval.

Each log record has a code or type that describes the event that recorded the record. There are also subtype codes to produce a more in-depth event description.

You can use mapping macros provided in macro **DSNDQJ00** in the **SDSNMACS** data set to interpret the log record formats for records and subtypes. Each macro is self-documenting with notes. You can also acquire log statistics from your monitor to calculate the minimum megabytes per second required to write to the active log data set to understand your logging requirements.

Size of the Active Log Data Sets

The frequency of offloading to the archive is key to determining the size of the logs. The CLIST uses the **UPDATE RATE** and **ARCHIVE LOG FREQUENCY** fields on installation panel **DSNTIPL** to determine the disk space required by the logs.

Basically, the size is calculated as follows to find the hours in the archive period for one log; you would double this result for dual logging:

*Disk space required by logs = (Data change log record size) * (Data change rate per hour) * (Hours in archive period)*

Log Utilities

DB2 9 includes enhancements to several stand-alone utilities related to the logs.

DSN1LOGP

The **DSN1LOGP** utility, which formats the contents of the recovery log for display, now detects possible erroneous recovery information. If you attempt to print a range of records but the range is no longer in the BSDS because the archive logs have rolled off, error message DSN1224I indicates that the range could not be found and returns an RC4.

When you specify the utility's **SUMMARY(YES)** option, the report shows whether objects are logged or not logged. This option might not be available if the specified range of log records does not include the Begin UR log record.

Note that a clone table's object identifier will have the eighth, or high-order, bit set on, so the OBID for the clone might be **x'8xxx'** and the base table would have **x'0xxx'** as the OBID. When reading the output of the **DSN1LOGP** utility, you need to be aware of this clone naming convention.

DSNJU003

You use the change log inventory utility, **DSNJU003**, to create conditional restart control records. In DB2 9, you can now use timestamps for your normal conditional restart and for the **RESTORE** system utility.

DSNJU004

The print log map utility, **DSNJU004,** runs as a batch job. You can use it to print the BSDS contents and the conditional restart record. You can also use this utility to determine the current log configuration. Each checkpoint that is displayed now shows the stored clock value in the checkpoint queue section. Each log record includes a suffix that describes how the record segments are placed in the physical control intervals.

The print log map utility output has changed regarding DDF. Several keywords related to request identification have been added. These changes are reflected in the output of utility **DSNJU003**. **DSNJU004** now prints the DDF information at the beginning of the output, before the log information.

To determine how much space is left in the log, obtain the high-written RBA in the log and then subtract it from **x'FFFFFFFFFFFF'**. If you have applied APAR PK27611, use RBA **x'FFFF00000000'** instead.

DSNJU004 provides an assortment of data you will find very useful. Its information includes:

- Names of active and archive log sets
- BSDS information
- Active logs available, log starting/ending RBA values
- Checkpoint record contents in BSDS
- System-level backup information (new in DB2 9)
- Checkpoint queue contents
- Utility and system timestamps
- Conditional restart control records
- Information in the system Coded Character Set Identifier (CCSID)

System Checkpoints

When you have a long-running unit of recovery, DB2 records a large number of log records from the beginning to the end of the transaction. Usually, the jobs running are doing a large number of updates without proper committing within the program. The **DSNTIJUZ** job includes a parameter, **URLGWTH**, that deals with long-running reader threshold. The parameter's default value is **0** (zero), which means that long-running UOR checking is not activated by default.

Installation panel **DSNTIPN** provides the value for checkpoint frequency (in the **CHECKPOINT FREQ** field). In DB2 9, system checkpoints now store information at the table level to track segmented table spaces independently. Stored in the UR checkpoint record along with table space and partition level, the checkpoints record information about each modified object uncommitted unit of recovery. This process assists in the back-out processing at start-up time.

In DB2 9, the updating of **SYSLGRNX** entries is deferred beyond the start-up, allowing faster restart of DB2. The entries are updated at the first system checkpoint that follows the restart.

Archive Logs

The archive logs are sequential data sets and support up to 10,000 archive log data sets per log copy. In DB2 9 CM, all active logs support BSAM to read the archive data sets. In NFM, archive logs can be defined as extended format (EF) data sets and must be SMS-managed. As a result of the extended formatting, compression and striping are allowed.

Conversion of Archive Log Processing from AMODE(24) to AMODE(31)

Before DB2 9, some customers reported running short of storage below the 16 MB line in the **MSTR** address space during archive log processing. Storage constraint relief and increased archive log processing are a result of converting using 31-bit mode in DB2. In addition, DB2 9 moves these buffers above the 16 MB line and, when possible, uses dual buffering for archive log reads or writes. This support is available starting in DB2 9 CM.

Bootstrap Data Set

The bootstrap data set is an inventory manager for the active and archive logs, passwords for the directory and catalog, and conditional restart and checkpoint record information. The BSDS is the only VSAM key-sequenced data set (KSDS) in DB2. It contains name and status information for DB2 and RBA range specifications for all active and archive log data sets.

Each time an active log is archived, a copy of the BSDS goes along with it. The BSDS is the first entry on the tape or disk archive log backup. You need take no special steps to keep the BSDS updated with records of DB2 logging events; the system handles this task automatically.

Each BSDS requires 3.5 MB of space. DB2 automatically allocates two BSDS copies at installation time. When moving to DB2 9, make sure you convert your BSDS by running the **DSNJCNVB** conversion utility, which is part of job **DSNTIJUZ**.

To migrate to DB2 9, your BSDSs must be in the new expanded format, which supports up to 10,000 archive log volumes and up to 93 active log data sets for each copy of the log. This new format became available beginning with DB2 8 NFM. When executing the job, expect a return code of **888** from this step if your BSDSs have already been converted. Job **DSNTIJUZ** accepts return codes of **0** and **888** from the **DSNTCNVB** step.

Your shop might require changes to active or archive logs that necessitate a corresponding change to the contents of the BSDS, such as:

- Adding more active log data sets
- Recovering a damaged BSDS
- Discarding outdated archive log data sets
- Copying active log data sets to newly allocated data sets
- Moving log data sets to other devices
- Adding or changing the DDF communications record
- Creating or canceling control records for conditional restart

The DB2 batch change log inventory utility, **DSNJU003**, lets you change the contents of the BSDS.

Do not run utility **DSNJU003** when DB2 is active. DB2 must be inactive, or unpredictable results may occur.

To change the BSDS:

1. Make sure you have a backup of the BSDS.
2. Issue the **STOP DB2 MODE(QUIESCE)** command to stop the DB2 subsystem.
3. Run utility **DSNJU003**.
4. Restart DB2 with the **START DB2** command.

Using the Access Method Services (IDCAMS) **REPRO** command, you can copy an active log data set, but only when DB2 is down. DB2 allocates the active log data sets as exclusive (**DISP=OLD**) at DB2 start-up.

Virtual Buffer Pools

Buffer pools are memory allocations for the storage of pages of information from table spaces and index spaces. The total storage in all buffer pools should not exceed 1 TB. In DB2 9, buffer pools have moved above the 2 GB bar. Make sure your buffer pools are backed up by real storage. Buffer pools are located and managed by the **DBM1** address space.

During installation or migration, you specify a name and size for each buffer pool. An operator command, **ALTER BP**, is available in case you need to change these values.

Buffer Pool Definition

Panel **DSNTIP1** (Figure 2.14) is the first of two installation/migration CLIST panels that deal with the buffer pools.

```
DSNTIP1          INSTALL DB2 - BUFFER POOL SIZES - PANEL 1
===>  _


 1 DEFAULT  4-KB BUFFER POOL FOR USER DATA ===> BP0        BP0    - BP49
 2 DEFAULT  8-KB BUFFER POOL FOR USER DATA ===> BP8K0      BP8K0  - BP8K9
 3 DEFAULT 16-KB BUFFER POOL FOR USER DATA ===> BP16K0     BP16K0 - BP16K9
 4 DEFAULT 32-KB BUFFER POOL FOR USER DATA ===> BP32K      BP32K  - BP32K9
 5 DEFAULT BUFFER POOL FOR USER LOB DATA   ===> BP0        BP0    - BP32K9
 6 DEFAULT BUFFER POOL FOR USER XML DATA   ===> BP16K0     BP16K0 - BP16K9
 7 DEFAULT BUFFER POOL FOR USER INDEXES    ===> BP0        BP0    - BP32K9
Enter buffer pool sizes in number of pages.
 8 BP0  ==> 20000     18 BP10 ==> 0        28 BP20 ==> 0
 9 BP1  ==> 0         19 BP11 ==> 0        29 BP21 ==> 0
10 BP2  ==> 0         20 BP12 ==> 0        30 BP22 ==> 0
11 BP3  ==> 0         21 BP13 ==> 0        31 BP23 ==> 0
12 BP4  ==> 0         22 BP14 ==> 0        32 BP24 ==> 0
13 BP5  ==> 0         23 BP15 ==> 0        33 BP25 ==> 0
14 BP6  ==> 0         24 BP16 ==> 0        34 BP26 ==> 0
15 BP7  ==> 0         25 BP17 ==> 0        35 BP27 ==> 0
16 BP8  ==> 0         26 BP18 ==> 0        36 BP28 --> 0
17 BP9  ==> 0         27 BP19 ==> 0        37 BP29 ==> 0
```

Figure 2.14: Installation panel DSNTIP1 – Buffer pool sizes (panel 1)

Here, you specify the default buffers for user data, LOB and XML data, and indexes in DB2 9. These settings apply to objects that are created implicitly and to objects that are created explicitly without the **BUFFERPOOL** clause. Table 2.6 lists the subsystem parameters and default values associated with these entries.

Table 2.6: Buffer pool size DSNZPARMs			
DSNZPARM	**Description**	**Acceptable values**	**Default**
DSN6SYSP TBSBPOOL	Default 4 KB buffer pool for user data	Any 4 KB buffer pool name	**BP0**
DSN6SYSP TBSBP8K	Default 8 KB buffer pool for user data	Any 8 KB buffer pool name	**BP8K0**
DSN6SYSP TBSBP16K	Default 16 KB buffer pool for user data	Any 16 KB buffer pool name	**BP16K0**
DSN6SYSP TBSBP32K	Default 32 KB buffer pool for user data	Any 32 KB buffer pool name	**BP32K**
DSN6SYSP TBSBPLOB	Default buffer pool for user LOB data	Any 4 KB, 8 KB, 16 KB, or 32 KB buffer pool name	**BP0**
DSN6SYSP TBSBPXML	Default buffer pool for user XML data	Any 16 KB buffer pool name	**BP16K0**
DSN6SYSP IDXBPOOL	Default buffer pool for user indexes	Any 4 KB, 8 KB, 16 KB, or 32 KB buffer pool name	**BP0**

Figure 2.15 shows the second installation/migration CLIST panel where you define the buffer pools, **DSNTIP2**. You use this panel to specify the total number of buffers for a given virtual buffer pool from **BP30** to **BP32K9**.

```
DSNTIP2          INSTALL DB2 - BUFFER POOL SIZES - PANEL 2
===>  _

Enter buffer pool sizes in number of pages.
  1 BP30  ==> 0      18 BP47   ==> 0       35 BP16K4 ==> 0
  2 BP31  ==> 0      19 BP48   ==> 0       36 BP16K5 ==> 0
  3 BP32  ==> 0      20 BP49   ==> 0       37 BP16K6 ==> 0
  4 BP33  ==> 0      21 BP8K0  ==> 1000    38 BP16K7 ==> 0
  5 BP34  ==> 0      22 BP8K1  ==> 0       39 BP16K8 ==> 0
  6 BP35  ==> 0      23 BP8K2  ==> 0       40 BP16K9 ==> 0
  7 BP36  ==> 0      24 BP8K3  ==> 0       41 BP32K  ==> 250
  8 BP37  ==> 0      25 BP8K4  ==> 0       42 BP32K1 ==> 0
  9 BP38  ==> 0      26 BP8K5  ==> 0       43 BP32K2 ==> 0
 10 BP39  ==> 0      27 BP8K6  ==> 0       44 BP32K3 ==> 0
 11 BP40  ==> 0      28 BP8K7  ==> 0       45 BP32K4 ==> 0
 12 BP41  ==> 0      29 BP8K8  ==> 0       46 BP32K5 ==> 0
 13 BP42  ==> 0      30 BP8K9  ==> 0       47 BP32K6 ==> 0
 14 BP43  ==> 0      31 BP16K0 ==> 500     48 BP32K7 ==> 0
 15 BP44  ==> 0      32 BP16K1 ==> 0       49 BP32K8 ==> 0
 16 BP45  ==> 0      33 BP16K2 ==> 0       50 BP32K9 ==> 0
 17 BP46  ==> 0      34 BP16K3 ==> 0
```

Figure 2.15: Installation panel DSNTIP2 – Buffer pool sizes (panel 2)

Remember that the total amount of your buffer pool storage cannot exceed 1 TB. In the 64-bit addressing space, DB2 can have up to 16 exabytes of virtual storage addressability by a single DB2 address space.

Buffer Pool Management

You can manage the buffer pools yourself through tuning and monitoring, or you can use the services of dynamic buffer pool size adjustments so that the system's memory resources can be more effectively used to achieve workload performance goals. This new service is available in conversion mode in DB2 9.

DB2 9 supports Workload Manager–assisted buffer pool management with z/OS 1.8. This WLM service assists in making dynamic buffer pool size adjustments on realtime monitored workloads. With dynamic buffer pool assist, a DB2 subsystem on the same LPAR might have non-critical buffer pools decreased in size while those pages are reassigned to a critical subsystem.

The automatic management of buffer pool storage provides sizing information to WLM. Buffer pools are registered with WLM, and DB2 communicates with WLM every time an allied agent encounters delays relating to read I/O and periodically reports the buffer pool size and random read hit ratios to WLM.

WLM projects the effect of making a change to the size of the buffer pool over time from collected data maintained in a histogram. It plots the size and hit ratio over time to determine whether work is achieving its goals and then determines the appropriate course of action.

WLM decides whether increasing the buffer pool size could help achieve the performance goal if I/O delays are occurring. If sufficient storage is available, WLM could decide to increase a buffer pool or even decrease one buffer pool and increase another. If the adjustment is made, the results will be just as though you had issued an **ALTER BUFFERPOOL VPSIZE** command.

To enable this feature, use the **AUTOSIZE(YES)** setting on the **CREATE TABLESPACE** command. You can modify individual buffer pools by using the **ALTER BUFFERPOOL** command with **AUTOSIZE(YES/NO)**. The default for automatic buffer pool adjustment is off (**NO**).

To summarize, DB2 takes the following steps to perform automatic management of buffer pool storage:

1. Registers the buffer pool with the WLM

2. Provides the sizing information to WLM

3. Communicates to WLM each time allied agents encounter delays due to read I/O

4. Periodically reports buffer pool size and random read hit ratios to WLM

Buffer Pool Details

Buffer pools temporarily store pages of data from table spaces or indexes in storage. DB2 buffer pool pages are not paged out; the EDM pools and the sort pool are held in real storage. For the DB2 buffer pools, the EDM pool, and working storage, the amount of real storage must be the same as the amount of virtual storage. Paging activity in the buffers is an indication of a problem.

DB2 lets you use up to 50 different 4 KB buffers and up to 10 different buffer pools each for 8 KB, 16 KB, and 32 KB buffers. You can set the size of each of these buffer pools separately during installation.

As of DB2 9, using above-the-bar real storage enables the use of very large buffers. As a result, applications can avoid a substantial amount of read and write I/O.

The following points summarize the process flow of an application with respect to the buffer pools:

1. The program accesses a row of a table.

2. DB2 places the page that contains that row in a buffer.

3. Is the data already in a buffer? If so, the application program does not have to wait for it to be retrieved from disk.

4. Has the row been changed? If so, data in the buffer must be written back to disk eventually. A write operation might be delayed until DB2 takes a

checkpoint or until one of the related write thresholds is reached. (The data-sharing environment writing mechanism differs somewhat.)

5. The data remains in the buffer until DB2 decides to use the space for another page. Data can be read or changed without a disk I/O operation until written.

Buffer Pool Analyzer and ALTER BUFFERPOOL Statement

You can use the Buffer Pool Analyzer for z/OS to obtain recommendations about buffer pool allocation changes and perform "what if" analysis of your buffer pools. To change the size and other characteristics of a buffer pool or to enable DB2 automatic buffer pool size management for a buffer pool, you use the DB2 **ALTER BUFFERPOOL** command. You can issue this command at any time while DB2 is running.

In DB2 9, you can specify 4 KB, 8 KB, 16 KB, or 32 KB buffer pools for user indexes. Indexes that are created during conversion mode require a 4 KB buffer pool. If you do not specify a 4 KB buffer pool in the **BUFFERPOOL** clause when you create an index in CM, DB2 issues the following error:

```
SQLCODE = -676, ERROR: ONLY A 4K PAGE BUFFERPOOL CAN BE USED FOR AN INDEX
```

Work File Database

The work file database is the only temporary database in DB2 9. It is used for all temporary tables. In DB2 9, the work file database merged with the **TEMP** database; the **TEMP** database is no longer used. Job **DSNTIJTM** creates data sets for the work file database.

The work file database **DSNDB07** houses work file table spaces that are logical work files used in sorting. This sorting could be the result of an SQL **ORDER BY**, **GROUP BY**, **DISTINCT**, **JOIN**, or other request. Multiple table spaces are defined for 4 KB and 32 KB sizes in DB2 9, requiring buffer pools to be assigned to these table spaces as well.

You should increase your space for 32 KB work files. You can reallocate the space by stopping the **DSNDB07** database, deleting the old work file data sets, and redefining the work file data sets as larger or increasing the number of data sets.

Next, issue the **CREATE TABLESPACE** statement for each new work file. Then, start the **DSNDB07** database.

When allocating multiple table spaces in the sort work file database, keep in mind that DB2 9 gives preference to the least recently used table space whose secondary quantity (**SECQTY**) is **0** (zero). It is advisable to allocate multiple work file table spaces with a **SECQTY** of **0** to facilitate efficient concurrent I/O.

When allocating the table spaces in the work file database for use by declared global temporary tables (DGTTs) in your applications, define the table spaces with a non-zero secondary quantity (**SECQTY>0**) in the work file. DGTTs do not span multiple table spaces; they are limited to one table space. Allocating your work files this way will minimize the contention for space in the work files. You will need to monitor and tune your definitions of the table spaces in the work file database to ensure efficient space use. For more information, see IBM Tech Note 1386786 and maintenance PK70060/UK46839 and PK67691/UK47354.

Utilities do not run against the work file database. Statistics are kept on the table spaces in columns **NACTIVE**, **SPACE**, and **EXTENTS** in the database.

When sorting begins, rows are written to work files. At the end of the input phase, the rows are sorted. If multiple work files are used, they are merged together to produce one work file at the end of the input phase.

When an application needs to sort data, the work files are allocated on a least recently used basis for a particular sort. These work files are logical work files (LWF) that reside in the work file table spaces in **DSNDB07** in a non–data-sharing environment. DB2 uses a buffer pool when writing to the LWF.

Only the buffer pool size limits the number of work files that can be used for sorting. DB2 can support large sorts by allocating a single logical work file to several physical work file table spaces. Very large buffer pools can also help avoid disk I/O.

If you think global temporary tables are monopolizing your sort pool, take a look at performance class 8 using IFCID 0311. Various factors can impact the performance of the sort process, such as the size of the sort pool, the size of the row being sorted, and whether I/O contention is occurring. Keep your work files in buffer pools separate from other data.

Things to Know About Work Files

DB2 uses 32 KB work file data sets when the total work file record size, which includes the record overhead, exceeds 100 bytes.

You can use the sort summary trace record (IFCID 0096) to show the number of sorted records, the record size, and whether a merge phase was required.

Using Parallel Access Volume (PAV) disk devices is a way to minimize I/O contention.

As I/Os occur in the merge phase of a sort, DB2 uses sequential prefetch to bring eight pages into the buffer pool. If there are insufficient pages in the work file buffer pool, DB2 reduces the prefetch quantity to four or less and might disable prefetching entirely.

In the buffer pool that supports only 4 KB or 32 KB work files, set **VPSEQT** (the sequential steal threshold) to 99 percent to avoid overwriting space maps. The default setting is 80 percent, which means 20 percent of the buffers can go unused.

If you have SQL that uses an in-memory sparse index scan as an access method, know that in-memory sparse index is based on the sorted work file. DB2 uses the sparse index to fetch records from the work file rather than a table space scan.

Increase the **DWQT** (deferred write threshold) and **VDWQT** (vertical deferred write threshold) values. If you reach the threshold set for these values, writes are scheduled.

You cannot use **RECOVER** on the **DSNDB07** work files (except in a data-sharing environment).

If **DSNDB01.DBD01** is stopped or inaccessible, the descriptor is not loaded into main storage, and the work file will not be allocated. To get around this situation, stop and restart the work file database after **DBD01** is available.

Remember that the default buffer pool for 4 KB sorting in DB2 is **BP0**. You should change the default from **BP0** to **BP07** or your choice of buffer pool.

During an **INSERT** statement, a temporary work file result table is populated, and it uses work file space. Until this work file space goes away, no other process can use that same work file space. The space can be released by the program at commit, rollback, or deallocation time. Use IFCID 0311 in performance trace class 8 to distinguish these tables from other uses of the work file. This IFCID is the global temp table usage trace. Among other things, it gives you the program name and information about the package that uses the global temporary table.

In prior releases, if you granted privileges on the TEMP database, you have to grant those privileges on the work file database to avoid authorization errors.

In DB2 9, the **DSNTIJTM** job creates the default storage group **SYSDEFLT**, defines the database that is for temporary work files, and binds DB2 REXX Language Support. By changing the parameters in the last step of installation job **DSNTIJTM**, you can specify a different user-managed storage group. You can create additional work file table spaces after running **DSNTIJTM** by using the **DSNTWFG** exec program in job **DSNTIST**. Check the comment block in this job step for information about the parameters for **DSNTWFG**.

If storage space is not a problem, wait to drop the temporary database. Falling back to DB2 8 will require you to re-create it.

You must define at least one of the table spaces in the work file database with a page size of 32 KB. Static scrollable cursor result tables and declared global temporary tables both require a 32 KB work file database table space. There are no 8 KB or 16 KB table spaces in the work file database. You will find a sample query to check your work file database in **SDSNSAMP** member **DSNTESQ**.

Rows of a declared global temporary table reside in a table space in a work file database. DB2 will not create an implicit table space for the DGTT table.

There cannot be more than 500 table spaces in the work file database for 4 KB or 32 KB work files.

For all agents on the local DB2, the number of declared global temporary table indexes cannot be greater than 10,000.

DB2 9 lets you use the installation CLIST to add table spaces to the work file database as part of the **MIGRATE** process. Earlier releases allowed this process only in **INSTALL** mode. The segment size of the table spaces is restricted to 16 until DB2 enters new-function mode. During migration, job **DSNTIJTC** creates and updates indexes on the catalog tables. The migration job will fail if you do not have enough storage.

Your buffer pool hit ratio for the work file buffer pool is a measure of how often a page access (a getpage) is satisfied without requiring an I/O operation. Make your buffer pools large enough to increase the buffer hit ratio.

Sort Pool

The sort pool is part of the database services address space. DB2 uses a tournament sort; in this technique (depicted in Figure 2.16), the algorithm produces logical work files called runs. These runs are intermediate sets of ordered data. If sufficient room exists, sorting is done in the sort pool; otherwise, the work file database is used.

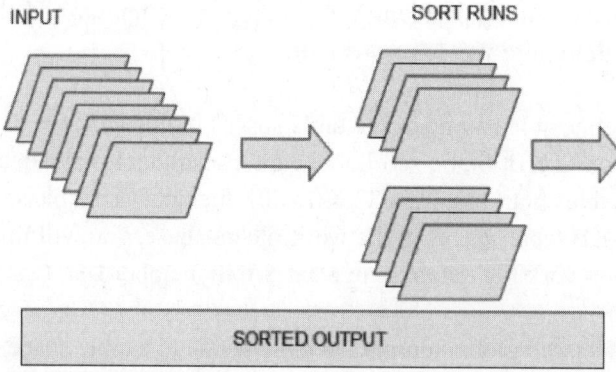

INPUT

SORT RUNS

SORTED OUTPUT

Figure 2.16: Sorted output

The **SORT POOL SIZE** field on installation panel **DSNTIPC** (or the subsystem parameter **SRTPOOL** in macro **DSN6SPRM**) sets the amount of storage required for the sort pool.

The buffer pools, sort pool, and RID pool have been moved above the 2 GB bar and are no longer included in the region size calculation. Local storage for the sort pool is created above the 2 GB bar at allocation time. The above-the-bar sort pool contains sort tree nodes. This local sorting can be invoked when a cursor within a program requires a sort; this usually is prompted by an **ORDER BY** clause.

DB2 allocates 240 KB as a minimum and 128 MB as a maximum for each concurrent sort. The default size of the sort pool is 2 MB. DB2 starts with 240 KB and then adds more storage until either the limit is reached or a maximum number of nodes is populated in the sort tree (32 KB). The DB2 in-memory sort work area maintains the storage boundaries for each concurrent sort operation.

You can change the sort pools and other CLIST calculations on installation panel **DSNTIPC** (Figure 2.17). Using the **SORT POOL SIZE** field, you can make the sort pool as large as possible. The default value, as previously noted, is 2 MB.

```
DSNTIPC          INSTALL DB2 - CLIST CALCULATIONS - PANEL 1
===>
You can update the DSMAX, EDMPOOL, EDMPOOL STATEMENT CACHE, EDM DBD CACHE,
EDM SKELETON POOL, SORT POOL, and RID POOL sizes if necessary.
                                      Calculated    Override
 1  DSMAX - MAXIMUM OPEN DATA SETS  =    9960                  (1-100000)
 2  DSNT485I  EDMPOOL STORAGE SIZE  =   13142 K            K
 3  DSNT485I  EDM STATEMENT CACHE   =   56693 K            K
 4  DSNT485I  EDM DBD CACHE         =   11700 K            K
 5  DSNT485I  EDM SKELETON POOL SIZE =   5120 K            K
 6  DSNT485I  BUFFER POOL SIZE      =     101 M
 7  DSNT485I  SORT POOL SIZE        =    2000 K            K
 8  DSNT485I  RID POOL SIZE         =    8000 K            K
 9  DSNT485I  DATA SET STORAGE SIZE =   17928 K
10  DSNT485I  CODE STORAGE SIZE     =   38200 K
11  DSNT485I  WORKING STORAGE SIZE  =   55800 K
12  DSNT486I  TOTAL MAIN STORAGE    =     238 M
13  DSNT487I  TOTAL STORAGE BELOW 16M =  1159 K WITH SWA ABOVE 16M LINE
14  DSNT438I  IRLM LOCK MAXIMUM SPACE =    2 G, AVAILABLE =   2 G
```

Figure 2.17: Installation panel DSNTIPC – CLIST calculations

To investigate further, take a look at IFCID 217 (storage sizes) to find out the total amount of storage available for storage manager pools.

System Error Reporting

In MVS, most messages are issued from the **JES2/JES3** subsystems, Data Facility Product (DFP), various system products, and application programs. The locations of these messages can be found at the console, hard-copy log, job log, or **SYSOUT** data set. Other messages can be found in the MVS system log data set (**SYSLOG**). In z/OS, the job log is used to show the start sequence of DB2.

The DB2 system administrator has the responsibility to debug problems within DB2. Sometimes these problems may be the DB2 software, a user job, or a transaction. To aid in determining which component has failed, you capture the memory contents in a dump. There are different ways to take these dumps and different data sets that store this information.

Dumps, along with other information (e.g., the console log), can provide information about where the components have failed. The information you collect can be written by MVS in four types of system data sets. Figure 2.18 shows the four types of error data that can be collected.

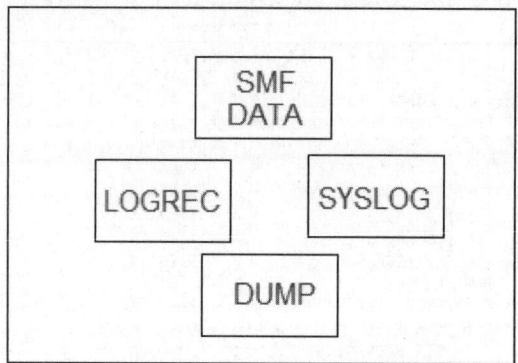

Figure 2.18: Locations of error data collected

SMF data produces analysis reports, **LOGREC** data contains statistical data about machine failures such as I/O errors, **SYSLOG** data (which resides in the **JES2/3** spool space), holds console messages and other system communications, and **DUMP** data sets record areas of virtual storage.

System Display and Search Facility

The z/OS System Display and Search Facility (SDSF) lets you monitor, manage, and control z/OS. You can control job processing, control output, browse jobs without printing, and manage system resources. Data is displayed on panels in tabular format. You select a desired function on an SDSF panel, or you can enter **SDSF** or system commands on the **COMMAND INPUT** line.

- You can manage jobs on the Status (option **ST**) panel. Here, you will see the status of jobs on any queue, including held and non-held output.

- **DA** shows only active jobs (address spaces).

- **O** (output) displays information about output that is ready to be printed.

- **H** (help output) shows the jobs on hold.

Operators and system programmers have a more robust SDSF Primary Option menu (Figure 2.19) that includes the system log, WLM resources, and more. You can use this menu to manage jobs.

```
   Display  Filter  View  Print  Options  Help
---------------------------------------------------------------
 ----------------- SDSF PRIMARY OPTION MENU  ----------
COMMAND INPUT ===> _

DA     Active users                    INIT   Initiators
I      Input queue                     PR     Printers
O      Output queue                    PUN    Punches
H      Held output queue               RDR    Readers
ST     Status of jobs                  LINE   Lines
                                       NODE   Nodes
LOG    System log                      SO     Spool offload
SR     System requests                 SP     Spool volumes
MAS    Members in the MAS
JC     Job classes                     ULOG   User session log
SE     Scheduling environments
RES    WLM resources
ENC    Enclaves
PS     Processes

END    Exit SDSF
```

Figure 2.19: Expanded SDSF Primary Option menu

Using SDSF, you can view the system log online, view a merged sysplex log (**LOG O**), view a separate display of system requests (including action messages and write to operator with reply messages, or WTORs), and search for specific information using SDSF commands.

The SDSF **FIND** command lets you search the system log. New log data is added to the bottom of the log, so you might want to repeat the find or enter a command that repeats the search at some time interval, such as **BOT &20**, which goes to the bottom of the log every 20 seconds.

SYS1.LOGREC

The **SYS1.LOGREC** data set is a repository of information about system-level software errors or hardware problems. You can use **LOGREC** as a starting point for diagnosing a system problem. You typically look at logs (which can include **SYSLOG**, **OPERLOG**, the job logs, and traces associated with the problem you are investigating) from the starting time frame of the problem. The problems in need of investigation can be varied and may include loops, abends, system hangs, performance problems, and output problems.

DB2 Tools for Problem Diagnosis

Several DB2 commands are available to assist in DB2 problem diagnosis:

- **DISPLAY DATABASE(*) USE/LOCKS LIMIT(*)**
- **DISPLAY UTILITY (*)**
- **DISPLAY THREAD(*) DETAIL**
- **D A,ALL** (or **D A,ssid*** or **D A,IRL***)
- **D GRS,CONTENTION**
- **D OPDATA**

The MVS system log data set (**SYSLOG**) contains the output from these commands; be sure to keep this information. The command output is also stored in the master trace table. The master trace table output in a dump includes the most recently issued system messages. Use these commands before performing a dump for the DB2 address spaces to capture information.

Data-sharing environments should find two additional commands useful in collecting information:

- **F irlmproc,STATUS,ALLI**
- **F irlmproc,STATUS,ALLD**

Running the DB2 **DIAGNOSE** utility with the **MEPL** option produces a Module Entry Point Listing, which shows the PTF level of the DB2 modules. The DB2 **MSTR** dump will contain this data as well.

If the DB2 subsystem or the **MSTR** address space is hung, the **DISPLAY** commands will not produce a response. In that case, the only other option is a dump of the related DB2 address spaces.

Dumps

Certain codes and messages generated by DB2 require you to dump the DB2 address spaces. You typically will dump the **DBM1**, **MSTR**, or **IRLM** address space. You may be asked to provide a DDF, DIST, or SPAS dump. When problems occur, look for all available diagnosis information, which might include traces, dumps, **SYS1.LOGREC** entries, error messages, hardware device problem information, and any other information you can assemble to help diagnosis the issue.

Several dump types are provided in z/OS:

- Abend
- Snap
- Stand-alone
- Supervisor call (SVC)
- Transaction

The type of dump you select depends on the problem you are experiencing and the data you may need to acquire.

If you experience a program problem or an abnormal end to an authorized program, you can request an *abend dump*. Three types of abend dumps can be produced:

- **SYSABEND** is the largest of the abend type dumps.
- **SYSUDUMP** is the smallest of the abend dumps.

- **SYSMDUMP** is the only abend dump you can format using the Interactive Problem Control System (IPCS). It contains a summary of the failing program and some system data relating to the task.

If you are testing a problem program and need a dump while the program is running, a *snap dump* is appropriate. This type of dump shows one or more virtual storage areas that a running program requests. Snaps are preformatted; you cannot use IPCS to format a snap dump.

A *stand-alone dump* is called for when a system problem occurs — for example, when system processing is slow or stops or when the system is in a wait or a loop.

If you have a system problem but the system continues to process, a *supervisor call dump* is recommended. There are two ways to use SVC dumps:

- When the system experiences an unexpected system error but continues to process

- When an operator or an authorized program requests an SVC dump

An SVC dump produces a summary dump with control blocks and system code and can be analyzed using IPCS.

A transaction dump is a CICS formatted dump for the program that was active at the time the dump was requested. A transaction dump indicates where the error occurred within the program.

Based on the error you receive (e.g., 04E or 04F abends), you may be asked to obtain a dynamic dump, which is sent to the **SYS1.DUMP***xx* data set. You might also be requested to copy the BSDS using the **DSNJU004** utility.

Under z/OS, DB2 supports IPCS and the DB2 dump formatter/printing routine, **DSNWDPRD**. To invoke **DSNWDPRD**, use the following command:

```
DB2 VERBEXIT DSNWDMP
```

The *DB2 Diagnosis Guide* and the z/OS dump and printing documentation provide more information about this control statement.

SMF

A DB2 trace produces SMF records. The DB2 Instrumentation Facility Component (IFC) provides a trace facility. The analysis of the trace records must take place outside DB2.

You can send data to SMF in several ways:

- By writing an application to read and report information from the SMF data set

- By using OMEGAMON to format, print, and interpret DB2 trace output

- By using Tivoli Decision Support for z/OS to collect data and create reports

SMF must be operational before you can send data to it. You use member **SMFPRM***xx* in **SYS1.PARMLIB** to activate SMF and indicate which types of records SMF will accept. Be sure to specify the **ACTIVE** parameter and the proper **TYPE** sub-parameter.

The EREP Program

The z/OS error facilities can collect information about hardware and software errors in the form of an error log. You can then use the Environmental Record Editing and Printing (EREP) program to produce reports from this data. The error log can be written to an MVS data set or, in a Sysplex environment, to a log stream in the coupling facility. Or, you may instead decide not to record the error log at all.

The **LOGREC** parameter of the **IEASYS***xx* member of **SYS1.PARMLIB** defines the location of the error log. The **ICFEREP1** utility offloads the log to a history data set, which you can then use to make periodic tape backups and to print reports. Another utility, **IFCOFFLD**, lets you perform an emergency offload of the EREP data set. This alternative is quick but does not record any statistical information. If the data set fills up, recording stops and Z/OS continues with no error log recording. The manuals detail the recommended methods for coding and scheduling the offload and reporting jobs.

When an internal error occurs, DB2 records it in **SYS1.LOGREC** — known as the "logrec" or the Error Recording Data Set (ERDS). You typically obtain a listing of **SYS1.LOGREC** data sets by executing program **IFCEREP1**, the EREP job. The EREP program can format error reports.

A downloadable tool called the Logrec Viewer lets you view the **LOGREC** using the Interactive System Productivity Facility (ISPF). For more information and the download link for this tool, go to *http://www-03.ibm.com/systems/z/os/zos/downloads/logrec_viewer.html*.

IPCS VERBX

You can use the EREP program or the IPCS **VERBX LOGDATA** command to format software records recorded in **SYS1.LOGREC**. The IPCS diagnostic tool is provided in MVS to help diagnose software failures. Its facilities include formatting and analysis support for the traces and dumps produced by MVS, program products, and applications running on MVS.

MVS dumps fall into two categories: formatted dumps and unformatted dumps. You can use IPCS to format and analyze unformatted dumps. IPCS does not work with formatted dumps.

IPCS services provide a tool to format dumps and traces in both batch and online mode. Commands provided by the facility let you interrogate components to review storage locations or control blocks. The most common IPCS command is **VERBX** (Verb Exit), which formats data by product. DB2 dumps that use IPCS can be processed with the **VERBX DSNWDMP** IPCS command, which formats the DB2 dump data.

IPCS LOGDATA

When searching the data, you can use IPCS subcommands to pinpoint the problem (e.g., a wait, loop, or abend), or you might look for a CSECT name or component name that, through systems and messages, directs you to the problem.

Before you can use the data, you need to format the dump. The **VERBX LOGDATA** command formats **SYS1.LOGREC** records from the storage buffer. Input to IPCS is either an unformatted stand-alone or SVC dump. Be aware that it must be a complete dump.

LookAt

IBM's LookAt facility runs on VM, TSO, and Microsoft Windows and takes the user directly to an online reference that opens to the section addressing a subject message ID. For more information about LookAt, go to *http://www.ibm.com/ eserver/zseries/zos/bkserv/lookat*.

DB2 Start-Up and Shutdown Messages

Console messages for the active address spaces provide an incredible amount information. You can view these messages using SDSF.

Prefixes on the messages indicate the component associated with the problem, such as **DFH** for CICS or **DSN** for DB2. Figure 2.20 shows an example of messages issued upon DB2 start-up, beginning with the job initiator message $HASP373.

```
$HASP373 xxxxMSTR STARTED
DSNZ002I - SUBSYS ssnm SYSTEM PARAMETERS
           LOAD MODULE NAME IS dsnzparm-name
DSNY001I - SUBSYSTEM STARTING
DSNJ127I - SYSTEM TIMESTAMP FOR BSDS= xx.xxx xx:xx:xx.x
DSNJ001I - csect CURRENT COPY n ACTIVE LOG DATA
           SET IS DSNAME=...,
           STARTRBA=...,ENDRBA=...
DSNJ099I - LOG RECORDING TO COMMENCE WITH
           STARTRBA = xxxxxxxxxxxx
$HASP373 xxxxDBM1 STARTED
DSNR001I - RESTART INITIATED
DSNR003I - RESTART...PRIOR CHECKPOINT RBA=xxxxxxxxxxxx
DSNR004I - RESTART...UR STATUS COUNTS...
           IN COMMIT=nnnn, INDOUBT=nnnn, INFLIGHT=nnnn,
.......more messages follow.....
```

Figure 2.20: DB2 start-up system messages

SYS1.DUMPxx

The **DUMP** command requests a system dump (SVC dump) of virtual storage. The data set can be a pre-allocated dump data set named **SYS1.DUMPxx**, or you can automatically allocate a dump data set based on your installation's specified naming convention. As previously noted, different types of dumps are available to analyze problems. The processes to acquire these dumps are discussed in a series of IBM Redbooks called the *ABCs of z/OS System Programming*.

If you are looking at an SVC dump of a DB2 address space, examine the **LOGREC** symptom string to help determine the failing DB2 component.

MVS Tracing

There is only one way to activate a Generalized Trace Facility (GTF) trace: you must enter the **START GTF** command from the console that has master authority. You select your cataloged procedure or IBM-supplied procedure for GTF. The IBM GTF cataloged procedure in located **SYS1.PROCLIB**. It defines the GTF operation, how much storage you will need, the output destination, and the trace data sets.

A GTF trace shows the system processing events over time. This type of trace uses more CPU time than a system trace. The trace operates in its own address space as a system task.

DB2 Tracing

To run a DB2 trace, you can issue the **START TRACE** command from an MVS console, a DB2I command panel, a DSN session, a CICS or IMS terminal, or an IFI program. You must have the proper authorization of **SYSADM**, **SYSCTRL**, or **SYSOPR**. The command must include a trace type option of **PERFM**, **STAT**, **AUDIT**, **ACCTG**, or **MONITOR**. For example:

```
-START TRACE (PERFM) DEST(GTF) PLAN(plan_name, ... ) CLASS(class)
```

DB2 Trace Output

The **START TRACE** command's **DEST** option specifies where the trace output is to be recorded. You typically will request that the trace be sent either to GTF or to SMF.

The MVS GTF record identifier for DB2 trace records is X'0FB9'. The SMF record type depends on the IFCID record:

IFCID record	SMF record type
1 (system services statistics)	100
2 (database services statistics)	100
3 (agent accounting)	101
202 (dynamic system parameters)	100
230 (data sharing global statistics)	100
239 (agent accounting overflow)	101
All others	102

To trace all performance class records and write to GTF, you would start the trace as follows:

```
-START TRACE(PERFM) DEST(GTF) CLASS(*)
```

Chapter 6 provides more information about tracing.

Storage Management Subsystem

Disk storage has changed rapidly over the past few years, resulting in the delivery of new functions and improved performance. To keep pace and make use of these disk improvements, DB2 has undergone many changes.

Extended Address Volume (EAV)

An Extended Address Volume (EAV) supports 223 GB per volume on z/OS 1.10 and the IBM System Storage DS8000 to address the problem of running out of z/OS addressable disk storage due to the four-digit device number limit. An EAV is 65,536 cylinders or larger. Data sets on an EAV are eligible to have extents in the extended addressing space. This includes the VSAM data types for DB2, both SMS and non-SMS managed. EAV provides constraint relief for DB2 applications that use large VSAM data sets.

Parallel Access Volume

DB2 9 also continues to use Parallel Access Volume and Multiple Allegiance features of the IBM TotalStorage Enterprise Storage Server (ESS) and DS8000. PAV enables more than one I/O operation to be processed on a single logical 3390 volume, significantly reducing device queue delays. This is done by assigning multiple addresses to volumes. Implementing PAV devices is accomplished using static or dynamic alias management.

With this support, your careful data set placement methodology of the past can be replaced with the use of PAV and SMS group policies for data separation. PAV reduces I/O responses by reducing I/O supervisor queue (IOSQ) time, and SMS can be used to "spread" data for partitions across volumes. Together, the two reduce I/O contention.

In addition, the SMS groups provide effective organization of data for recoverability when you use the **BACKUP** and **RESTORE** system utilities. SMS grouping can also aid in the cloning of systems.

PAV requires a fiber channel connection (FICON) attachment feature. It is possible to vary the number of parallel accesses to a PAV.

DSVCI

DB2 8 introduced the ability to have control interval sizes that are the same size as the page being allocated. You enable this support through the online updatable DSNZPARM **DSVCI**. Making the CI size the same as the page size allows for data integrity because you can be sure that the whole row is intact when it is externalized.

Before this enhancement, there were some instances of data integrity exposures for 8 KB, 16 KB, and 32 KB objects when writing to disk at the extent boundary. The integrity exposure caused DB2 not to allow these objects to use VSAM multi-striping and required you to run a **SET LOG SUSPEND** command when doing split mirror design backups. In addition, concurrent copy required **SHRLEVEL REFERENCE** for 32 KB pages and did not allow **CHANGE**. With **DSVCI**, the integrity issue has been resolved, and these functions are now available for all page sizes.

SMS Storage

SMS storage lets the operating system take over storage tasks that we usually do manually. To implement SMS, you define a volume pooling structure made up of storage groups. Routines are executed by the system to control the allocation of the storage groups. Automatic class selection (ASC) routines define which data sets can be allocated in which storage group.

DFSMS implements the policies put in place regarding how hardware resources and space should be handled. Installation panel **DSNTIPA3** (Figure 2.21) lets you define the SMS data class, management class, and storage class associated with your data sets in DB2.

```
DSNTIPA3        INSTALL DB2 - DATA PARAMETERS PANEL 2
===>  _

Check parameters and reenter to change:
 1  PERMANENT UNIT NAME    ==> 3390          Device type for MVS catalog
                                              and partitioned data sets
 2  TEMPORARY UNIT NAME    ==> SYSDA         Device type for
                                              temporary data sets


                                   --------------- SMS ---------------
                           VOL/SER  DATA CLASS   MGMT CLASS   STOR CLASS
                           -------  ----------   ----------   ----------
 3  CLIST ALLOCATION    ==> DSNV01  ==>          ==>          ==>
 4  NON-VSAM DATA       ==> DSNV01  ==>          ==>          ==>
 5  VSAM CATALOG, DEFAULT, ==> DSNV02 ==>        ==>          ==>
    AND WORK FILE DATABASE
 6  DIRECTORY AND CATALOG ==>       ==>          ==>          ==>
    DATA
 7  DIRECTORY AND CATALOG ==>       ==>          ==>          ==>
    INDEXES
 8  LOG COPY 1, BSDS 2  ==>         ==>          ==>          ==>
 9  LOG COPY 2, BSDS 1  ==>         ==>          ==>          ==>
```

Figure 2.21: Installation panel DSNTIPA3 – SMS data parameters

SMS Classes and Groups

The constructs within the basic structure of SMS consist of classes and groups: data class, management class, storage class, storage group, aggregate group, tape library, optical library, and optical drives, as well as a base configuration for the systems and groups.

Data classes actually apply to non-SMS or SMS managed data sets. You can specify space parameters associated with your data sets.

Storage classes are only for SMS managed data sets, supplying information about dynamic cache management, concurrent copy, or sequential data set striping.

The management class applies to SMS data sets, which supply a list of migration information about backup and retention. The DFSMS Hierarchical Storage Management (DFSMShsm) tool uses these attributes for storage management.

Storage groups apply to SMS and relate to the physical storage for data sets and objects. The six types of storage groups are pool, object backup, tape, dummy, VIO, and object.

These classifications allow service levels for data sets to be assigned and permit the system to be managed automatically.

Parallel Sysplex and DB2

Parallel Sysplex is a clustering approach for S/390 systems. A group of IBM mainframes linked in this type of environment is called a system complex, or sysplex.

Applications running on more than one DB2 subsystem can write and read to the same databases concurrently and share the same DB2 catalog. Data sharing gives the ability to cluster together up to 32 DB2 subsystems to provide shared data, availability, and workload management and to take advantage of parallel sysplex on the zSeries and z/OS. The parallelism across participating DB2 members and the ability to add processors to scale vertically provides a near-linear support.

Coupling Facility

A coupling facility (CF) consists of one or more processors running specialized code that coordinates events across multiple members of the data-sharing group. Three structures make up the CF, and all three reside in one or more CFs:

- Group buffer pools
- Shared communications area (SCA)
- Lock structure

The group buffer pools contain data and index pages being accessed across the data-sharing group. The SCA is for recovery and startup across the group. The lock structure maintains the integrity of the data across members. Data sharing in DB2 is an option.

Large Mainframe Systems and Hardware Resources

The IBM z9 Integrated Information Processor (zIIP) is a specialty engine for the System z9 mainframe. The z/OS operating system manages and directs the work between general-purpose processors and the zIIPs. DB2 9 redirects more processing to the zIIP engine. The zIIP engine is designed so that a program can work with z/OS and have all or a portion of its enclave SRB work directed to the zIIP.

DB2 8 for z/OS was the first DB2 version to exploit the zIIP with System z9 109 and z/OS 1.6 or later. No changes are required for DB2 8 for z/OS applications to use the zIIP. The PTFs listed in info APAR II14219 provide more information about the requirements for DB2 8 and DB2 9 of DB2.

Workloads Benefiting from zIIP

Workloads in DB2 that benefit the most from the zIIP engines are business intelligence (BI), enterprise resource planning (ERP), customer relationship management (CRM), data warehousing, and DB2 utilities.

For data warehousing, those requests that use parallel queries, including star schemas, benefit from the offloading of work to the zIIP. The DB2 utility functions used to maintain index maintenance structures also benefit. Applications such as BI, CRM, and ERP and other applications that use DRDA over a TCP/IP connection (enclave SRBs, not stored procedures or user-defined functions) also benefit from the offloading of work to the zIIP engine.

Estimates show the following possible reductions in Class 1 CPU time with the zIIP:

- **REBUILD INDEX**: 5 to 20 percent
- **LOAD** or **REORG** of a partition with one index only: 10 to 20 percent
- **LOAD** or **REORG** of an entire table space: 10 to 20 percent
- **REBUILD INDEX** of a logical partition of a non-partitioning index: 40 percent
- **REORG INDEX**: 10 to 20 percent
- **LOAD** or **REORG** of a partition with more than one index: 30 to 60 percent
  - » When **LOAD** or **REORG** is used with many partitions or indexes and CPU enclave SRB during index rebuild phase: less than 10 percent

Workload Manager

The Workload Manager component of z/OS implements dynamic workload management. WLM buffer pool management is also available in conversion mode.

In DB2 9, the maximum name length of the default WLM environment (defined in subsystem parameter **DSN6SYSP**, macro **WLMENV**) is increased from 18 to 32 characters.

WLM can dynamically redistribute or allocate server resources such as I/O, memory, and CPU across workloads (groupings of work) based on defined goals and resource demand within a z/OS image.

WLM manages workloads by assigning goal and work priorities based on your business requirements. WLM uses these goals to dynamically adjust access to storage and processor resources.

WLM uses several constructs in managing workloads. These include service definitions, service policies, service classes, report classes, and resource groups.

- *Service definitions* contain a set of classification rules that separate incoming work into distinct service classes and multiple service policies. A service definition deals with the management of work that needs to be identified and grouped into classes.

- A *service policy* is a named set of goals associated with the service classes. A policy applies to all work running in a sysplex. You can have one policy active at a time.

- *Service classes* are associated with a base goal.

- *Report classes* provide greater granularity than service classes. You can define up to 999 report classes.

- *Resource groups* control the CPU service units per second consumption of a set of classes. They define a minimum and maximum amount of service that the service classes should not exceed. Resource groups are not required.

You use the WLM ISPF application panels to define a service definition. Then, from the menus, you create your workloads, policies, resource groups, service classes, and other definitions.

Service Classes

Service classes are a named collection of work within a workload. They define the runtime requirements for that work. Assigning an importance to each service class gives the workloads within it a preference; this is the first step in separating work into distinct service classes. WLM examines all service classes every 10 seconds to determine which classes might need help with resources. Be careful not to over-allocate service classes, or WLM may need to make too many adjustments to your work assignments.

Each service class is associated with a goal and an importance to manage work. Goals for service classes can be defined as average response time, execution velocity (the acceptable amount of work delay), percentile response time (ending work within a certain time limit), or discretionary (when there is no specific goal definition or no specific importance for work in the service class).

An appropriate installation-defined service goal for the DB2 address spaces **MSTR**, **DBM1**, and **DIST** is a high velocity goal. Most of the DB2 thread work applies to the user goal. User work runs under separate goals for the enclave.

Work is classified into distinct service classes by subsystem type, which usually is related to an application. You define the service classes and goals in a service definition.

The two primary system service classes are **SYSTEM** and **SYSSTC**. Classify address spaces that support the system or its operation as service class **SYSSTC**, and classify all system-related address spaces as service class **SYSTEM**.

• •

A third class, named **SYSOTHER**, is predefined in the system. You should classify all work so that **SYSOTHER** is not used.

• •

Enclave

We previously discussed enclaves as they relate to DDF. DB2, WebSphere, and other major components and middleware applications on z/OS also exploit enclave management. In enclave management, all functions are given to the end user in defining goals, monitoring execution, and observing the progress of work in the system. WLM can manage the enclave directly, independently of the address spaces where the execution units belong.

Stored Procedures

The stored procedure type dictates the process used to create a stored procedure. DB2 for z/OS supports the following types of stored procedures:

- *Native SQL procedure*: The body of this type is written in SQL, and no C program is generated by DB2. Native SQL procedures are WLM-managed.

- *External SQL procedure*: The body of an external SQL procedure is written in SQL, and DB2 does generate an associated C program.

- *External stored procedure*: These are written in a host language.

In addition, Java stored procedures and user-defined functions can contain SQL statements. A client program written in any supported language invokes the Java stored procedure. Java Database Connectivity (JDBC) type 4 connections are recommended to engage the zIIP engine. JDBC requests are sent to DB2 using JDBC driver type 2 or driver type 4.

Administrative Tasks

You can use the administrative task scheduler to run tasks, which can be JCL jobs or stored procedures. Once defined, these tasks are stored in two redundant task lists: **SYSIBM.ADMIN_TASKS** and a VSAM data set defined in **ADMTDD1**.

You manage the scheduler task list using DB2 stored procedures that add or remove tasks (**ADMIN_TASK_ADD** and **ADMIN_TASK_REMOVE**). DB2 also provides user-defined functions that help you monitor the task list (**ADMINT_TASK_LIST**) and the status of tasks in DB2 (**ADMIN_TASK_STATUS**).

The scheduler is a started task named in DB2, and it starts when DB2 is brought up. The scheduler's name is **ADMTPROC**.

Because the scheduler manages two redundant task lists, it can continue working even if one of the task lists becomes damaged or unavailable. If a task list is corrupted, you will receive the message DSNA679I. You can recover the VSAM data set for the **ADMIN_TASKS** task list. As soon as this data set is available, the scheduler will perform an autonomic recovering of the contents.

z9 Processor and Specialty Engines

IBM's zIIP specialty engine is a less expensive alternative to CPU costs. Workloads are eligible to be offloaded to zIIPs if they run under a z/OS enclave SRB. Workload Manager in z/OS manages the workloads that are eligible for offloading. WLM directs the work between the zIIP and the central processor without any changes to your programs.

zIIPs and Workloads

Workloads that can offload work to the zIIP include native stored procedures, some portions of star-schema parallel queries, and parts of the index build and maintenance process of the **REORG**, **LOAD**, and **REBUILD INDEX** utilities. IFI includes DB2 support to reflect zIIP- and CPU-related performance information. WLM algorithms verify the buffer pool size, adjust it (if necessary) to prevent out-of-storage conditions, and try first to take storage from other buffer pools to make the adjustment.

WLM Services and zIIP

Stored procedures, DDF, and buffer pools are all managed by WLM. SMF records for enclave reporting are types 30 and 72:

- Type 30: The record contains the resources consumed at the address space level.

- Type 72: Have a service class record and a report class if it is in the service policy. So, with WLM, you can separate the enclaves into different classes, either report or service, to get a better idea how the work is being done in DDF.

Activating zIIP for DB2

Hardware zIIP engines z9 BC and z9 EC models have the zIIP engines available. No further action is required to implement zIIP use once the hardware and software are installed.

RMF

The Resource Measurement Facility Workload Activity report summarizes resource consumption by workload and by service class periods within workloads. The **PROJECTCPU=YES** option enables RMF to monitor DB2 to assess how zIIP consumption would be used. You can run this projection capability at any time.

The **PROJECTCPU=YES** option enables z/OS to collect zIIP usage data as though a zIIP was configured when the target workload is being run. When you use this parameter, RMF and SMF show the calculated zIIP time, which is used to gain an accurate zIIP projection.

Practice Questions

Question 1

Name the three major groups of subcomponent code structure in DB2.

○ A. SSAS, DBAS, DDF

○ B. SSAS, DBAS, IRLM

○ C. SSAS, DBAS, SPAS

○ D. SSAS, DBAS, WLM

Question 2

At DB2 address space termination, what happens to the DB2 shared memory object area?

○ A. It continues to run, but the VSO is deleted.

○ B. It is freed, and interest in the VSO is deleted.

○ C. It will continue to be available on the next start-up of DB2.

○ D. It will not be affected.

Question 3

An inactive connection in DB2 was previously called:

○ A. Type 2 inactive thread

○ B. Inactive DBAT

○ C. Active DBAT

○ D. Type 2 active thread

Question 4

When trying to establish the total number of threads that can access data in DB2, what should you do?

○ A. Add **MAXDBAT** and **CTHREAD**.

○ B. Subtract **CTHREAD** from **MAXDBAT**.

○ C. Divide **MAXDBAT** by **CTHREAD**.

○ D. Check **MAXDBAT** only.

Question 5

Native stored procedures, if invoked from DRDA TCP/IP connections to DB2, may:

○ A. Be eligible for zap processing

○ B. Be eligible for zIIP processing

○ C. Be eligible for zIIP and zap processing

○ D. Are not eligible for either zIIP or zap processing

Question 6

What are the associated pools in the EDM pool (RDS)?

○ A. **EDMDBDC, EDMSTMTC, EDM_SKELETON_POOL**

○ B. **EDMDBDC, EDMSTMTC**

○ C. **EDMDBDC, EDM_SKELETON_POOL**

○ D. **EDMDBDC**

Question 7

The DSNZPARM parameter **MAXKEEPD** is used to:

○ A. Limit the number of threads

○ B. Limit the number of dynamic statements held in the cache

○ C. Limit the number of statistics kept on dynamic cache

○ D. Limit the number of threads to keep

Question 8

Which DSNZPARM defines the number of RID blocks in the RID pool storage?

○ A. **CONDBAT**

○ B. **URLGWTH**

○ C. **NUMTCB**

○ D. **MAXRBLK**

Question 9

What buffer sizes are supported for the **DSNDB07** database?

○ A. 4 KB, 8 KB, 16 KB, 32 KB

○ B. 4 KB, 32 KB

○ C. 4 KB, 16 KB

○ D. 4 KB, 8 KB

Question 10

What are the types of dumps in z/OS?

○ A. Transaction, abend, stand-alone

○ B. SVC, transaction, abend, stand-alone, snap

○ C. Stand-alone and snap

○ D. Stand-alone, abend, snap, dump

CHAPTER 3

Installation and Migration

Section 1 of the DB2 9 System Administrator for z/OS certification exam tests your knowledge of DB2 9 for z/OS installation and migration procedures and issues. This part of the exam makes up 15 percent of the overall test.

This chapter takes you through the steps involved in getting the system ready for installation or migration and reviews the System Modification Program/Extended (SMP/E) installation utility methods. We also discuss the purpose of the jobs in the installation and migration process and how to plan for the way these procedures could affect your current DB2 systems.

Preparing to Install or Migrate

To install or migrate your DB2 environments, you must meet hardware and software requirements and also satisfy storage requirements for virtual storage and data sets. Be sure to review the program directory document to learn the latest requirements.

DB2 9 for z/OS requires 128 GB of 64-bit shared virtual storage for each DB2 subsystem. The virtual storage requirement for the common service area (CSA) below the 16 MB line is less than 40 KB for each DB2 for z/OS subsystem and 24 KB for each Internal Resource Lock Manager subsystem. If your system activity is fairly high or you experience high contention, you may need a larger CSA.

The extended common service area (ECSA) is where DB2 common data resides. The extended private area above the 16 MB line and above the 2 GB bar houses most of the DB2 modules, buffers, and control blocks.

If you have DB2 8 for z/OS installed, moving to the next release requires a migration process. The migration process differs from the installation process you perform for new installations of DB2 9. IBM's *DB2 Version 9.1 for z/OS Installation Guide* (GC18-9846) provides the documentation for both of these procedures. You should review this manual and study the sections that are associated with your installation or migration. There is really no substitute for reading this book. In this chapter, we will revisit sections of the installation guide to make sure we touch on the important issues about which you will be tested.

Planning for Storage

In looking at the requirements for DB2 9, you need to consider any additional or new storage requirements. Table 3.1 shows default storage values that can be used to calculate space requirements associated with the following types of installations:

- Small site: Supports a small number of DB2 users

- Medium site: Supports more extensive use of DB2 databases

- Large site: Supports heavy use of DB2

- Extra-large site: Supports very heavy use of DB2

Table 3.1: Default storage estimates

Site	# of plans	# of application databases	# of tables
Small	100	50	1,000
Medium	200	200	4,000
Large	400	400	8,000
Extra Large	600	600	12,000

For more information about the specific estimates, refer to the DB2 program directory and the installation guide.

Program Directories

The DB2 program directories provide information about the material and procedures associated with installing the various components of DB2. They are intended to assist the DB2 system programmer who is responsible for program installation and maintenance.

IBM's Technical Resources page for DB2 for z/OS lists the program directories for DB2 components for Versions 9, 8, and 7 of DB2. These directories are also shipped with each product you order. To view this documentation online, go to IBM's DB2 for z/OS Web site (*http://www-01.ibm.com/software/data/db2/zos*) and click the **Product documentation** link. You can also reach the Technical Resources page directly by going to *http://www-01.ibm.com/support/docview. wss?rs=64&uid=swg27011656*.

Figure 3.1 shows the list of program directories for DB2 9 for z/OS.

Program Directories for DB2 Version 9.1 for z/OS				
Title (Order Number)	**Published**	**HTML**	**PDF**	**Updates**
DB2 9 for z/OS Program Directory GI10-8737-02	Apr 2009		🗎	
DB2 Accessories Suite for z/OS Program Directory GI10-8749-03	June 2009		🗎	
Data Studio Workbench Program Directory GI10-8773-01	June 2009		🗎	
DB2 Utilities Suite for z/OS, V9R1, Program Directory GI10-8746-00	Feb 2007		🗎	
DB2 Management Clients Package Program Directory GI10-8738-00	Mar 2007		🗎	
z/OS Application Connectivity to DB2 for z/OS GI10-8739-00	Mar 2007		🗎	

Figure 3.1: Program directories for DB2 9 for z/OS

Each listed item represents a function modification identifier (FMID), or product code. The DB2 9 list contains the following items:

- DB2 9 for z/OS Program Directory

- DB2 Accessories Suite for z/OS Program Directory

- Data Studio Workbench Program Directory

- DB2 Utilities Suite for z/OS, V9R1, Program Directory

- DB2 Management Clients Package Program Directory

- z/OS Application Connectivity to DB2 for z/OS

If you are installing DB2 for the first time on z/OS, you need to know whether you have ordered the DB2 for z/OS Value Unit Edition (VUE). This cost-saving edition of DB2 contains exactly the same code as the regular edition, but the pricing is different. This is a one-time charge pricing model available for new applications or workloads for VUE. The workload must be deployed in one or more System z New Application License Charges (zNALC) logical partitions (LPARs), and an existing workload cannot be transferred or migrated to the zNALC LPAR(s).

Figure 3.2 shows the three VUE program directories.

Program Directories for DB2 9 for z/OS Value Unit Edition				
Title (Order Number)	**Published**	**HTML**	**PDF**	**Updates**
DB2 9 for z/OS VUE Program Directory GI10-8779-02	Apr 2009		🗎	
DB2 Management Clients Package VUE Program Directory GI10-8780-00	Feb 2008		🗎	
z/OS Application Connectivity to DB2 for z/OS VUE Program Directory GI10-8781-00	Feb 2008		🗎	

Figure 3.2: Program directories for DB2 9 for z/OS Value Unit Edition

In addition to the program directories for both the regular and VUE editions of DB2 for z/OS, the Technical Resources page lists documentation for the DB2 Accessories Suite for z/OS, including information for tools such as OmniFind Text

Search, the Optimization Service Center (OSC), and Spatial Support for DB2 for z/OS.

As you examine the various program directories, you will notice that they have a common look and feel. The first-page description references the component (e.g., DB2 Accessories Suite for z/OS) and the version, program number, FMIDs, and document date. As you look through the document, you will see information about the installation of the particular program component and all necessary steps. Read these directories carefully to ensure a successful installation or migration. They detail installation requirements, service levels, machine requirements, programming requirements, operational requisites, and installation instructions.

DB2 Products and Features

When you order DB2, the following items are included:

- DB2

- Internal Resource Lock Manager (IRLM) 2.2

- Java Database Connectivity (JDBC)

- Structured Query Language for Java (SQLJ)

- Open Database Connectivity (ODBC)

- Extensible Markup Language (XML) Extender

 With the introduction of native XML data store in DB2 9, the XML Extender has been deprecated. This feature is still supported in DB2 9, but it will be discontinued at some point in the future. In DB2 9, you can use the new XML data type instead.

Figure 3.3 summarizes the DB2 product and no-charge features.

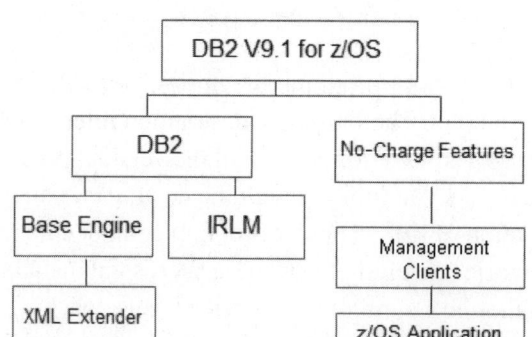

Figure 3.3: DB2 product and no-charge features

The DB2 Management Clients Package and z/OS Application Connectivity to DB2 for z/OS are separately ordered, non-chargeable items. If you plan to run Java on z/OS, you will need the z/OS Application Connectivity to DB2 for z/OS feature.

Figure 3.4 shows the components of the DB2 Management Clients Package, which include DB2 Administration Server for z/OS, DB2 for z/OS Control Center Enablement, and DB2 Connect, all of which are delivered on CD-ROM.

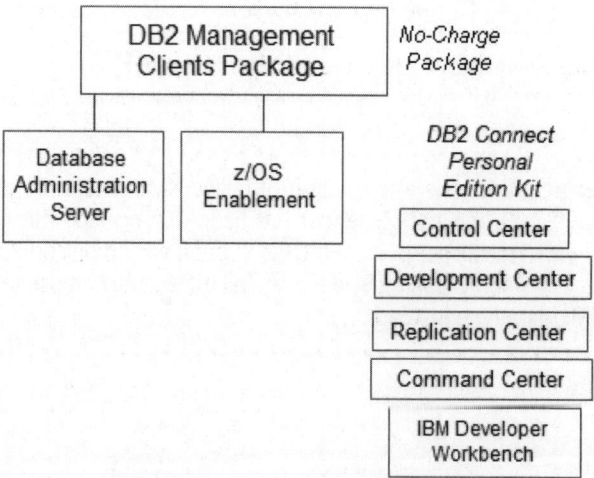

Figure 3.4: DB2 Management Clients Package

You will need the Clients package if you want to run the Control Center. In addition to the Control Center, this package supports the Development Center, Replication Center, Command Center, and more. It also contains the z/OS enablement for stored procedures, user-defined functions, and batch programs, as well as the DB2 Connect Personal Edition Kit, which gives you a "limited use" copy of DB2 Connect 9.

Notice that the client package CD-ROM also includes the IBM Developer Workbench (DWB).

There are a few packaging changes we should talk about here. The Developer Workbench is the successor to the Development Center. In DB2 9, the DWB has a new name, the Data Studio Developer, and it has been rolled into the Optim Development Studio 2.2. You can download a stand-alone version of the Data Studio Developer for free (after registration) from *https://www14.software.ibm. com/webapp/iwm/web/preLogin.do?lang=en_US&source=swg-dm-db2dwb*. This Web site "directs" you to the download page for the stand-alone version of the Data Studio Developer product.

Figure 3.5 shows the components of another no-charge feature, the DB2 Accessories Suite (product number 5655-R144).

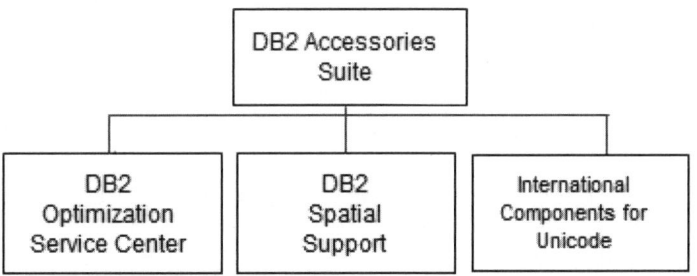

Figure 3.5: DB2 Accessories Suite

The Optimization Service Center is part of the DB2 z/OS Accessories Suite. Much of the capability that was formerly in OSC is now being provided in either Data Studio (stand-alone) or the Optim query tuning products.

Within the Accessories Suite, the OSC is used for monitoring and tuning SQL statements running on DB2 9 for z/OS and DB2 8 for z/OS. This workstation tool can identify and analyze SQL statements at the workload level. A no-charge item, OSC is also available for download from *https://www14.software.ibm.com/webapp/iwm/web/preLogin.do?lang=en_US&source=swg-db2zosc*. You can install OSC on a Windows workstation, connect to a DB2 subsystem, and work with your SQL queries and workloads to improve the performance.

Another component of the Accessories Suite, DB2 Spatial Support for DB2 9 for z/OS, can generate, analyze, manage, and store spatial information about geographic features. Spatial data types, user functions, and stored procedures for spatial queries are provided in this support.

Your SMP/E software installation processes depend on the packaging category of your software products order. When you place your order, the products can be packaged in a variety of ways. The packages are grouped into categories (e.g., CBPDO, FunctionPac, ProductPac, ServerPac, SystemPac) that are listed on the ShopzSeries Web site, *https://www14.software.ibm.com/webapp/ShopzSeries/ShopzSeries.jsp*. You can use this site to draft and place orders, check on orders in process, and view completed orders. You can access the product catalog on ShopzSeries by product code and FMID.

You will have SMP/E jobs for the different FMIDs, such as the chargeable utility products. A set of core utility products comes with DB2 at no charge. There is only one FMID on a single tape for the utility products. In DB2 9, the DB2 Utilities are contained in a single FMID.

Table 3.2 lists the product codes and FMIDs for DB2 (English).

Table 3.2: Product codes and FMIDs			
Product code	**Description**	**FMID**	**Notes**
5635-DB2	DB2 9 for z/OS	HDB9910	
		HIY9910	Information Management System (IMS) Attach Facility; must be installed, even if you don't have IMS
		HIZ9910	Subsystem initialization
	Internal Resource Lock Manager (IRLM)	HIR2220	Base code
		HDRE910	Resource Access Control Facility (RACF) authorization exit

Table 3.2: Product codes and FMIDs (continued)			
Product code	**Description**	**FMID**	**Notes**
		JDB9914	English panels
	REXX		Shipped with base code
	XML Extender		Shipped with base code
5635-DB2	DB2 Management Clients Package		Workstation-based client tools; no charge
	Database Administration Server	HDAS910	
	z/OS Enablement for DB2 Control Center	JDB991D	
	DB2 Connect Personal Edition Kit	CD-ROM	Limited Connect 9.1 included, single Windows o/s connection
5655-N97	DB2 Utilities Suite	JDB991K	Chargeable
	z/OS Application Connectivity to DB2 for z/OS	HDDA211	Java type 4 Java Database Connectivity (JDBC) driver (see GI10-8738 program directory); no charge
5655-R14	DB2 Accessories Suite		No charge; optional
	DB2 Optimizer Service Center	H2AG110	
	DB2 Spatial Support	J2AG110	
	International Components for Unicode	H2AF110	
5697-P12	DB2 9 for z/OS Value Unit Edition (VUE)	JDB991Z	
Optional FMIDs	JDBC/SQLJ	JDB9912	
Optional FMIDs	Kanji Panels	JDB9911	
Optional FMIDs	Open Database Connectivity (ODBC)	JDB9917	
Optional FMIDs	XML Extender	JDB991X	

Release Information for DB2 9 for z/OS

Before you begin the installation or migration process, you must know the current release level and maintenance support level of your DB2 8 environment. You should also be aware of any release-to-release incompatibilities that IBM has documented.

The latest version of DB2 is DB2 9 for z/OS. The product announcement letter is USA 207-041, dated March 6, 2007. The DB2 9 for z/OS program directory document, which is available online and also shipped with the product, provides information about the current packaging.

Determining Your Current Support Level for DB2 for z/OS

If you came into a new job as a DB2 system administrator and wanted to determine the "release" level of the DB2 components, how would you find this information? One way is to use DB2's **DIAGNOSE** utility. You can use this tool to list all the DB2 components and their service levels.

The **DIAGNOSE** utility is a diagnostic tool that generally is used under the direction of IBM Support to help analyze system problems. In this case, we will use only the utility's **DISPLAY** statement to obtain the information we need.

Figure 3.6 shows the syntax of the **DISPLAY** statement. (The DB2 command syntax diagrams that appear in this book are reproduced, with permission, from IBM's *DB2 Version 9.1 for z/OS Command Reference*, SC18-9844.)

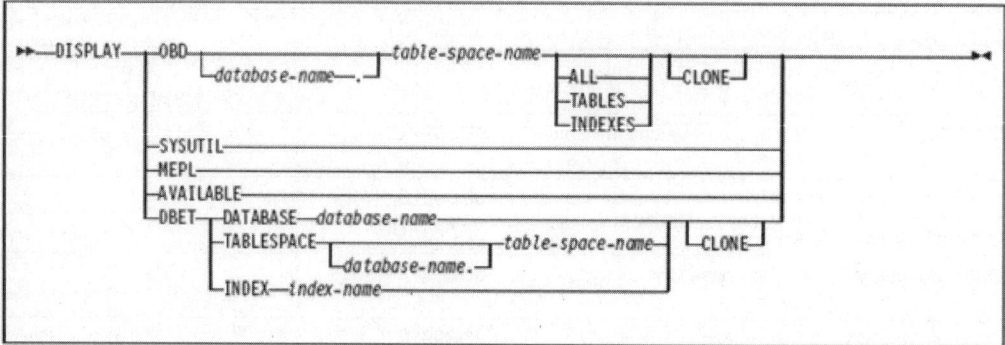

Figure 3.6: DIAGNOSE utility's DISPLAY statement syntax

We are interested in two options: **MEPL** and **AVAILABLE**.

The **DISPLAY MEPL** utility control statement specifies that the DB2 module entry point lists (MEPLs) are to be displayed:

```
DIAGNOSE
DISPLAY MEPL
```

You can use the output from this statement to determine the service level of a specific DB2 module. The output lists each module, the most recent PTF or APAR that was applied to the module, and the date when the PTF or APAR was installed. Note that when you run **DIAGNOSE** with the **DISPLAY MEPL** option, a difference could exist between what is in the **LOAD** library and what is in modules that are picked up in memory. (**LOAD** modules might have changed and not be reflected in memory.)

The **DISPLAY AVAILABLE** utility control statement displays the utilities that are installed on the subsystem:

```
DIAGNOSE
DISPLAY AVAILABLE
```

This option reports the installed utilities in both bit-map and readable format. The presence or absence of the IBM DB2 Utilities Suite for z/OS (5655-N97) affects the results of this display. Message DSNU862I contains the output.

Another way to determine the service level of a DB2 module is to use SMP/E to view the libraries for the installation date, PTF, or APAR level for a specific DB2 module. You can also use the DB2 sample program **DSN8ED7**, which generates a list of current DB2 parameter settings. This program formats data from the called stored procedure **DSNWZP** and returns a report that lists the macro name, parameter name, and current parameter setting.

How the DB2 Support Level Is Maintained

The SMP/E utility supports the installation and upgrade processes for z/OS system products. This utility keeps track of all system elements and any modifications to them and provides a tool for installing, servicing, and maintaining your inventory of software.

We need to look at SMP/E jobs and what you do to set up the target and distribution libraries; however, this won't be a complete course on SMP/E. You can find more information about SMP/E at the z/OS Internet Library (*http://www-03. ibm.com/systems/z/os/zos/bkserv*). Additional details are available in the *SMP/E User's Guide for z/OS and S/390* (SA22-7773) and related publications.

The DB2 software products and maintenance processes for SMP/E come from software products and product packages that you order. DB2 product orders are shipped as customized offerings; for example, you might order a CBPDO, a ServerPac, or a SysPac. Products that become generally available will be included in the next ServerPac and SystemPac monthly update. The media type for this software is chosen during the customized offering process based on your customer environment.

The packages consist of elements such as modules, macros, and source code. Utilities, such as link editors or assemblers, process these elements to create load modules that contain executable code.

All modifications, updates, and new elements are identified to SMP/E through *modification identifiers*. SMP/E uses these identifiers to track all system modifications (SYSMODs) installed on your system:

- A function modification identifier, or FMID, is a SYSMOD that introduces an element into the system.

- A replacement modification identifier (RMID) is the last SYSMOD that replaced an element.

- An update modification identifier (UMID) identifies the last SYSMOD update of an element.

SYSMODs are a combination of elements and control information used as input data to SMP/E. System updates are packaged as SYSMODs, and SMP/E ensures that the updates are installed in the proper sequence.

SYSMODs contains information that SMP/E uses to track and install your system modifications. SYSMODs have four classifications (PTF, FUNCTION, APAR, and USERMOD), which we'll talk about further later.

There are two types of SYSMODs: base function and dependent function. A base function SYSMOD might replace an entire set of base system functions, such as JES2. A dependent function SYSMOD might provide an addition to an existing system function. At the point of installing a dependent function, you would already have a base function installed.

Structure of the SMP/E Libraries

When we speak of installing a function SYSMOD, we are referring to the placement of all the product's elements in the system data sets, or system libraries. All code and its modifications are located in the SMP/E database called the *consolidated software inventory (CSI)*, which consists of one or more VSAM data sets. (Don't confuse this CSI with the consolidated service test, which we discuss later.) The CSI data set contains all the information about the target and distribution libraries — not the element itself, but a description of what the element represents; the element name, history, and type; and a pointer to the distribution and target libraries.

In SMP/E, there are two types of libraries: distribution and target. Distribution libraries contain all the elements, such as modules and macros, that are used as input for running your system. One important use of the distribution libraries is backup. The target libraries contain the executable code that is needed to run the system. These distribution and target libraries are grouped based on their installation status.

SMP/E Zones

Next, we need to talk about zones. First, we will look at what the global zone, target zone, and distribution zone are in SMP/E.

The SMP/E *global zone* contains information about SMP/E processing status for all SYSMODs that SMP/E has started to process. Entries describe each target and distribution zone to SMP/E. Entries in the global zone can have exception data for SYSMODs that are in error or need special handling.

When we talk about exception data, we are usually talking about HOLDDATA, such as a PTF in error. Various values define this data and indicate the processing that the SYSMOD requires; these values are **ACTION**, **AO**, **DELETE**, **DEP**, **DOC**, **EC**, **EXRF**, **Facility**, **FULLGEN**, **IOGEN**, **MSGSKEL**, and **MVSCP**. For more detailed information about these IDs, consult the *SMP/E Reference* (SA22-7772).

The *target zone* contains all the executable code that is needed to run the system.

The *distribution zone* contains the elements that are used to run the system. This is your backup in case you have an element with a problem; in that event, you can replace the element from the distribution libraries (**DLIB**s).

The way the SMP/E environment is set up can differ from shop to shop. You might have all the products under one global zone and then have a target and distribution zone for each product. Or, you might have all products in their own global, target, and distribution zones. You might even have a global zone for each software vendor. This is a shop-to-shop preference that you will need to understand. To direct SMP/E to a specific zone, you specify the zone name on the **SET** command.

Management of SMP/E Maintenance

SMP/E uses three commands to accomplish the installation process: **RECEIVE**, **APPLY**, and **ACCEPT**. You can run SMP/E using either batch jobs or dialogs under Interactive System Productivity Facility/Program Development Facility (ISPF/ PDF). With the SMP/E dialogs, you can interactively query the SMP/E database and create and submit jobs to process SMP/E commands.

After you place an order for DB2 and associated products, you will receive either a tape or a cartridge. (If you order a custom-built product delivery offering, or CBPDO, your order may differ from what is described here.) Your first step is to copy the SMP/E jobs from that medium to a disk so that you can edit them. The jobs you copy will allocate your DB2 libraries and then load data from the cartridge or the tape.

To copy the jobs from tape to disk, you invoke the z/OS utility job **IEBCOPY**, an IBM data set utility program. Input is a partitioned data set, a partitioned data set extended (PDSE), or an unload data set that has members to be copied, merged, or unloaded; the output is data sets. Figure 3.7 reproduces the example from the installation manual that copies all the members for the SMP/E installation using **IEBCOPY**.

```
//STEP1 EXEC PGM=IEBCOPY
//SYSPRINT DD SYSOUT=*
//IN DD DSN=IBM.HDB9910.F3,UNIT=tunit, VOL=SER=DB9910,
// LABEL=(6,SL),DISP=(OLD,KEEP)
```

```
//OUT DD DSNAME=jcl-library-name,
// DISP=(NEW,CATLG,DELETE),
// VOL=SER=dasdvol,UNIT=SYSALLDA
// DCB=*.STEP1.IN,SPACE=(TRK,(20,10,10))
//SYSUT3 DD UNIT=SYSALLDA,SPACE=(CYL,(1,1))
//SYSIN DD *
COPY INDD=IN,OUTDD=OUT
/*
```

Figure 3.7: Copying the SMP/E jobs

For more information about **IEBCOPY** (and **IEBPTPCH**, which prints each job), see the *Data Facility Storage Management System (DFSMS) Utilities* (SC26-7414) guide. This manual describes the space management, tape management, backup/recovery, and other functions of this data set utility program.

You can edit this job, make changes, and submit it, and as a result you will have a list of jobs copied to disk. The sample JCL copies all the members that are necessary to complete the SMP/E process. Note that there are no **JOB** statements, so you will have to create your own. Then, once you have all the JCL in order, you submit the job to run.

The SMP/E jobs exist in a partitioned data set called **IBM.HDB9910.F3** on a tape with the volume serial number (**VOLSER**) DB9910. On the tape or cartridge, there will be a list of SMP/E jobs that can be edited to execute the **RECEIVE**, **APPLY**, and **ACCEPT** process as well as a program directory describing any changes to the ordered medium. Each tape will have one or more FMIDs; for example, IRLM will have its own FMID for shipping. If you ordered a CBPDO or ServerPac, refer to the documentation that accompanied it.

If you plan to use DB2 ODBC or DB2 for z/OS Java Edition, you will need to run additional installation jobs. Two IBM DB2 product references document these jobs: *DB2 V9.1 for z/OS ODBC Guide and Reference* (SC18-9850) and *DB2 V9.1 for z/OS Application Programming Guide and Reference for Java* (SC18-9842).

Structure of the SMP/E Jobs

Before you start working with the SMP/E installation jobs, you should refer to the DB2 9 for z/OS program directory. In this document, look for the Preventative Service Planning (PSP) information. After reviewing the specifications, you can use the ServiceLink facility of IBMLink or ShopzSeries to check the latest service information for DB2. (To obtain access to IBMLink, contact IBM Software Support.)

You must first copy the jobs and then edit and execute them. The steps listed in Tables 3.3 and 3.4 list the jobs that are copied from the tape.

Table 3.3: Overview of SMP/E installation jobs			
Step	**Description**	**Job/s**	**Job type**
1	Copy, edit the SMP/E jobs.	IEBCOPY	
2	*Optional*: Initialize the SMP/E environment for DB2. *Note*: Some data sets are in partitioned data set extended (PDSE) format. This step creates DB2 target and distribution zones and defines SMP/E control data sets in these zones and in the SMP/E global zone. Check with the systems programmer if you need help managing the SMP/E data sets.	DSNTIJAA	SMP/E
3	Allocate the libraries. This step creates the DB2 target and distribution libraries and defines these libraries in the SMP/E target and distribution zones for DB2 for required and optional FMIDs.	DSNALLOC	ALLOCATE
4	Run the RECEIVE jobs. This step loads the DB2 program modules, procedures, macros, IRLM, JDBC, ODBC, SQLJ, and DB2I Kanji into temporary data sets (SMPTLIBs). *Important*: Before starting these jobs, back up your DB2 8 distribution and target libraries and your SMP/E data sets.	DSNRECV1, DSNRECV2, DSNRECV3, DSNRECV4, DXXRECEV	RECEIVE (DB2) RECEIVE (IRLM) RECEIVE (ODBC, etc.) RECEIVE(Kanji) RECEIVE(XML extender)
5	*Optional*: Run the cleanup job. This delete process should be done before you install DB2 9 (job DSNAPPL1); Run it if you are migrating from DB2 8 to DB2 9.	DSNTIJUD	Optional
6	Run the APPLY CHECK job. This step copies and link odito the DB2 program modules, procedures, and macros into DB2 target libraries for required FMIDs and additional FMIDs.	DSNAPPL1	APPLY

Table 3.3: Overview of SMP/E installation jobs (continued)			
Step	Description	Job/s	Job type
7	Run the SMP/E ACCEPT job. This step ACCEPTs all the required and additional FMIDs into the DB2 distribution libraries (DLIBs), letting you apply corrective service later.	DSNACEP1	ACCEPT
8	*Optional*: Unload the jobs for the additional FMIDs.		
9	*Optional*: Run the RECEIVE jobs for the additional FMIDs.	DSNRECV1, DSNRECV2, DSNRECV3, DSNRECV4	RECEIVE
10	*Optional*: Run the APPLY job for the additional FMIDs.	DSNAPPL1	APPLY
11	*Optional*: Run the ACCEPT jobs for the additional FMIDs.	DSNACEP1	ACCEPT
12	RECEIVE and APPLY any maintenance shipped with the product. *Important*: DB2 8 must be at the proper maintenance level before migration to DB2 9.		

Table 3.3: Additional SMP/E jobs			
Step	Description	Job/s	Type
Sample	Invoke the supplied DSNAMKDR EXEC to allocate hierarchical file system (HFS) paths for DB2 base.	DSNASMKD	MKDIR
Sample	Invoke the supplied DSNAMKDR EXEC to allocate HFS paths for MQListener.	DSNLSMKD	MKDIR
Sample	Invoke the supplied DSNWMKDR EXEC to allocate HFS paths for the Web Services Object Runtime Framework (WORF).	DSNWSMKD	MKDIR
Sample	Invoke the supplied DSNMKDIR EXEC to allocate HFS paths for JDBC/SQLJ.	DSNISMKD	MKDIR
Sample	Define SMP/E DDDEFs. Check the program directory for entries you delete that are no longer used in DB2 9.	DSNDDEF1	DDDEF

DB2 9 for z/OS and IRLM V2R2 are assumed to be in the same zones. If they are not, you will have to edit jobs **DSNALLOC**, **DSNAPPL1**, and **DSNDDEF1**and make the modifications to the jobs. In addition, in job **DSNAPPL1**, which performs the SMP/E **APPLY CHECK** for DB2 9 for z/OS, you should have the latest Enhanced HOLDDATA. This data is available at *http://service.software.ibm.com/holdata/390holddata.html*.

You want to install the FMIDs regardless of the status of unresolved High Impact Pervasive (HIPER) PTFs. However, you should analyze any unresolved HIPERs before deploying the software. Where you have **++HOLD** statements for HIPERs and you must complete the FMID installation, you have two options:

- **BYPASS** the specific ERROR HOLDs and continue the FMID installation. (You will have to do some research to complete this step.)

- Add the **BYPASS(HOLDCLASS(HIPER))** operand to the **APPLY** command. The FMID will be installed even though HIPER ERROR HOLDs exist against it. This option is quicker, but subsequent review of the **REPORT ERRSYSMODS** command output is required to investigate the HIPERs.

••
Appendix A of the program directory for DB2 9 for z/OS V09.01.00 (program number 5635-DB2) provides a list of included PTFs for each FMID.
••

There are a few steps to do before you execute the jobs. Each job needs your JOB card statements added. You will also need to check the link list options. If you did not place the *prefixxxx*.**SDSNLOAD** in the **LNKLST*xx*** member of library **SYS1. PARMLIB**, you will need a **STEPLIB** or **JOBLIB** statement in your Time Sharing Option (TSO) or batch jobs.

Edit each of the DB2 SMP/E jobs, and follow the directions in the header notes of each job to specify the names of the SMP/E data sets. If you want to add a suffix, edit the SMP/E procedures and allocation jobs. The prefix cannot exceed 18 characters, and the suffix cannot exceed 17 characters minus the length of the prefix. In addition, any data set names that exceed eight characters must be specified in groups of no more than eight characters, separated by periods. The qualified data set name cannot exceed 44 characters.

DB2 V9 includes fewer SMP/E jobs than DB2 8 because the DB2 utilities are now contained in a single FMID. Jobs **DSNACCPM**, **DSNACCPS**, **DSNAPPLM**, **DSNAPPLS**, **DSNRECVM**, and **DSNRECVS** are deleted.

Once you have the tape loaded and the SMP/E jobs edited, submitted, and checked, you can move to the maintenance process.

Table 3.4 lists the distribution libraries that are loaded from your SMP/E work. These libraries contain the master copy of all elements for your DB2 system.

Table 3.4: DB2 distribution libraries	
Distribution libraries	**Contents**
prefix.ADSNBASE	Jobs required to complete SMP/E installation
prefix.ADSNENU or *prefix*.ADSNDKF	DB2 English task panels/DB2 Kanji task panels.
prefix.ADSNLOAD	Individual object module for every DB2 load module. Contains IRLM modules if you choose to install IRLM in the same distribution libraries as DB2. This must be a PDSE data set.
prefix.ADSNLOD2	PDSE data set containing JDBC and SQL DDLs.
prefix.ADSNHFS	Data to be copied into z/OS UNIX System Services.
prefix.ADSNIVPD	Installation verification procedure (IVP) input data and expected output for sample applications.
prefix.ADSNMACS	DB2 macros, sample programs and data, initialization data, Time Sharing Option (TSO) CLISTs, Interactive System Productivity Facility (ISPF) panels, ISPF messages.
prefix.ADSNXML	Data used from IBM Managed System Infrastructure (msys) for Setup DB2 Customization Center. Note that msys for Setup DB2 Customization Center is deprecated; use the installation panels instead.
prefix.ADXRLOAD	Individual object module for every IRLM load module.
prefix.ADXRSAMP	Installation procedures for installing IRLM V2.

Table 3.5 shows the DB2 target libraries that are loaded from your SMP/E work. These libraries contain the various DB2 components and are updated when you apply corrective service.

Table 3.5: DB2 target libraries	
Target libraries	**Contents**
prefix.SDSNBASE	Jobs required to complete SMP/E installation.
prefix.SDSNC.H	Header files; a command line interface (CLI) requirement, usable by C language programs.
prefix.SDSNCLST	TSO CLIST library/code to simplify installation/migration, use of utilities, use of DB2I.
prefix.SDSNDBRM	System database request modules (DBRMs) for DB2 9.
prefix.SDSNEXIT	Empty when first created; install jobs put DSNHDECP, the DSNZP*xxx* load module, and exit modules into this library.
prefix.SDSNIVPD	IVP input data and output for sample applications.
prefix.SDSNLINK	Early code for DB2 9.
prefix.SDSNLOAD	Load modules for DB2 9; must be a PDSE data set.

Table 3.5: DB2 target libraries (continued)	
Target libraries	**Contents**
prefix.SDSNLOD2	PDSE data set containing JDBC and SQLJ DDLs.
prefix.SDSNMACS	Macro library needed for CICS and IMS attachment facilities, initialization parameter macros, data-mapping macros for some applications.
prefix.SDSNPFPE or *prefix*.SDSNPFPK	English/Kanji task and help panels.
prefix.SDSNSAMP	Initialization library, sample applications/data, migration and installation jobs, default installation and migration parameters, and catalog initialization data for DB2. The Job Control Input (JCLIN) for each FMID is stored in this library.
prefix.SDSNSPFM	DB2 ISPF message library, which contains messages issued during installation or migration process.
prefix.SDSNSPFP	DB2 ISPF library for installation task/help routing panels.
prefix.SDSNSPFS	ISPF skeleton library for DB2 used to produce EDIT JCL.
prefix.SDSNSPFT	ISPF command table library.
prefix.SDXRRESL	IRLM load modules; can be empty if you choose to install IRLM elsewhere.
prefix.SDXRSAMP	IRLM sample library; can be empty if you choose to install IRLM elsewhere.

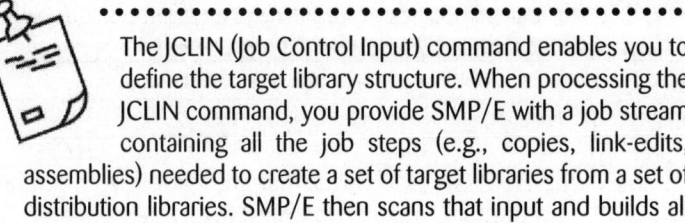

The JCLIN (Job Control Input) command enables you to define the target library structure. When processing the JCLIN command, you provide SMP/E with a job stream containing all the job steps (e.g., copies, link-edits, assemblies) needed to create a set of target libraries from a set of distribution libraries. SMP/E then scans that input and builds all required entries to define the target system structure.

How, Where, and When Do You Apply Maintenance?

The z/OS systems programmer is responsible for all software products and modifications on the system, but in many shops the DB2 system administrator performs the DB2 SMP/E work. Before installing DB2, check the PSP updates listed in the program directory. Be sure that you apply all the maintenance (corrective service) to your system before migrating from DB2 8 to DB2 9.

This SMP/E responsibility and critical problem resolution for DB2 requires the DB2 system administrator to receive and apply fixes or modifications to DB2 SMP/E libraries. These types of elements fall into four categories:

- *Program temporary fix (PTF):* PTFs are IBM-supplied corrections for some type of reported problem. PTF SYSMODs always depend on the installation of a function SYSMOD. Sometimes, a PTF SYSMOD may also depend on the installation of other PTF SYSMODs. Such dependencies are known as prerequisites.

- *Authorized program analysis report (APAR):* APARs are temporary corrections for some defect in an IBM licensed program or system control program that affects a specific user. For example, say you have a severe problem in a system control program or licensed program, but there is not a PTF that is ready to correct the problem. In this case, IBM will supply a quick corrective fix in the form of an APAR. An APAR SYSMOD always has the installation of a function SYSMOD as a prerequisite and can also depend on the installation of other PTF or APAR SYSMODs.

- *FUNCTION:* A function SYSMOD could be an updated product, a release of a product, or even a new version of a product. All types of SYSMODs are dependent on a function SYSMOD, so there are two types of function SYSMODs: base function, when you are replacing all of a product's elements in system data sets or system libraries when installing a function SYSMOD, and dependent function, which is an addition to an existing function.

- *User modification (USERMOD):* You create a USERMOD to add some type of independent function to the system or possibly to change IBM code.

The SMP/E processes keep up with all the service levels for all the elements and use the SYSMOD hierarchy to determine the correct service order for accomplishing the updates.

Pre- and Post-Requisites

Some PTFs and APARs can have corequisites, and there can also be prerequisites. PTF, APAR, and USERMOD SYSMODs all have the function SYSMOD as a prerequisite. We sometimes have a PTF or even an APAR that depends on other PTF SYSMODs; this is called a corequisite. Sometimes, a PTF contains multiple element replacements. When you think about keeping track of all the system elements and their modifications, the importance of handling these elements in a z/OS system becomes readily apparent.

Figure 3.8 shows IBM's Technical Help Database for mainframe operating environments, available at *http://www14.software.ibm.com/webapp/set2/ srchBroker/views/srchBroker.jsp?rs=112.*

Technical help database
for mainframe operating environments

Search for technical documents related to the mainframe operating systems.
To include software products that run in the mainframe operating environment, select a product or group of products using the **"Expand search to other product categories"** or **"Quick Selects"** options below.

Search mainframe systems:

[   ] (Go)

Sort results by:

[Date - newest first ▼]

Other databases
→ Subscription services
→ Preventive Service Planning buckets
→ Redbooks

Expand search to other product categories:

Collaboration & Knowledge
Database & Data Management
e-Learning Software
Enterprise Messaging
Host Transaction Processing
Monitors, Terminals

Quick Selects:
All Categories
Collaboration
Data Management
Development Software
Hardware
Software Management
Transaction Software
Web Software

Limit search to selected documents:

☐ APARs   ☐ Flashes
☐ FAQs   ☐ Preventive service planning
☐ Product information   ☐ Redbook abstracts
☐ Education   ☐ Solutions
☐ Technotes   ☐ White Papers

Figure 3.8: Technical Help Database page

This handy Web site offers two ways to find the PSP bucket(s) for DB2. You can also use this page to search for APARs and other information.

The first PSP search method is very simple. Under **Other databases**, select **Preventive Service Planning buckets**; then, on the next page, enter DB2's FMID, which is HDB9910, and press **Enter**. The list of PSPs will appear on the next page.

The second method is to expand the search to other product categories and select **Database & Data Management** from the drop-down list; then, under **Limit search to selected documents**, select the **Preventive service planning** check box.

The second method typically produces a shorter list of items to look through than the first method. In either case, when you click **Go** or press **Enter**, a list of PSPs will appear. Review the list for items that might impact your system. Included in the list are upgrade FUNCTIONs that deal with the z/OS family of products. Find the latest DB2 upgrade that should be "after" the date your tape was shipped.

Figure 3.9 shows a sample extract of listed items.

2.	Upgrade FUNCTION, Subset CAPPROV - Extract File Extract File [More items like this found in z/OS family]	2009-03-27
3.	Upgrade TWSZOS850, Subset JWSZ501 - Extract File Extract File [More items like this found in z/OS family]	2009-03-27
4.	Upgrade FUNCTION, Subset HCHECKER FUNCTION Bucket HCHECKER [More items like this found in z/OS family]	2009-03-27
5.	Upgrade OMXEI5420 Version 4, Release 2, Modification 0 for IBM TIVOLI OMEGAMON XE FOR IMS on z/OS [More items like this found in z/OS family]	2009-03-27
6.	Upgrade FUNCTION, Subset XRCSCA FUNCTION Bucket XRCSCA [More items like this found in z/OS family]	2009-03-27
7.	Upgrade ZOSV1R9, Subset CSIP Communications Srvr IP Version 1, Release 9, Modification 0 [More items like this found in z/OS family]	2009-03-27
8.	Upgrade FUNCTION, Subset ZIIP - Extract File Extract File [More items like this found in z/OS family]	2009-03-27
9.	Upgrade DB2910 Version 9, Release 1, Modification 0 for DB2 for z/OS [More items like this found in z/OS family]	2009-03-27
10.	Upgrade FUNCTION, Subset HCHECKER - Extract File Extract File [More items like this found in z/OS family]	2009-03-27

Figure 3.9: Program upgrade list

This panel contains a list of upgrades that might impact your installation. You should carefully evaluate this list of products and upgrades. It gives you a feel for the information that is available to you for more than just DB2. Note that HIPER APAR information about DB2 9 is included under item 9.

If you select item 9, **Upgrade DB2910**, you will see a document that explains each upgrade associated with the PSP (Figure 3.10).

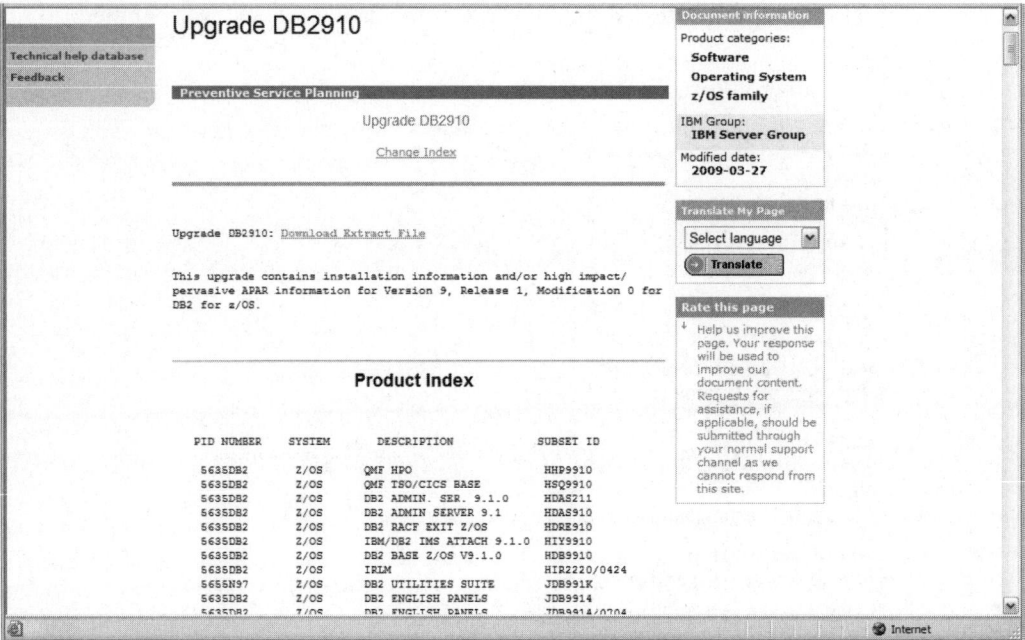

Figure 3.10: Product upgrade list

You use the document's **Download Extract File** link to obtain the PSP upgrades. Click this link to see the list of APARs with FMID, FIX, UPG, and SUB headings.

If you click on the PSP document's **Change Index** link, you will see the date, subset altered, and comments about each fix within the document. Figure 3.11 shows a sample Change Index list. Notice that the dates in the first column appear in descending order. This display provides an ongoing list of fixes you can check.

Change Index

```
    DATE          SUBSET ALTERED     COMMENTS

292 09/03/27   HDB9910/0704       SECTION 4, ADDED ITEM 221 PK82013 UK44791
               HDB9910/0704       SECTION 4, ADDED ITEM 222 PK76834 UK44770
291 09/03/26   HDB9910/0704       SECTION 4, ADDED ITEM 220 PK68878 UK41583
290 09/03/25   HDB9910/0704       SECTION 4, ADDED ITEM 218 PK79775 UK44662
               HDB9910/0704       SECTION 4, ADDED ITEM 219 PK79463 UK44665
289 09/03/23   HDB9910/0704       SECTION 4, ADDED ITEM 217 PK80572 UK44561
288 09/03/20   HDB9910/0704       SECTION 4, ADDED ITEM 216 PK81404 UK44529
287 09/03/18   HDB9910/0704       SECTION 4, ADDED ITEM 214 PK79236 UK44461
               HDB9910/0704       SECTION 4, ADDED ITEM 215 PK73345 UK42873
286 09/03/16   HDB9910/0704       SECTION 4, ADDED ITEM 212 PK78463 UK44410
               HDB9910/0704       SECTION 4, ADDED ITEM 213 PK75926 UK44440
```

Figure 3.11: Change Index list in descending date order

An FAQ document available at *http://www-01.ibm.com/support/docview.wss?rs =64&context=SSEPEK&dc=DB560&dc=DB520&uid=swg21210011&loc=e n_US&cs=UTF-8&lang=en&rss=ct64db2* provides a set of keywords to help you search for APAR text. This is a handy way to make sure that what you are asking for is what IBM is searching for in the APAR text.

We generally think of doing maintenance on a schedule. Some shops, for example, perform maintenance each quarter. You should consider how this strategy fits into your preventative maintenance planning. Recommended Service Upgrade (RSU) is IBM's method for keeping up with the latest maintenance.

Notice the HDB9910 subset shown in the preceding figure. You can click on a highlighted PK*xxxxx* (APAR) or UK*xxxx* (PTF) item on the right side of this display to go to the technical support page where you can view the item's definition. Figure 3.12 shows a sample result.

Results		
Technical support	Information centers	Publications

1 - 1 of 1 items found*		Modified date
1.	PK82013: ABEND=0C4-4 IN DSNIKESE+14A8 DUE TO SINGLE BIT OVERLAY Abend occurs if, for packages bound before V6, DSNITCUS will turn off MSIXMLSELLK before checking to see if an extension [More items like this found in Data Servers (Database Management Systems)]	2009-10-19
1 - 1 of 1 items found*		Modified date

Figure 3.12: Sample PK item description

Click on the item's title here to see the entire fix document. The documentation reports the status of the APAR and provides an error description, local fix, recommendation, problem summary, problem conclusion, and comments. In addition, the APAR information that follows the comments section reports the status, submitted date, and closed date.

Level of Support

The product levels documented in both the program directory and the PSP bucket (Figure 3.8 under the selection **Other databases**) are the levels with which DB2 9 for z/OS was tested. You can tell the level of support you have when the product is shipped to you by the service level, which in this case is PUT level 0803.

Program level refers to the APAR fixes incorporated into the program. *Service level* refers to the PTFs incorporated into the program. So you have APAR fixes incorporated into the product tapes for DB2. For more information about specific APARs incorporated into PUT level 0803, see the program directory at *http:// publibfp.boulder.ibm.com/epubs/pdf/i1087372.pdf*.

"PUT level" (PUT stands for Program Update Tape) is an older term that has been replaced by the term Recommended Service Upgrade. PTFs may take a little time to get to the RSU list, but a HIPER fix will show up immediately on the next RSU order. So, when we say RSU or PUT level, the meaning is the same. New products, such as z/OS 1.9 and related products, would be "upgraded" to PUT level 0803.

All products consist of maintenance that is in a closed status. A PTF that is still open will not be in the base code. So, the functions of the DB2 V9.1.0 base are at PUT level 0803. The product levels documented in both the program directory and the PSP bucket are the levels with which DB2 9 for z/OS was tested.

DB2 SMP/E Data Sets

In the DB2 9 installation panels, the prefix and suffix of the data sets in SMP/E and the installation-defined data sets need not use the same prefix and suffix. Panel **DSNTIPA1** in the installation command list (CLIST) lets you specify different prefixes and suffixes for both types of these data sets.

System Managed Storage

On installation panel **DSNTIPA2**, you specify whether System Managed Storage (SMS) will control the data sets created by the installation, migration, and verification process. DB2 9 does not require you to explicitly define all device types and volume IDs for migration, installation, or verification. Now, you have the option to also define the following:

- SMS data class

- SMS management class

- SMS storage class

You define these on installation panel **DSNTIPA3**, if you indicated on panel **DSNTIPA2** that you wanted to use SMS for the data sets.

Consolidated Service Test (CST)

IBM has a software service testing environment called Consolidated Service Test (CST). This cross-product testing environment puts the software maintenance for z/OS and OS/390 platforms through a testing process to ensure the quality of maintenance service for greater coordination between the products and each level of service. This testing occurs in addition to individual PTF testing and does not replace the current testing done at the product level.

CST uses industry-like workloads to test products such as z/OS and OS/390, Information Management System (IMS), MQSeries for OS/390, CICS Transaction Server for OS/390, and DB2 for z/OS. A monthly RSU is then produced. Each quarter, all the service (which includes severity 1, 2, 3, and 4 APARs) is put through a CST test cycle and becomes the recommended service level. Each month, you should also look at HIPER PTFs.

Monthly and quarterly RSUs follow the naming convention of RSU*yymm* as a SOURCEID notation (where *yy* = year and *mm* = month). So when you are looking for the quarterly RSUs, look to the month value (i.e., RSU*yy*03, RSU*yy*06, RSU*yy*09, RSU*yy*12) to decide on the quarter. IBM recommends that you roll out the quarterly RSU product by product on any single system to eliminate complicating the task of dealing with any problems that might occur.

IBM's CST Web site, *http://www-03.ibm.com/systems/z/os/zos/support/servicetest*, provides additional information about the Consolidated Service Test.

Acquiring Fixes

When working with fixes, acronyms and terminology can sometimes be confusing. The term "SUP TAPE" (SUP stands for "Superseded") is the older naming convention for service, which is now referred to as an RSU. You will also hear terms such as "corrective service" or "preventative maintenance," but it all amounts to an RSU or an individual PTF or APAR that you're looking for. You will also encounter the term "PE" (program error); this is a PTF-in-error.

A HIPER PTF is issued to correct a severe problem. A SUP APAR, or superseded APAR, is another term you will come across. SPE stands for Small Programming Enhancements; the required fallback APAR for DB2 8 is called an SPE APAR.

To keep up with service, you can also monitor IBM's Red Alerts by subscribing to the e-mail notification service at *http://www14.software.ibm.com/webapp/set2/ sas/f/redAlerts/home.html*. It is a good practice to sign up for Red Alerts from IBM on zSeries, which include DB2 Red Alerts.

You can also sign up on the CST Web site to be notified about new RSUs. After registering, you will receive an e-mail with a notification similar to the one shown in Figure 3.13 whenever a new RSU becomes available.

Figure 3.13: Sample new RSU notification
You registered on IBM's Consolidated Service Test (CST) Web site asking us to notify you when we've completed testing of a new RSU. I'm writing to tell you we've updated our Web site for the latest RSU service package tested, RSU0903. Refer to your service deliverable (such as ShopzSeries or CBPDO) for RSU availability.
RSU0903 includes:
PE resolution or HIPER/Security/Integrity/Pervasive PTFs and their associated requisites and supersedes through February 2009.

Obtaining RSUs Using ShopzSeries

You can use the ShopzSeries Web tool to acquire the next RSU for z/OS and OS/390 service. Figure 3.14 shows the ShopzSeries welcome page, *https://www14. software.ibm.com/webapp/ShopzSeries/ShopzSeries.jsp*.

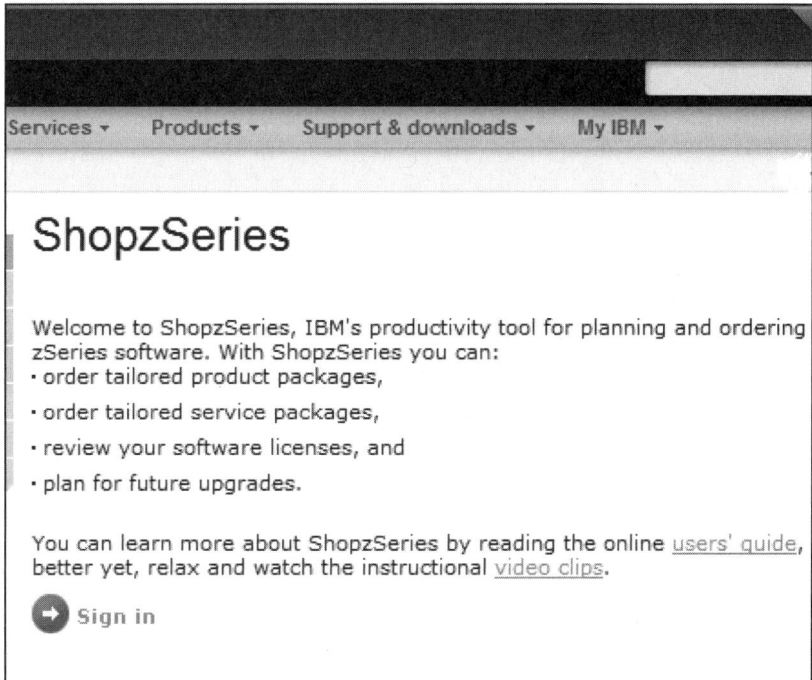

Figure 3.14: ShopzSeries welcome page

To begin using ShopzSeries, you must sign in to the tool. Doing so requires an IBM ID and password. Once signed in, you can create new orders for services or products, view draft orders that you have not sent, check orders you've placed, and review completed orders. Figure 3.15 shows the panel used to create a new order.

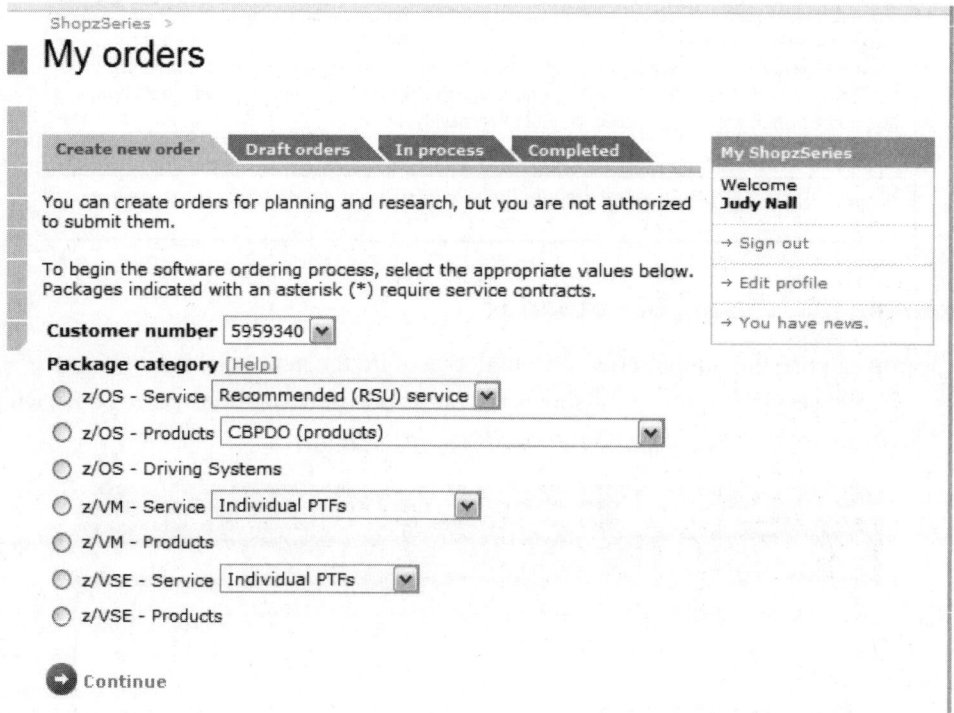

Figure 3.15: My orders panel

Just remember that when you order preventive service, the service you receive will be for all the products you have in your "profile." You can always update your profile to reflect changes in your software.

If you order service for products that are not tested in the CST environment, you will still receive all the service specified in your profile. In addition, you will receive RSU **++ASSIGN** statements for all the service — both CST-tested and non–CST-tested service.

Software Subscription and Support at IBM

Note that the term "Software Subscription and Support" has replaced the term "Software Maintenance" in the current release. To take advantage of Software Subscription and Support, your company must have an active IBM software maintenance contract, and you must be authorized to submit a problem to IBM. There are two ways to handle this: You can go online, or you can contact IBM by phone.

Online support is handled through two license acquisition methods for Software Subscription and Support offerings: Passport Advantage and Passport Advantage Express (*http://www-01.ibm.com/software/lotus/passportadvantage*). Take the time to look over the Web site and ask within your company what the company's license agreement is with IBM for software support. From the Web site, you can obtain Web software support by opening a service request. If you need to talk, your customer support is a telephone call away.

Before beginning an installation or migration, use Information/Access or the ServiceLink facility of IBMLink to check for PSP updates to the information contained in the DB2 program directory about DB2 and other products. Contact the IBM Support Center if you do not have access to IBMLink.

The IBM Support Portal (*http://www-947.ibm.com/support/entry/portal/Overview/ Software/Information_Management/DB2_for_z~OS*) provides features that make it easier to find the exact support information or tool you need. Check here for a link to downloads, to open a service request, and for other support. To connect to the ServiceLink/IBMLink Web site, select the **Open service request** task. You must sign in to access this site. You can also view prior service requests (SRs). To access this Web site, you must have a software maintenance contract, user ID, and password.

V8-to-V9 Release Incompatibilities and Preplanning

The *DB2 Version 9.1 for z/OS Installation Guide* includes a section on changes and release incompatibilities. Take a look at this material to obtain a complete list of considerations for preplanning and incompatibilities. The latter topic is divided into seven categories: application, utility, commands, storage, and other incompatibilities and functions that are no longer supported or are deprecated.

You also need to look carefully at the program directory for additional preplanning information and incompatibilities. We will address most of the storage and other incompatibilities here, as well as some of the functions that are no longer supported or are deprecated.

You must consider new, obsolete, and updated functions carefully in the migration process. You also need to take into account IBM's documented recommendations in migrating from DB2 8 to DB2 9. One of those recommendations is the binding of plans and packages before you migrate.

Several jobs need to be run and their output evaluated before migration. Job **DSNTIJPM** is shipped with each release of DB2 and identifies plans that were not bound before DB2 7. Job **DSNTIJP9** is the same as DB2 9's **DSNTIJPM** but is shipped with DB2 8 to maximize the time available to prepare the DB2 8 catalog for migration to DB2 9. Both jobs contain a series of SQL statements that check the catalog for inconsistencies. Examine each SQL output to ensure you have no issues. This is a good health check to perform in preparing to migrate to DB2 9.

If you use the Resource Access Control Facility (RACF), the **DSNR** resource class must be active, and you might have to create additional RACF profiles in the class.

Maintenance Information

The following paragraphs summarize key maintenance items related to DB2 9 for z/OS.

Informational APAR II14401

Informational APAR II14401 is the DB2 8 migration/fallback informational APAR for DB2 9. It details the APARs required for migration and fallback to and from DB2 9. The APAR contains changes to the **DSNTIJP9** job and is dated 2008-10-04. Note that several corrections were made to the SQL in these jobs; a quick check of these would be in order first.

PK77228

The PK77228 APAR contains miscellaneous fixes to DB2 for DB2 9 dated 2009-04-06. You need to take a look at the latest maintenance. The list can be obtained with ShopzSeries.

PK39850

In DB2 8, PK39850 is a preconditioning corrective fix for future functions for z/OS Utility users.

SPE APAR PK11129 (UK90008)

Preparing DB2 8 for migration requires application of the SPE APAR PK11129 NEW FUNCTION. In the migration process, you must be in DB2 8 new-function mode (NFM) with the fallback PK11129 applied to the subsystem and the subsystem restarted. This requirement, dated 2009-03-20, applies to DB2 8 users migrating to DB2 9.

Non–data-sharing DB2 subsystems must also run with this fallback SPE and be restarted before you attempt migration to DB2 9. If you are data sharing, you must apply this APAR to all members of a data-sharing group and start DB2 V8R1 on all members before one of the members can be started with DB2 V9 to migrate the DB2 catalog. Required for coexistence of DB2 8 and DB2 9 in a data-sharing environment, the APAR must be applied and the subsystem must be started.

At DB2 start-up time, the code level of the DB2 subsystem is compared with the code level required by the DB2 catalog. If there is a mismatch, you will receive message DSNX208E, and the start-up will be terminated. In a data-sharing group, the code level is compared with the starting subsystem each time you start a subsystem. If a mismatch exists with the code level of the catalog, you will receive either message DSNX208E (in a non–data-sharing environment) or message DSNX209E (in a data-sharing environment). Message DSNR045E is issued when DB2 is started and the fallback SPE APAR PK11129 has not been applied.

For more information about fallback, see informational APAR II14224 (prior is APAR II12423) and these specific APARs: PK33664, PK38799, PK39850, PK44884, and PK74494.

PK83585

This fix ensures that universal table spaces (UTSs) are created in reordered row format (RRF), preventing UTS table spaces or partitions in basic row format (BRF) under all conditions.

PK78958

This fix disables RRF conversion for compressed page sets.

PK31841

This fix contains a correction to the pre-migration job **DSNTIJP9**.

PK62178

This fix provides a new function describing the maximum number of implicit databases.

PK76532

APAR PQ93353 was not put into DB2 9. The PK76532 fix relates to use of the **START DATABASE** command by **SYSOPR**.

PK52522 (Plan Stability)

The PK52522 APAR lets you plan your migration using plan stability. In the event that you needed to fall back, you would need to know whether your packages were bound at DB2 8 or DB2 9. To facilitate this process, you need to apply some APARs. The IBM-recommended strategy is to rebind the packages in DB2 8 and then rebind them in DB2 9.

Rebind in DB2 8, and, after moving to conversion mode (CM), don't forget to run the **RUNSTATS** utility before converting to DB2 9 NFM. In DB2 9, you can store three versions of the package, so you can have a current version, a previous version, and an original version (if migrating, this is DB2 8).

In DB2 9, the term *conversion mode* replaces the term *compatibility mode*.

If you use this strategy in fallback to DB2 8 from DB2 9 after binding, the binds must be specified as **SWITCH(PREVIOUS)** to enable return to the DB2 8 level — good to know! Once you are in DB2 9 and want to establish a new original version, you would use **FREE PACKAGE ... ... PLANMGMTSCOPE(INACTIVE)** to free the original package and the previous version. Now, you can begin your plan stability strategy in DB2 9.

One more thing: If you intend to have these three versions, make sure you have enough disk space in the catalog to store three times the size of your current **SPT01** directory table space when using **REBIND PACKAGE EXTENDED**.

Preconditioning Fixes

Make sure you have PK52522. This preconditioning APAR for plan stability should be applied to all DB2 8 NFM systems.

Also, DB2 9 PK52523 introduces plan (package) stability and allows for a safe way to **REBIND** (fall back) for plan stability. A new **REBIND PACKAGE** option, **SWITCH**, lets you revert to an older copy of a package, undoing the prior **REBIND**. Just remember that if DB2 Service advises you to do a **REBIND PACKAGE**, this functionality is not recommended.

A few other things to note along this line:

- Be sure you have the DB2 8 plan table information before you start the DB2 9 CM migration.

- In CM on DB2 9, set the DSNZPARM called **PLANMGMT** to **EXTENDED**.

- Run **RUNSTATS** on DB2 9 CM before you **REBIND** on DB2 9.

- Set the DB2 9 **STATCLUS** DSNZPARM to **ENHANCED**.

- If you need to fall back to DB2 8, **REBIND** with **SWITCH(ORIGINAL)**, which takes you to the DB2 8 version of the package.

PK80375 enables ESA compression for **SPT01** and the reorganization of **SPT01**. Entries are placed in this skeleton package table as you **BIND** or **REBIND**. Sometimes, the space requirements are an inhibitor to using plan/package stability. Compression should be very helpful in this regard. This fix should also help those large packages that have more than 200 sections (which can be a critical bottleneck) by compressing them. This APAR adds an opaque DB2 subsystem parameter called **COMPRESS_SPT01** (value **YES** or **NO**) to macro **DSN6SPRM**.

PK62876 converts plans with database request modules (DBRMs) to packages.

Some new functions require z/OS 1.8, such as volume-based utility enhancements and database roles and trusted contexts.

The DSNDB07 Database

You will need to increase the size of the **DSNDB07** database. The temporary database goes away in DB2 9, and the processes that used it (declared global temporary tables and static scrollable cursors) now use **DSNDB07**. Before dropping the temporary database, be sure you will not be falling back to DB2 8.

In DB2 9, the switch from 4 KB work files to 32 KB work files for sorting is now at 100 bytes. In DB2 8, the switch was at 4,000 bytes. This extensive increase in the 32 KB pages in DB2 9 will require you to increase the pages allocated to 32 KB work files. If no pages are available in the 32 KB work files and the row length is less than 4 KB, DB2 uses the 4 KB work files. Also check the sizes of your buffer pools for the 4 KB and 32 KB work files associated with **DSNDB07**.

Bootstrap Data Set

You must have expanded the bootstrap data set (BSDS) in DB2 8 NFM before you migrate. See job **DSNJCNVB** in DB2 8 to make the changes. DB2 now supports 10,000 archive log data sets and up to 93 data sets for the active logs. It is a good idea to back up your BSDSs before running the conversion utility.

Buffer Pools and Indexes

DB2 9 supports 4 KB, 8 KB, 16 KB, or 32 KB buffer pools for user indexes. You need to have a 4 KB buffer pool during conversion mode. This support for larger than 4 KB buffer pools is also for compression for indexes. The subsystem parameter **IDXBPOOL** assigns the default buffer pool for indexes. To support compression on indexes, the size of the buffer pool must be greater than 4 KB. You can run the DB2 **DSN1COMP** utility against an index in DB2 9 for compression estimates. You will receive an **SQLCODE** of **-676** if you do not have a buffer pool larger than 4 KB and try to **ALTER** an index using **COMPRESS YES**.

Stored Procedures

Remember that DB2-managed stored procedures are going away; in DB2 9, they must be managed by Workload Manager for z/OS (WLM). DB2-established stored procedure address spaces are no longer supported. You will need to convert all your existing stored procedures that run in the DB2-managed stored procedure address space (SPAS) to the WLM SPAS. If you don't, any SP defined with **NO WLM ENVIRONMENT** will fail after migration to DB2 9 CM, and the **SQLCODE -471/00E7900A** will be given.

Simple Table Spaces

Simple table space creation is removed from support in DB2 9. If you cannot change these table spaces to segmented table spaces, at least **ALTER** them with **RESTRICT ON DROP**. There is no real recovery on a simple table space **DROP**; you must change the table spaces to segmented or partitioned. Data definition language (DDL) for a simple table space will create a segmented table space with a default of **SEGSIZE 4**. The usual recommendation is to convert such table spaces to partition-by-growth universal table spaces. In addition:

- Make sure no incomplete object definitions exist in the DB2 8 catalog.
- Complete or drop objects that are incomplete in their structure.
- **REORG** your catalog before migration to speed the conversion process.

Catalog/Directory Space

You should examine the size of the VSAM clusters that support your catalog and directory to make sure you have enough space. You can run the tailored job **DSNTIJIN** to define data sets of the new catalog, table spaces, and indexes.

Just to review, two steps are involved in migrating the catalog from DB2 8 to DB2 9. First is the migration to conversion mode; this job, **DSNTIJTC**, runs the **DSNUTILB** utility program with the parameters **CATMAINT UPDATE**, specifying the update to the catalog.

Second, in enabling-new-function mode (ENFM), job **DSNTIJEN** performs an online **REORG** of the catalog spaces **SYSIBM.SYSOBJ** and **SYSIBM.SYSPKAGE**. It converts **SYSOBJ** from 8 KB to 16 KB page size and completes the Real Time Statistics (RTS) tables in the catalog.

Following these steps, you run **DSNTIJNF** to switch to new-function mode, specifying control card option **CAFTNFM COMPLETE**. Remember that you can always run **DISPLAY GROUP DETAIL** to find the mode of DB2. Just to note, there is also an **UPDATE VCAT SWITCH** option in the **CATMAINT** utility, so your VCAT names for indexes, table spaces, and storage groups can be switched.

As in each release, the size of the DB2 catalog increases with additional table spaces, tables, indexes, columns, and table check constraints. Then, you need to make sure you do a **REORG** on the catalog before migration. So, consider increasing the size of the underlying VSAM data sets for the catalog and directory. It is recommended that you run **DSN1CHKR** to check for broken links. You can use the sample job **DSNTIJCX** to check the catalog and directory indexes for consistency.

Default Databases

You can no longer explicitly create a database name with **DSN*xxxxx***. If you try to **CREATE** a database name with **DSN** followed by five digits, you will receive **SQLCODE -20074 (SQLSTATE 42939)**.

In addition, DB2 implicitly creates a database if none is given on the **CREATE** statement without an **IN** clause. The numbering scheme that DB2 uses for these implicit databases is **DSN00001**, **DSN00002**, and so on up to **DSN60000**. PK62178 lets you change this range. With the PTF, the numbering limit is lowered to 10,000. When DB2 gets to **DSN10000** and it is not available, the *nnnnn* is set to **00001** and DB2 tries the database name **DSN00001**. Just know that when you drop the table, the implicit database is not dropped.

Resource Limit Facility

DB2 9 for z/OS provides two Resource Limit Facility (RLF) tables:

- *authid*.**DSNRLST***nn*

- *authid*.**DSNRLMT***nn*

For the latter table, you must have **DSNRLST***nn* in CM, or the command **START RLIMIT** will terminate.

When you are in NFM, either RLF table permits the **START RLIMIT** command to be executed successfully.

Real Time Statistics

RTS tables are now part of the catalog in DB2 9. DB2 moves the tables into the catalog when you execute the job **DSNTIJEN** in ENFM. DB2 does not use the user-defined tables, and at some point after you migrate, you can drop these tables. If you fall back to conversion mode* (CM*) — the asterisk (*) indicates that your system at one time was in ENFM or NFM — the RTS stays in the catalog tables and does not revert to your user-defined tables. The catalog tables that are used are **SYSIBM.SYSTABLESPACESTATS** and **SYSIBM.SYSINDEXSPACESTATS**.

DSNHDECP

As has been mentioned, the migration module **DSNHDECP** is not compatible between DB2 8 and DB2 9. In preparing for migration, you should reassemble all copies of this module in your system. If you have code that loads **DSNHDECP** and maps it with macros, you should plan to change that code because some current use of **DSNHDECP** has been deprecated.

Your assembly of the DSNZPARMs, which includes **DSNHDECP**, is stored in **SDSNEXIT** library. Incompatibility between DB2 8 and DB2 9 in fallback will cause a problem. You also might want to consider allocating separate **SDSNEXIT**s for each member in a data-sharing environment from the DB2 8 library you have now.

Fallback

In DB2 9, once you start the process of ENFM, you can fall back only to CM*. You will not be able to fall back to DB2 8 NFM.

To return to CM*, follow these steps:

1. Run job **DSNTIJCS** with the control statement option **CATENFM CMON**.

2. If you have already run job **DSNTIJNF**, then after running **DSNTIJCS**, run **DSNTIJNG** with option **DSNHDECP NEWFUN=NO** to rebuild your **DSNHDECP** module.

V8-to-V9 Migration and Installation: Changes and Incompatibilities

Installation doesn't deal with modes, regression, or preexisting data, which means you can take advantage of all the new functions of the new release right away. Migration, on the other hand, can involve a DB2 subsystem or a data-sharing group, requiring the conversion of the catalog and directory and user data to DB2 9. Some features are deprecated and some items are new in DB2 9, and these two processes — installation and migration — have a different flow to them. We will walk through each as we go along.

> As you move through your upgrade, you will be looking at activity on the system. A change to the **DISPLAY THREAD** command issued from the MVS console now imposes a default of 512 lines of output. If you have automated jobs that use this output, you might need to change them.

DB2 Early Code

You need to make sure that the link list options for your load modules are correct. For DB2 9, **SDSNLINK**, a load module library, contains the modules known as DB2 early, or ERLY, code. Job **DSNTIJMV** makes changes to the **SYS1.PARMLIB** library. The early code preconditioned PTFs are applied to the system before you migrate.

This library must be in the link list because the modules are loaded up at subsystem initialization time (IPL). The other libraries are **SDSNLOAD**, **SDSNLOD2**, and **SDSNEXIT**.

Customer Information Control System (CICS) needs to include the DB2 libraries in the CICS initialization JCL. Refer to the *CICS Transaction Server for z/OS DB2 Guide* (SC34-7011) for details. If you are using DB2 with CICS, you should probably put *prefix*.**SDSNLINK**, not *prefix*.**SDSNLOAD**, in the **LNKLST***xx* member of **SYS1.PARMLIB**. Then, place the needed **STEPLIB** or **JOBLIB** statements in the CICS procedures.

If this is the first time you start DB2 (e.g., if you are a new installation), you must IPL z/OS and then start the DB2 subsystem. Library **SDSNLINK** contains the early code. The modules in this library must be placed in the link list lookaside address space (LLA). The DB2 9 code is downward-compatible to DB2 8.

REFRESH Command

If you are migrating, any maintenance or installation of early code requires you to IPL z/OS to execute the early program. If no **PARMLIB** updates exist and the early code is at the correct level, no IPL is required for migration. You can use the **REFRESH** command to activate the new early code modules and rebuild the early code control blocks. Library **SYS1.PARMLIB** contains control parameters for z/OS and for some program products. There may be other libraries concatenated with it.

In DB2 9, you use the **REFRESH DB2,EARLY** DB2 command to accomplish this activation of code. If you are data sharing, you should execute the command on every instance:

```
-REFRESH DB2,EARLY
```

You can issue the **REFRESH** command only while DB2 is shut down. If you try to execute the command with the DB2 system started, you will receive message DSNY003I, which informs you of the failure. **SYSLOG** will contain messages associated with the command:

```
-REFRESH DB2,EARLY
DSNY003I SUBSYSTEM IS ALREADY ACTIVE
DSN9023I DSNYSCMD 'REFRESH DB2' ABNORMAL COMPLETION
```

Technical Requirements and New Functions

DB2 9 operates on any processor that supports 64-bit z/Architecture, including Systems z9 and z10, System z 890, System z 990, and zSeries z800, z890, z900, and z990 families of processors or a comparable processor. z/OS 1.7 is the minimum requirement to run DB2 9, the Data Facility Storage Management Subsystem (DFSMS) V1R7, Language Environment Base Services, RACF

1.7, IRLM 2.2, and z/OS Unicode Services. If you are going to use volume-based utilities, you need z/OS 1.8, DFSMS Hierarchical Storage Management (DFSMShsm) V1R8, DFSMS Data Set Services (DFSMSdss), and FlashCopy V2.

Tailoring DB2 Jobs and the Installation CLIST

At this point, let's assume you have performed SMP/E work steps 1 through 12, applied the necessary maintenance, consulted the program directory for any prereqs or coreqs, made sure you have all incompatibilities reconciled, obtained the early code, and applied preconditioning PTFs. You are now ready to proceed through the installation CLIST.

The installation CLIST displays a series of ISPF panels. In each panel, you supply parameters or accept defaults for the displayed values to describe the DB2 operating characteristics for your installation or migration. The CLIST edits the values you enter to ensure they are within the range of acceptable values. If these values need to change later, you can use an update function to change them.

Figure 3.16 summarizes the installation CLIST flow.

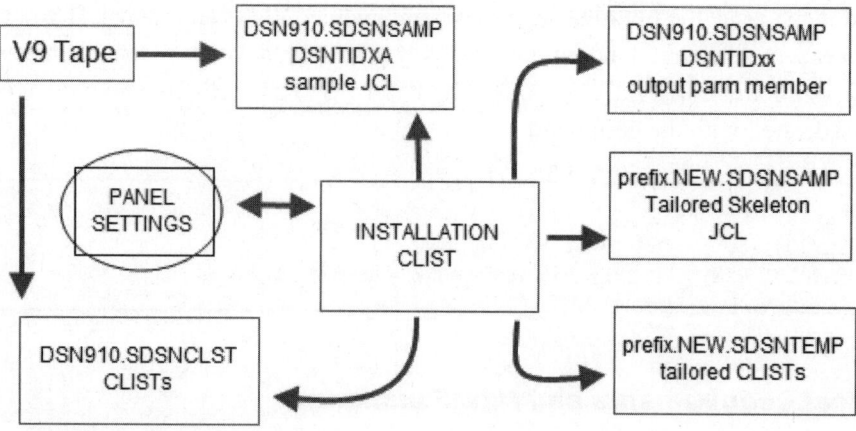

Figure 3.16: Installation CLIST flow

Before invoking the CLIST, you have a few preparation steps. First, check your TSO region size; it should be at least 2 MB. Then, invoke ISPF. When the main ISPF panel appears, choose item 6 and then invoke the CLIST by specifying

```
EXEC 'prefix.SDSNCLST(DSNTINST)''CONTROL(LIST)'
```

If you don't want to see the messages that trace the process, remove **'CONTROL(LIST)'**.

Your data sets can be allocated on panel **DSNTIPA2**, and your TSO user ID should have the authority to allocate these data sets. Output from the panel session produces the following items:

- A new data set member (if you want), that has the parameter values you entered during the session stored in *prefix*.**SDSNSAMP**

- A new data set, *prefix*.**NEW.SDSNSAMP**, the edited JCL with the values you entered on the panels

- A new data set, *prefix*.**NEW.SDSNTEMP**, with the tailored CLISTs for input to job **DSNTIJVC**, which is run during installation or migration

Job **DSNTIJVC** will merge unchanged CLISTs from *prefix*.**SDSNCLST** with the tailored CLISTs from *prefix*.**NEW.SDSNTEMP** and then place all the CLISTs in *prefix*.**NEW.SDSNCLST**.

The customization process takes you through the ISPF panels, prompting you to enter values and then moving to the next panel. The values you provide on the panels are placed into macros for substitution in job streams that you run to finalize your installation or migration. The values you enter reflect the application environment, IRLM, stored procedures, and storage that make up your DB2 subsystem environment. As you proceed through the panels, remember that pressing the **End** key will prevent changes to the original panel copies of your install jobs.

The jobs you execute after stepping through the panels depend on which task you are performing: installing, migrating, or updating. Each of these tasks executes a different set of jobs. Instructions are provided in each job for recovery in the event that a job fails.

After keying your values into each panel, you proceed to executing the set of jobs that use these parameters as input. Usually, you edit the jobs, check job cards, and then execute the jobs in the required order.

One of the jobs, **DSNTIJUZ**, assembles the DSNZPARMs, which are your "startup" parameters for DB2. This job's output name is used to start the DB2 subsystem. To manage that, you use the **START DB2** command, providing the subsystem command prefix you defined for the DB2 subsystem and specifying the named DSNZPARM you have assembled as an input parameter.

Here is an example of starting DB2 from the z/OS console:

```
-DSN1 START DB2 PARM(DSNZPxxx)
```

Panels, Values, and Dependencies

Figure 3.17 shows the starting CLIST panel, **DSNTIPA1**, which will be displayed again at the end of your CLIST processing. The values you key into the panels tailor and load the migration and installation jobs. The entries on the main panel control input to and output from the installation CLIST.

```
DSNTIPA1 DB2 VERSION 9 INSTALL, UPDATE, MIGRATE, AND ENFM - MAIN PANEL
===> _

Check parameters and reenter to change:
 1  INSTALL TYPE          ===> INSTALL    Install, Migrate, ENFM, or Update
 2  DATA SHARING          ===> NO         Yes or No (blank for ENFM or Update)

Enter the data set and member name for migration only. This is the name used
from a previous Installation/Migration from field 9 below:
 3  DATA SET(MEMBER) NAME ===>

For DB2 SMP/E libraries (SDSNLOAD, SDSNMACS, SDSNSAMP, SDSNCLST, etc.), enter:
 4  LIBRARY NAME PREFIX   ===> DSN910
 5  LIBRARY NAME SUFFIX   ===>

For install data sets (NEW.SDSNSAMP, NEW.SDSNCLST, RUNLIB.LOAD, etc.), enter:
 6  DATA SET NAME PREFIX  ===> DSN910
 7  DATA SET NAME SUFFIX  ===>

Enter to set or save panel values (by reading or writing the named members):
 8  INPUT MEMBER NAME     ===> DSNTIDXA  Default parameter values
 9  OUTPUT MEMBER NAME    ===>           Save new values entered on panels
PRESS:   ENTER to continue   RETURN to exit   HELP for more information
```

Figure 3.17: Main CLIST panel – DSNTIPA1

If you are running DB2 Value Unit Edition (FMID JDB991Z), you will next see panel **DSNTIP01**, which asks you to indicate whether DB2 is to operate under a one-time license charge. Panel **DSNTIP02** is then displayed for you to accept the OTC license for VUE.

DSNZPARM Settings: Understanding the Flow and Purpose

The subsystem parameter module is generated by job **DSNTIJUZ** each time you install, migrate, or update DB2. Seven macros expand to form this data-only parameter load module:

- **DSN6ENV**: DB2 environmental settings

- **DSN6ARVP**: Settings for archive dataset

- **DSN6LOGP**: Logging parameters

- **DSN6FAC**: Distributed Data Facility (DDF) settings

- **DSN6SPRM**: Database manager installation parameters

- **DSN6SYSP**: Other system parameters

- **DSN6GRP**: Data-sharing parameters

These macros are located in *prefix*.**SDSNMACS** (e.g., **DSN910. SDSNMACS(DSN6SYSP)**).

Job **DSNTIJUZ** also generates the data-only load module **DSNHDECP**, which contains the application programming defaults. The DSNZPARMs are in the **SDSNEXIT** library. If you select the update process on the first CLIST panel, you generate only one job: **DSNTIJUZ**.

Changing DSNZPARM Parameters

Some subsystem parameters can be changed dynamically online. Others still require DB2 to be re-cycled after the changing and assembly of the DSNZPARMs. After modifying parameters, you assemble and link-edit the DSNZPARM module. Now you need to have the new values loaded. We can do this now without re-cycling DB2.

You should save all your jobs from the original installation or migration in a different data set from the enable jobs. If you save them in *prefix*.**NEW.SDSNSAMP**, your jobs might be overwritten.

To dynamically load the DSNZPARM start-up load member, you can issue the command **SET SYSPARM LOAD** from the z/OS console, a DB2 Commands DB2I panel, a default subsystem name (DSN) session under TSO or CICS, or an IMS terminal. You must have the **SYSADM**, **SYSCTRL**, or **SYSOPER** privilege to execute this command.

The **SET SYSPARM RELOAD** command loads the last named DSNZPARM module. The options are:

- **SET SYSPARM LOAD**: Load a new system parameter load module

- **SET SYSPARM RELOAD**: Reload previous load module (this option always reloads a load module with the same name as the current active one)

- **SET SYSPARM STARTUP**: Reload load module used at start-up (this option resets the parameters to values taken from the load module specified during DB2 start-up; these values are taken from the copy of the load module in storage, and MEPL displays these values)

DB2 can maintain up to three DSNZPARM modules in storage at any one point in time. Remember, you can dynamically change the selected DSNZPARM to be executed.

The installation verification procedure (IVP) sample job **DSNTEJ6Z** job generates the report of current subsystem parameter settings by executing the C-language caller program **DSN8ED7**. The subsystem parameter settings stored procedure **DSNWZP** is the stored procedure called by **DSN8ED7**. You must have this stored procedure created. The install job **DSNTIJSG** rebinds packages and DB2-supplied stored procedures, including this one.

There is one thing to remember here, and that is that installation job **DSNTEJ6Z** is not edited by the CLIST unless you specify a non-blank value for **WLM ENVIRONMENT** on panel **DSNTIPX** and specify **AUTO** or **COMMAND** for the **DDF STARTUP OPTION** field on panel **DSNTIPR**. You will not generate a whole set of jobs in phase 6 of the job unless this WLM name is provided.

New and Changed Panels

Several CLIST panels are either new or changed in DB2 9 for z/OS. The following discussion reviews the affected panels and parameters.

Panel DSNTIP9: Work File Database

Panel	DSNZPARM	Macro	Panel field	Job
DSNTIP9	MAXTEMPS	DSN6SPRM	MAX TEMP STG/AGENT	DSNTIJTM

Parameter **MAXTEMPS** sets the maximum amount of temporary storage that is available to a single agent. The default value is 100 MB, and the valid range is 0–2147483647. A value of **0** indicates no limit. You can enter a value in gigabytes using the form nG (e.g., **4G** to indicate 4 GB).

As of DB2 9, there is one work database; the **TEMP** database space has been merged into the **WORKFILE**. There are only two sizes of work space, 4 KB and 32 KB, and they are both managed by DB2. If you are installing, these work files are created; if you are migrating, they are added. You must have at least one 4 KB and one 32 KB work file space. The amount of space for each table space cannot exceed 64 GB.

When migrating, you will want to drop the **TEMP** database after you are secure in your NFM. The **WORKFILE** size should be large enough to support the combined space. You can add additional work file table spaces. These work files are shared database table spaces. In migration, the IDCAMS allocation step is missing in job **DSNTIJTM**.

In previous DB2 releases, the **DSNTIJTM** job was run at install time to create work file table spaces. In DB2 9, the job optionally creates additional table spaces for the work file database.

If you exceed the limit on space used by an agent, you will receive **SQLCODE -904**. IFCID 0343 for performance class 3 and statistics class 4 records information about the agent exceeding the **MAXTEMPS** value.

Panels DSNTIP01 and DSNTIP02: OTC License Usage

Panels	DSNZPARM	Macro	Panel field
DSNTIP01, DSNTIP02	OTC_LICENSE	DSN6SYSP	LICENSE TERMS ACCEPTED

You will see panels **DSNTIP01** and **DSNTIP02** only if you are using the DB2 Value Unit Edition. If you ordered this special licensing edition, you must now indicate that you accept the one-time license charge. On panel **DSNTIP01**, enter a **1** (No) or a **2** (Yes) to indicate whether the DB2 subsystem or data-sharing member is to be configured to operate using the one-time charge (OTC) license.

Panel **DSNTIP02** defines the license charge, and you must enter **YES** for the **LICENSE TERMS ACCEPTED** field (**OTC_LICENSE** DSNZPARM) to accept the terms. This panel appears only if you have indicated on panel **DSNTIP01** that you are using VUE of DB2 9.

Panel DSNTIPA2: Data Parameters

Panel	DSNZPARM	Macro	Panel fields	Jobs
DSNTIPA2	CATALOG	DSN6SPRM	CATALOG ALIAS, DEFINE CATALOG, USE SMS	DSNTIJCA, DSNTIJDE, DSNTIJEN, DISNTIJIN, DSNTIJOC, DSNTIJOS, DSNTIJTM, DSNTEJ1, DSNTEJ2A, DSNTEJ3M

The **CATALOG** subsystem parameter sets the VSAM high level used by the DB2 catalog and directory. The value you specify here is used by installation and migration jobs to define the high-level data set naming convention, such as **DSNCAT.BSDS** on panel **DSNTIPH**. The parameter's default value is **DSNCAT**, or you can enter a different value from one to eight characters in length.

The value of the **DEFINE CATALOG** field determines whether DB2 should create a new integrated catalog facility (ICF) catalog. The default value of **YES** instructs ICF to build a new catalog using the alias name. If you enter **NO**, CLIST docs not build a new ICF catalog.

The **USE SMS** field (default value **NO**) indicates whether data sets are controlled by SMS. If you set **USE SMS** to **YES**, panel **DSNTIPA3** (Figure 3.18) is displayed.

```
DSNTIPA3               MIGRATE DB2 - DATA PARAMETERS PANEL 2
===>


Check parameters and reenter to change:
 1 PERMANENT UNIT NAME    ==> 3390           Device type for MVS catalog
                                             and partitioned data sets
 2 TEMPORARY UNIT NAME    ==> VIO            Device type for
                                             temporary data sets


                                  ---------------- SMS ----------------
                          VOL/SER    DATA CLASS    MGMT CLASS    STOR CLASS
                          -------    ----------    ----------    ----------
 3 CLIST ALLOCATION      ==> SBOX9A ==>           ==>           ==>
 4 NON-VSAM DATA         ==> SBOX9A ==>           ==>           ==>
 5 VSAM CATALOG, DEFAULT, ==> SBOX9A ==>           ==>           ==>
   AND WORK FILE DATABASE
 6 DIRECTORY AND CATALOG ==> SBOX9A ==>           ==>           ==>
   DATA
 7 DIRECTORY AND CATALOG ==> SBOX9A ==>           ==>           ==>
   INDEXES
 8 LOG COPY 1, BSDS 2    ==> SBOX9A ==>           ==>           ==>
 9 LOG COPY 2, BSDS 1    ==> SBOX9A ==>           ==>           ==>
```

Figure 3.18: Panel DSNTIPA3 — Data parameters

Fields 3 through 9 here each have four values associated with them. If you change field 1, **PERMANENT UNIT NAME**, during migration, the change does not affect the ICF catalog, directory, logs, or catalog, but the new value is used for data sets that are created in the migration process.

The entries on this panel define your storage management choices for the storage groups and data sets that are created during migration and installation. During migration, you cannot change items 8 and 9.

Panel DSNTIPC: CLIST Storage Calculations

Panel	DSNZPARM	Macro	Panel field
DSNTIPC	EDMPOOL_SKELETON_POOL	DSN6SPRM	EDM SKELETON POOL SIZE

Panel **DSNTIPC** displays the CLIST storage calculations. A new DSNZPARM, **EDMPOOL_SKELETON_POOL**, lets you specify the minimum size of the environmental descriptor manager (EDM) skeleton pool. The range of acceptable values is 5,120 to 2,097,152 KB; the default is 5,120. This skeleton pool is located above the bar and is used for storing skeleton package tables and skeleton cursor tables. You can set this value using the **SET SYSPARM** command.

Panel DSNTIPE: Thread Management

Panel	DSNZPARM	Macro	Panel field
DSNTIPE	LRDRTHLD	DSN6SPRM	LONG-RUNNING READER

Main storage sizes are calculated from the entries on DB2 panel **DSNTIPE**. In DB2 9, all the values on this panel are updatable.

Item 11 on this panel is parameter **LRDRTHLD**, field **LONG-RUNNING READER**. This parameter specifies the number of minutes a read claim is held by an agent before DB2 writes a trace record to show it as a long-running reader. You can specify from 0 to 1,439 minutes, **0** being the default. If you specify **0**, DB2 does not report the long-running readers. The value is specified in **DSN6SPRM LRDRTHLD** in **DSNZP*xxx***.

Item 13, the **MAX OPEN FILE REFS** field, corresponds to the **MAXOFILR** subsystem parameter. This setting specifies the maximum number of data sets for large object (LOB) file references that can be open concurrently for processing. This parameter is located in macro **DSN6SYSP** and is updatable online.

Job DSNTIJSG Changes

Job **DSNTIJSG** creates the Resource List (RLST) database **DSNRLST** during installation. During migration, the DDL for creating the RLST is typically removed by the installation CLIST. There is DDL commented out in job **DSNTIJSG** for creating a new **DSNRLMT*nn*** table and **DSNMRL*nn*** index. If you try to create a new table without the RLF database, you will receive **SQLCODE -204**.

An XML schema repository (XSR) of tables in database **DSNXSR** is created during installation or migration. Job **DSNTIJSG** creates this XSR database and all the associated objects. To validate and store XML documents in DB2 tables, this XML repository must be available.

DSN6SYSP.DBPROTCL in the DSNZPARMs has been eliminated from DB2 9. There is no default private protocol bind for plans and packages. A tool called **DSNTP2DP** can help you convert from private protocol to Distributed Relational Database Architecture (DRDA). **DSNCOLLID** is defined to be a generic collection ID to maintain remote packages. You should run **DSNTP2DP** on your DB2 8 system. It will generate commands that you can run later to convert objects that have a dependency on private protocol. You can run these generated commands after you run **DSNTIJTM**.

Job **DSNTIJSG** creates a generic collection ID, **DSNCOLLID**, with job step **DSNTICC**. You must uncomment this job step to execute the create of **DSNCOLLID**. Do not try to manually edit **DSNTIJSG** and run it during a migration, or you might receive an **SQLCODE -4700**. Instead, use **DSNTIJNX** for migration.

You might use the default collection name, **DSNCOLLID**, when converting plans and packages from private protocol to DRDA. The purpose of this new generic collection ID is to reduce the tasks required to maintain collections for remote packages. Be aware that you are not required to use this default collection name. You would need to **GRANT** privileges to the public on this collection name to enable generic remote binding.

Finally, in DB2 9, **DSNTIJSG** does not handle creating the **STOGROUP SYSDEFLT**.

Job DSNTIP5 Changes

In DB2 9, the **DBPROTOCOL** setting is **DRDA** by default, and the **DBPROTCL** DSNZPARM has been removed from **DSN6SYSP**.

Job DSNTIJOS

The new job **DSNTIJOS** consists of several job steps in DB2 9 that create the database objects that support Optimization Service Center, Optimization Expert, or the IBM Data Studio Developer on DB2 9 subsystem. The functions in this job include creating table spaces, tables, indexes, stored procedures, and aliases; binding packages; and granting privileges. You should customize this job to fit your system requirements. The sample JCL includes documentation for what to review before you submit the job for execution.

Tables maintained in the **DB2OSC** database record the content of workloads, maintain definitions, and monitor profiles for the workload control center in OSC. The table names follow with the naming conventions **DB2OSC.DSN_WCC_*xx_xx*** and **DB2OSC.DSN_WSA_*xx_xx***, which are used exclusively by the OSC workload advisor tools. There are also additional **EXPLAIN** tables that the SQL optimization tools, such as IBM Data Studio (the strategic replacement for DB2 Visual Explain) or DB2 **EXPLAIN**, might use. Profile tables enable the monitoring of query performance as well.

Job DSNTIJDE

Job **DSNTIJDE** deletes the previously created data sets for the DB2 catalog and directory. This job is not in the normal installation process and should not be run during migration or fallback. **DSNTIJDE** will not work if job **DSNTIJSG** or **DSNTIJTM** has been executed.

DSNZPARM Notes

This section looks at some of the more interesting, hidden, opaque, and noteworthy subsystem parameters. Note that any of these parameters can be changed with IBM maintenance as time moves on, so always check to see whether they have been modified.

ACCUMACC (Macro DSN6SYSP)

Parameter **ACCUMACC** in macro **DSN6SYSP** relates to the accounting data being accumulated for DDF and Recovery Resource Services Attachment Facility (RRSAF) threads. Its value specifies the accounting intervals for a given user for the accounting rollup blocks. This is rollup accounting data (aggregated according to parameter **ACCUMUID**). The default **ACCUMACC** setting is 10; values from 2 to 65535 are permitted.

&SPRMRSMX (Macro DSN6SPRC)

Use this hidden parameter only with IBM guidance. It comes into play if you have a massive storage leak problem and want to avoid a system wait state.

&SPRMRRF (Macro DSN6SPRC)

Before migrating your first system or data-sharing group to DB2 9 NFM, you could consider disabling reordered row format on a temporary basis and then re-enabling it after migrating all systems and data-sharing groups. The first method to achieve this has been around for a while as the hidden DSNZPARM **&SPRMRRF**. In DB2 9, APAR PK87348 (described below) replaces hidden parameter. Check with IBM Support first before performing the following procedure, and proceed with caution!

Method #1

To disable RRF:

1. Locate the **&SPRMRRF** parameter in macro **DSN6SPRC** in library **SDSNMACS**.

2. Look for the following statement:

```
.&SPRMRRF SETC .1. 1=Enable High Perf Row Option
```

3. Edit the macro, setting **&SPRMRRF** to the **.O.** value.

4. Rerun **DSNTIJUZ**.

Disabling RRF with parameter **&SPRMRRF** has the following effects:

- Any table spaces created in DB2 9 NFM will be created as basic row format.

- When a basic row format table space is reorganized, it will remain in BRF.

- Page sets/partitions already in RRF will remain in RRF (note this point carefully).

- **REORG** will not convert to BRF using this method.

Method #2

APAR PK87348 changes the **SPRMRRF** DSNZPARM from hidden to opaque (APAR PK87348 9/09, V9 NFM, HOLDDATA for DB2 9.1 RSU level 0910). If you have used Method #1 above to disable RRF formatting, know that PK87348 removes the entry from the **DSN6SPRC** macro in the **SDSNMACS** library only.

You will need to add the setting **RRF=ENABLE** or **RRF=DISABLE** to the **DSN6SPRM** macro in your **DSNTIJUZ** job.

APAR PK87348 adds a new keyword to the **LOAD** and **REORG TABLESPACE** utilities called **ROWFORMAT BRF/RRF** (in DB2 9 NFM only). When specified, this keyword overrides the existing **SPRMRRF** setting in these utilities.

EN_PJSJ (Macro DSN6SPRM)

APAR PK76100 provides the new subsystem parameter **EN_PJSJ**, which enables pair-wise star join, also known as dynamic index **AND**ing for star join. See APAR II14468 for additional APARs to be applied. Setting **EN_PJSJ** to **ON** enables the new star join method in DB2 9 for the subsystem. DB2 will consider this access path at query optimization time along with the existing methods for star joins. To locate the APAR for **EN_PJSJ**, you can search for the "**SQLPAIRWISEJOIN**" keyword.

OPTIOWGT (Macro DSN6SPRM)

Changing the **OPTIOWGT** parameter could impact the access paths of queries that are otherwise stable. For more advice about how to set this parameter, contact IBM Software Support. APAR PK61277 (fixing UK39140) added this support in the DB2 9 optimizer in the **DSN6SPRM** macro. The default parameter value is **DISABLE**, which tells the optimizer to choose the traditional cost formula in the optimizer. Value **ENABLE** instructs DB2 to use an "enhanced" formula for CPU and I/O cost balancing in the optimizer. This option is designed to help reflect the speed of new hardware, such as the z9 and z10. PK75643 changes the default **OPTIOWGT** value from **DISABLE** to **ENABLE**. To make this parameter available for static applications, remember to rebind.

The HOLDDATA for DB2 9.1 PUT level 0809 contains explicit instructions for adding the keyword parameter in your DSNZPARM modules and library entries. You can modify parameter **OPTIOWGT** by using profile tables. Profile table **SYSIBM. DSN_PROFILE_ATTRIBUTES** and a new keyword, **IO WEIGHTING**, are allowed in the **KEYWORDS** column; these updates are also described in this PUT level.

OPTJBPR (Macro DSN6SPRM)

PTF UK39139 corrects an access path costing issue that could cause an ineffective index to be chosen on an inner table when a buffer pool size increases. Setting parameter **OPTJBPR** to **ON** enables the new function; the parameter is **OFF** by default. Refer to APAR II13979 for more information before applying this PTF.

OPTIXOPREF (Macro DSN6SPRM)

PTF UK39744 permits a new setting of **YES** for parameter **OPTIXOPREF**, which governs index preference logic. No action is required if you prefer to maintain the current setting.

Note that parameter **OPTIXOPREF** is deprecated in DB2 9. IBM recommends that all current DB2 9 for z/OS customers who use **OPTIXOPREF=OFF** now convert to **OPTIXOPREF=ON**.

UTIL_TEMP_STORCLAS (Macro DSN6SPRM)

APAR PK41711 adds the new storage class parameter **UTIL_TEMP_STORCLAS** for the temporary data sets for utilities.

Use of **CHECK INDEX/DATA/LOB SHRLEVEL CHANGE** (online check) allocates a shadow data set in the same storage class as the production page set, potentially causing system overhead. **UTIL_TEMP_STORCLAS=storclass** causes the **CHECK** utilities to pass the storage class supplied by **UTIL_TEMP_STORCLAS** to DFSMS, providing a way to allocate a shadow data set on non–Peer-to-Peer Remote Copy (PPRC) volumes. The DSNZPARM is passed to the Data Facility Data Set Services (DFDSS) command that is used to create the copy.

REOPTEXT (Macro DSN6SPRM)

For the **REOPT(AUTO)** option to work, subsystem parameter **REOPTEXT** must be set to **YES**. If **REOPTEXT** is set to **NO**, the system ignores **REOPT(AUTO)**. The **REOPT(AUTO)** option applies only for dynamic statements that can be cached. This enhancement takes effect when **REOPTEXT** is turned on.

PK46054/UK29645 removes the obsolete **REOPTEXT** parameter from DB2 9 for z/OS and from installation panel **DSNTIP8** (field 15). For more information, see informational APAR II14401.

MXDTCACH (Macro DSN6SPRM)

The new **MXDTCACH** parameter sets the maximum size for data caching in memory. The default setting is 20 MB, and the range of acceptable values 0 MB to 512 MB. If you allocate a value, the memory comes from above the 2 GB bar. If you specify **0**, DB2 does not use caching, and sparse index is used instead. **MXDTCACH** replaces the existing installation parameter **SJMXPOOL**, and the space for star join has been moved to the local pool above the 2 GB bar.

DSNZPARMs Not on Installation Panels

"Visible," or regular, DSNZPARMs can be changed or adjusted by running the installation CLIST (**DSNTINST**). These visible parameters appear on the installation panels. Certain other DSNZPARMs do not appear on the install panels and are accessible only through other means.

"Hidden" DB2 subsystem parameters are added to the DSNZPARM macros by the system administrator; they are not part of the CLIST generation. The hidden DSNZPARMs involve special cases that require code changes by directly editing the macros to solve a problem or improve performance. To implement them, you add them to your DSNZPARM macros and reassemble. You must obtain IBM guidance on working with these parameters.

"Opaque" parameters do not appear on the installation panels but can be added manually to the **DSNTIJUZ** (DSNZPARM) job.

New DSNZPARMs can be introduced via a maintenance stream (PTF). These parameters often do not appear on installation panels and may be hidden, opaque, or regular DSNZPARM parameters. The following subsystem parameters are defined by job **DSNTIJUZ** in DB2 9 and did not appear originally on any installation panels at the release of DB2 9.

ADMTPROC (Macro DSN6SPRM)

The started procedure name of the administrative scheduler is saved in parameter **ADMTPROC**. If you specify null, you disable this scheduler. You cannot update **ADMTPROC** online.

CACHEDYN_FREELOCAL (Macro DSN6SPRM)

The default **CACHEDYN_FREELOCAL** value of **1** indicates that DB2 can free cached dynamic statements to relieve **DBM1** below-the-bar storage. This parameter applies only when the **KEEPDYNAMIC(YES)** bind option is active. If you specify **0**, DB2 does not free cached dynamic statements.

COMCRIT (Macro DSN6SPRM)

The default **COMCRIT** value of **NO** does not change DB2 behavior for the Common Criteria environment. When **COMCRIT** is set to **YES**, all tables that you create must have multilevel security. This setting does not apply to created global temporary tables, declared global temporary tables, and auxiliary tables. PK53477 allows **COMCRIT** to be online and updatable.

DISABSCL (Macro DSN6SPRM)

The **DISABSCL** default value of **NO** indicates that **SQLWARN1** and **SQLWARN5** are set for non-scrollable cursors on **OPEN CURSOR** and **ALLOCATE CURSOR** statements.

HONOR_KEEPDICTIONARY (Macro DSN6SPRM)

The **HONOR_KEEPDICTIONARY** setting determines whether DB2 honors the **LOAD** and **REORG** parameter **KEEPDICTIONARY** when tables are converted from basic row format to reordered row format. If **HONOR_KEEPDICTIONARY** is set to **YES**, DB2 respects the **KEEPDICTIONARY** setting. If it is set to **NO**, DB2 ignores **KEEPDICTIONARY** when converting tables from BRF to RRF.

INLISTP (Macro DSN6SPRM)

The **INLISTP** parameter lets you specify the maximum number of elements in an **IN**-list for certain **IN**-list predicate optimizations to occur. The default value is **50**.

MAX_CONCURRENT_PKG_OPS (Macro DSN6SPRM)

Parameter **MAX_CONCURRENT_PKG_OPS** indicates the maximum number of automatic bind requests that can be processed simultaneously. Be aware that if the value of the **AUTO BIND** field on panel **DSNTIPO** is **NO**, the value of **MAX_CONCURRENT_PKG_OPS** has no effect. The parameter's default value is **10**.

MAX_OPT_STOR (Macro DSN6SPRM)

The system checks the hidden subsystem parameter **MAX_OPT_STOR** to ensure that enough storage is available to complete multi-index access processing. APAR PK56686 was introduced on 2008-07-30 for DB2 8 and DB2 9; for DB2 9, the default parameter value is **40**. APAR UK40287 now checks to determine whether too much storage is being used to optimize multi-index access. Be sure to check UK35163 as well.

MAX_UTIL_PARTS (Macro DSN6SPRM)

The **MAX_UTIL_PARTS** parameter changes the behavior of the **LOAD** command to allow processing of more than 254 partitions (compressed) when the **COMPRESS YES** option is specified. The parameter specifies the number of partitions of a compressed table space that **LOAD** processes without limit. Valid values are **254** through **4096**; the default is **254**.

This parameter was provided in PK51853 in DB2 8. DB2 9 no longer imposes this limit and uses virtual storage more effectively. It is recommended that you watch your virtual storage when loading table spaces with many compressed partitions. Note that the limit does not apply if a **PART** range is specified on the **REORG** command or if the **PART** keyword is used on **INTO TABLE** statements for **LOAD SHRLEVEL NONE**.

NPGTHRSH (Macro DSN6SPRM)

The system-wide parameter **NPGTHRSH** specifies whether DB2 is to use special access path selection for tables under a given size. The parameter value is an integer that indicates the number of pages within the tables that DB2 favors for matching index access.

Matching index access for SQL can sometimes be more costly than table space scan or non-matching index access. If the statistics indicate a small table but the table is large when the query takes place, DB2 will choose an inefficient access path. If you cannot run the statistics and get the SQL to favor the correct access path, setting **NPGTHRSH** to favor matching index access over a table space scan or non-matching index access is an option. The default value of **0** indicates that this option is not to be used; instead, the standard cost optimization is used. Other values indicate the number of pages on which rows appear in the table. You can also set **NPGTHRSH** to **-1**, which almost disables the DB2 cost-based optimization, and this is not the value of choice.

Note that the parameters **NPGTHRSH** and **VOLATILE** work together. **VOLATILE** (a keyword on the **CREATE TABLE** and **ALTER TABLE** statements) forces index use for volatile tables even if **NPAGES** exceeds **NPGTHRSH**. The default **VOLATILE** value is **0**, which means that no special access path selection is used. The other thing you can do is to fudge the value for **CARDF** in the catalog tables. Acceptable values are:

CARDF value	Description
-1	Every table qualifies as small.
0	No table qualifies as small (default).
1	Only tables with zero pages qualify as small.
2	Tables with less than two pages qualify as small.
10	Tables with less than 10 pages qualify as small.
502	Tables with less than 502 pages and tables that have not had statistics collected qualify as small (e.g., when **NPAGES** = -1).

OJPERFEH (Macro DSN6SPRM)

The **OJPERFEH** parameter specifies whether to disable the performance enhancements for outer join operations. See notes in PQ18710 and APAR PQ48485, added in DB2 7. The parameter's default value is **NO**, which means the enhancements are disabled; **YES** enables them. The **YES** value can improve outer join performance. In this process, DB2 does not try to reduce work file usage for outer joins. It does use transitive closures for the predicates in the **ON** in outer joins.

OTC_LICENSE (Macro DSN6SYSP)

For those who are using VUE special pricing for DB2, the **OTC_LICENSE** parameter specifies whether the DB2 subsystem or data-sharing member operates under the OTC license. Valid values for this parameter are **NOT USED** and **TERMS ACCEPTED**. The default **NOT USED** indicates that the OTC license is not in effect on this subsystem or data-sharing member. **TERMS ACCEPTED** indicates that you accept the terms of the OTC license for this subsystem or data-sharing member. To update the **OTC_LICENSE** parameter, you must stop and restart DB2.

PLANMGMT (Macro DSN6SPRM)

The **PLANMGMT** parameter affects the behavior of the **REBIND PACKAGE** and **REBIND TRIGGER PACKAGE** commands. Possible values are **OFF**, **BASIC**, and **EXTENDED**. The default value, **OFF**, results in little change to the existing **REBIND** behavior.

When you use a **PLANMGMT** value of **BASIC** or **EXTENDED**, the binding results have a slightly altered behavior. **REBIND** automatically saves copies of all relevant records from catalog tables and directories pertaining to the existing package. The primary difference between the **BASIC** and **EXTENDED** values is the number of copies of a package that are retained.

The value **BASIC** retains up to two copies of a package: a copy of the currently active copy and one for the previous copy. Each time you run **REBIND** ... **PLANMGMT(BASIC)**, any previous copy is discarded, and the current copy becomes the previous copy. The new copy then becomes the current copy.

When you specify a value of **EXTENDED**, DB2 retains up to three copies of a package: the currently active copy, a previous copy, and an original copy. The original copy is the one that existed when the **REBIND PLANMGMT(EXTENDED)** command was first run, and this copy is created only once. Unlike the previous copy, it is never overwritten.

For a package **REBIND** with a value of **BASIC** or **EXTENDED** for **PLANMGMT**, the following options must stay the same: **OWNER**, **QUALIFIER**, **DBPROTOCOL**, **ENABLE**, **DISABLE**, **PATH**, **PATHDEFAULT**, and **IMMEDWRITE**. If any of these options is changed when **PLANMGMT** is set to **BASIC** or **EXTENDED**, DB2 issues an error.

PTASKROL (Macro DSN6SYSP)

The **PTASKROL** value indicates whether to roll up accounting trace records from a parallel query task into the originating task's accounting trace. The recommended default value of **YES** means the originating task should generate an additional accounting trace record with all the roll-up values from parallel tasks. A **NO** value causes each parallel task to produce its own accounting trace record. IFCID 221 gives you a subpipe breakdown; IFCID 222 gives the number of rows that qualified by subpipe; and IFCID 231 gives CPU/Elapsed by parallel task.

SJTABLES (Macro DSN6SPRM)

When star join processing is enabled and the number of tables joined meets the **SJTABLES** threshold, star join and pair-wise join are considered along with nested loop, merge, and hybrid join based on cost estimates. These are System z Integrated Information Processor (zIIP) offloadable, and some parallelism is supported even when the degree is **1** (one).

The **SJTABLES** value specifies when DB2 should enable star join processing. The default setting is **10**. This value indicates that when the total number of tables in a query block, including the fact table, dimension tables, and snowflake tables, is equal to or greater than 10, the star join method is enabled.

Table 3.6 lists the possible **SJTABLES** values and their meanings. You can change the parameter value online by using the **SET SYSPARM** command.

Table 3.6: Star join values	
SJTABLES value	**Description**
0	The default value (**10**) is used.
1, 2, 3	Star join is always considered.
4 to 225	Star join is considered for query blocks having at least the specified number of tables.
>226	Star join is never enabled.

SJMISSKY (Macro DSN6SPRM)

APAR PK16800 introduced the hidden subsystem parameter **SJMISSKY** to improve star join query performance when a dimension table is not highly normalized or when the join column on a dimension table is not the primary key. To enable this fix, you add the keyword **SJMISSKY=ON**. Before enabling this setting, be sure to review PK06964/UK05802/UK10374 for more information about additional effects of turning on **SJMISSKY**.

SMF89 (Macro DSN6SYSP)

Parameter **SMF89** specifies whether DB2 should do detailed tracking for measured usage pricing. A **YES** value causes DB2 to perform detailed measured usage tracking if System Management Facility (SMF) type 89 records are activated. DB2 invokes a z/OS service on every entry into or exit out of DB2 to ensure accurate tracking.

The default value of **NO** means that DB2 does not perform detailed measured usage tracking. If the SMF type 89 record is activated, only high-level tracking is recorded in the record. Selecting **NO** reduces CPU usage but increases the amount of time spent in DB2 as measured by SMF 89. You should use **SMF89 YES** only if you employ measured usage pricing.

SMSDCFL (Macro DSN6SPRM)

Parameter **SMSDCFL** holds the SMS data class name keyword for all table space data sets. It specifies a DFSMS data class for table spaces. If you specify either **SMSDCFL** or **SMSDCIX** (covered next), all corresponding table spaces and/or index spaces will be allocated as SMS-managed, DB2-storage-group–defined VSAM data sets. This function lets you define DB2 VSAM linear data sets (LDSs) with a DFSMS data class name.

Before using parameter **SMSDCFL**, you need to define the data classes for your table space data sets. You may also need to code SMS automatic class selection (ACS) routines to assign indexes to one SMS storage class and table spaces to another.

When you use DFSMS and DB2 storage groups, you can use parameter **SMSDCFL** to assign table spaces to different DFSMS data classes. If you assign a value to

SMSDCFL, DB2 specifies that value when it uses Access Method Services to define a data set for a table space. If the **SMSDCFL** value is one or more blanks, DB2 does not specify a data class when it creates data sets for table spaces. The parameter's default value is a blank; valid values are one to eight characters long.

SMSDCIX (Macro DSN6SPRM)

Parameter **SMSDCIX** specifies an SMS data class name for all index space data sets. When you use DFSMS and DB2 storage groups, you can use subsystem parameters **SMSDCFL** and **SMSDCIX** to assign table spaces and indexes to different DFSMS data classes. If the **SMSDCIX** value is one or more blanks, DB2 does not specify a data class when it creates data sets for indexes. The parameter's default value is a blank; valid values are one to eight characters long.

Both **SMSDCFL** and **SMSDCIX** were introduced in APAR PQ32414. They allowed DB2 users to define DB2 VSAM LDSs with an SMS data class name. Later, PQ44569 provided these parameters as new DSNZPARMs, and IFCIDs were supplied and supported.

UTIL_TEMP_STORCLAS (Macro DSN6SPRM)

Parameter **UTIL_TEMP_STORCLAS** specifies the storage class, if any, that the **CHECK DATA**, **CHECK INDEX**, and **CHECK LOB** utilities are to use when allocating temporary shadow data sets. (These utilities allocate shadow data sets when you specify the **SHRLEVEL CHANGE** option.) The default parameter value is spaces, which indicates that the shadow data sets are to be defined in the same storage class as the production page set. If you specify any other value for **UTIL_TEMP_ STORCLAS**, that value must be a valid storage class that exists in the active SMS configuration. Specifying an explicit storage class for **UTIL_TEMP_STORCLAS** can improve performance, especially when the system uses paired disk volumes for peer-to-peer remote copy.

ZOSMETRICS (Macro DSN6SPRM)

To have DB2 gather z/OS metrics, including CPU usage and storage metrics, by using the z/OS Resource Measurement Facility (RMF) interface, code a value of **YES** for **ZOSMETRICS**. The parameter's default value is **NO**.

Do not set **ZOSMETRICS** to **YES** unless you have applied APAR OA24404 for
the z/OS RMF. Check APAR PK62116 as well for dependencies. Also, see the
information in the HOLDDATA for DB2 9.1 PUT level 0809 for more details.

DSNZPARM Summary

Tables 3.7 and 3.8 provide a key to the subsystem parameters available for
DB2 for z/OS DB2 9. The last column of each table indicates the status of each
DSNZPARM:

Table 3.7: DSNZPARMs Changed, Added, Deleted, or of Interest (Table 1 of 2)

MACRO	PARAMETER NAME	DELETED VALUE	OLD VALUE	NEW VALUE	
DSHHDECP	DEF_DECFLOAT_ROUND_MODE			ROUND_HALF_EVEN	N
DSN6FAC	PRGSTRIN (APAR PK46079)			ENABLE	N
DSN6FAC	SQLINTRP (V9 APAR PK59385)			ENABLE	C
DSN6LOGP	MAXARCH		1000	10000	C
DSN6SPRM	ADMTPROC			DSNADMT	N
DSN6SPRM	CACHEDYN_FREELOCAL	(UK15493 in V8)	0	1	C
DSN6SPRM	COMCRIT	NO			D
DSN6SPRM	DISABSCL			NO	
DSN6SPRM	EDM_SKELETON_POOL		-	102400 KB	N
DSN6SPRM	EDMPOOL_ABOVE_2GB		-		D
DSN6SPRM	HONOR_KEEPDICTIONARY		-	NO	N
DSN6SPRM	IDXBPOOL		4KB	8,16 or 32KB	C
DSN6SPRM	INLISTP			50	
DSN6SPRM	MAX_CONCURRENT_PKG_OPS		-	10	N
DSN6SPRM	MAX_OPT_ELAP				D
DSN6SPRM	MAX_OPT_STOR	20		40	C
DSN6SPRM	MAX_UTIL_PARTS	(PK51853)			N
DSN6SPRM	MINSTOR		NO	YES	C
DSN6SPRM	MXDTCACH			20MB	N
DSN6SPRM	MXQBCE		32767	1023	C
DSN6SPRM	MAXTEMPS			0 (MB or GB)	N
DSN6SPRM	MGEXTSZ		NO	YES	C
DSN6SPRM	NPGTHRSH		-1	0	C
DSN6SPRM	OJPERFEH	II12836		NO	
DSN6SPRM	OPTCCOS4	OFF			D
DSN6SPRM	OPTIOWGT (PK61277)		DISABLE	ENABLE	C
DSN6SPRM	OPTIXIO		OFF	ON	C
DSN6SPRM	OPTXOIRC	OFF			D
DSN6SPRM	OPTXQB			ON	N
DSN6SPRM	PARAPAR1	YES			D
DSN6SPRM	PLANMGMT			OFF	N

*Key: N = New DSNZPARM, C = Changed DSNZPARM, D = Deleted DSNZPARM, Blank = Parameters of
interest*

Table 3.8: DSNZPARMs Changed, Added, Deleted, or of Interest (Table 2 of 2)

MACRO	PARAMETER NAME	DELETED VALUE	OLD VALUE	NEW VALUE	
DSN6SPRM	RELCURHL	NO			D
DSN6SPRM	REOPTEXT		PK46054		D
DSN6SPRM	RESTORE_RECOVER_FROMDUMP			NO	N
DSN6SPRM	RESTORE_TAPEUNITS			NOLIMIT	N
DSN6SPRM	RPITWC			YES	N
DSN6SPRM	SJMXPOOL	20			D
DSN6SPRM	SJTABLES			10	
DSN6SPRM	STATCLUS			ENHANCED	N
DSN6SPRM	SUPPRESS_TS_CONV_WARNING	NO			D
DSN6SPRM	SYSTEM_LEVEL_BACKUPS			NO	N
DSN6SPRM	TABLES_JOINED_THRESHOLD	16			D
DSN6SPRM	UTILS_DUMP_CLASS_NAME			blank	N
DSN6SPRM	UTIL_TEMP_STORCLAS	(PK41711)			N
DSN6SPRM	ZOSMETRICS	(APAR OA24404)		NO	
DSN6SYSP	DBPROTCL				D
DSN6SYSP	EN_PJSJ	(PK76100)			N
DSN6SYSP	IMPDSDEF			YES	N
DSN6SYSP	IMPTSCMP			YES	N
DSN6SYSP	OTC_LICENSE			YES/NO	N
DSN6SYSP	MAXOFILR		100		N
DSN6SYSP	PTASKROL			YES	
DSN6SYSP	RESTORE_RECOVER_FROMDUMP			NO	N
DSN6SYSP	STORPROC				D
DSN6SYSP	TBSBP32K		BP32K0		N
DSN6SYSP	TBSBP8K		BP8K0		N
DSN6SYSP	TBSBPK16K		BP16K0		N
DSN6SYSP	TBSBPLOB			BP0	N
DSN6SYSP	TBSBPXML			BP16K0	N
DSN6SYSP	WLMENV		18 CHARs	32 CHARs	C
DSN6SYSP	XMLVALA			204800KB	C
DSN6SYSP	XMLVALS			10240MB	C
DSNSPRC	SPRMIFS				D
DSNSPRC	SPRMKFC	(PK42809)	10	100	C

Key: N = New DSNZPARM, C = Changed DSNZPARM, D = Deleted DSNZPARM, Blank = Parameters of interest

Installation, Migration, Fallback, and Remigration

In DB2 9, you use the same general approach for installing and migrating as with DB2 8. There are four CLIST modes:

- **INSTALL**: Use this option to install a brand-new DB2 9 subsystem.
- **MIGRATE**: Use this option if you have existing DB2 8 systems that you want to migrate to DB2 9. Run the **MIGRATE** option for each member of the data-sharing group to get each member into DB2 9 conversion mode.

- **ENFM**: Use this option to enable a new function for a subsystem or an entire data-sharing group. **ENFM** is a group-wide enablement.

- **UPDATE**: Use this option when you want to update or change DSNZPARMs.

Installing DB2 9

Table 3.9 lists the installation steps for DB2 9 for z/OS and the jobs associated with the installation process. You must not use secondary authorization IDs to perform any of these steps. After running the CLIST, remember to review each job before you submit it to be executed.

Table 3.9: Installation job steps		
Step	Description	Job(s)
1	Define DB2 to z/OS	DSNTIJMV
2	Define the ICF catalog and alias	DSNTIJCA
3	Define system data sets	DSNTIJIN
4	Define DB2 initialization parameters	DSNTIJUZ
5	Initialize system data sets	DSNTIJID
6	Define user authorization exit routines	DSNTIJEX (optional)
7	Record DB2 data to SMF	(optional)
8	Establish subsystem security	(optional)
9	Connect DB2 to TSO	DSNTIJVC
10	Connect IMS to DB2	(optional)
11	Connect CICS to DB2	(optional)
12	IPL z/OS	
13	Start the DB2 subsystem	
14	Tailor the DB2 catalog	DSNTIJTC
15	Create default storage group, define temp work files, and bind DB2 REXX language support	DSNTIJTM
16	Define and bind DB2 objects	DSNTIJSG
17	Create and bind objects (OSC, OE, Data Studio)	DSNTIJOS
18	Populate the user-maintained databases	DSNTIJSG (optional)
19	Back up the DB2 directory and catalog	DSNTIJIC
20	Set up the administrative scheduler	DSNTIJMV (customize)
21	Verify a successful installation	Series of jobs
22	Enable additional capabilities for DB2, such as communications network, Java support, installing a second DB2 subsystem on same operating system	See steps in installation manual for complete details

The first process invokes **DSNTINST** (the install or migrate panels), which generates data sets and members. Among the items generated are **DSNTIJUZ**, the job to create the DSNZPARM data, and **DSNTID*xx***, which is an updated set of parameters. The table lists the jobs that are part of the generated data sets and members for the installation process to DB2 9. You run these jobs in the order they are listed, checking each for a successful completion. Once the jobs have been completed, you then begin your system verification procedure jobs (IVP).

Migrating to DB2 9

Table 3.10 lists the job steps that are used in the migration process to conversion mode (CM).

Table 3.10: DB2 9 migration jobs		
Step	**Description**	**Job(s)**
1	Perform pre-migration actions	DSNTIJPM
2	Run link checker on DB2 8 table spaces	(Optional)
3	Check for plan/package invalidation	(Optional)
4	Check consistency between catalog tables	(Optional)
5	Take image copies of directory and catalog	DSNTIJIC
6	Connect DB2 to TSO and batch	DSNTIJVC
7	Connect IMS to DB2	(Optional)
8	Connect CICS to DB2	(Optional)
9	Stop DB2 8	(None)
10	Back up DB2 8 volumes	(Optional)
11	Define DB2 initialization parameters	DSNTIJUZ
12	Establish subsystem security	(Optional)
13	Define DB2 9 to z/OS	DSNTIJMV
14	Define system data sets	DSNTIJIN
15	Define user authorization exit routines	DSNTIJEX (optional)
16	IPL z/OS	(None)
17	Start DB2 9	(None)
18	Tailor DB2 9 catalog	DSNTIJTC
19	Perform DB2 catalog check	DSNTIJCX, DSN1CHKR
20	Rebuild indexes	DSNTIJRI (optional)
21	Enable change data capture	

Step	Description	Job(s)
	Table 3.10: DB2 9 migration jobs (continued)	
22	Prepare dynamic SQL program	DSNTIJTM
23	BIND SPUFI, DCLGEN	DSNTIJSG
24	Create and bind OSC, OE, and Data Studio Developer objects	DSNTIJOS
25	Migrate objects for OSC	DSNTIJOM
26	Verify views	Query
27	Copy CM catalog	DSNTIJIC
28	Administrative scheduler setup	Multiple job dependencies
28	Verify CM	DSNTEJ*xx* (optional)
30	Enable stored procedures	(Optional)

Here is an overview of the jobs you run to migrate:

- **DSNTIJTC** is used to migrate from DB2 8 to DB2 9.

- **DSNTIJEN** moves DB2 from CM to ENFM or completes the changes that are made in ENFM. If for some reason this job cannot be completed, you can simply resubmit it; it will continue from where it was stopped.

- **DSNTIJES** takes DB2 to ENFM* from CM* or NFM. Once this job is run, exploiting new function is no longer allowed (if DB2 went from NFM to ENFM*). You can access objects created while in NFM.

- **DSNTIJCS** returns DB2 to CM* from ENFM, ENFM*, or NFM. After the job has been run, exploiting new function is no longer allowed (if DB2 went from NFM to CM*).

- Objects created in NFM can still be accessed. All members must remain at DB2 9 in a data-sharing system.

- **DSNTIJNF** takes DB2 to NFM.

Falling Back to DB2 8

If you are thinking about falling back from DB2 9 to DB2 8, you need to consider which mode you are currently in and what is allowed at this point in the migration process. The diagram in Figure 3.19 depicts the fallback support in each migration mode of DB2.

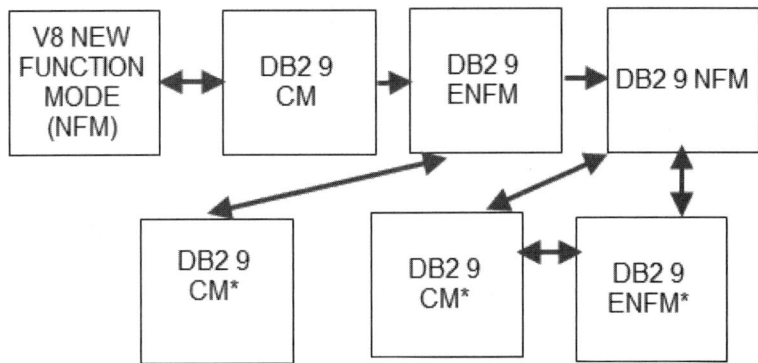

Figure 3.19: Fallback modes in DB2

If you have problems with the migration process and are in ENFM or NFM, you can revert to CM*. The DB2 9 catalog is used in DB2 8 after fallback.

Fallback to DB2 8 NFM with fallback SPE PK11129 applied to DB2 8 is supported only from DB2 9 CM. Be sure to read the HOLDDATA on PK11129. There may be prerequisite APARs, which may or may not be related to fallback.

As long as job **DSNTIJCS** has been completed successfully, you can fall back.

Fallback procedures involve a few steps. You must:

1. Stop all DB2 9 activity

2. Terminate all utilities running on DB2 9

3. Rename the cataloged procedures (**DSNTIJFV**)

4. Reactivate DB2 8, reconnect TSO, IMS, and CICS to DB2 8

5. Start DB2 8

6. Verify the fallback with the **DSNTEJ***xx* jobs

The early code from DB2 9 is compatible with DB2 8, so this issue is not a problem.

Here is what you can and can't do for fallback:

- You can fall back to DB2 8 only after successfully migrating using **DSNTIJTC** to CM.

- You cannot fall back to DB2 8 or CM DB2 9 if you enter ENFM or NFM.

- You cannot use the new DB2 facilities until you are in NFM.

- You might have frozen objects after fallback; these are unavailable.

The **CATENFM** utility, whose syntax is shown in Figure 3.20, enables a DB2 subsystem to enter into ENFM and NFM. It also allows the return to ENFM from NFM.

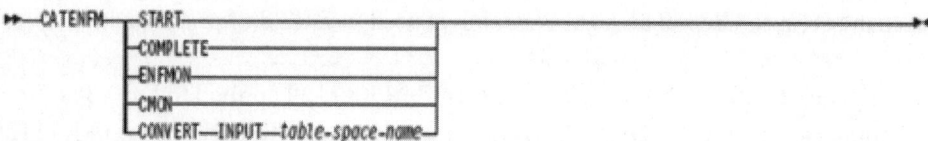

Figure 3.20: CATENFM utility

The **CMON** parameter returns DB2 to conversion mode. If you are in ENFM, **CMON** returns you to CM*. You cannot fall back to DB2 8 from CM*.

Considerations When Falling Back

Basically, there is no IBM-approved fallback. Before proceeding with a fallback procedure, you need to think about backing up the DB2 volumes of your system beforehand. It is your responsibility to provide backup for your system. If you have flash copy available, this would be the easier choice for copying the system; the copy steps can be tedious otherwise.

Don't forget to copy BSDSs and active logs. You may be using DFDSS dump and restore or **DSN1COPY** to handle these data sets. Be aware that your data sets during this process will be at different level IDs. By resetting the level ID, you are asking DB2 to accept the down-level data sets.

In DB2, a level ID is associated with every page set or partition. When you fall back, the level ID for a data set or partition will differ. In the CLIST panels, the

LEVELID UPDATE FREQ option on panel **DSNTIPL** (parameter **DLDFREQ** in macro **DSN6SYSP**) lets you control down-level detection. This field specifies how often, in number of checkpoints, the level ID should be updated for a partition or data set. Setting the field to **0** disables the down-level detection.

When you restart DB2, you might receive the following message:

```
DSNB232I csect-name - UNEXPECTED DATA SET LEVEL ID ENCOUNTERED
```

This message could be generated during any type of normal operations or during utility processing. Resetting the level ID is necessary in a situation such as fallback or when picking up earlier data sets to be used in **DSN1COPY** jobs. If you use **DSN1COPY** to copy or move data in this type of situation, you need to correct the down-level ID. In **DSN1COPY**, the **RESET** option resets the level ID. You can use the **REPAIR** utility with the **LEVELID** option to correct the level ID problem. This option resets the level identifier in the table space partition, table space, or index space partition to a new level identifier.

Remigrating to DB2 9 CM

The remigration process involves going back to DB2 9 CM after falling back to DB2 8. If you run the DB2 command **DISPLAY GROUP DETAIL** after remigrating, you will see the "mode" of CM*. You can use this display command in both data-sharing and non–data-sharing environments.

A Closer Look at Migration Modes

DB2 8 supported three migration modes: conversion mode (CM, formerly called compatibility mode), enabling-new-function mode (ENFM), and new-function mode (NFM). DB2 9 introduces two new migration modes: conversion mode* (CM*) and enabling-new-function mode* (ENFM*). The asterisk, as noted earlier, indicates that a system was previously in ENFM or NFM at some earlier time.

Conversion Mode

Running job **DSNTIJTC** takes you through to the conversion mode of DB2 9. You can run the **CATMAINT UPDATE** utility in **DSNTIJTC** to update the catalog while DB2 is operating, but take care to do so in a non-peak environment. In data sharing, all members can be active when you run **CATMAINT**.

DSNTIJTC adds the following items:

- New catalog table spaces and tables
- New columns to existing catalog tables
- New check constraints for catalog columns
- New definitions to existing catalog columns
- New indexes for new and existing catalog tables

In addition, the job revises existing check constraints for catalog columns.

Enabling-New-Function Mode

Before you begin the next step in the migration process, which is moving to ENFM, *all* members of a data-sharing group *must* have been migrated successfully to DB2 9 CM. Also, once you convert to NFM, you cannot fall back to DB2 8, so you need to make sure that you have done everything required in ENFM and have tested before moving to NFM. The code base for DB2 9 ENFM and NFM is the same as for CM.

Before enabling new-function mode, you need to create a point of consistency for the catalog and directory. Typically, you don't allow changes to the catalog and directory while enabling new-function mode. This is a good rule to follow.

The ENFM process converts the DB2 8 catalog to DB2 9 format, in job **DSNTIJEN**. If the RTS database **DSNRTSDB** does not exist, **DSNTIJEN** will fail. Steps in this job load data from the database to the catalog.

At ENFM, your data-sharing groups must have only DB2 9 members. You will use the CLIST with the ENFM option.

Before you begin, you should copy the DB2 9 CM catalog and directory (at a minimum) for system backup purposes. A flash copy works nicely for this purpose.

You run the installation CLIST using the **ENFM** option in the **INSTALL TYPE** field on panel **DSNTIPA1** (Figure 3.21).

```
DSNTIPA1 DB2 VERSION 9 INSTALL, UPDATE, MIGRATE, AND ENFM - MAIN PANEL
===>

Check parameters and reenter to change:
 1  INSTALL TYPE          ===>        Install, Migrate, ENFM, or Update
 2  DATA SHARING          ===> NO     Yes or No (blank for ENFM or Update)

Enter the data set and member name for migration only. This is the name used
from a previous Installation/Migration from field 9 below:
 3  DATA SET(MEMBER) NAME ===>

For DB2 SMP/E libraries (SDSNLOAD, SDSNMACS, SDSNSAMP, SDSNCLST, etc.), enter:
 4  LIBRARY NAME PREFIX   ===> DSN910
 5  LIBRARY NAME SUFFIX   ===>

For install data sets (NEW.SDSNSAMP, NEW.SDSNCLST, RUNLIB.LOAD, etc.), enter:
 6  DATA SET NAME PREFIX  ===> DSN910
 7  DATA SET NAME SUFFIX  ===>

Enter to set or save panel values (by reading or writing the named members):
 8  INPUT MEMBER NAME     ===> DSNTIDXA  Default parameter values
 9  OUTPUT MEMBER NAME    ===>           Save new values entered on panels
```

Figure 3.21: Panel DSNTIPA1

For the **INPUT MEMBER NAME** field, enter the value you specified as the output member during conversion mode. After keying in this information, press **Enter**.

The next panel that appears is **DSNTIPT** (Figure 3.22).

```
DSNTIPT         INSTALL DB2 - DATA SET NAMES PANEL 1
===> _

Data sets allocated by the installation CLIST for edit
 1  TEMP CLIST LIBRARY ===> prefix.NEW.SDSNTEMP
 2  SAMPLE LIBRARY     ===> prefix.NEW.SDSNSAMP
Data sets allocated by the installation jobs:
 3  CLIST LIBRARY        ===> prefix.NEW.SDSNCLST
 4  APPLICATION DBRM     ===> prefix.DBRMLIB.DATA.suffix
 5  APPLICATION LOAD     ===> prefix.RUNLIB.LOAD.suffix
 6  DECLARATION LIBRARY===> prefix.SRCLIB.DATA.suffix
Data sets allocated by SMP/E and other methods:
 7  LINK LIST LIBRARY  ===> prefix.SDSNLINK.suffix
 8  LOAD LIBRARY       ===> prefix.SDSNLOAD.suffix
 9  MACRO LIBRARY      ===> prefix.SDSNMACS.suffix
10  LOAD DISTRIBUTION  ===> prefix.ADSNLOAD.suffix
11  EXIT LIBRARY       ===> prefix.SDSNEXIT.suffix
12  DBRM LIBRARY       ===> prefix.SDSNDBRM.suffix
13  IRLM LOAD LIBRARY  ===> prefix.SDXRRESL.suffix
14  IVP DATA LIBRARY   ===> prefix.SDSNIVPD.suffix
```

Figure 3.22: Panel DSNTIPT – Data set names

On this panel, choose the output **SDSNSAMP** data set. Only the **SAMPLE LIBRARY** value can be changed on this panel. Press **Enter** to continue.

The CLIST calculates space allocations for shadow data sets and then displays its results on panel **DSNTIP00** (Figure 3.23). Accept these recommendations by pressing **Enter**.

```
DSNTIP00                 ENABLE NEW FUNCTION MODE FOR DB2
===>

Enter storage management properties for defining ENFM shadow data sets:
                   VOL/SER      DATA CLASS      MGMT CLASS      STOR CLASS
                   --------    ----------     ----------     ----------
 1 TABLE SPACES ===> DSNV01   ===>           ===>           ===>
 2 INDEXES       ===> DSNV02   ===>           ===>           ===>

Enter space for defining the ENFM shadow data sets for SYSOBJ:
 3 PRIMARY RECS ===> 708        SECONDARY RECS ===> 708

Enter space for defining the ENFM shadow data sets for SYSPKAGE:
 4 PRIMARY RECS ===> 1241       SECONDARY RECS ===> 1241

Enter storage management properties for defining ENFM image copy data sets:
                   DEVICE       DATA CLASS      MGMT CLASS      STOR CLASS
                   --------    ----------     ----------     ----------
 5 IMAGE COPY   ===> SYSDA    ===>           ===>           ===>
Enter the data set prefix for the ENFM image copy data sets:
 6 PREFIX       ===> DSN910.IMAGCOPY
```

Figure 3.23: Panel DSNTIP00 – Enable new function mode for DB2

Two additional panels, **DSNTIP03** and **DSNTIPC1**, show you the calculated space allocations and a summary of space requirements. At this point, you can press **Enter** to save the values or press **Return**.

Once you press **Enter**, the CLIST generates the ENFM job and sample jobs. The CLIST customizes several jobs, including **DSNTIJCS**, **DSNTIJEN**, **DSNTIJES**, **DSNTIJNF**, **DSNTIJNG**, and **DSNTIJNX** as well as the sample jobs.

Job **DSNTIJEN** executes the **CATENFM START** utility, which enables new-function mode, converting DB2 to ENFM* or ENFM. During this process, DB2 is placed in enabling-new-function mode. **DSNTIJEN** performs several functions, including the following:

- Adds **BIGINT** and **VARCHAR** columns to **SYSTABLESPACESTATS** and **SYSINDEXSPACESTATS**

- Copies RTS from user spaces to new table spaces in the DB2 catalog

- Creates a **DSNRTX03** index on **SYSINDEXSPACESTATS**

- Changes the buffer pool page size for the **SYSOBJ** table space

The first time **DSNTIJEN** runs **CATENFM START**, DB2 saves the relative byte address (RBA) or log record sequence number (LRSN) of the system log in the bootstrap data set. In ENFM, the **REORG** utility reorganizes **SYSOBJ** and **SYSPACKAGE** table spaces. This statement indicates the start of enabling-new-function mode. You can run the **CATENFM** utility as many times as needed.

After successfully running **DSNTIJEN**, take a copy of the DB2 catalog and directory. Job **DSNTIJIC** copies the catalog and directory; this is a tape backup. If you modified this job for disk backup, you might want to change it from the two volumes to which it is limited. To modify the number of volumes, use volume serial numbers instead of the **VOL=REF=*.jobstep**.

You can stop the **CATENFM** process by using the **TERM UTILITY** command. You can stop the ENFM processing by issuing **CATENFM HALTENFM**; this statement stops enabling-new-function mode at the completion of the next step in the processing.

New-Function Mode

Do not convert to new-function mode until you are sure you will not need to fall back to DB2 8. After successful activation of ENFM, you can move to NFM. In NFM, all new functions in DB2 9 are available. These are the jobs you run:

- **DSNTIJNF**: Activates NFM

- **DSNTIJNG**: Enables the DB2 precompiler to accept NFM SQL

- **DSNTIJNX**: Creates objects for the XML Schema Repository

New-function mode is activated by steps ENFM9700 and **DSNTICA** in job **DSNTJNF**. When the preceding jobs have been run and you have executed the

CATENFM COMPLETE utility, DB2 9 new-function mode can be used in your DB2 subsystem.

ENFM9700 verifies that the catalog and directory conversion is complete. **DSNTICA** alters the definition of **SYSPROC.DSNWZP**, ensuring that the external module is **DSNWZP** not **DSNWZPR**. In NFM, **DSNHDECP** should have **NEWFUN=YES** set.

You can generate NFM from ENFM, CM*, or ENFM*. You cannot fall back to DB2 8 or DB2 9 CM after going to NFM.

If you fall back from NFM or ENFM, any objects that were created and any new SQL features you exploited will still function in ENFM* or CM*, but no new objects or new functions can be exploited until you return to NFM.

When converting to new-function mode, the CLIST tailors the jobs listed in Table 3.11.

Table 3.11: New-function jobs			
DSNTIJEN	DSNTIJNF	DSNTIJNX	DSNTIJES
DSNTIJCS	DSNTEJ*xx*	DSNTIJNG	DSNTIJCS

Enhancements to the Installation CLIST and Panels

The DB2 9 installation CLIST features several usability enhancements. Just to review the process, you have SMP/E jobs to run, maintenance, prerequisites to resolve, and then the process of using the CLIST to step through panels and migrate/install. These macros are then externalized into *prefix*.SDSNMACS. The CLIST tailors job values that are used in the execution and finally in the assembly and link-editing of DSNZPARMs in job **DSNTIJUZ** to complete the process.

Basically, we have the same installation and migration methodology, with two additional modes for migration (CM* and ENFM*) added in DB2 9.

Migration Path

Before migrating to DB2 9, run the pre-migration job **DSNTIJP9** on your DB2 8 system to do a check. This job was delivered via the service stream in APAR PK31841. After applying this PTF, you must reassemble and link-edit **DSNHDECP** to integrate the changes in module **DSNARIB**. You will receive output from **DSNTIJP9** that indicates which tables have incomplete definitions. Also check PK73441 for DB2 9 changes for **REPORT09** of **DSNTIJPM**.

You should take a look at PK73081 for SQL changes in jobs **DSNTIJP9** and **DSNTIJPM**.

If each DB2 data-sharing member of the group has its own **DSNHDECP** module, you need to repeat the following steps for each member to update **DSNHDECP**:

1. Create a separate job containing only the **DSNTIZP** and **DSNTIZQ** steps from the job **DSNTIJUZ** previously edited by the install CLIST.

2. Run your newly created job to produce a new **DSNHDECP** by re-assembling and link-editing the **DSNHDECP** load module.

3. Stop and start your DB2 8 system.

If you migrate, the CLIST tailors the jobs listed in Table 3.12.

Table 3.12: Migrate tailored jobs				
DSNTIJFV	DSNTIJIC	DSNTIJIN	DSNTIJMV	DSNTIJSG
DSNTIJOM	DSNTIJTC	DSNTIJTM	DSNTIJUZ	DSNTIJVC
DSNTIJCX	DSNTIJRI	DSNTIJOS		

Migration also tailors the **DSNH, DSNHC, DSNU,** and **DSNEMC01** CLISTs.

Installation Path

Jobs in DB2 9 have changes to them, and some additional jobs have been added. Always use the installation guide as your guide for these jobs.

When you install DB2, the CLIST tailors the jobs listed in Table 3.13.

Table 3.13: Installation tailored jobs				
DSNTIJMV	DSNTIJCA	DSNTIJIN	DSNTIJUZ	DSNTIJID
DSNTIJEX	DSNTIJVC	DSNTIJTC	DSNTIJDE	DSNTIJTM
DSNTIJSG	DSNTIJIC	DSNTIJOS	DSNTEJ0	DSNTEJ1
DSNTEJ1L	DSNTEJ1P	DSNTEJ1S	DSNTEJ1T	DSNTEJ2A
DSNTEJ2C	DSNTEJ2D	DSNTEJ2E	DSNTEJ2F	DSNTEJ2P
DSNTEJ2U	DSNTEJ3C	DSNTEJ3P	DSNTEJ4C	DSNTEJ4P
DSNTEJ7	DSNTEJ71	DSNTEJ73	DSNTEJ75	DSNTESA
DSNTESC	DSNTESD	DSNTESE	DSNTEJ1U	DSNTEJ61
DSNTEJ62	DSNTEJ3M	DSNTEJ76	DSNTEJ77	DSNTEJ78

If you have activated DDF, the CLIST also tailors job **DSNTEJ6**.

If you specify a default WLM name in install panel **DSNTIPX**, the jobs listed in Table 3.14 are edited.

Table 3.14: WLM install panel DSNTIPX				
DSNTEJ6D	DSNTEJ6S	DSNTEJ6P	DSNTEJ6R	DSNTEJ6T
DSNTEJ6U	DSNTEJ6V	DSNTEJ6W	DSNTEJ6Z	DSNTEJ6
DSNTEJ64	DSNTEJ65	DSNTEJ66		

If you select CICS, the CLIST edits jobs **DSNTEJ5A**, **DSNTEJ5C**, and **DSNTEJ5P**. If you select data sharing, the CLIST edits jobs **DSNTIJFT** and **DSNTIJGF**. The installation CLIST also tailors the **DSNEMC01**, **DSNH**, **DSNHC**, and **DSNU** CLISTs.

Practice Questions

Question 1

In the migration/installation process, which is the logical sequence of events if you need to fall back from ENFM?

○ A. ENFM to CM* to CM

○ B. ENFM to CM to CM*

○ C. ENFM to CM*

○ D. ENFM to CM

Question 2

What is the FMID for the base code for DB2 9 for z/OS (not VUE)?

○ A. JDB991Z

○ B. HDB9910

○ C. HDRE9910

○ D. JDB991K

Question 3

Which target library contains the DB2 early code?

○ A. *prefix*.SDSNLINK

○ B. *prefix*.SDSNLOAD

○ C. *prefix*.SDSNEXIT

○ D. *prefix*.SDSNIVPD

Question 4

Which mode converts the DB2 catalog?

○ A. CM

○ B. ENFM

○ C. NFM

○ D. CM*

Question 5

Which job assembles DSNZPARMs?

○ A. **DSNTIJUZ**

○ B. **DSNTIJEN**

○ C. **DSNTIJMS**

○ D. **DSNTIJTC**

Question 6

Which job is used to check DB2 release incompatibilities in DB2 9?

○ A. **DSNTIJTC**

○ B. **DSNTIJIC**

○ C. **DSNTIJP9**

○ D. **DSNTIJPM**

Question 7

Which job is used to convert the BSDS to the new format for DB2 9?

○ A. **DSN1COPY**

○ B. **DSNJU003**

○ C. **DSNJCNVB**

○ D. **DSNJU004**

Question 8

Which command reloads a previous DSNZPARM load module?

- ○ A. **-SET SYSPARM RELOAD**
- ○ B. **-SET SYSPARM LOAD**
- ○ C. **-SET SYSPARM STARTUP**
- ○ D. **-SET SYSPARM AGAIN**

Question 9

What is the size or sizes of the work files in DB2 9?

- ○ A. 4 KB, 8 KB, 16KB
- ○ B. 4 KB, 32 KB
- ○ C. 4 KB, 8 KB, 16 KB, 32KB
- ○ D. 4 KB

Question 10

From panel **DSNTIPA1**, what are the four types of changes you can make through CLIST generation?

- ○ A. **INSTALL, MIGRATE, UPDATE, NFM**
- ○ B. **INSTALL, MIGRATE, ENFM, DELETE**
- ○ C. **INSTALL, MIGRATE, UPDATE, CM**
- ○ D. **INSTALL, MIGRATE, ENFM, UPDATE**

CHAPTER 4

Security and Auditing

In this chapter, we review some of the methods for securing and auditing data. Company requirements and software support for data security and auditing can vary from shop to shop. The methods discussed here are those you should be familiar with for Section 2 of the DB2 9 System Administrator for z/OS certification exam (Security and Auditing). This part of the exam makes up 7 percent of the overall test.

IBM Security Solutions

Within the IBM Security Framework, there are five security solution areas:

- Security compliance
- Identity and access
- Information security
- Application security
- Infrastructure security

Information security addresses the challenges of protecting and securing organizations' information assets. Security management is the process of setting up the controls to protect and secure those assets.

Data Security in DB2

On z/OS and DB2, we separate roles and responsibilities to provide a secure data environment. By limiting the privileges associated with each user's roles and responsibilities, we divide the security risks. For example, a DB2 system administrator's responsibilities and level of access to DB2 data are essentially different from those of the security administrator. This separation of tasks and security is a necessary part of good overall data security management.

A variety of methods are available to help you implement a security philosophy in DB2 9 for z/OS:

- Encryption to secure backups, logs, and data for recovery

- Role-based security to grant object privileges to roles

- Trusted security context

- A multilevel security scheme that enables row-level security checks and the classification of data into different categories

- Hardware support for encryption (tape drives and disk)

- Resource Access Control Facility (RACF) data set rules for data security

- Use of explicitly granted privileges

- Industry-recognized, standard encryption algorithms supported at the hardware level: American Encryption Standard (AES) and Triple Data Encryption Standard (TDES)

Encryption Solutions for DB2

The purpose of encryption is to protect data confidentiality. By transforming data from plain text, encryption renders the data unreadable to anyone except those who possess the decryption key. There are two aspects of encryption:

- Encryption and decryption

- Key management

Key management is the more difficult task.

Two encryption options are available for DB2 for z/OS:

- Built-in encryption (column-level)
- Tools and edit procedures

DB2 8 for z/OS introduced encryption at the column level. If an encrypted column is associated with an index, the index column is also encrypted.

Protecting data at the column level presents some handling difficulties and brings up some performance issues:

- SQL can result in index scans to materialize results.
- Predicates that depend on the sequence of encrypted columns can generate incorrect results.
- The use of range predicates can increase performance cost considerably.

The result is that DB2's built-in encryption is not widely used in the application programming environment.

Tools provide a good alternative for implementing encryption without requiring program changes. One such tool is IBM's Data Encryption for IMS and DB2 Databases. This facility implements encryption through the use of edit procedures (EDITPROCs) in DB2. The only drawback of this approach is that although the table row is encrypted, the associated index is left in clear-text (not encrypted).

When transmitting data, we use native data stream encryption that is supported in the database protocols; at the network level, Secure Sockets Layer (SSL) protocol is used. For SSL, DB2 for z/OS exploits the z/OS Communications Server's Application Transparent Transport Layer Support (AT-TLS) service. Native data stream encryption uses the Data Encryption Standard (DES) to provide a level of performance over SSL. DRDA encryption is single DES and is not recommended for reasonable security.

Encryption of data on disk comes in two forms:

- DB2 native encryption and decryption column functions
- The IBM Data Encryption for IMS and DB2 Databases tool

The built-in encryption functions work only for data that is stored and retrieved from the same DB2 subsystem. These encryption processes do not work for data passed into and then out of a DB2 subsystem. Distributed Relational Database Architecture (DRDA) data encryption handles the latter task, which is separate from the built-in data encryption functions.

When you offload backups and archive logs, encryption is built in-to the tape drives to protect the archive tape. The drives exploit System z cryptographic hardware features that are built in-to z/OS. Encryption support is provided by the TS1130 tape drive; the DR550 tape drive with encrypting tape and write once, read many (WORM) support; and ES8000 encrypting disks.

Specifying a Secure Port to DB2

When using TCP/IP with SSL, you can specify a secure port to DB2 in one of two ways.

The first method is to specify the TCP/IP port number in the DRDA **SECURE PORT** field of the **DSNTIP5** installation panel (Distributed Data Facility Panel 2) during DB2 installation. You use this field to specify the port number (1–65534) to be used for accepting TCP/IP connection requests from remote DRDA clients that want to establish a secure connection using the SSL protocol. The specified port number must be different from the values specified for the panel's **DRDA PORT** and **RESYNC PORT** fields. If you leave the **SECURE PORT** field blank, SSL verification support is disabled, and the DB2 TCP/IP SQL Listener does not accept any inbound SSL connections on the secure port.

The second way to specify a secure port is to use the **DSNJU003** (change log inventory) stand-alone utility to update the **SECPORT** parameter of the Distributed Data Facility (DDF) statement in the bootstrap data set (BSDS). The **SECPORT** parameter specifies a port number (0–65535) for the DB2 TCP/IP SQL Listener service to use to accept inbound SSL connections. If the parameter value is **0**, SSL verification support is disabled, and the DB2 TCP/IP SQL Listener does not accept inbound SSL connections on the secure port.

User Authentication

To access DB2 data, users must be authenticated. Access is controlled by secured layers of security. Allied agents with different connection methodologies, such as Customer Information Control System (CICS), Information Management System (IMS), and Time Sharing Option (TSO), can have distributed conversations through DRDA to DB2. The initial point of entry into DB2 from other DB2 systems and platforms is the distributed relational database server. For DRDA distributed access and remote procedures, DB2 establishes the security context and manages the work.

You can protect data sets in DB2 by using Resource Access Control Facility (RACF). RACF-managed security controls the connections to DB2 by using the RACF resource class **DSNR**. RACF assigns identity, and the DB2 primary authorization ID is an RACF identity.

The RACF access control module activated at the DB2 authorization exit point **DSNX@XAC** controls access to DB2 objects, commands, and utilities. DB2 commands, utilities, and SQL are each associated with a set of privileges and authorities. A user's initial primary authorization ID remains the primary ID, the SQL ID is set equal to the primary ID, and the list of DB2 secondary IDs is set to the list of group names to which the RACF user ID is connected.

Trusted Context and Role-Based Security

DB2 9 for z/OS provides two new features in the area of user ID authentication: trusted security context and database roles.

Trusted Security Context

A DB2 *trusted context* is an object defined by the database administrator (DBA). It contains a system authorization ID and a set of trust attributes. For a z/OS server, the user identity must be the RACF ID. In a trusted context, the user is trusted by the server to open a connection, and the identity of the end user is preserved while the application server interacts with the database. The trusted context should be enabled for the DB2 database before you enable a trusted connection. The users defined in this context can also be defined to obtain a database role.

Network trusted context is an object that gives users a specific set of privileges. It is available when a user connects to the database through a trusted connection. A series of trusted attributes are evaluated to determine whether a specific context can be trusted. Once trust has been established, you can define a unique set of interactions between DB2 and the external entity. A different user can use the existing database connection without requiring authentication of the new connection user.

Before the availability of trusted context, one system user ID was used to establish the connection, and that system user ID performed all transactions on behalf of all users. Now, the application receives a trusted connection through the trusted context. Users' identities can be passed to the database server. This trusted context then lets you create a unique set of interactions between DB2 and the application.

New DDL Statements

Several new DDL statements support trusted context in DB2 9:

- **CREATE TRUSTED CONTEXT**

- **ALTER TRUSTED CONTEXT**

- **DROP TRUSTED CONTEXT**

- **COMMENT ON TRUSTED CONTEXT**

- **GET DIAGNOSTICS**

A new value, **T**, for the **DB2_AUTHENTICATION_TYPE** field of the **GET DIAGNOSTICS** information indicates trusted context authentication.

The **CREATE TRUSTED CONTEXT** statement defines a trusted context at the current server. Trusted context lets multi-tier applications connect to DB2 and switch the authorization ID without having to re-logon or provide a password. The authorization IDs to which the connection switches must exist in RACF.

You can embed the **CREATE TRUSTED CONTEXT** statement in an application program or issue it interactively. The statement can be prepared dynamically only if **DYNAMICRULES** run behavior is implicitly or explicitly specified. The privilege set that is defined by the statement must include **SYSADM** authority.

When the statement is embedded in an application program, the owner of the package or plan is the privilege set. If the statement is bound in a trusted context with the **ROLE AS OBJECT OWNER** clause specified, the role is the owner; otherwise, an authorization ID is the owner.

New Catalog Tables

Three new catalog tables support trusted context in DB2 9:

- **SYSIBM.SYSCONTEXT** contains one row for each trusted context and includes the context name, context ID, and other context related information.

- **SYSIBM.SYSCTXTTRUSTATTRS** holds the attributes for a given context.

- **SYSIBM.SYSCONTEXTAUTHIDS** stores the authorization IDs that can be switched to in a trusted connection.

These three catalog tables, along with **SYSIBM.SYSROLES** and **SYSIBM. SYSOBJROLEDEP**, provide the information related to the trusted contexts and roles.

Database Roles

DB2 9 enables DBAs to manage objects owned by roles, allowing a more precise control of security. Trusted network context and roles let a DBA create and manage objects without ownership. The role exists as an object independently of its creator.

A *role* is a database entity to which one or more DB2 privileges can be granted or revoked. A database role is a virtual authorization ID that is assigned to an authorization ID through an established trusted connection. A role is available only in a trusted context. You can associate primary authorization IDs with a role in the definition of the trusted context and then use the SQL **GRANT** statement with the **ROLE** option to grant privileges to the role. To make a role a grantor, you would specify **ROLE AS OBJECT OWNER** when defining the trusted context. You can implement databases, table spaces, tables, indexes, and views in a trusted context with a role as the owner of the created objects.

Roles provide a way for users to acquire context-specific privileges. When associated with a role and using a trusted connection, an authorization ID inherits all the privileges that the role grants. Within a trusted connection, DB2 permits only one role to be associated with a thread at any point in time. The authorization must include either **SYSADM** or **SYSCTRL** authority.

DB2 extends the SQL **GRANT** and **REVOKE** statements to support roles in a trusted context and provide the ability to add roles to the list of authorization names to which privileges are granted and revoked. An established trusted connection can have privileges granted to and revoked from a role with the **GRANT** and **REVOKE** statements (as shown in Figure 4.1).

```
GRANT/REVOKE (collection privileges) TO ROLE role-name
GRANT/REVOKE (distinct type or JAR privileges) TO ROLE role-name
GRANT/REVOKE (function or procedure privileges) TO ROLE role-name
GRANT/REVOKE (sequence privileges) TO ROLE role-name
GRANT/REVOKE (system privileges) TO ROLE role-name
GRANT/REVOKE (table or view privileges) TO ROLE role-name
GRANT/REVOKE (use privileges) TO ROLE role-name
GRANT/REVOKE (package privileges) TO ROLE role-name
GRANT/REVOKE (plan privileges) TO ROLE role-name
GRANT/REVOKE (schema privileges) TO ROLE role-name
```

Figure 4.1: Granting/revoking privileges to a role

Roles can own and create objects. A role becomes the owner of objects created in a trusted connection if the trusted context definition specifies the **ROLE AS OBJECT OWNER** parameter. All the privileges necessary for the role to create the objects must exist. Outside the context, a user requires a **GRANT** to access an object owned by a role.

Roles can be assigned to and removed from individuals through the trusted authorization context as needed, permitting control over the activities of DBAs. A role can be used to assign privileges to a database administrator for a certain amount of time, and the role can be revoked later. The user's activities can be audited, providing controlled access to sensitive data.

Defining a Role

Figure 4.2 demonstrates the creation of a role as object owner and the creation of a trusted context.

```
CREATE ROLE PRODA_DBA;

GRANT DBADM ... TO PRODA_DBA;

CREATE TRUSTED CONTEXT DBA1 ...
DEFAULT ROLE PRODA_DBA WITH ROLE AS OBJECT OWNER AND QUALIFIER;
```

Figure 4.2: Defining a role and trusted context

Auditing trails are available for verification by a security administrator or auditor.

Revoking a Role

By dropping the role itself or using the **REVOKE** statement, you revoke all privileges assigned to a role. Before you attempt a drop, make sure the role does not own any objects; the **DROP** statement is rolled back if the role owns objects. If the role does not own any objects, the role is dropped, privileges held by the dropped role are revoked, and the revocation is cascaded.

Defining Trusted Contexts

You can use roles and trusted context to provide added security for your network-attached application servers. The role object ownership in a trusted context eliminates object dependency on authorization IDs.

Using roles and trusted context, you can implement DBA privileges that can easily be disconnected and reconnected to individual employees. A trusted context is an independent database entity that you define based on a system authorization ID and connection trust attributes that include IP address, domain name, server authorization, or job name of a local client. This functionality gives the ability to control where, when, and how local and remote requesters communicate with DB2.

You define a trusted context by using a system authorization ID and connection trust attributes before you create a trusted connection. You can establish a trusted connection to a local DB2 subsystem by using the Recovery Resource Services Attachment Facility (RRSAF) or the DSN command processor under TSO and the DB2 Interactive (DB2I) service.

A system authorization ID is the DB2 primary authorization ID that is used to establish the trusted connection. Table 4.1 shows the system authorization IDs for local connections.

Table 4.1: System authorization IDs	
Source	**System authorization ID**
TSO	TSO logon ID
BATCH	**USER** parameter on **job**
Started task RRSAF	**USER** parameter on job or RACF **USER**

Trusted Connections

A trusted connection is defined as a database connection:

- Incoming connection attributes match the attributes of a unique, enabled trusted context defined at the server.

- Trust attributes identify a set of characteristics about the specific connection. These attributes are required for the connection to be considered a trusted connection.

- A connection and a trusted context are established when the connection to the server is first created, and this relationship remains for the life of the connection.

When attributes of the trusted context are altered, the changes take effect on the next new connection or when a switch user request is issued within an existing trusted connection.

Creating Local Trusted Connections

You can establish a trusted connection to a local DB2 subsystem by using RRSAF or the DSN command processor under TSO and DB2I. TSO and batch connections using RRSAF, DSN, and utilities are determined by DB2 to be trusted or not. If a matching context is found, the connection is established as trusted.

Here is the series of steps that occurs as a local trusted connection is established:

1. DB2 searches for a trusted context that matches the primary authorization ID and the job or started task name you supply.

2. If a matching trusted context is found, DB2 checks whether the **DEFAULT SECURITY LABEL** attribute is defined in the trusted context.

3. If the **DEFAULT SECURITY LABEL** attribute is defined with a security label, DB2 verifies the security label with RACF. This security label is used for multilevel security verification for the system authorization ID.

   a. If verification is successful, the connection is established as trusted.

   b. If the verification is not successful, the connection is established as a normal connection without any additional privileges.

DB2 online utilities can run in a trusted connection if the following three conditions are true:

- A matching trusted context is defined;

- The primary authorization ID matches the authorization ID specified in the **SYSTEM AUTHID** clause of the trusted context definition; and

- The job name matches the **JOBNAME** attribute defined for the trusted context.

Establishing Remote Trusted Connections by DB2 for z/OS Requesters

A DB2 for z/OS requester can establish a trusted connection to a remote location by setting up the new **TRUSTED** column in the **SYSIBM.LOCATIONS** table. How DB2 obtains the system authorization ID to establish the trusted connection depends on the following values:

- The **SECURITY_OUT** value in the **SYSIBM.IPNAMES**

- The **TRUSTED** column value in **SYSIBM.LOCATIONS**

- The **TYPE** column value in **SYSIBM.USERNAMES**

With the trusted connection successfully established, DB2 obtains the translated authorization ID for the primary authorization ID from the row in the **SYSIBM. USERNAMES** table whose **TYPE** value is **O** for outbound. DB2 sends the user switch request on behalf of the primary authorization ID using RACF pass-ticket authentication.

If for any reason the **SECURITY_OUT** option is not set up correctly, DB2 will return an error.

Establishing Remote Trusted Connections to DB2 for z/OS Servers

When the DB2 for z/OS server receives a remote request to establish a trusted connection, DB2 checks to see whether an authentication token accompanies the request. The authentication token can be a password, an RACF pass-ticket, or a Kerberos ticket.

The requester goes through the standard authorization processing at the server. If the authorization is successful, DB2 invokes the connection exit routine, which associates the primary authorization ID, possibly one or more secondary authorization IDs, and an SQL ID with the remote request. DB2 searches for a matching trusted context.

If the validation is successful, DB2 establishes the connection as trusted. Otherwise, the connection is established as a normal connection without any additional privileges, and DB2 returns a warning with the **SQLWARN8** set.

Setting Authorization in DB2 Security

The **GRANT** and **REVOKE** statements grant privileges to and remove privileges from authorization IDs or roles if you are running in a trusted context. You **REVOKE** a privilege that was explicitly given with **GRANT**.

Privileges can be explicitly or implicitly given to a user in DB2. For example, you might explicitly grant a user a privilege of **CREATE** for tables; when a create is then executed, the creator has implicit select privileges on the table.

Implicit privileges are related to the ownership of an object and are different for each different object type. When the user is the owner of the DB2 object, the user implicitly holds certain privileges over that object that are set at object creation time.

Giving Privileges to Authorization IDs or Roles

Five DB2 catalog tables show the **GRANT** information that is recorded in the catalog:

- **SYSCOLAUTH** (privileges by users on column level)
- **SYSDBAUTH** (privileges by users over databases)
- **SYSTABAUTH** (privileges by users on the table level)
- **SYSRESAUTH** (privileges on resources, such as buffer pools and storage groups)
- **SYSUSERAUTH** (system privileges by users)

Administrative Authorities

In DB2, administrative authorities are a set list of authorities and associated privileges. You grant administrative authorities to an authorization ID by using the **GRANT** statement:

```
GRANT DBADM ON DATABASE PROD23 TO AUSER
```

Table 4.2 lists the administrative authorities and their associated privileges.

Table 4.2: DB2 administrative authorities and associated privileges	
Authority	**Privileges**
Installation **SYSADM**	No additional named privileges
SYSADM	**EXECUTE** privileges on all plans All privileges on all packages **EXECUTE** on all routines **USAGE** on distinct types
SYSCTRL	*System privileges:* **BINDADD, BINDAGENT, BSDS, CREATEALIAS, CREATEDBA, CREATEDBC, CREATESG, CREATEMTAB, MONITOR1, MONITOR2, STOSPACE** *Privileges on all tables:* **ALTER, REFERENCES TRIGGER, INDEX** *Privileges on catalog tables:* **SELECT, INSERT, UPDATE, DELETE** *Privileges on all plans:* **BIND** *Privileges on all collections:* **CREATEIN** *Privileges on all schemas:* **CREATEIN, ALTERIN, DROPIN** *User privileges on:* **BUFFERPOOL, TABLESPACE, STOGROUP**
PACKADM	*Privileges on a collection:* **CREATEIN** *Privileges on all packages in a collection:* **BIND, COPY, EXECUTE**
DBADM	*Privileges on tables and views in one database:* **ALTER, INSERT, DELETE, SELECT, INDEX, UPDATE, REFERENCES, TRIGGER**
Installation **SYSOPR**	*Privileges* **ARCHIVE, STARTDB** (cannot change access mode)
SYSOPR	*Privileges* **DISPLAY, STOPALL, RECOVER, TRACE** *Privileges on routines:* **START, STOP, DISPLAY, STOPALL, TRACE**
DBMAINT	*Privileges on one database:* **CREATETAB, STARTDB, CREATETAB, STATS, DISPLAYDB, STOPDB, IMAGCOPY**

Security authorizations in DB2 are structured in a hierarchy, which is depicted by the diagram shown in Figure 4.3.

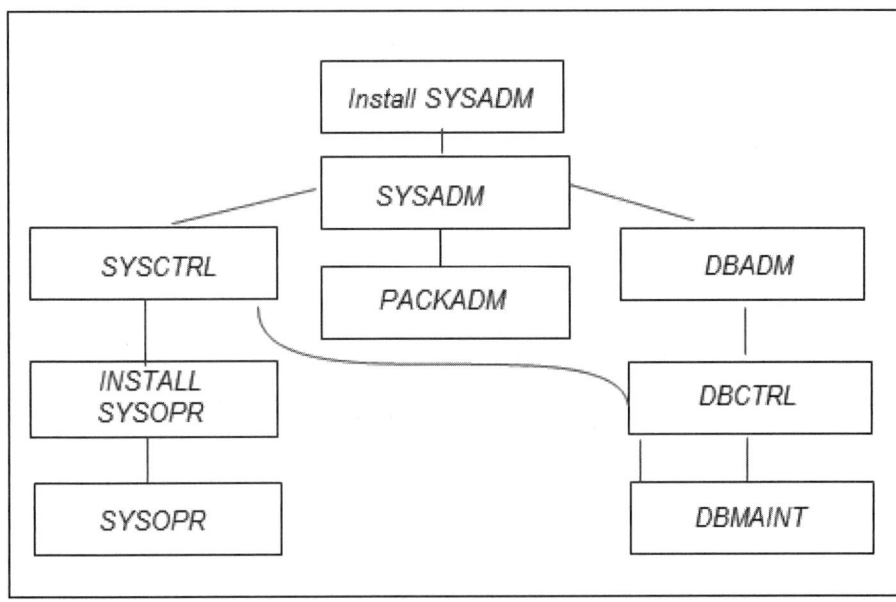

Figure 4.3: DB2 administrative authorities

Each administrative authority includes the associated privileges listed in the preceding table, plus the privileges of the lower authorities in the same branch of the hierarchy. The exception is the installation **SYSOPR**, which includes some privileges of **SYSADM** and **SYSCTRL**. The **DBADM**, **DBCTRL**, and **DBMAINT** authorities are database-dependent. **PACKADM** is collection-independent.

In addition to the administrative authorities shown in the diagram, one or two IDs are assigned the installation **SYSADM** authority, and one or two IDs are assigned the installation **SYSOPR** authority. These extra **SYSADM** and **SYSOPR** authorities are not recorded in the catalog by DB2; they are defined in the DSNZPARM subsystem initialization parameter module. These are special installation authorities, and no other ID can revoke these authorities in DB2. Special actions such as starting the directory and catalog when they are in restricted state or stopped, running all utilities against databases, running the **CATMAINT** utility, and accessing DB2 when the subsystem is started in **MAINT** mode are some of the special tasks these authorities can perform.

The **SYSADM**, **SYSADM2**, **SYSOPR**, and **SYSOPR2** authorities can be changed only by using the **SET SYSPARM** command with the current **SYSADM** authority. You can change only the install **SYSADM** (**SYSADM** and **SYSADM2**) subsystem parameters using **SET SYSPARM** with the current install **SYSADM** authority. If you lack the proper authority, DB2 issues message DSNZ015 for each ID you try to change, and the current value of the load module parameter will remain in effect. The rest of the load module is unaffected, and all other changes will take effect. If your primary or any secondary authorization ID has an install **SYSADM** authority, you can change **SYSOPR** or **SYSOPR2** if you use the **SET SYSPARM** command.

Remember when you look at the hierarchy for the privileges that the privileges "below" your authority are also included in your list of privileges. For instance, if you wanted to run DB2 commands, create or drop objects, run utilities on any database, bind plans and packages, and have access to DB2 when it is started with the **ACCESS(MAINT)** command, you would need to be at the **SYSCTRL** level. Notice how some of these privileges fall under **DBCTRL**. Note also the fact that **DBMAINT**'s authority is included in **DBCTRL**'s authorizations.

A Note About SYSCTRL and Authorization Privileges

The **SYSCTRL** authority is designed for administering a system that contains sensitive data. A user with **SYSCTRL** authority has nearly complete control of the DB2 subsystem. However, that user cannot access user data directly unless the privilege to do so is explicitly granted.

Group privileges in DB2 can be by table, plan, package, collection, database, system, user, schema, distinct type, and routine. Within each group is a set of privileges that can be granted. With table privileges, for example, you can use the **GRANT** or **REVOKE** statement to grant or remove **ALTER**, **DELETE**, **INDEX**, **INSERT**, **REFERENCES**, **SELECT**, **TRIGGER**, **UPDATE**, or **GRANT ALL** privileges on the table.

Authorization Checking with RACF

When you access DB2 from outside DB2 — as an allied agent, for instance — one way to control access is through RACF. Before you can use RACF, you need to install the RACF access control module. This module checks the RACF profiles that correspond to a set of privileges and authorities.

The authority checking performed by the RACF access control module simulates DB2 authority checking:

- DB2 object types map to RACF class names.

- DB2 privileges map to RACF resource names for DB2 objects.

- DB2 authorities map to the RACF administrative authority class (**DSNADM**) and RACF resource names for DB2 authorities.

- DB2 security rules map to RACF profiles.

The RACF access control module is supplied in member **DSNXRXAC** of library *prefix*.**SDSNSAMP** and provides access control using a combination of RACF and DB2 checking. You can alter the DB2 installation process by modifying the **DSNTIJEX** job to assemble the RACF access control module rather than the default DB2 exit routine. The default assembler RACF access control module is a DB2 exit routine called **DSNX@XAC** in library *prefix*.**SDSNLOAD**. To clarify the names of the RACF modules:

- The source code for the default DB2 exit routine is the **DSNXSXAC** member of *prefix*.**SDSNSAMP**.

- The sample exit code routine is **DSNXRXAC**.

- The load module name is **DSNX@XAC** in library *prefix*.**SDSNLOAD**.

> **IRR@XACS**, the RACF access control module in releases prior to DB2 8, is no longer shipped with RACF in **SYS1. SAMPLIB**. You cannot use this exit with DB2 9. The exit has changed substantially and is now shipped with DB2 9 as FMID HDRE910 (DB2 RACF Authorization Exit). You must migrate to the new RACF access control module for DB2 9.

The DB2 installation process assembles the RACF access control module into *prefix*.**SDSNEXIT**. You can use the **SDSNEXIT** library to implement separate levels of DB2 for the separate DB2 versions.

The default DB2 exit routine at exit point **DSNX@XAC** returns a code to the DB2 authorization module indicating that an installation-defined access control authorization exit routine is not available. DB2 will then perform native authorization checking and will not try to invoke this exit routine again.

You must match the code version of the RACF module to the DB2 version you are running. You can run multiple DB2 versions against the same RACF database provided the code versions match.

Code contained in **DSNXRXAC** ensures that the routine is invoked by the correct DB2 version. **DSNXRXAC** maps resource accesses to the same-format RACF resource names in the same classes. The only exception is that if the RACF resource name contains both a schema name and another long name (e.g., a JAR name), the schema name is truncated.

To protect DB2 objects, the RACF access control module uses three values to format resource and class names: **&CHAROPT**, **&CLASSNMT**, and **&CLASSOPT**.

Once installed, the RACF control module will become active on the next DB2 restart as long as you have one RACF class associated with DB2 at the time of restart. Before you restart, be sure that your implementation team has already defined appropriate RACF resources in the active DB2 classes; otherwise, unintended DB2 authorization failures or exposures can occur.

Planning RACF

The responsibilities of the RACF administrator include:

- Planning RACF classes for use with DB2
- Defining RACF resources to protect DB2 objects and administrative authorities
- Activating the RACF classes for DB2

The RACF resource class for DB2 is **DSNR**. This class is contained in the RACF descriptor table. Resources included in the class are profiles for access to a DB2 subsystem from one of these environments: the Call Attachment Facility (CAF), CICS, DDF, IMS, TSO, or batch. Profiles allow controlled access to a DB2 subsystem from a specific environment.

The secondary authorization IDs depend on whether the RACF "list of groups" option is active. If RACF and the list of groups are active, the routine sets the list of DB2 secondary IDs to the list of group names to which the RACF user ID is connected. Keep in mind that RACF user IDs that are in **REVOKE** status do not become DB2 secondary IDs. The maximum number of supported groups is 245.

The subsystems **DBM1**, **DIST**, and **MSTR**, as well as your Workload Manager (WLM) subsystem, must be associated with an RACF user ID. There are two ways to associate RACF with user IDs and groups. One way is to use the started procedures table **ICHRIN03**; the other is to use the RACF **STARTED** class.

If you use **ICHRIN03** to associate RACF user IDs and group names with the DB2 procedures address space, you will need to reassemble the **ICHRIN03** started procedures table to include your group names and user IDs. Using **ICHRIN03** requires an IPL for the changes to go into operation. The **STARTED** class takes effect without an IPL.

Table 4.3 lists the DB2 address spaces and associated RACF user IDs and group names.

Table 4.3: RACF user IDs and group names		
Address space	**RACF user ID**	**RACF group name**
DSNMSTR	SYSDSP	DB2SYS
DSNDBM1	SYSDSP	DB2SYS
DSNDIST	SYSDSP	DB2SYS
DSNWLM	SYSDSP	DB2SYS
DB2TMSTR	SYSDSPT	DB2TEST
DB2TDBM1	SYSDSPT	DB2TEST
DB2TDIST	SYSDSPT	DB2TEST
DB2TSPAS	SYSDSPT	DB2TEST
DB2PMSTR	SYSDSPD	DB2PROD
DB2PDBM1	SYSDSPD	DB2PROD
DB2PDIST	SYSDSPD	DB2PROD
CICSSYS	CICS	CICSGRP
IMSCNTL	IMS	IMSGRP

Authorization Checks Mapped to RACF

The DB2 9 class **DSNR** specifies the relationship between DB2 objects (e.g., tables, databases, views) and the RACF resource classes. The DB2 objects correspond to RACF general resource classes. The DB2 privileges are a part of RACF profile names, and the DB2 administrative authorities are profiles within RACF general resource classes.

Table 4.4 lists the RACF resource classes.

Table 4.4: RACF resource classes	
RACF resource class	Description
DSNADM	DB2 administrative authority class
DSNR	Control access to DB2 subsystems
GDSNBP	Grouping class for DB2 buffer pool privileges
GDSNCL	Grouping class for DB2 collection privileges
GDSNDB	Grouping class for DB2 database privileges
GDSNJR	Grouping class for Java Archive files (JARs)
GDSNPK	Grouping class for DB2 package privileges
GDSNPN	Grouping class for DB2 plan privileges
GDSNSC	Grouping class for DB2 schemas privileges
GDSNSG	Grouping class for DB2 storage group privileges
GDSNSM	Grouping class for DB2 system privileges
GDSNSP	Grouping class for DB2 stored procedures
GDSNSQ	Grouping class for DB2 sequences
GDSNTB	Grouping class for DB2 table, index, or view privileges
GDSNTS	Grouping class for DB2 table space privileges
GDSNUF	Grouping class for DB2 user-defined function privileges
GDSNUT	Grouping class for DB2 user-defined distinct type privileges
MDSNBP	Member class for DB2 buffer pool privileges
MDSNCL	Member class for DB2 collection privileges
MDSNJR	Member class for Java Archive files (JARs)
MDSNPK	Member class for DB2 package privileges
MDSNPN	Member class for DB2 plan privileges
MDSNSC	Member class for DB2 schema privileges
MDSNGN	Member class for DB2 storage group privileges
MDSNSM	Member class for DB2 system privileges

Table 4.4: RACF resource classes (continued)	
RACF resource class	**Description**
MDSNSP	Member class for DB2 stored procedures privileges
MDSNSQ	Member class for DB2 table, index, or view privileges
MDSNTS	Member class for DB2 table space privileges
MDSNUF	Member class for DB2 user-defined function privileges
MDSNDB	Member class for DB2 database privileges
MDSNUT	Member class for DB2 user-defined distinct type privilege

Authorization Routine Exits

The processing of remote attachment requests to DB2 uses RACF to check and verify the requesting ID and then accept or reject the request accordingly. This is the first level of authorization checking performed. In the flow of remote attachment, the sign-on exit routine, **DSN3@SGN**, then follows.

DB2 provides two exit points for authorization routines: one for connection processing and one for sign-on processing. Both exit points are used in the assignment of values to primary IDs, secondary IDs, and SQL IDs. You must have a routine for each exit; default routines are provided for both. The default exit routine for connections is **DSN3@ATH**, and the default exit routine for sign-on is **DSN3@SGN**.

Multilevel Security in DB2

DB2 multilevel security defines a relationship between DB2 users and DB2 objects. In the context of multilevel security, an object is any system resource to which access must be controlled. These objects can be data sets, tables, rows and columns. A user is an entity that requires access to these system resources.

Multilevel security lets you define a hierarchy between DB2 objects by assigning *security labels* to the objects. Access to an object is then restricted based on the security level of that object.

DB2 also provides an implementation of multilevel security at the row level. To implement this level of security, you add a table column that acts as the security label (**SECLABEL**), assigning the **AS SECURITY LABEL** attribute to the column. This implementation enables you to perform row-level security, giving you the ability to control which users are authorized to view, modify, or perform other actions on specific rows of data.

The security labels are defined within RACF (in the **SECLABEL** resource class) and can be assigned to users, systems, data sets, and other objects. The security-checking process retrieves the security label from RACF and compares it with the security label in the row. If access is allowed, data is returned. To minimize processing time, the security label values are cached.

Trusted Contexts, Roles, and Multilevel Security

A trusted context can exist without multilevel security. Together, these capabilities enable a user to be automatically switched to one of his or her defined **SECLABEL**s for the duration of work within a trusted connection.

You can specify a default **SECLABEL** for the trusted context to associate a default **SECLABEL** to users not assigned one. This must be a valid **SECLABEL** for the users. Combining the network trusted context, roles, and multilevel security permits more precise control of security.

DB2 Column-Level Encryption

Starting with DB2 8, DB2 for z/OS provides several built-in functions that let you encrypt data at the column level. Functions for encrypting data in DB2 include:

- **ENCRYPT_TDES** (or **ENCRYPT**) function to encrypt data in a column
- **DECRYPT_BIN** and **DECRYPT_CHAR** functions to decrypt the data in its appropriate format
- **GETHINT** function to retrieve the hint for the password

Create and Insert

The **SET ENCRYPTION PASSWORD** statement lets you specify a password as a key to the encryption functions. In the example shown in Figure 4.4, column **EMPNO** in table **EMPX** is encrypted with a password in DB2.

```
CREATE TABLE EMPX
(EMPNO VARCHAR(64) FOR BIT DATA,
EMPNAME CHAR(20),
CITY CHAR(20) NOT NULL DEFAULT 'GULF SHORES',
SALARY DECIMAL(9,2))
IN DSNDBXX.JUDYTEST ;
COMMIT ;
SET ENCRYPTION PASSWORD = 'PWENCR' WITH HINT 'AFOCUS';
INSERT INTO EMPL(EMPNO,EMPNAME, SALARY)
VALUES (ENCRYPT('77777'),'GARY SPRINGS',20000.00) ;
INSERT INTO EMPL(EMPNO,EMPNAME, SALARY)
VALUES (ENCRYPT('88888'),'MARIE DESTIN',20000.00) ;
```

Figure 4.4: Specifying a password for the encryption functions

When you create a column for data encryption, you must define the column as type **VARCHAR FOR BIT DATA**. The length of the **VARCHAR** column depends on the password and the password hint. Assuming column **EMPNO** is **VARCHAR(6)** before encryption, you can compute the final length.

Encryption at the Hardware Level

The System z platform provides encryption support at the hardware level with standard and optional hardware cryptographic devices. Devices are available with the proper software components in the different operating systems. These solutions provide applications with APIs to invoke the system's hardware cryptography and key repository management facilities.

Cryptographic Hardware

IBM products implement cryptographic algorithms in hardware. The following cryptographic hardware products are available for mainframe servers:

- Central Processor Assist for Cryptographic Functions (CPACF)
- Cryptographic Coprocessor Feature (CCF)
- Cryptographic Express2 Coprocessor (CEX2C)
- Cryptographic Express2 Accelerator (CEX2A)

- Peripheral Component Interconnect Cryptographic Coprocessor (PCICC)

- Peripheral Component Interconnect Cryptographic Accelerator (PCICA)

- Peripheral Component Interconnect - Extended Cryptographic Coprocessor (PCIXCC)

In over-the-network protection by the hardware or within z/OS, DB2 9 features the implementation of AT-TLS, Internet Protocol Security (IPSEC), or SSL encryption for sending and receiving data.

Tools for Auditing

The U.S. Sarbanes-Oxley Act and many other regulations require the IT staff to fulfill auditor requests for various views and reports of data. Auditors now need to track, analyze, and report on the status of legal and regulatory compliance efforts. To access the data they need, auditors rely on the IT department for data.

IBM provides several tools that address the auditing and compliance needs of auditors, security administrators, and database administrators. DB2 also offers tools to encrypt, test, audit, and safely archive data for long-term retention. These IBM tools include:

- DB2 Audit Management Expert for z/OS

- Data Encryption for IMS and DB2 Databases

- Log Analysis Tool

- Performance tools

Other products to be aware of include the Tivoli zSecure Suite and Tivoli Security Information and Event Manager. In addition, IBM Optim for z/OS provides facilities that automatically archive, browse, compare, copy, and edit related data. In general, these functions rely on IBM DB2 relationships, supplemented by user-defined relationships, to manipulate sets of relational data. The following Optim products may provide solutions for your shop:

- IBM Optim Data Growth Solution for z/OS

- IBM Optim Data Privacy Solution

- IBM Optim Test Data Management Solution

- IBM Optim Database Relationship Analyzer

DB2 Audit Trace

DB2's trace facility gives you the ability to collect monitoring, auditing, and performance information about your data and environment. This type of tracing produces reports about the access to DB2 data that is taking place.

Using the audit trace, you can trace different events or categories of events by authorization IDs and object ownerships. After you start the audit trace, it records certain types of actions and sends the report to a named destination.

As with other types of DB2 traces, you can specify the following options for the audit trace:

- Event categories

- Authorization IDs or plan IDs

- Ways to start and stop the audit trace

- Destinations for audit records

In general, you use audit traces to identify a process by its primary authorization ID. The audit trace records the primary ID before and after invocation of an authorization exit routine. The System Management Facility (SMF) and Generalized Trace Facility (GTF) accept SMF type 102 audit trace records.

Starting Audit Trace

You choose whether to audit the activity on a table by specifying the **AUDIT** clause in the **CREATE TABLE** or **ALTER TABLE** statement. You can specify **AUDIT ALL**, **AUDIT CHANGES**, or **AUDIT NONE**.

You can set the **AUDIT TRACE** field on installation panel **DSNTIPN** to start the audit trace, or you can start an audit trace at any time by issuing the **START TRACE** command. You can choose which audit classes to trace, specify the destination for trace records, and include an identifying comment. The overhead imposed by the audit trace is typically less than 5 percent.

To see which audit traces are active, use DB2's **DISPLAY TRACE** command:

```
-DISPLAY TRACE (AUDIT)
```

To stop a particular trace, specify its trace number in the **TNO** option of the **STOP TRACE** command:

```
-STOP TRACE (AUDIT) TNO(3)
```

When you start an audit trace, you choose which events to audit by specifying one or more audit classes. Table 4.5 lists the audit classes and the events they include.

Table 4.5: Audit classes		
Audit class	**Traced events**	**Activated IFCIDs**
1	Access attempts denied due to inadequate authorization	140
2	Explicit **GRANT** and **REVOKE** statements	141
3	**CREATE, ALTER,** and **DROP** operations against audited tables	142
4	First change of audited object	143
5	First read of audited object	144
6	**BIND** time information about SQL statements that involve audited objects	145
7	Assignment or change of authorization ID	53, 83, 87, 69, 319
8	Utility jobs	23, 24, 25, 219, 220
9	Installation-defined audit record	146
10	Trusted context	269, 270
11–29	Reserved	
30–32	Available for local use	

In DB2 9, the new audit class 10 audits trusted context events, using IFCID 269 for trusted connections and switch use and IFCID 270 for **CREATE TRUSTED CONTEXT** and **ALTER TRUSTED CONTEXT** statements. You should use these trusted context audit records whenever trusted contexts exist.

Here is an example of how to run the audit trace; keep in mind that read accesses are class 5:

```
-START TRACE AUDIT CLASS(4,5)

ALTER OWNER, TABLEX AUDIT ALL
```

IFCID 314: Authorization Exit Parameters

DB2 trace record IFCID 314 is useful when you are debugging an authorization exit. This information, which is generated after the authorization exit is called, shows the contents of the parameter list. You will see the stored clock before and after values when the exit was called, an address work area, a reason code from the user-defined exit, an authorization ID, an object owner, an object name, an access control environment element (ACEE) token (if available), and the parameters specific to the exit.

Practice Questions

Question 1

Name the two encryption options available for DB2 for z/OS:

- ○ A. FIELDPROC and SSAS encryption
- ○ B. Built-in encryption and FIELDPROC
- ○ C. Built-in encryption at the column level and EDITPROC
- ○ D. FIELDPROC and EDITPROC

Question 2

When creating a column for data encryption, you must define the column as:

- ○ A. **CHAR**
- ○ B. **VARCHAR FOR BIT DATA**
- ○ C. **DECIMAL**
- ○ D. **INTEGER**

Question 3

Why is trusted security context important to establishing connections? Identify *two* reasons:

- ○ A. User identity can be passed to the database server.
- ○ B. Trusted security is an object that gives users a specific set of privileges.
- ○ C. Trusted security context is only for DDF.
- ○ D. Trusted security context does not require an RACF ID.

Question 4

Which *two* of the following statements are true of role-based security:

○ A. A role is a database entity.

○ B. One role can be associated with one thread at any point in time.

○ C. More than one role can be associated with a thread.

○ D. You cannot use **GRANT** and **REVOKE** with **ROLE**.

Question 5

SYSCTRL authority is designed:

○ A. To be an administrator in a system that contains sensitive data

○ B. To allow access to all data directly in DB2

○ C. Not to be a part of the administrative authorizations

○ D. So that group privileges cannot be granted to **SYSCTRL**

Question 6

What is the sample exit code routine that supports RACF in DB2?

○ A. **DSNX@XAC**

○ B. **IRR@XACS**

○ C. **DSNTIJEX**

○ D. **DSNXRXAC**

Question 7

What is the RACF resource class for DB2?

○ A. **RADB**

○ B. **DSNR**

○ C. **RSNR**

○ D. **DADB**

Question 8

What are the default exit routines for authorization and connection and for a sign-on process in DB2? Choose *two* answers:

○ A. **DSN3@ATH**

○ B. **DSNAUTH**

○ C. **DSN3@SGN**

○ D. **DSNSGON**

Question 9

Which SMF type are the audit trace records?

○ A. 101

○ B. 102

○ C. 103

○ D. 104

Question 10

If you are using an audit trace in DB2, how much overhead is typical?

○ A. More than 5 percent

○ B. Less than 5 percent

○ C. More than 20 percent

○ D. Less than 20 percent

CHAPTER 5

System Backup and Recovery

DB2's **BACKUP** and **RESTORE** utilities support system data recoverability. In DB2 9 for z/OS, the DB2 backup and restore process is improved significantly with enhancements to these utilities and the use of FlashCopy. To prepare you for Section 4 (Backup and Recovery) of the DB2 9 System Administrator for z/OS certification exam, this chapter reviews the z/OS system requirements for backup and restore and examines the enhancements that provide system recoverability in DB2 9. This part of the exam makes up 20 percent of the overall test.

System-Level Requirements

The objective of disaster recovery is to recover DB2 data operations without (or with little) loss to data and in as timely a way as possible. To achieve this goal, you need a devised and tested backup and recovery strategy that you periodically review to maintain recovery capability.

When we think about the methods for DB2 recovery, one possible scenario is a total loss of the data center that requires you to recover an entire system from a fixed point in time. We also think of systems failures that cause data center and DB2 problems that must be resolved on a day-to-day basis. User database failures due to program errors, DB2 code problems, and operator errors also can occur and must be resolved. To prepare for all these types of failures, you must establish a copy procedure that provides the necessary backup of your data to enable the appropriate type of recovery for each situation (at either your own or a remote site). You must also understand the point in time when the data was backed up and know how to recover to a point in time.

Disaster recovery involves the entire z/OS operating system and components. Local system failure and DB2 failures, be they data or system, also require recovery backup methodologies. The two do not necessarily constitute the same strategies, but similarities do exist.

The basics involved are the knowledge and use of utilities in DB2 such as **BACKUP**, **COPY**, **LOAD**, **RECOVER**, **RESTORE**, and **UNLOAD** that might play into the scenarios for recoverability. Without an understanding of how these utilities work, the best of strategies is useless.

You also need a knowledge of the structure of the DB2 database management system at a physical level to be able to back up the proper table spaces for catalog, directory, and user data. An understanding of DB2 logging and a knowledge of the bootstrap data set, active logs, and archive logging strategies — all this and more comes into play when you plan your backup and recovery strategies.

This chapter focuses on the strategies that implement features in DB2 9 for z/OS, but we begin with a review of some of the basics to get things started.

REPORT RECOVERY Utility

When run using the **RECOVERY** option, DB2's online **REPORT** utility provides a tool to obtain the recovery history of a table space, which is a good starting point for assessing your recovery strategy for objects. The information produced by this utility comes from the **SYSCOPY** catalog table, the **SYSLGRNX** directory table, and the BSDS.

You can use **REPORT** information in recovering user table spaces, the catalog, and the directory. The information produced contains all **SYSCOPY** records, the log ranges from the **SYSLGRNX** directory table, log data sets from the BSDS, and all the table space names in a table space set. By specifying the appropriate parameter, you can obtain this information for the local system (**LOCALSITE**), the recovery system (**RECOVERYSITE**), or both.

The report also shows image copies of the **DBD01**, **SYSCOPY**, and **SYSUTILX** table spaces that are not recorded in **SYSCOPY**. When executing **REPORT RECOVERY** on the catalog and directory, be sure to specify the **CURRENT** option to avoid additional archive tape mounting. Omitting this parameter causes DB2 to search all **SYSCOPY** records in the log and on the archive tapes. If you specify **CURRENT** and the last recovery point does not exist on the active log, you will be prompted to mount archive tapes until this point is found. Only the **SYSCOPY** entries from the last full image copy (last recovery point) of a table space are reported when you specify **CURRENT**.

You can use the **REPORT** utility's **TABLESPACESET** option to obtain the names of the table spaces and tables in a referential structure. Using the **LISTDEF** utility, you could report on all the tables in a specific database:

```
LISTDEF RELIST INCLUDE TABLESPACES DATABASE DB0101
REPORT RECOVERY TABLESPACE LIST RELIST
```

When you use the **TABLESPACESET** or **REPORT RECOVERY** utility syntax, information relating to cloned table spaces is displayed in a special section of the report.

With your **REPORT RECOVERY** information, you can determine whether image copies are available. The report shows information about image copy data sets and archive log data sets that could be required in a recovery. Also check the **SYSTEM-LEVEL BACKUPS** field on panel **DSNTIP6** for the value **YES**. This setting enables the system-level backups to be used for object-level recovery. If the field is set to **YES**, take a look in the BSDS at your system-level backup information if you have taken system-level backups. By using both pieces of information, you can determine your recovery baseline.

Check the report carefully, examining the listed image copy events, and make sure you look at the values in the **STYPE** and **IC TYPE** fields. These values indicate whether an event happened after the image copy that would put the table space in a state that makes the image copy unusable. This might be the case, for example, if you took a **COPY** and some subsequent event put the table space in **REORG**-pending status, making the **COPY** invalid.

MODIFY RECOVERY Utility

The **SYSIBM.SYSCOPY** catalog table contains entries for utilities, such as the **COPY** utility, that have run against table spaces and index spaces. Over time, you should clean out old entries in this table that no longer relate to your recovery strategies. You have backups, logs, and entries in **SYSCOPY** whose retention you need to coordinate to ensure your data is available.

You likely will use the **REPORT RECOVERY** utility to see which objects are available for recovery purposes and then use the **MODIFY** utility with the **RECOVERY** option to delete old data from **SYSCOPY**, related records from **SYSLGRNX**, and entries from the DBD. The **MODIFY** utility also recycles DB2 version numbers for reuse.

Your JCL might contain statements similar to the following to print and then report recovery information for the specified contents:

```
//SYSIN      DD *
     LISTDEF A1 INCLUDE TABLESPACE DB1AAA.T*
REPORT RECOVERY TABLESPACE LIST A1
```

By analyzing the resulting entries and assessing what is no longer useful for recovery, you can then eliminate old entries using the **MODIFY** utility. In the same job stream as above or a later one, you would specify the necessary parameters to remove the old copies from **SYSCOPY**:

```
MODIFY RECOVERY LIST A1
     DELETE DATE(*)
```

In DB2 9, **MODIFY RECOVERY** deletes entries from **SYSLGRNX** even though no records are deleted in **SYSCOPY**. Deleting works by date, not by timestamps, and you have the keyword options **DELETE AGE** and **DELETE DATE**.

A new DB2 9 parameter, **RETAIN**, provides a more straightforward approach than other deletion criteria. This keyword is available only in new-function mode of DB2 9. You can use the **RETAIN** parameter with the **GDGLIMIT**, **LAST**, **LOGLIMIT** option to simplify the retention and deletion of entries in **SYSCOPY** and **SYSLGRNX**.

This utility is your maintenance for recovery information.

System Disaster Recovery Process

In planning for disaster recovery, you must find your recovery point. In other words, if you were to lose the system, what point in time (PIT) would you have as a backup for your system and user data, and how long would it take to recover that data and bring the copies you have up to that point in time? In this section, we look at the different methods of backup and recovery as well as the tools that exist in DB2 to provide these services.

The Traditional Approach

In the traditional strategy for disaster recovery, you need to know what to **COPY**, what to **RECOVER**, and in what order these steps should be done. In the system backup, you **COPY** the system components in a specific order specified by DB2. Remember to set system parameter **DEFER** to **ALL** to postpone processing of all databases during the initial DB2 restart.

Some of the these **DSNDB06** catalog table spaces must be specified in a single **COPY** statement, completely by themselves. If you find it necessary to perform a point-in-time recovery of the catalog and directory databases, make sure you **QUIESCE DSNDB06.SYSCOPY** separately from all the other table spaces.

Table 5.1 shows the exact sequence of the recovery of table spaces for the **RECOVER** utility. Notice that **SYSCOPY** comes last.

Table 5.1: RECOVER sequence
DSNDB01.SYSUTILX
DSNDB01.DBD01
DSNDB01.SCT02
DSNDB01.SPT01
DSNDB01.SYSDBASE
DSNDB06.SYSDBAUT
DSNDB06.SYSGPAUT
DSNDB06.SYSGROUP
DSNDB06.SYSPLAN
DSNDB06.SYSPKAGE
DSNDB06.SYSUSER
DSNDB06.SYSSTR

Table 5.1: RECOVER sequence (continued)
DSNDB06.SYSVIEWS
DSNDB06.SYSSTATS
DSNDB06.SYSDDF
DSNDB06.SYSOBJ
DSNDB06.SYSSEQ
DSNDB06.SYSSEQ2
DSNDB06.SYSHIST
DSNDB06.SYSGRTNS
DSNDB06.SYSJAVA
DSNDB06.SYSJAUXA
DSNDB06.SYSJAUXB
DSNDB06.SYSALTER
DSNDB06.SYSEBCDC
DSNDB01.SYSLGRNX
DSNDB06.SYSCOPY

The **COPY** utility is the method of backing up system and user data using the traditional approach. One of the most important things to keep in mind is that you always want to make sure the table spaces or index spaces are not in a restrictive state before you try to run the **COPY** utility.

You can terminate a **COPY** utility, but be aware that DB2 will insert an **IC TYPE** of **T** in the **SYSCOPY** catalog table if you do so. You cannot take an incremental copy while this **T** exists; you must take a full image copy. The copies produced by the **COPY** utility are available to the **RECOVER** utility to provide your backups.

All the data in the system, including the directory and catalog, can be copied by using the **BACKUP SYSTEM** utility. This method permits updates to data, so a system-level backup could have uncommitted data.

After copying the table spaces, you would want to archive the DB2 active log by using the following command:

```
-ARCHIVE LOG
```

In addition to archiving the log, this command makes a copy of the BSDS. You can use this copy as a way to recover the BSDS if it is damaged and you cannot restart DB2. The interesting thing to remember is that the BSDS will not have the corresponding archive log recorded in it in this traditional approach.

It is recommended that you execute an SQL query that selects the table space names by database from the catalog, with the corresponding tables, indexes, and object identifiers for each. Also, run the stand-alone utility **DSNJU004** (print log map) to print the BSDS, and make sure all this information goes off-site with your backups; documentation is part of your backup, too.

This completes the backup for the traditional system piece. You are still responsible for making sure all the system and user databases are copied on a schedule to maintain system integrity.

When you performed the traditional recovery, you would restore the ICF catalogs used for the DB2 catalog and directory from a backup. Before starting the DB2 recovery, you would run IDCAMS with the **DELETE NOSCRATCH** option for all DB2 VSAM data sets.

RECOVER Using an Earlier Copy

The **RECOVER** online utility lets you specify the latest point in the log from which a copy will be selected during recovery. A new keyword, **RESTOREBEFORE**, supports this option.

RECOVER always tries to allocate the latest copy that resides in **SYSCOPY**. If that copy has been damaged or lost, you need a way to redirect the utility to another copy. The **RECOVER RESTOREBEFORE** option directs the utility to use a recovery base that is earlier than the system-level backup. The value of the **SYSTEM-LEVEL BACKUPS** field on installation panel **DSNTIP6** must be **YES** to support this functionality.

When you use the **RESTOREBEFORE** option, you instruct the **RECOVER** utility to restore the object to its current state and apply the log records to a specified **TOLOGPOINT** or **TORBA** value that you select and provide in the **RESTOREBEFORE** syntax:

```
RECOVER LIST RCBILIST RESTOREBEFORE X'nnnnnnnnnnn'
```

You can check the log record sequence number (LRSN) or relative byte address (RBA) value using the **REPORT RECOVERY** utility.

The system compares the **RESTOREBEFORE** value you provide with the LRSN or RBA value in the **START_RBA** column of the **SYSIBM.SYSCOPY** record for the copies (image copy, concurrent copy, or system-level backup). So, for example, you can avoid the most recent copy by providing the number (LRSN or RBA value) to which you want DB2 to restore in the **RESTOREBEFORE** parameter. The system compares the **RESTOREBEFORE** value with the LRSN or RBA value in the **START_RBA** column in the **SYSIBM.SYSCOPY** records for the copies.

System-level backups do not "fall back" to a previous copy (backup), so the ability to recover to an earlier copy can be very helpful in a system-level backup situation, especially if the image copies have been moved off to tape and are unavailable.

RECOVER Syntax

Figure 5.1 shows the syntax of the **RECOVER** utility control statement.

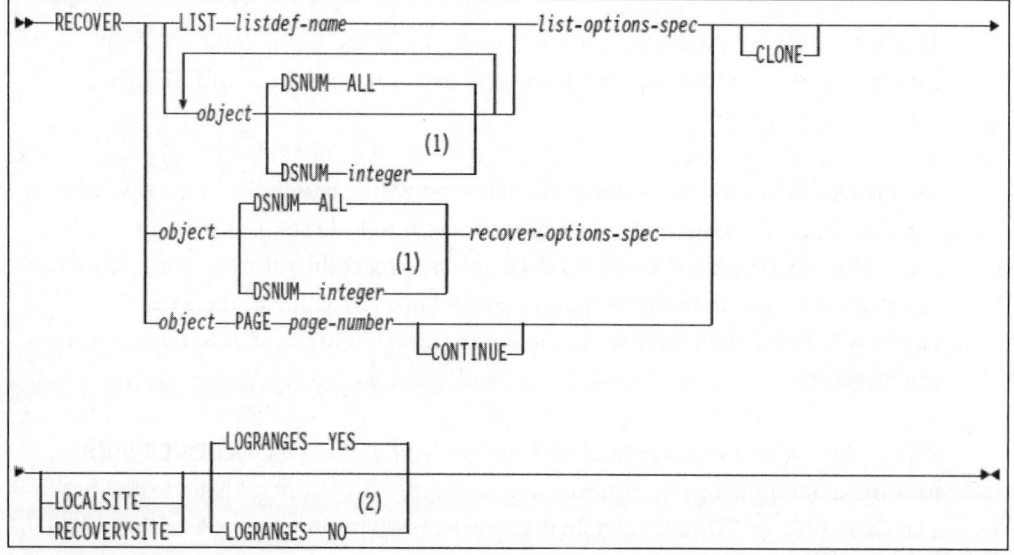

Figure 5.1: RECOVER syntax

When you recover an object from a system-level backup that resides on disk, the object is passed to DFSMS Hierarchical Storage Management (DFSMShsm) before being restored from image copies or concurrent copies. When the system-level backup is on tape, **RECOVER** can restore the objects from the image copies, system-level backups, and concurrent copies at the same time. **RECOVER** can also use backups made with the **BACKUP SYSTEM** utility as well as image copies.

Output from RECOVER

Data output recovered by the **RECOVER** utility can consist of a table space, index, partition or data set, error range, or page within a table space. **RECOVER** puts any associated index spaces in **REBUILD**-pending status if you use the recover option parameter **TOCOPY**, **TOLASTCOPY**, or **TOLASTFULLCOPY** to recover to a point in time.

Used with the list option parameter **TOLOGPOINT** or **TORBA**, **RECOVER** puts indexes in **REBUILD**-pending status if they are not recovered with their table spaces. To remove the pending status, you run the **REBUILD INDEX** utility.

In NFM of DB2 9, if you have used **TOLOGPOINT** or **TORBA**, DB2 detects any work that was uncommitted at the point in time selected for recovery. To support this capability, two new execution phases have been added after the **LOGAPPLY** phase for **RECOVER TORBA** and **RECOVER TOLOGPOINT** operations: **LOGCSR** and **LOGUNDO**.

The **LOGCSR** phase is run for each DB2 member with an active unit of recovery (UR); if no UR was active, this phase is skipped. URs that have not completed are identified. Once all URs have been determined, the **LOGUNDO** phase is executed. This phase backs out any changes made on recovered objects with active URs. In data-sharing environments, this back-out occurs one member at a time.

Added support in the **TERM UTIL** command lets the **RECOVER** utility phases of **LOGAPPLY**, **LOGCSR**, and **LOGUNDO** end at the next commit point. This new support lets the utility terminate; in previous releases, **TERM UTIL** was ignored. You will see DSNU1555I messages appear as the **LOGUNDO** phase processes the URs.

Remember that if you are recovering to a point in time and the object is referentially tied to other objects, you must ensure that you recover the entire set of table spaces associated with that object. Otherwise, **RECOVER** will set **CHECK**-pending status for all the dependent table spaces, LOBs, and base table spaces in the referential set.

Image copies taken with **TOCOPY**, **TOLASTCOPY**, or **TOLASTFULLCOPY** to be used by the **RECOVER** utility should be made with the **SHRLEVEL REFERENCE** option. You should know that the entry in the catalog table **SYSCOPY** column **PIT_RBA** stores the "finish time" of the share level change copy. The system uses this value to locate the image copy with which to start recovery if you are using a specific timestamp.

The system uses column **STYPE** in **SYSCOPY** to determine whether a recover to a PIT was done with or without consistency. The **STYPE** column value in combination with that of column **IC TYPE** indicates the consistency level.

Advanced Recovery Concepts

To shut down the DB2 subsystem, you use this command:

```
-STOP DB2 MODE(QUIESCE)
```

Recovery from Different System Failures

If you were to lose both copies of the active log during a DB2 shutdown, you could safely use a DB2 cold start to bring DB2 back up without the active logs. With a conditional restart record that does not create a gap in the log, you should take image copies of all the table spaces after the cold start. This situation represents a unique condition, not one that is typical, but it is an interesting example of the recovery process.

When you look the basics, the successful recovery of DB2 involves you first taking image copies of your user table spaces, DB2 catalog, and directory; then truncating the active log; and then performing an MVS catalog backup.

Recovery Manager and Recovery Log Manager

The DB2 recovery manager (RM) subcomponent manages processes related to checkpoint, restart, abort, and commit. These services support the subcomponents in the system services address space. RM controls the communications between resource managers when data is recovered and tracks the LRSN for each member of a data-sharing group.

The DB2 recovery log manager (RLM) subcomponent supports the system services tasks of log offloading, BSDS access, archive log read tasks, the log command, and log timer services. RLM maintains the DB2 recovery log, the BSDS, and the archiving of the active logs and supports other DB2 resource managers by reading and writing data on the DB2 recovery log. RLM also supports the copying of active log data sets to archive log data sets as the active log data sets become full.

DB2 supports dual data sets for your active log, archive, and BSDS. Log records are assigned ascending RBAs in non–data-sharing environments and mapped into physical data sets as described by the BSDS.

If you need to print the active log, the log must not be allocated to DB2. Issue the following commands to ensure that the active log is not allocated to DB2:

```
-STOP DATABASE
-STOP DB2
```

Then, you can use the **DSN1LOGP** stand-alone utility to print the active log.

BSDS Dual Mode Restore

You may encounter a message from DB2 that indicates that a subsystem is in single BSDS mode. The procedure to restore dual BSDS mode after deleting and redefining a damaged BSDS is to issue the **RECOVER BSDS** command.

Messages will alert you to any problems you might have at the start-up of your DB2 system related to the BSDS, such as the BSDSs not having the same timestamp. In this case, DB2 will start up, try to resynchronize the BSDS, and then re-enable dual BSDS mode.

Active Logs Running Out of Space

If a failure from the archive logging offload process occurs due to an out-of-space condition on one copy of the archive log, DB2 will continue to offload in single-archive mode. If that offload is successful, only one copy of the archive log is recorded in the BSDS.

Active Logs

If you determine that the system is running low on active logs, you can allocate a new active log data set using IDCAMS. You would then stop DB2, add the active log names, and restart DB2.

If you encounter hardware problems (e.g., a DASD controller error), the active logs may be left in a stopped state. After resolving the hardware problem, delete all active logs from the BSDS, and then use the **DSNJU003** (change log inventory) utility to re-add the active logs to the BSDS.

You can use utility **DSN1LOGP** to process the log and then identify the starting and ending LRSNs or RBAs. Be sure to verify the RBA values against the BSDS to confirm whether the **ENDRBA** value matches or not.

Utility **DSNJU003** is also used to create conditional restart records. If you ever need to perform a cold start, you can use this utility with the **CRESTART** control statement and a **STARTRBA** value equal to **ENDRBA**. You can also use **CRESTART** to find the **ENDLRSN** for data sharing.

If you are requiring DB2 to recover to a point in time, you will need to decide on the non–data-sharing **ENDRBA** number. Utility **DSNJU004** is the tool to use to determine this information. The usual cold restart method for data sharing is to specify the following command:

```
CRESTART CREATE, ENDLRSN=xxxxxxxxx, FORWARD=YES, BACKOUT=YES
```

Of course, you will need to determine the **ENDLRSN** for all members in the data-sharing environment and choose the lowest LRSN as your truncation point.

Other conditions, such as a DB2 failure due to an exceptional peak in normal workload, can cause a conditional restart. The normal restart then abends in the log apply phase whenever DB2 is started. In this case, you must perform a DB2 conditional restart.

IN DB2 9, you can initiate log truncation by timestamp using two new parameters of the **DSNJU003** utility's **CRESTART** statement. Parameter **SYSPITRT** lets you add a timestamp, in the **ENDTIME** format, to truncate logs for a PIT recovery restart. You use parameter **SYSPITR** to establish a log truncation point when preparing to run the **RESTORE SYSTEM** utility.

If you have performed a conditional restart of DB2, the system is in a system recover pending mode. What that means is that only the **RESTORE SYSTEM** utility is allowed to execute. All data remains unavailable until the **RESTORE SYSTEM** has finished.

If you are running in a data-sharing environment, you need to restart all members with **SYSPITR CRCR**, which specifies the same log truncation LRSN. After conditionally restarting each member, you can execute the **RESTORE SYSTEM** utility on a member. You must re-cycle DB2 and bring down all data-sharing members to reset the system recover pending mode.

• •
Two queues of records are associated with the conditional restart in the BSDS, in addition to describing the active and archive logs. You use the offline utility **DSNJU004** to read the conditional restart information and issue a report.
• •

DSNDB07: Work Files

Work files are critical for data sorting in DB2. If you encounter a space failure for one of the data sets in **DSNDB07**, you need to create an additional 4 KB or 32 KB table space in **DSNDB07**. Messages on the system log will alert you to space problems.

Application Abends

An application that abends after running for a very long time without any committing process can be a problem. This situation usually occurs with batch jobs that update critical tables whose data may be used by many applications. As the back-out starts running, it begins to take a very long time to complete successfully. How do you resolve this problem?

In this type of scenario, it is best if you can let DB2 continue with the back-out process. If back-out cannot complete successfully, the process begins to restore the data. Ideally, you have already designed this recovery process and can implement it quickly.

Active Logs in Recovery, Advisory Pending State, and DBETE

When you restart the DB2 subsystem, the system uses log information to determine the status of objects. DB2 start-up consists of four phases of execution. The second phase rebuilds the database exception table (DBET).

The system processes the logs to assemble information about the status of indexes and table spaces. If the object condition cannot be verified, a DBET is rebuilt from log records.

The DBET error status, **DBETE**, is a new advisory pending state that requires you to take further action to reset the error status on an object experiencing a DBET error. Once you recover or rebuild the object, the **RECOVER** utility removes the pending state: page set rebuild pending (**PSRBD**), rebuild pending (**RBDP**), or recovery pending (**RECP**).

This functionality was designed to reduce DBET abends, a state that occurs when an internal structure or logical inconsistency exists. Certain DBETs can cause an abend during a restart or **RESTORE SYSTEM** operation. DB2 9 tolerates the DBET error and puts the page set into a restrictive state, reducing the problems associated with DBETs causing abends. This exception state does require the object to be recovered.

DB2 checks the condition of the object's log records, and if the status cannot be guaranteed at that time, a DBET is rebuilt from the log records. During this processing, DB2 issues message DSNI046I to the console to inform you that there is a problem with the object. The message will contain either the RBA or the LRSN of the log record at the time of the error.

A DSNI046I message condition has the following format:

```
module-name DBET ENTRY IN ERROR REASON reason-code ERQUAL erqual-value
NAME object-name DBID dbid OBID obid LRSN lrsn-or-rba
```

Because the DBET states were being modified during a log apply, this error prohibits DB2 from successfully updating the DBET states. The index space or table space is placed in **RBDP** or **RECP** status and in **DBETE** status. DB2 then abends with a reason code and generates a dump. The response is to report the problem to IBM and then determine how to handle the exception state error.

What all this means is that DB2 accepts or tolerates the exception state so that a restart or **RESTORE SYSTEM** utility can continue.

You can reset the **DBETE** condition and then restart DB2 by issuing the following command (an abbreviated form of the **START DATABASE** command):

```
-STA DB(xxxx) SP(xxxx) ACCESS(FORCE)
```

To let you know the status on the restart, a new message, DSNI045I, indicates the object involved and allows restart and remedial action:

```
DSNI045I OPEN FAILED FOR DB dbname SPACE NAME tsname, PART partno
```

DB2 Restart

DB2 restart needs to be quick and clear-cut. To help with this goal, DB2 9 initiates a "page set open" earlier in the forward log phase. The asynchronous page set open is done at read time rather than waiting until the log apply phase. **SYSLGRNX** range closing is deferred until after the restart.

QUIESCE

The online **QUIESCE** utility provides a consistent recovery point for a page set to use for point-in-time recovery processing. You may be able to eliminate the need to use **QUIESCE** by using the **RECOVER** utility to back out any uncommitted changes from the recovery point. This process will also roll back uncommitted URs. The **RECOVER** alternative does not apply to **TOCOPY** recovery processes.

Object-Level Recovery

In DB2 9, you can use **RECOVER** to perform a single object-level recovery from a system-level backup. The **RECOVER** utility can also use the volume-level flash copy made by the **BACKUP SYSTEM** utility.

DB2 9 provides no **REPORT RECOVERY** support for object-level recovery. You can use the **REPORT** utility to obtain information about the catalog and directory as well as information about recovery of a page set. You can also use the DFSMShsm **LIST COPYPOOL** command with the **ALLVALS** option and the **DSNJU004** utility to determine whether the data is still on DASD or has been dumped to tape.

To view the **RECOVER** utility log apply progress, you can use the command:

```
-DISPLAY UTILITY
```

DSN1LOGP

The **DSN1LOGP** stand-alone utility formats and displays the extracted portions of the recovery log and can also prepare a summary for all units of recovery within the specified portion of the log. The extracted information can be about checkpoints and conditional restart control records.

The DB2 data manager uses the recovery log manager to write and read records into the DB2 log. These log records describe data modifications that have been made, such as before and after images of an SQL update, or a system state, such as a database that has been stopped.

These data modification records of undo or redo changes are used to roll back uncommitted updates during rollback or at system restart time. At restart time, log records that describe the system state are then used to restore the system to its previous state.

Two queues in the BSDS have associated conditional restart records. You can use utility **DSN1LOGP** to read and extract this information for use in your conditional restarting of DB2.

Helpful Commands

Next, we will look at some DB2 commands that are useful when working with recovery and restarting of DB2:

- **DISPLAY UTILITY**

- **TERM UTILITY**

- **DISPLAY DATABASE**

- **DISPLAY THREAD**

- **CANCEL THREAD**

The **DISPLAY UTILITY** command lists the currently running utilities in DB2. At a restart, you can use this command in either of the following forms to see whether there are any stopped utilities:

```
-DISPLAY UTILITY
-DIS UTIL(*)
```

In DB2 9, the display command also shows the progress of the **RECOVER LOGAPPLY** phase. This command gives you the utility identifier, user identifier, utility type, phase, and status. You can use it to check the restricted status of objects when restarting DB2. This information can help you estimate the time it will take to complete the recovery job. If no utilities are running, a message will let you know this as well.

The command provides the starting and ending RBAs or LRSNs and reports the last **COMMIT** point RBA or LRSN for the **RECOVER** utility in the **LOGAPPLY** phase. In addition, it displays the elapsed time based on the starting time of the **LOGAPPLY** phase.

The **TERM UTILITY** (or **TERM UTIL**) command cleans up and releases resources that were in a restricted status as a result of stopping DB2:

```
-TERM UTIL(xxxxx)
```

The **DISPLAY DATABASE** command lets you see databases that are in a possible restricted status, table spaces in a check pending (**CHKP**) state, and table spaces and indexes in a recovery pending (**RECP**) state. The command also indicates the **DBET** status for an object if it is in error.

```
-DISPLAY DATABASE
```

Another display command, **DISPLAY THREAD**, lets you take a look at the number of system agent threads, the subsystem status, and other information that reveals the general health of the DB2 that is running the command. The command displays system agent information to aid in problem assessments.

```
-DISPLAY THREAD(*) TYPE(SYSTEM)
```

In DB2 9, the **DISPLAY THREAD** command has been extended to include a storage option. This enhancement is part of the health monitor feature and can be useful in diagnosing problems:

```
-DISPLAY THREAD(*) SERVICE(STORAGE)
```

The **CANCEL THREAD** command cancels the processing of database commands, a function that can be useful when a page set is left in stop-pending status:

```
-CANCEL THREAD
```

Data Sharing

Before DB2 9, the log record sequence number in data sharing had to be unique at the subsystem level. DB2 used the store clock value (**STCK**) synchronized across the members of a data-sharing group with the Sysplex Timer to derive this value. If a duplicate was derived, the **STCK** instruction was repeated until a unique value was generated. This process, known as LRSN spin, caused log latch contention while generating the log record. The latch was driven by code that moved the log record to the output buffer and could be monitored by latch class (LC) 19.

In DB2 9 new function mode, the LRSN value is unique at the index or data page level, reducing LRSN spin and lock contention. DB2 now hangs on to the log latch (class 19) while the LRSN is incremented and reduces the LC.

When you are in a disaster recovery situation and are using the **RESTORE SYSTEM** utility, the conditional restart control record (CRCR) that you build for the **SYSPITR** option must be the same for each DB2 member. This point brings up the fact that when you use utility **DSNJU003**, the latest LRSN you can use is the last written record for all the members participating in a restart. Before starting the first member, you would use the **SETXCF FORCE** command to purge DB2 coupling facility structures.

In a traditional image copy disaster recovery, you would use the **DEFER=ALL** option for the first restart and the z/OS **SETXCF FORCE** command.

BACKUP SYSTEM and RESTORE SYSTEM

DB2 8 introduced the **BACKUP SYSTEM** and **RESTORE SYSTEM** utilities. This method of backup and recovery provides the ability to make fast volume-level backups of an entire DB2 subsystem or data-sharing group. With this support, you can recover a subsystem or data-sharing group to any point in time, even though you may or may not have uncommitted units of recovery work. These uncommitted URs are resolved during the forward and backward recovery phase at the DB2 restart.

The **BACKUP SYSTEM** utility provides fast volume-level copies (versions) of DB2 databases and logs. The **RESTORE SYSTEM** utility provides the ability to recover a DB2 system to an arbitrary point in time and can automatically handle any

CREATEs, DROPs, and **LOG NO** events that may have occurred between the backup and the recovery PIT. Both **BACKUP** and **RESTORE** utilities use FlashCopy.

These utilities exploit the fast replication services of DFSMShsm, and the data sets you copy need to be SMS-managed data sets. The facilities of z/OS 1.8 or later are a requirement, and you must have disk control units that support IBM TotalStorage Enterprise Storage Server (ESS) FlashCopy.

You can use the **BACKUP SYSTEM** utility to copy all data for a single application. When you use **BACKUP SYSTEM**, all the data sets you copy must be SMS-managed data sets. You can later run the **RESTORE SYSTEM** utility to recover the entire backed-up system. Both **BACKUP SYSTEM** and **RESTORE SYSTEM** use z/OS DFSMShsm copy pools, V1R8 functions of z/OS DFSMShsm, and the disk volume FlashCopy backups.

Several requirements apply when you use the **BACKUP SYSTEM** utility. One is the use of copy pools, which are a defined set of storage groups that contain data that DFSMShsm can back up and recover collectively. When using **BACKUP SYSTEM**, you can have up to two copy pools, one for databases and one for logs. The utility makes volume copies based on the parameters you set and the copy pools associated with the database, the logs, or both.

To use tape for the **BACKUP SYSTEM** utility, you must have z/OS DFSMShsm V1R9 or higher. You can use incremental FlashCopy, but the dump that goes to tape is always a full dump.

FlashCopy enables your **BACKUP SYSTEM** operation to go directly to tape. When you specify the **DUMP** or **DUMPONLY** option, the output is directed to a dump class in DFSMShsm, which in this case is tape. **DUMP** lets the copy to tape start before the completion of the FlashCopy. You can have up to five dump classes in DB2, each with its own set of copy pools, giving you the flexibility to keep one backup copy locally and send another off-site for disaster recovery purposes.

Keep in mind that although the option to use tape may let you to keep your data longer, if circumstances require you to restore a full system, this operation could take some time coming from tape.

On a data-sharing group, you must issue the **DISPLAY UTILITY** command from the member on which you invoke **BACKUP SYSTEM**; otherwise, the current utility information will not be displayed. The utility also provides a **FORCE** parameter; if the previous dump has not been completed, the use of **FORCE** lets a new dump be started. Specify this option when you need to take another copy and are more concerned about completing the new dump than the previous one.

The **BACKUP SYSTEM** utility produces as output a copy of the volumes on which the DB2 data and log information resides. **BACKUP SYSTEM** history is recorded in the BSDS.

A DB2 9 enhancement lets you to recover a subset of the system-level backups. To enable the **RECOVER** utility to use the system-level backups, you must alter indexes to specify **COPY YES**. **RECOVER** itself requires no changes unless the **BACKUP SYSTEM** went to tape. If the copy before the recovery point is a system backup, the data will be extracted and then restored by DFSMShsm.

With the ability to use **RECOVER** to recover individual data sets and system-level backups, you may not have to run image copies individually on your data sets. Obviously, you should evaluate the impact of adopting this practice at your shop. For example, **LOAD REPLACE** or **REORG LOG NO** copies would still be required.

DFSMS Enhancements

In DB2 9, the **CREATE STOGROUP** statement supports SMS storage classes, providing help in managing data sets. Three new columns in the **SYSIBM. SYSSTOGROUP** DB2 catalog table — **DATCLASS**, **MGTMCLAS**, and **STORCLAS** — reflect the SMS classes you specify on the **CREATE STOGROUP** or **ALTER STOGROUP** statement, reflecting the storage class, management class, and data class parameters to pass to SMS. DB2 does not check the classes you give it on the **STOGROUP** statement; it passes this information to DFSMS, which does the work. DB2 must be in new-function mode to make use of this new support.

When you back up and recover data sets, you must have SMS-managed data sets. DB2 8 required DFSMShsm V1R5 copy pool enhancements. In DB2 9, the utilities rely on new functions of z/OS DFSMShsm V1R8.

To use fast replication operations, you must define the log and database copy pools and associated source and backup storage groups. You may need to see the storage system administrator for help. Fast replication refers to the FlashCopy function supported by IBM ESS disk and the SnapShot function supported by IBM RAMAC Virtual Array (RVA) disk.

The log copy pool should contain the active logs and the BSDS. The database copy pool should contain DB2 catalog, directory, and user data. These SMS copy pools are defined using DB2 naming conventions and are identified by a token passed to DB2 via the **BACKUP SYSTEM** utility.

FlashCopy

Incremental flash copy support is an addition that requires z/OS DFSMShsm V1R8 and an APAR (OA17314) for z/OS to use. With FlashCopy, changes from the incremental copy are applied immediately to the previous full copy. This does not reduce your disk volume requirements. The tracks that have changed since the last copy was taken are the only tracks that are copied, and this content is what replaces the previous content on the source volume.

Keep in mind that a one-to-one relationship exists between the disk volume and the incremental, and note that there are a defined number of versions to a copy pool. So if a copy pool has more than one version, the versions will be full backups.

The **BACKUP SYSTEM** utility includes two new keywords that accommodate FlashCopy. Use the keyword **ESTABLISH FCINCREMENTAL** once for a database copy pool to establish a persistent incremental FlashCopy relationship for a database copy pool version and a full copy. The **END FCINCREMENTAL** keyword takes the last incremental copy and withdraws the FlashCopy relationship.

Copy Pools

When you begin to use the new **BACKUP** and **RECOVER** methods in DB2, you need to understand about SMS copy pools. Copy pools are used for system-level point-in-time recovery.

A copy pool is a new SMS storage group that is used as a container for copy pool volumes that you can back up and restore with a single command. Each copy pool storage group volume will have a corresponding volume in the copy pool backup storage group. For each copy pool volume, there are as many backup volumes defined.

You assign one copy pool for your databases and one for logs. The naming convention follows the format **DSN$*locn-name*$*cp-type***, where:

- **DSN** is the unique DB2 product identifier
- **$** is a delimiter
- *locn-name* is the DB2 location name
- *cp-type* is the copy pool type: **DB** for database copy pool or **LG** for log copy pool

When implementing system-level PIT recovery, you need to know what you can copy and recover. Let's first take a look at the two copy pools.

The **LOG** copy pool contains volumes for the active logs, BSDS, and the ICF catalog associated with these data sets. The **DATABASE** copy pool holds all volumes used for the databases and the ICF catalog associated with these data sets. The ICF data resides on a different volume than for logs.

After the copy pools are set up, the **FRBACKUP PREPARE** statement is issued for each copy pool to validate the fast replication environment for DFSMShsm. A system administrator typically executes this statement.

You can determine whether your database copy pool is still on DASD or has been dumped to tape by first issuing the DFSMShsm **LIST COPYPOOL** command with the **ALLVALS** option and then running the **DSNJU004** stand-alone utility to obtain output that contains the DB2 system-level backup. For a data-sharing system, run the utility with the **MEMBER *** option to obtain system-level backup information from all members.

Next, we'll review the new commands in DFSMShsm. The **FRBACKUP** command creates a backup version for each volume in the copy pool you specified. **FRRECOV** lets you recover a single volume or a pool of volumes from the backup versions. **FRDELETE** deletes unneeded fast replication backup versions.

LIST and **QUERY** are two commands that help with the monitoring of backup versions. Other commands have also changed in DB2 9 to provide new information related to the DFSMShsm fast replication function.

Flow of BACKUP SYSTEM

The diagram in Figure 5.2 depicts the flow of the **BACKUP SYSTEM** utility.

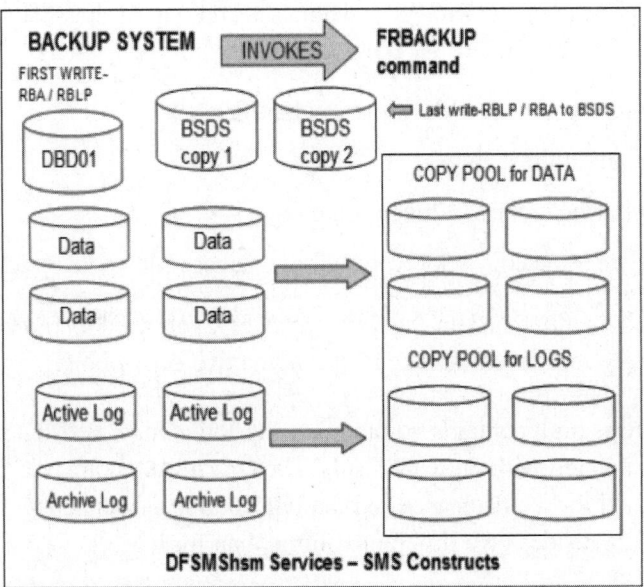

Figure 5.2: BACKUP SYSTEM utility flow

At the start and during the backup of the copy, the RBA or recovery base log point (RBLP) is written to the directory in **DBD01** in the header page. Each time a backup is taken, the **DBD01** RBA/RBLP is overwritten in the header page; it is also recorded in the BSDS and in the DFSMShsm control data sets. Because this value is recorded before the copy is started, it can be used as a log point after a restore if necessary. The information for data sharing is also written in the shared communications area (SCA).

Active logs usually reside on different DASD and copy pools than archive logs, and if they do not, they are part of the data copy pool. The logging process does not stop while the **BACKUP SYSTEM** process is going on.

The **BACKUP SYSTEM** process takes only a few seconds to execute, and with the **VERSIONS** parameter you can specify up to 85 copies to be maintained on disk. At this point, the system writes the RBA or RBLP to the BSDS and issues a message to let you know the process has been completed:

```
BACKUP SYSTEM Utility Completed.
```

BACKUP SYSTEM FULL vs. DATA ONLY

There are two ways to use the **BACKUP SYSTEM** syntax. One way is to back up the data only (**BACKUP SYSTEM DATA ONLY**); the other is to perform a full system backup (**BACKUP SYSTEM FULL**).

BACKUP SYSTEM FULL backs up both the logs and the databases. So you would have an SMS copy pool that contains the catalog, directory, and user data, and you would have another copy pool that contains the BSDS and the active logs. You would recover the system to the PIT at which the copy was taken. You are not required to use the **RESTORE SYSTEM** utility to do so, but you can. After restoring the backups, you can use a normal restart to bring the system to a consistent state. Using the **FULL** option, you copy the database copy pools first and copy the log copy pool last. DSNU messages show the status of the utility as it runs. You also will see DFSMShsm messages in the syslog for the **BACKUP** when the **FRBACKUP** commands are executed.

The **BACKUP SYSTEM DATA ONLY** command copies only the database copy pool; it does not copy the log copy pool. This type of backup is referred to as a data-only system backup. Using **RESTORE SYSTEM** and this type of backup, you could recover your system to an arbitrary PIT. It does not matter whether you use **FULL** or **DATA ONLY**; in both cases, backups are recorded in the BSDS, and the **DBD01** header page is updated with the RBA or RBLP.

BACKUP SYSTEM Utility Steps

The following steps summarize the **BACKUP SYSTEM** utility process:

1. First, DB2 takes a new lock type of exclusive lock to ensure that no other backup utility can execute. If you are running data sharing, DB2 takes a global lock.

2. Next, any 32 KB page writes created prior to NFM are suspended. You can avoid this write suspension by reorganizing (**REORG**) these objects. In a data-sharing environment, all members are notified.

3. DB2 suspends all deletions, renamings, creations, and extensions of data set objects. You don't want to have **CREATE**s or processes such as **TRUNCATE TABLE** trying to run at this point because these operations could actually cause a wait situation to occur when you try to run the **BACKUP SYSTEM** utility.

4. System checkpoints are suspended. In a data-sharing environment, all members are notified.

5. Data sets are prevented from pseudo-closing. In a data-sharing environment, all members are notified.

6. The **DBD01** header page is updated with the RBA, RBLP, or LRSN, and the page is then written to DASD. In data sharing, the system checkpoint prior to the lowest LRSN of all active members is used.

7. The BSDS is updated with the system backup information. In data sharing, only the BSDS for the submitting member is updated.

8. The FlashCopy of the database copy pool is invoked from DFSMShsm.

9. If this is a full system backup, DFSMShsm is invoked to take a FlashCopy of the log copy pool.

10. All suspended activities from the preceding steps are resumed. In a data-sharing environment, all members are notified.

11. The exclusive lock is released. In a data-sharing environment, all members are notified.

12. A message is issued indicating that the backup has been completed.

BACKUP SYSTEM Tape Support

The **BACKUP SYSTEM** utility provides three options for tape support:

- **DUMP**

- **DUMPONLY TOKEN X'...'**

- **FORCE**

You can **DUMP** the data to tape when the copy pool (or pools) is logically complete. If you use **DUMPONLY TOKEN**, you create a dump on tape for an existing backup of a copy pool that is on DASD. If you don't specify a token, the most recent copy pool backup goes to tape. The **FORCE** syntax allows the overlaying of the oldest copy pool that has not been completed. The **DUMP** and **DUMPONLY** parameters also support the **DUMPCLASS** option.

You must invoke the **BACKUP SYSTEM** utility twice for tape support: first, to perform a **DUMP** to initiate the copy pool backup on disk and, second, with the **DUMPONLY** option to initiate the dump to tape.

If you use **BACKUP SYSTEM** and then dump the backup to tape, you can specify the **RESTORE_RECOVER_FROMDUMP** system parameter with the **NO** setting to retrieve the backup from disk.

BACKUP SYSTEM Syntax

Figure 5.3 shows the **BACKUP SYSTEM** syntax.

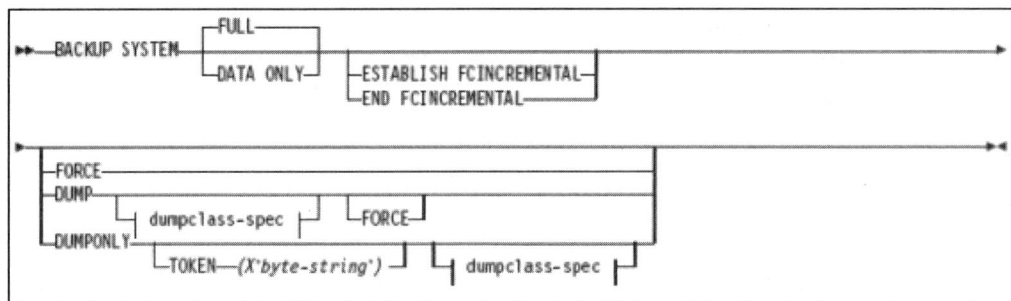

Figure 5.3: BACKUP SYSTEM syntax

Here are a few suggested system parameter settings for system backup and restore:

- **RESTORE_RECOVER_FROMDUMP = NO**

- **RESTORE_TAPEUNITS = NOLIMIT**

- **SYSTEM_LEVEL_BACKUPS = NO** (restricts the system-level backup to use by only the **RESTORE SYSTEM** utility during an object-level recovery)

- **UTILS_DUMP_CLASS_NAME** = blank

RESTORE SYSTEM

The **RESTORE SYSTEM** utility invokes z/OS DFSMShsm V1R8 to recover a DB2 subsystem or a data-sharing group to a previous point in time. To perform the recovery, the utility uses data that is copied by the **BACKUP SYSTEM** utility. All data sets that you want to recover must be SMS-managed data sets.

In DB2 9, the **RECOVER** utility permits using a backup taken at the system level as the recovery base, and the most recent recovery base is chosen. The recovery base can be an image copy, concurrent copy, log yes event, or copy pool backup. This is a subsecond restore if the backup data resides on DASD. The data is restored to the same volumes on which it resided at the time of the backup.

If the data or the table space or index space has moved since the copy pool was backed up, the copy pool backup cannot be used as the recovery base. This situation can occur if utilities such as **REORG** or **LOAD REPLACE** move the objects. In that case, the PIT recovery will be the previous recovery base.

If you use the **FROMDUMP** option in your syntax, the data sets are restored from tapes. Remember that **RESTORE_RECOVER_FROMDUMP** is a subsystem parameter that you can override during execution of the **RESTORE SYSTEM** utility with the **FROMDUMP** keyword.

You can run **RESTORE SYSTEM** from any member in a data-sharing group, including a member that is usually quiesced when backups are taken. If a data-sharing group is active and at or beyond the log truncation point, it must be restarted. The logs must be truncated to the **SYSPITR** LRSN point.

You can specify the **SYSPITR** LRSN point in the **CRESTART** statement of the **DSNJU003** utility. If there is a data-sharing member that is beyond the log truncation point or is not active, that member need not be restarted. Specifying a **SYSPITR** value of **FFFFFFFFFFFF** will cause a system point-in-time recovery to occur for a data-sharing group without log truncation. Data-sharing group members do not need to be restarted if they are normally quiesced at the time of the backups and are not active or beyond the log truncation point.

To be able to use system-level backups and the incremental FlashCopy that have been dumped to tape, your DFSMShsm level must be V1R8 or later. The restore of the copy pool from tapes occurs in parallel. There is integrated tape management between DFSMShsm and DB2.

The subsystem parameter **LOGAPSTG** in macro **DSN6SYSP** sets the maximum amount of **DBM1** storage that the fast log-apply process can use. The default of 100 MB of storage allows sufficient storage for 10 concurrent **RECOVER** jobs to execute.

You can use the DFSMShsm **LIST COPYPOOL** command with the **ALLVOLS** option and utility **DSNJU004** to determine whether the system-level backups are on disk or tape. If the system-level backups are dumped to tape, those tapes can later be used by the **RESTORE SYSTEM** utility.

Figure 5.4 shows the **RESTORE SYSTEM** syntax.

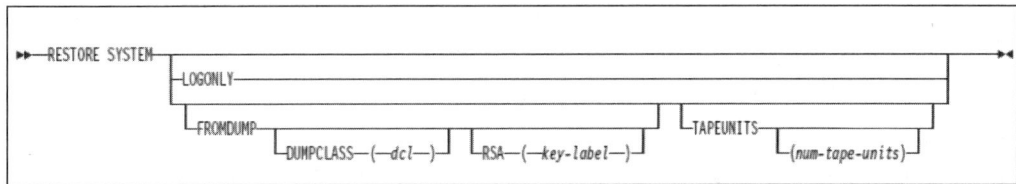

Figure 5.4: RESTORE SYSTEM syntax

Here are a few additional notes about the utility:

- DB2 must be started for **RESTORE SYSTEM** to run.
- **RESTORE SYSTEM** deals only with the database copy pool.
- **RESTORE SYSTEM** never restores logs from the log copy pool. **BACKUP SYSTEM FULL** does create copies of both the data and the logs. (Restore the logs by another method.)
- By default, **RESTORE SYSTEM** recovers the data from the database copy pool during the **RESTORE** phase and applies logs to the point in time at which the existing logs were truncated during the **LOGAPPLY** phase.

Recovery Point

The recovery point, or point in time, to which you decide to recover your system or data depends on what type of system backup is available and which PIT you go back to. It is your responsibility to find the PIT. We will look at the ways to restore a DB2 system to the PIT of a prior system-level backup and also to an arbitrary PIT.

The **BACKUP SYSTEM** utility lets you take system-level backups. The **RECOVER** utility, which requires z/OS 1.8 or later, can use these system-level backups for object-level recoveries. The use of the system-level backup by the **RECOVER** utility is prohibited if any of the following utilities have been run since the system-level backup base was run:

- **REORG TABLESPACE**
- **REORG INDEX**
- **LOAD REPLACE**
- **RECOVER** from image copy or concurrent copy
- **REBUILD INDEX**

Finding the PIT

To find a PIT and the LRSN or RBA that you will use in the conditional restart record, you need to do a few things. You are looking either for the RBA of the last valid log record or for the RBA of the latest checkpoint end.

Mission: You are looking for the **SYSPITR** RBA on the last archive log. The **SYSPITR** is the log truncation point.

RBA of Last Valid Log Record

To find the RBA of last valid log record, issue the **SET LOG SUSPEND** command or the **SET LOG RESUME** command to obtain a log truncation point, which is the point to which you want to recover. This step updates the RBLP in **DBD01**, temporarily freezing all updates in the DB2 subsystem so the logs and database can be copied with FlashCopy. All update activity on the subsystem is halted.

For a non–data-sharing group, you use the RBA value. For a data-sharing group, use the lowest LRSN from the active members.

To find the RBA of the last valid log record, you can use the **DSN1LOGP** stand-alone utility either like this:

```
RBASTART(nnnnnnnnnnn) SUMMARY(ONLY)
```

or like this:

```
RBASTART(nnnnnnnnnnn) SUMMARY(NO) DBID(FFFF)
```

Search the **DSN1LOGP** printout for a phrase similar to the following: "LAST LOG RBA ENCOUNTERED 0000563EF201." This statement contains the RBA of the last valid log record as a SYSPITR. This should represent the latest checkpoint end.

Next, you can look for the RBA of the latest checkpoint; you'll find this in the **BEGIN** *xxxxx* statement. Then, look for the latest checkpoint in **END** *yyyyyyy*.

Run **DSN1LOGP** again, specifying the RBA you just found as the **STARTRBA** value. The resulting output will show you the RBA of the last valid log record.

RBA of Latest Checkpoint End

To determine the RBA of the latest checkpoint end, execute utility **DSNJU004**. The print log map utility will list your BSDSs and the last archive you have. In DB2 9, the output will also include system-level backup information and **BACKUP SYSTEM** utility history. You can run the utility whether DB2 is running or not. To ensure the accuracy of the information, DB2 is usually stopped.

After executing **DSNJU004**, examine the printout to find the checkpoint queue. Next, locate the latest complete checkpoint on the last archive log (this usually is the second one in the queue); then find its **END CHECKPOINT RBA**. You have the SYSPITR.

Recovery Scenarios

Now, let's take a look at a few non–data-sharing recovery procedures.

Restoring to a PIT of a Prior System-Level Backup

When you use the **RESTORE SYSTEM** utility in a non–data-sharing environment, the system must be in system recover pending mode. A DB2 system goes into this mode after using a conditional restart control record.

You must have a **FULL** or **DATA ONLY** backup to restore. You must recover to the exact RBA of the backup used as the PIT in a non-data-sharing environment. The RBA is a six-byte, hexadecimal value.

To restore the system to the point where the backup was taken, use DFSMShsm to perform the restore of the database and the log copy pools. You can then perform normal restart recovery processing to back out in-flight URs:

```
FRRECOV COPYPOOL (cpname) GEN(gen)
```

Restore to a Previous Backup

To restore to a previous backup, you will need to stop the DB2 subsystem and deallocate the ICF catalog that is associated with the data and the log copy pools. Use DFSMS Data Set Services (DFSMSdss) commands to restore the database and log copy pools from the **BACKUP SYSTEM FULL** utility. The **TOKEN** parameter identifies these values:

```
FRRECOV * COPYPOOL(DSN$locn$DB) VERIFY(YES) TOKEN(nnnnnn)
FRRECOV * COPYPOOL(DSN$locn$LG) VERIFY(YES) TOKEN(nnnnnn)
```

You can add volumes to a copy pool. If you do so, the added volumes are automatically included in the next backup versions made. If volumes have been added to the data copy pool since the time of the backup, you will need to delete them because the ICF catalog did not reflect them at the time of the backup.

Now, you can perform a normal restart of the DB2 subsystem. To view the status of any utilities, use the display and terminate commands:

```
-DISPLAY UTIL
-TERM UTIL
```

You should also check to see whether any objects are in a restricted state. To do so, use this display command:

```
-DIS DB(*) SPACE(*) LIMIT(*) RESTRICT
```

Note that this entire procedure does not involve the **RECOVER** utility.

Restoring to an Arbitrary Point in Time

Prior to restoring to an arbitrary PIT, you must have used the **BACKUP SYSTEM DATA ONLY** utility to take a backup of the system.

To perform the restore, first stop the DB2 subsystem and deallocate the ICF catalogs that are associated with the data copy pool. You can add volumes to a copy pool; if you do so, the volumes are automatically included in the next backup versions made. If volumes have been added to the data copy pool since a backup was made, you will need to delete them because the ICF catalog did not reflect them at the time of the backup.

Next, determine the point in time to which you want to recover the system, and find the RBA that corresponds to this PIT. You will specify this information in utility **DSNJU003** for the **CRESTART SYSPITR** parameter, using the log truncation point you find.

Next, start the DB2 subsystem; it will start in recover pending mode. Submit the **RESTORE SYSTEM** job, and when it ends successfully, stop DB2. This resets the system recover pending status. Now, start the DB2 subsystem again.

To see the status of any utilities, use the display and terminate commands:

```
-DISPLAY UTIL
-TERM UTIL
```

You should also check for objects in a restricted state:

```
-DIS DB(*) SPACE(*) LIMIT(*) RESTRICT
```

At this point, you want to start the process of recovering the objects that might be in recovery pending, rebuild pending, or rebuild indexes state. You may need to rebuild objects or recover objects in the logical page list (LPL). Check statuses and conditions on the catalog and directory; if any restricted states exist, you must recover the objects or rebuild the page sets.

DB2 Tracker

One last topic we need to cover in this chapter is the DB2 tracker site. The DB2 tracker site is a separate DB2 subsystem that exists in the event that a disaster occurs at your local site. The tracker site is the "takeover" site — in other words, your disaster recovery site. Its only purpose is to keep shadow copies of the primary site's data. To keep the shadow data up-to-date, the tracker site periodically runs **LOGONLY** recoveries.

The tracker site shadows the work on the local site and, because you would not have to use image copies for recovery, represents a potentially faster method of recovering your site. That means you do not have to recover all the database objects to recover. The tracker site scans and processes the logs in parallel from you, using **RESTORE SYSTEM LOGONLY** for the recovery process.

Recovering from a system-level backup on disk occurs virtually instantaneously. Objects to be recovered from a system-level backup on tape volumes take much longer.

Some restrictions apply at the tracker site. No independent work takes place on this site; its sole purpose is backup. You cannot update the directory or the catalog. You can, however, run the **DIAGNOSE, REBUILD, RECOVER INDEX, RECOVER TABLESPACE, REPORT**, and **RESTORE SYSTEM LOGONLY** utilities. You must keep the objects on the tracker system consistent with the log data, so do not run any DDL or DCL on the system (only **SELECT** from DML).

The tracker system is a production configuration that is a complete second site. It is unavailable for any other use and requires careful planning, testing, and maintenance. However, it enables a simple process for recovery with the **RESTORE SYSTEM LOGONLY** utility.

Practice Questions

Question 1

What resources does the **REPORT** utility use to give you the recovery history of a table space?

○ A. **SYSCOPY, SYSLGRNX, BSDS**

○ B. **SYSTABLESPACE, SYSCOPY, BSDS**

○ C. **SYSTABLE, SYSCOPY, BSDS**

○ D. **SYSUTILX, SYSCOPY, BSDS**

Question 2

What is the first table space in the system that you recover using the **RECOVER** utility?

○ A. **DSNDB01.SYSUTILX**

○ B. **DSNDB01.DBD01**

○ C. **DSNDB01.SYSDBASE**

○ D. **DSNDB06.SYSCOPY**

Question 3

What are the two new phases in the **RECOVER** utility in DB2 9?

○ A. **TOLOGPOINT** and **TORBA**

○ B. **LOGCSR** and **LOGUNDO**

○ C. **COMLOG** and **COMRBA**

○ D. **UNDO** and **REDO**

Question 4

If you lose one of the archive logs during the offload process — for example, due to an out-of-space condition — what will DB2 do? Choose *two* answers:

○ A. Stop processing until the log is restored and then resume

○ B. Record only one copy in the BSDS if offload is successful

○ C. Continue to process without the log

○ D. Does not record in the BSDS

Question 5

Which offline utility do you use to create a conditional restart record?

○ A. **DSNLOG1P**

○ B. **DSNJU003**

○ C. **DSNJU004**

○ D. **DSN1COPY**

Question 6

If you perform a conditional restart of DB2, what type of mode is the system in?

○ A. Ready mode

○ B. System recover pending mode

○ C. system recover mode

○ D. Stopped mode

Question 7

The new advisory pending state of **DBETE**:

○ A. Reduces DBET abends

○ B. Increases start-up time

○ C. Causes the system to restart

○ D. Automatically removes pending states

Question 8

What is the purpose of **DSN1LOGP**?

○ A. Updates the active logs

○ B. Formats and displays the active logs

○ C. Truncates the active logs

○ D. Switches the active logs

Question 9

Which command displays a list of currently running utilities and the **RECOVER LOGAPPLY** phase progress?

○ A. **-DIS UTIL(*)**

○ B. **-DISPLAY DATABASE**

○ C. **-DISPLAY THREAD(*) TYPE(SYSTEM)**

○ D. **-DISPLAY THREAD(*) SERVICE(STORAGE)**

Question 10

How many disk copy pools can you have when using the **BACKUP SYSTEM** utility?

○ A. Four copy pools: two for data, two for logs.

○ B. Two copy pools: one for data, one for logs.

○ C. You can assign as many as you need.

○ D. You are allowed only one for the utility.

CHAPTER 6

Performance and Tuning

System administration requires careful attention to performance monitoring. Your attention to the details of monitoring, using commands, and observing trends in how the system is running is key to keeping DB2 performing at its peak.

In this chapter, we look at the elements and methods involved in tuning DB2 9 for z/OS from a systems perspective and discuss what to do with the information you collect in your monitoring. This background will help prepare you for Section 5 of the DB2 9 System Administrator for z/OS certification exam (Performance and Tuning). This part of the exam makes up 21.5 percent of the overall test.

Key Elements in Tuning

You can improve the response time and throughput of DB2 applications and queries by reducing I/O, shortening overall elapsed I/O time, and cutting processor consumption. To reduce I/O, for example, you manage **RUNSTATS** statistics, which are used to determine access paths for SQL, and you make sure your buffer pools are large enough to handle system workloads.

Managing these and other system resources requires the use of proper monitoring techniques, which in DB2 means using traces. Keep in mind that running traces causes system overhead. For this reason, you need to decide which traces to run (and why) and how long to run them. In addition, you must decide how to keep the resulting data and how to report it to management and staff.

Companies use baselines or service level agreements (SLAs) to establish acceptable system operating parameters. For example, an SLA might include a policy that requires 99.99 percent system availability by month or one that dictates no more than a three-second delay for SQL responses. Once determined and put into place, such policies serve as your guidelines for judging acceptable system performance.

Tracing DB2

Trace enhancements in DB2 9 for z/OS include new filter types in the **START TRACE**, **STOP TRACE**, and **DISPLAY TRACE** commands. Types for user ID, application name, workstation name, package, location, collection ID, connection ID, correlation ID, and role are now available. You can also exclude and include trace records by filter type.

Trace Destinations

You can write trace information to any of six destinations, specified by the **DEST** parameter of the trace command. Table 6.1 lists the possible **DEST** values and their meanings.

Table 6.1: Trace destinations	
DEST value	Description
GTF	The z/OS Generalized Trace Facility (GTF); part of z/OS used to store volumes of trace data
RES	The default destination for the global trace records in DB2; a wraparound table that resides in memory
SMF	The System Management Facility (SMF); the most common destination for traces in DB2
SRV	Used by IBM support personnel for service
OP*n*	One of up to eight output buffer areas used by the Instrumentation Facility Interface (IFI)
OPX	A generic output buffer that uses the first free OP*n* slot

Types of Traces

In DB2, a *trace class* captures information about certain types of subsystem events that are identified by IFCIDs. The data set *yourprefix*.**SDSNMACS** that is shipped with DB2 contains the IFCID descriptions.

DB2 traces can record six types of data:

- Accounting data
- Audit data
- Global data
- Monitor data
- Performance data
- Statistics data

Accounting Trace

Accounting traces collect application program information and are key to determining a task's activity and whether you are experiencing a DB2 performance problem. An accounting trace produces information about:

- Processor resources consumed
- The number of times certain SQL statements are issued
- Thread wait times for various events, including thread termination
- Start and stop times
- Number of commits and aborts
- Number of buffer pool requests
- Resource limit facility statistics
- RID pool processing
- Distributed processing
- Counts of certain locking events

The collection of accounting data starts when a thread connects to DB2. An accounting record is written when a thread terminates, when authorization changes (i.e., upon thread reuse), when a commit occurs in a program, when a database access thread (DBAT) becomes inactive, or when a parallel task is completed.

Of the 10 groups of accounting trace classes, those listed in Table 6.2 are the ones most commonly used. The table also indicates the estimated overhead imposed by each of these trace classes.

Table 6.2: Accounting trace classes		
Class	**Description**	**Estimated trace overhead**
1	Elapsed time	3–5%
2	Time spent in DB2	20% for fetch-intensive applications; 5–10% otherwise
3	Elapsed wait time	1–5%
7	CPU time for packages	<5%
8	Suspension times per package or database request module (DBRM)	<5%

Accounting trace classes 1 and 7 must be active to accumulate information about packages and database request modules (DBRMs). Class 8, when combined with class 1, collects information about how long an agent was suspended for each executed package.

For minimal package accounting, you would use classes 7 and 8. If you need more detail — about SQL, for example — use classes 7, 8, and 10. Be aware, though, that the latter combination increases CPU cost and the number of accounting trace records written to SMF.

Accounting class 3 monitors elapsed wait time. This data includes I/O wait time (both synchronous and asynchronous), latch time, and lock wait time — information that plays a key part in watching for locking problems. For a more detailed look at wait time, you can use the deadlock or timeout traces from statistics trace class 3 and the lock suspension report produced by the performance trace.

Accounting class 2, together with accounting classes 1 and 3, provides additional detail related directly to the accounting record IFCID 0003. You must have class 1 (elapsed time of the accounting interval or application time) activated for DB2 to externalize the collected information. Class 2 (time spent in DB2) also records the thread level entry into and exit from DB2, letting you separate DB2 times from application times. This is an important point to remember because you want to separate the DB2 time spent from the application time spent. Running accounting class 2 adds to the processing cost, but it does report DB2 time. Looking at the report from, say, DB2 Performance Expert (PE) or Performance Monitor (PM), you would see application class 1 statistics and DB2 class 2 statistics.

The calculated difference between the class 1 and class 2 elapsed time is the amount of time spent outside DB2, but it is within the accounting interval. More specifically, if you have only class 2 and class 3 times, you can calculate the not-accounted time as follows:

Not-accounted time = Class 2 elapsed time – Class 2 CPU time – Total Class 3 time

Keep in mind that this application could be one that reuses threads, which would increase the class 1 elapsed time.

Accounting class 8 is useful in situations where an application is running longer than normal, possibly as a result of some type of wait. Using accounting class 8 can help detect this change in performance. This trace gives you the number of asynchronous and synchronous read I/Os for individual packages.

The overhead from running the accounting traces depends on how much and what type of SQL an application issues. An online transaction incurs an additional 2.5 percent of overhead when running with accounting class 2; a typical batch query application incurs about 10 percent overhead when running with accounting class 2. If most of your work occurs through CICS, the class 1 and class 2 times will be very close, so you might not run with class 2.

Audit Trace

The 10 trace classes listed in Table 6.3 support audit tracing.

Table 6.3: Audit trace classes	
Class	**Description**
1	Default; access attempts that were denied
2	Explicit **GRANT/REVOKE**
3	**CREATE/DROP/ALTER** against an audited table
4	Only changes to audited tables
5	Reads to tables identified with **AUDIT ALL**

Table 6.3: Audit trace classes (continued)	
Class	Description
6	**BIND** of dynamic or static SQL statements
7	Change or assignment of authorization ID
8	Utility job start or end
9	Records written to IFCID 0146
10	**ALTER/CREATE TRUSTED CONTEXT** statements

You can run audit trace for a particular authorization ID or specific ID, object ownership, the start of a utility job, execution of **CREATE/ALTER TRUSTED CONTEXT** statements, table changes, **CREATE/ALTER/DROP** operations against a table, and more. You should evaluate these traces carefully before deciding which to use in implementing security policies for your installation.

You can generate audit reports by starting the audit trace for all classes. Doing so provides information about unsuccessful access attempts, **GRANT**s to critical information, and use of sensitive data.

The performance impact of auditing depends directly on the amount of audit data produced. Typical audit trace overhead is less than 5 percent. In general, an audit trace for a started transaction with all audit trace classes turned on imposes an overhead of 5 percent to 10 percent.

Monitor Trace

The monitor trace class records data for online monitoring with user-written programs. It provides 10 groups of trace classes.

In general, monitor tracing adds about 2 percent to 5 percent overhead on the system. The recommendations are to always run class 1 (elapsed time) and to run classes 2 (time spent in DB2) and 3 (elapsed wait time) by starting and stopping tracing as needed.

Monitor trace classes 2 through 8 let you collect information about DB2 resource usage. Using class 5, for example, you can find out how much time the system is spending processing Instrumentation Facility Interface (IFI) requests. Monitor trace classes 2, 3, and 5 are identical to accounting trace classes 2, 3, and 5.

Performance Trace

The performance traces consist of 20 groups of trace classes. System overhead can be high with these traces. For example, performance classes 1 and 2 can impose a 20 to 30 percent overhead. Class 3 can impose up to 100 percent or more!

The combined overhead of all performance classes runs from about 20 percent to 100 percent. The overhead for performance trace classes 1 through 3 typically ranges from 5 percent to 30 percent.

In performance class 8, IFCID 125 provides details about list prefetch for indexes used in prefetching. This information can be useful in determining the method of access that is taking place for an SQL statement.

You should turn on only those performance trace classes that are required to address a specific performance problem. Try to qualify the trace as much as possible to limit the gathered data to just the data you need. For example, qualify the trace by the plan name and IFCID. Other suggestions are to suppress other trace options (e.g., TSO or CICS) to reduce overhead.

Statistics Trace

The good news about statistics tracing is that the records are written only at the statistics time interval specified (in minutes) in the **STATIME** subsystem parameter, so overhead is negligible. The bad news is that statistics tracing is performed system-wide, so you cannot use this type of tracing for a purpose such as charge-back accounting. You can, however, use the statistics trace in capacity planning for DB2 storage use.

DB2 supports 10 groups of statistics traces. Statistics trace classes 1, 3, 4, 5, and 6 (Table 6.4) are the default classes for the statistics traces.

Table 6.4: Default statistics trace classes	
Class	**Description**
1	System services and database statistics; shows system parameters that were in effect when the trace was started
3	Deadlocks and timeouts information (if you are experiencing a lot of deadlocks, this is the trace type to use to analyze the problem)
4	Exceptional conditions
5	Data-sharing information
6	Storage statistics for the **DBM1** address space

Specifying **YES** for the **SMF STATISTICS** field on installation panel **DSNTIPN** causes statistics tracing to start automatically when DB2 is started. The statistics data is recorded in SMF type 100 and 102 record types.

To start data collection for the default classes, you use the following command:

```
-START TRACE(STAT) CLASS(1,3,4,5,6)
```

If you are monitoring a problem, set the value of the **STATIME** subsystem parameter to **1** (minute) to allow meaningful statistics collection; otherwise, the DB2 9 default setting of **5** is acceptable.

You should also consider increasing the Internal Resource Lock Manager (IRLM) **TIMEOUT** value if the statistics report shows a high occurrence of timeouts. You can use the **MODIFY** *irlmproc*,**SET** command to increase this value. The information gathered with the statistics trace can be used to tune a set of DB2 programs or to help in capacity planning.

Global Trace

Global tracing aids in diagnosing problems in DB2. It is wise to leave the **TRACE AUTO START** field on panel **DSNTIPN** set to its default value of **NO**, which prevents the global trace from starting automatically when DB2 is started. If you need to use this trace for service, you can run the **START TRACE** command.

Overall Trace Recommendations

Run the traces for accounting classes 1, 2, and 3 (optional 7, 8) and statistics classes 1, 3, 4, and 5 (6 if data sharing) in your DB2 system in your normal day-to-day environment.

Traces That Start Automatically

Several types of traces can be set to run automatically when DB2 is started. Figure 6.1 shows the portion of installation panel **DSNTIPN** where you specify this option. In DB2 9, the default for the **STATISTICS TIME** field (item 6) has changed from 30 minutes to 5 minutes. Check your DSNZPARMs when you migrate to see what this value is by looking at value **STATIME**.

```
DSNTIPN        INSTALL DB2 - TRACING PARAMETERS

===>  _
Enter data below:

  1  AUDIT TRACE        ===> NO      > Audit classes to start. NO,YES,list
  2  TRACE AUTO START   ===> NO      > Global classes to start. YES,NO,list
  3  TRACE SIZE         ===> 64K       Trace table size in bytes. 4K-396K
  4  SMF ACCOUNTING     ===> 1       > Accounting classes to start. NO,YES,list
  5  SMF STATISTICS     ===> YES     > Statistics classes to start. NO,YES,list
  6  STATISTICS TIME    ===> 5         Time interval in minutes. 1-1440
  7  STATISTICS SYNC    ===> NO        Synchronization within the hour. NO,0-59
  8  DATASET STATS TIME ===> 5         Time interval in minutes. 1-1440
  9  MONITOR TRACE      ===> NO      > Monitor classes to start. NO,YES,list
 10  MONITOR SIZE       ===> 256K      Default monitor buffer size. 256K-16M
 11  UNICODE IFCIDS     ===> NO        Include UNICODE data when writing IFCIDS
 12  DDF/RRSAF ACCUM    ===> 10        Rollup accting for DDF/RRSAF. NO, 2-64K
 13  AGGREGATION FIELDS ===> 0         Rollup accting aggregation fields

PRESS:    ENTER to continue   RETURN to exit   HELP for more information
```

Figure 6.1: Installation panel DSNTIPN – Tracing parameters

The panel lists trace parameters associated with accounting, audit, global, and monitor traces and DB2 system checkpoint frequency. Your basic tracing can be set on automatically in DB2 using DSNZPARMs.

At installation time, you:

1. Request that DB2 pass accounting, audit, and statistics data to SMF

2. Update member **SMFPRM***xx* in **SYS1.PARMLIB** to specify the **ACTIVE** parameter

3. Specify the proper **TYPE** subparameter of **SYS** and **SUBSYS**

At DB2 execution, you can then use the SMF **SET** command to change the SMF parameter values.

IFCIDs

You can choose which subsystem events you want to collect data about, or "trace." You define the limits of your tracing in DB2 using IFCIDs, which identify all DB2 trace records.

Member **DSNWMSGS** in library **SDSNIVPD** contains the IFCIDs and trace field definitions. This member also includes DDL and load card statements you can use to build tables with the IFCID definition information. Once these tables are built, you can run SQL to retrieve descriptions. Keep in mind that because IFCIDs can be changed or added during DB2 maintenance, a refresh might be in order.

DB2 9 for z/OS includes three new IFCIDs:

- IFCID 0239 (audit trace class 10) records information about the establishment and reuse of a trusted connection.

- IFCID 0343 (performance trace class 3 and statistics trace class 4) records agent information when system parameter **MAXTEMPS**, which specifies the maximum amount of work file storage an agent can use, is exceeded.

- IFCID 0346 records package detail.

DB2 9 also includes changes to several IFCIDs, some of which involve support of clone tables. For details about the changes for clone support, see *DB2 Version 9.1 for z/OS What's New?* (GC18-9856).

You use the **TRACE SIZE** field (item 3) on installation panel **DSNTIPN** to specify the size, in bytes, of the default destination for the global trace records in DB2 (the **RES** trace table). The default size is 64 KB. Subsystem parameter **TRACTBL** in macro **DSN6SYSP** specifies the same information.

Most trace records require 32-byte entries. Events with more than three data items require 64-byte entries. You can use the abbreviation **K** for multiples of 1,024 bytes; the value you specify is rounded up to a multiple of 4.

You can collect statistics about dynamic SQL in the dynamic statement cache by activating IFCID 0318. Collecting these statistics increases the processing cost of the statements, so if you do not need to monitor this cache, you should turn off the trace for IFCID 0318.

Recording SMF Trace Data

Before you can send data to SMF, the facility must be running. To make SMF operational, you must update member **SMFPRM***xx* to indicate which types of SMF records it will accept and whether SMF is active. You may have to ask the z/OS system programmer to help you with this task.

The z/OS operator command **SETSMF** lets you alter SMF parameters that were previously specified in member **SMFPRM***xx* in **SYS1.PARMLIB**. For example, you could use the command

```
SETSMF SYS(TYPE(100:102))
```

to record statistics (record type 100), accounting (record type 101), and performance (record type 102) data to SMF.

The SMF trace records produced by DB2 need to be processed. To accomplish this step, you can develop your own application, use the SMF program **IFASMFDP** to dump the records to a sequential data set, or use a monitor (e.g., OMEGAMON).

Collecting DB2 performance trace data can generate a lot of data. If you are going to send the data to SMF, you should make sure the SMF buffer settings are adequate. If the facility encounters a buffer shortage, it rejects the trace records. You will see messages DSNW133I and DSNW123I should this situation occur. To determine whether trace data has been lost, examine the DB2 statistics records with an IFCID of 0001 (mapped by macro **DSNDQWST**). These records will show whether any data has been lost and why.

You can send report trace records to SMF in several ways:

- Use Tivoli Decision Support for z/OS to collect the data
- Write an application program to read and report information from the SMF data set
- Use OMEGAMON

OMEGAMON

IBM OMEGAMON XE for DB2 Performance Expert on z/OS (called DB2 Performance Expert for z/OS in previous releases) is a tool that conducts performance monitoring, reporting, and buffer pool analysis and provides a performance warehouse.

OMEGAMON also includes an online monitor that gives you a snapshot view of your currently running DB2 subsystem. Both a host- and a workstation-based monitor are provided.

The Workstation Online Monitor improves usability substantially and simplifies online monitoring and problem analysis. For example, you can examine the access paths and processing methods chosen by DB2 for the currently executing SQL statement. The SQL might be performing poorly, causing performance problems in DB2. Using **EXPLAIN** and the IBM Optimization Service Center for DB2 for z/OS, you can analyze the query to determine tuning recommendations.

Other software vendors offer performance tools. Examples include BMC Software's MainView product and CA's Insight Performance Monitor.

Trace Commands

You can issue trace commands from a DSN session, a z/OS console, a DB2 DB2I panel, IMS, a CICS terminal, or a program that uses IFI. When using tracing, you should have a reason for obtaining trace information — that is, a specific need associated with the type of trace and class you are running. If you run a performance trace, do so using the classes, IFCIDs, plans, and authorization IDs you want to trace. This approach will help minimize the trace's impact on DB2 performance.

All commands, including the trace commands, require the appropriate security to execute. For each command's full syntax and security requirements, consult the *IBM DB2 for z/OS Command Reference* (SC18-9844).

Let's take a closer look at some of the trace commands available in DB2.

START TRACE

You use the DB2 **START TRACE** command to start a DB2 trace. The only way a performance trace can be started is by using this command.

Figure 6.2 shows the syntax diagram for the **START TRACE** command.

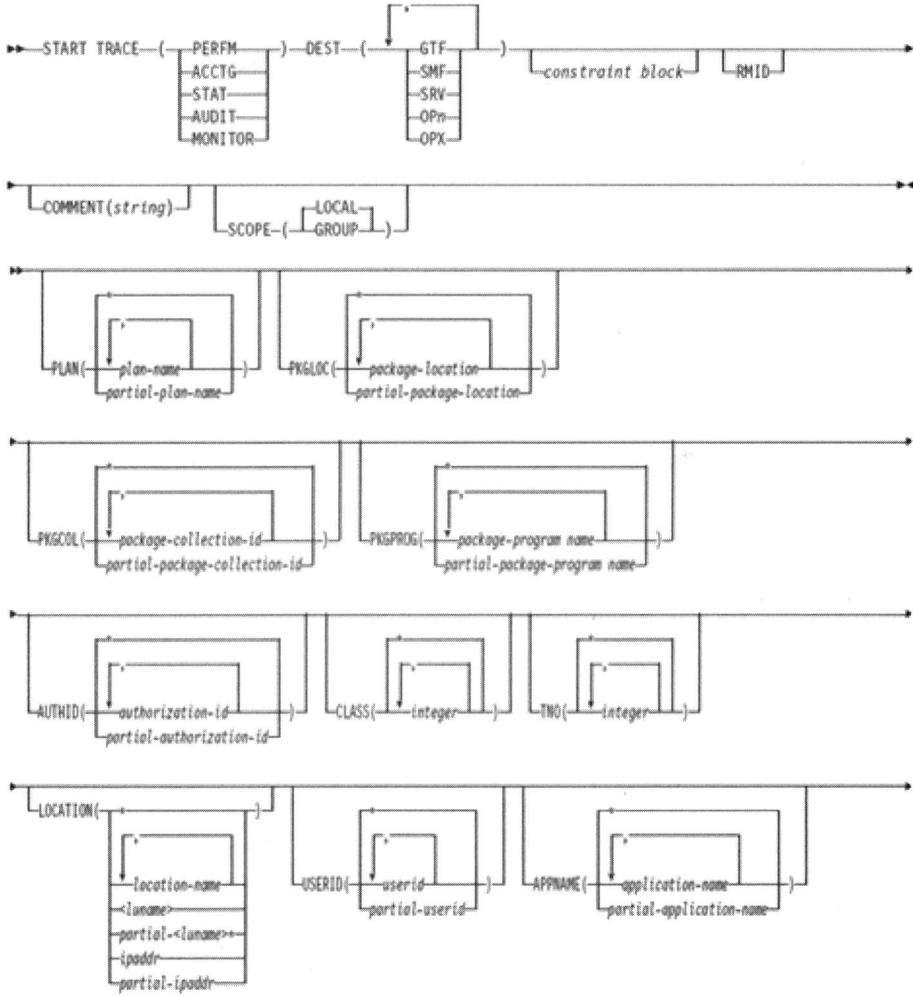

Figure 6.2: START TRACE syntax

DISPLAY TRACE

The DB2 **DISPLAY TRACE** command displays information about invoked traces, including the options that were selected and are in effect. You can use this command to find out which monitors are active and which events are being traced. Several other forms of the **DISPLAY** command are also useful:

```
-DISPLAY THREAD
-DISPLAY DATABASE
-DISPLAY DDF DETAIL
-DISPLAY LOCATION
```

You can use parameters with the **DISPLAY TRACE** command to specify which traces to display. Each option you specify, except the option **TNO** (trace number), limits the effect of the command to active traces that were started using the same option, either explicitly or by default, with exactly the same parameter values.

When you use **TNO**, you do not need to specify any other keywords or parameters. For example, the command

```
-DISPLAY TRACE TNO(7)
```

displays the seventh trace you invoked. Specifying the trace number provides a level of detail that is enough for DB2 to stop or display trace activity.

MODIFY TRACE

The **MODIFY TRACE** command changes the trace events (IFCIDs) being traced for any active trace. The command actually stops the existing trace and then starts the specified trace.

For example, the following command modifies trace number 1 to collect only data from IFCIDs 106 and 131 (utility trace data and system parameters in effect at trace invocation). Any other data that was being collected is stopped.

```
-MODIFY TRACE(GLOBAL) CLASS(3) IFCID(106,131) TNO(1)
   COMMENT('SYS PARMS AND UTILITY TRACE')
```

The command makes the specified changes to the trace events, stops the previous trace, and writes statistics records. If several traces are active, be sure you specify enough qualifying information to isolate the trace you want to change.

STOP TRACE

To terminate trace activity, you use the **STOP TRACE** command. When stopping a trace, you might not need to specify all the keywords you used when starting the trace (because you may have multiple traces running at the same time). The idea is to provide just enough detail to stop the particular trace you want to stop. However, the following command is invalid:

```
-STOP TRACE
```

To stop all active traces, you must issue this command:

```
-STOP TRACE (*)
```

To stop a particular trace (whether it was started explicitly or by default), the **STOP TRACE** command should specify the same parameter values with which the trace was started:

```
-STOP TRACE (AUDIT) CLASS (1) DEST (GTF)
```

If you are not sure which traces you started, use the **DISPLAY TRACE** command first to find out what has been started. This command displays the trace number, type, class, destination, and qualifier. With this information, you can determine exactly which trace you want to stop. You can then stop the desired trace (or traces) using the **STOP TRACE** command's **TNO** (trace number) parameter and restart with a different class or classes.

New Filter Types

DB2 9 for z/OS adds new filter types in the constraint block of the **DISPLAY TRACE**, **START TRACE**, and **STOP TRACE** commands:

- **APPNAME** (application name)
- **CONNID** (connection ID)
- **CORRID** (correlation ID)
- **PKGCOL** (collection ID)
- **PKGLOC** (location)
- **PKGPROG** (package)
- **ROLE** (role)
- **USERID** (user ID)
- **WKRSTN** (workstation name)

In addition to the new filter types, you can exclude trace records by filter type. Here are the exclusion keywords, which all start with the letter "X".

- **XAPPNAME**
- **XCONNID**
- **XCORRID**
- **XPKGCOL**
- **XPKGLOC**
- **XPKGPROG**
- **XROLE**
- **XUSERID**
- **XWRKSTN**

You can also perform exclude filtering by authorization ID (**XAUTHID**), location (**XLOC**), and plan name (**XPLAN**).

By specifying any of the filtering keywords, you can include or exclude trace records to tailor the command results to your needs. For example, the following statement excludes trace records for the plans named D, E, and F:

```
-START TRACE(ACCTG) XPLAN(D,E,F)
```

Performance and the EDM Pool

A previous chapter discussed the environmental descriptor manager (EDM) pool storage and changes that were implemented in DB2 9. Here, we look at some of the performance and tuning aspects of the EDM pool.

First, in the DB2 world, it is imperative that you have some type of monitoring tool. Handling the amount of data collected and ensuring timely reporting makes this requirement necessary. Many monitoring products are available, each with their own style and methods. You will have to evaluate the choices to determine which one is right for you.

New Applications and Storage Concerns

When you bind a new set of packages for a new application you are implementing, you should be concerned with the size specified for the **EDMPOOL** and **EDM_SKELETON_POOL** subsystem parameters. You want to effectively use the storage but not over-allocate it. Without a methodology, this setting becomes an interesting "guesstimate" of how much space is enough.

The storage in the EDM pool that is "in use" is stealable, and the percentage of free pages should be low; 10 percent to 20 percent is about right. What you need to know is how much space the new application will use in the EDM pool so that you can assess the amount of space required for database descriptors (DBDs), package tables (PTs), and skeleton package tables (SKPTs).

If you are working with a "test" environment, you should be able to assess (through SQL from the catalog or administration tools) the current size of the packages in the application and the average segments in the plan associated with it. The problem is that you do not know how often these segments will be used or loaded into the EDM pool and how many users might be working with them at one time, so you are still making your best guesstimate.

The installation estimates recommend making the EDM pool 10 times larger than the largest DBD or plan. The CLIST generates the value for this pool.

The calculation used to determine total EDM pool storage space for plans, packages, dynamic statements, and DBDs relies on the following values:

- The number of concurrently executing plans (*CPLANS*)
- The maximum number of plans in the pool at one time, or one quarter of the total number of plans (*MPLANS*)
- The average plan size (*APLAN*)
- The number of concurrent databases (from installation panel **DSNTIPE**) (*CDB*)
- The DBD size (*SDBD*)

Here is the equation:

EDM pool storage space =
  ((CPLANS + MPLANS) + 50 KB for overhead * APLAN + (CDB * SDBD)

Accepting the default values suggested by the installation yields the following result:

((200 + 200) + 50 KB overhead) * 25 + (100 * 223) = 33,550 KB

The CLIST then adds another 50 KB for overhead, arriving at 33,600 KB as the default value.

Note that the EDM pool size must be four times larger than the maximum DBD size. In addition, the size of the DBRM has an impact on the EDM pool, as does the value of the **RELEASE** parameter, which determines when packages are released from the EDM pool. **RELEASE(DEALLOCATE)** causes packages to be held longer, thereby consuming storage.

Region Size in DB2

The region size calculation in DB2 has changed in DB2 9 for z/OS. For the **DBM1** storage requirements, the sort pool, buffer pool, and RID pool values are no longer supported in the region size calculation.

In addition, part of the EDM pool has moved above the 2 GB bar. Therefore, the sum of the sizes of the EDM pool, VSAM data set control blocks, and working storage plus a fixed code size determines the amount of main storage.

Most of the virtual storage for DB2 is in extended private storage. This includes the buffer pool, most of the code, the EDM pool, and a significant amount of working storage.

Below-the-Bar EDM Pool

In DB2 9, you size the EDM pool for peak usage and add a cushion for any fragmentation you might encounter. It is thus possible to encounter a situation where a message indicating that the EDM pool full condition exists. If you experience this problem, use IFCID 31 to trace the EDM pool full condition. There is no way to dynamically change the size of the EDM pool, but you can modify it using a DSNZPARM.

In both below-the-bar and above-the-bar storage in DB2 9, you have 30 variable-length storage pools that handle the dynamic SQL statement storage. Therefore, the SQL storage is split between above the bar and below the bar. No separate IFCID exists for the 30 above-the-bar cache pools. The parameter **MAXKEEPD** limits the number of SQL statements to hold in the cache.

This is one of the biggest storage issues in below-the-bar storage in the EDM pool. Monitoring with IFCID 225 provides the pool summary statistics, which are produced at the interval set in subsystem parameter **STATIME**. This information gives you the peak number of statements usage, which will help you understand what is driving your storage use below the bar.

Also available is also a below-the-bar cache management DSNZPARM, **CACHEDYN_FREELOCAL**. This parameter indicates when to "free" the SQL cache below the bar. As you work with this parameter, you will find the level that is right for you to "trigger" the freeing of SQL cache storage below the bar.

Measuring the Efficiency of the EDM Pool

For dynamic SQL to be cached, you must have caching turned on to acquire the statistics for your SQL statements. If you turn on caching for dynamic SQL, the

EDM storage statistics provide information that can help you determine how successful your applications are at finding statements still held in the cache. DB2 8 for z/OS made extensive changes to the EDM pool statistics. The mapping macro **DSNDQISE** in **SDSNMACS** provides descriptions of the fields for the EDM pool statistics from the **DBM1** address space.

Through your tracing, statistics are recorded in monitors that let you calculate the efficiency of the EDM pool. Monitors such as OMEGAMON usually gather information to establish the ratios from these statistic records that are being measured to evaluate the efficiency of the EDM pool, EDM statement cache, and DBD cache.

In general, statistics in the form of a statistics report from a monitor or from your own application give you the CT, PT, DBD, and statement hit ratios. Your ratios from these statistics depend on the workload. A value of 80 percent is generally acceptable for a hit ratio; this number means that 80 percent of the work was done without I/O.

Along this same line, then, you should see statistics showing the number of free pages in the EDM pool at a ratio of about 20 percent. If this number is greater during peak periods, you can probably reduce the number of pages allotted for the pools. Mapping macro **DSNDQISE** provides the instrumentation data for mapping the EDM pool statistics.

Skeleton Tables and Locks

From earlier discussions, you know that the **SCT02** table space resides in the DB2 directory and that the skeleton cursor tables (SKCTs) that are the SQL package statement structures from your application plans are also housed here. The SKPT is stored in **SPT01** for your plans as well.

BIND, FREE, and **REBIND** operations use exclusive locks for the SKPT and SKCT structures when these tables are being changed. Locking is also in effect when you change the authorization level or drop associated objects upon which packages and plans depend. This locking impacts processing, so the programs cannot be executing during this time. You can avoid locks on static SQL statements by caching the statements in the EDM pool.

Database Descriptors and Locks

A DBD is located in the **DBD01** directory table and represents the database and its objects. In general, when you execute utilities or dynamic SQL statements, the DBD is in a shared locking mode. When you update objects, the associated DBD is also updated, which requires an exclusive lock. Therefore, your utilities and dynamic SQL will be suspended.

Automated Memory Monitoring

Messages that begin with "DSNV" identify and communicate information about the agent services manager. At DB2 start-up, the agent services establish the tasking structure for the control and resource manager address spaces. An internal DB2 memory monitor task measures below-the-bar storage thresholds. A part of this built-in monitor checks at one-minute intervals for critical threshold-level storage increases based on thresholds of 88 percent, 92 percent, 96 percent, or 98 percent of used available storage below the bar. Messages DSNV508I, DSNV510I, and DSNV512I are issued to alert you to the current storage consumption and tell you which agents are using the most storage.

Virtual Buffer Pools

Located in the data management subsystem, buffer pools have moved above the 2 GB bar. You define buffer pools through the installation/migration panels or using the **ALTER BUFFERPOOL** DB2 command.

With virtual storage addressability, a single DB2 address space can use up to 16 exabytes of storage. Real storage available on your particular mainframe will have hardware limits; for example, the z990 mainframe can support only up to 256 GB of memory. In DB2 9, you have 4 KB, 8 KB, 16 KB, and 32 KB buffer pools that you can assign.

The 4 KB buffer pools are named **BP0-BP49**. Buffer pool **BP0** serves the catalog and directory; nothing else should use this buffer pool. Buffer pool **BP7** is generally dedicated to sort work; the **DSNDB07** database is used for DB2 sorting.

The 8 KB buffer pools are named **BP8K0-BP8K9**. The 16 KB buffer pools are **BP16K0-BP16K9**. The 32 KB buffer pools are **BP32K** and **BP32K1-BP32K9**.

As you know, you will need real storage to back buffer pools; otherwise, paging I/Os will affect performance. If you see the buffer pool being paged to auxiliary storage, decrease the size of the buffer pool to reduce this paging.

The database virtual buffer pools can have any or all three of the following types of pages at any given instant:

- In-use pages: Pages currently being updated or read that contain data available for use by applications.

- Updated pages: Pages whose data has been changed but that have not yet been written out to disk.

- Available pages: Pages considered for new use that can be overwritten by an incoming page of new data. In-use pages and updated pages are unavailable because they are not considered for new use.

Figure 6.3 shows how DB2 manages the data pages in a buffer pool. In subsequent sections of this chapter, we will discuss the management of the buffer pools and the settings of the variable and static thresholds that make up the detail in this diagram.

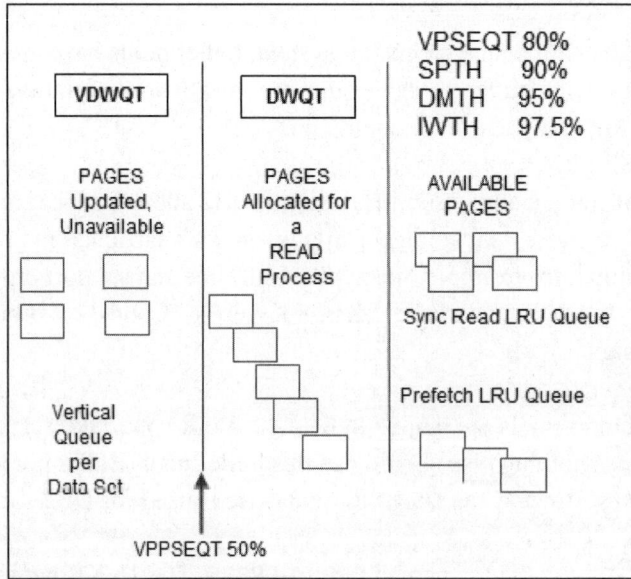

Figure 6.3: Buffer pools and pages

Read Methods

DB2 uses three read methods: normal read, sequential prefetch, and list sequential prefetch. Each method has different least-recently-used queues for available pages, so sequential prefetching of pages does not monopolize the pool.

DB2 uses a normal read when retrieving just one page or a few consecutive pages. The unit of transfer for a normal read is one page, and the read is executed under the user task control block (TCB).

To read sequential data, DB2 uses a process called *dynamic prefetch*, which includes the read methods of sequential prefetch and list sequential prefetch. Prefetching is controlled by the buffer pool size (**VPSIZE**), the type of prefetch, and the number of buffers.

Physical I/O is one component of elapsed time. You can check the wait time for prefetch I/O using IBM's SQL Performance Analyzer or another monitoring tool.

Sequential Prefetch

The object of sequential prefetching is to bring a sequential set of pages into the buffer pool so that these acquired pages are in memory before they are needed. Sequential prefetch reads several pages with a single I/O operation. This method allows central processor (CP) and I/O operations to be overlapped. The prefetching is performed concurrently with other operations of the originating application program.

Sequential prefetch can be used to read data pages, by table space scans or index scans with clustered data reference. It can also be used to read index pages in an index scan. The index-clustering ratio must be higher than 80 percent for sequential prefetching to be turned on. The **PLAN_TABLE** column of DB2 **EXPLAIN** indicates whether sequential prefetch is in effect (**PREFETCH=S**).

As Table 6.5 indicates, the number of buffers and the buffer pool size dictate how many pages DB2 actually reads for each asynchronous I/O. For example, for a 4 KB buffer pool with more than 1,000 buffer pages, the pages read by prefetch would be 32 pages. The **LOAD**, **RECOVER**, **REORG** utilities can use twice as many pages on a sequential prefetch.

Table 6.5: Sequential prefetching chart		
Page size	**Buffer size**	**Prefetch**
4 KB	<=223 buffers 224–999 buffers 1000+ buffers	8 pages 16 pages 32 pages
8 KB	<=112 buffers 113–499 buffers 500+ buffers	4 pages 8 pages 16 pages
16 KB	<=56 buffers 57–249 buffers 250+ buffers	2 pages 4 pages 8 pages
32 KB	<=16 buffers 17–99 buffers 100+ buffers	0 pages 2 pages 4 pages

Using the **DISPLAY BUFFERPOOL** command with the **DETAIL** option, you can see the number of times sequential prefetch was requested.

List Sequential Prefetch

List sequential prefetch, or simply list prefetch, is the reading of data pages that are not contiguous, by table space scan or index scans through non-clustered indexes. List prefetch can be used with either single or multiple index access.

List prefetch reads a set of data pages determined by a list of RIDs taken from one or more indexes. The RIDs are sorted (except for a hybrid join where **SORTN_JOIN** is **N**, which would mean that the page numbers might not need sorting before the data pages are accessed).

In a single list prefetch, the maximum number of pages DB2 prefetches is 32. If it is a utility that is running, the maximum is 64 pages. Incremental image copies also use list prefetch.

Column **PREFETCH=L** in the **PLAN_TABLE** from **EXPLAIN** indicates a list sequential prefetch.

WRITE Operations

Write operations in DB2 usually occur asynchronously with the user request. Write operations for updated pages are queued until:

- A checkpoint is taken

- The percentage of updated pages reaches the vertical deferred write threshold

- The unavailable pages exceed the deferred write threshold limit

DB2 writes in a single I/O operation. Up to thirty-two 4 KB pages or four 32 KB pages can be written in a single I/O operation.

Buffer Pool Thresholds

DB2's use of a buffer pool is governed by preset values called *thresholds*. Each threshold is a level of use that, if exceeded, causes DB2 to take some action. Some DB2 buffer pool thresholds might indicate a buffer pool shortage problem, while others may just report normal buffer management.

Fixed Thresholds

DB2 *fixed thresholds* are expressed as a percentage of the buffer pool that unavailable pages might occupy. You cannot change the percentages assigned to the fixed thresholds. Reaching these thresholds can affect I/O and processor consumption.

There are three fixed thresholds in DB2:

- Immediate write threshold (**IWTH**): 97.5 percent (danger zone)

- Data management threshold (**DMTH**): 95 percent (avoid reaching this level)

- Sequential prefetch threshold (**SPTH**): 90 percent (bad, but not as bad as the previous two)

Because the fixed thresholds are critical for performance (even more so than the variable thresholds, discussed below), you should monitor your buffer pool usage to see when and how often your system is reaching these thresholds. Set your buffer pool sizes large enough to avoid reaching the fixed thresholds, except occasionally.

Note that increasing the size of a buffer pool with the **ALTER BUFFERPOOL** command can affect other buffer pools, depending on the total amount of real storage available for your buffers. IFCID 2 collects the statistics values associated with buffer pools.

Immediate Write Threshold: 97.5%

Reaching the immediate write fixed threshold has a significant effect on processor usage and I/O resource consumption. DB2 checks this threshold whenever a page is to be updated. If the threshold is reached, the writes are performed synchronously; once they are completed, the application can proceed. While a write operation takes place, it is one write for one update. Therefore, even if you have multiple rows on a page, the updates are done individually and are written individually.

Data Management Threshold: 95%

DB2 checks the data management threshold before reading or updating a page. If you are constantly reaching the data management threshold, you need to figure out which objects are monopolizing the buffer pool. It is best to avoid this threshold because when it is reached, DB2 reads the page for every retrieved or updated row. As you can imagine, this process affects CPU usage significantly.

All **GETPAGE** and **RELEASE** operations on pages occur at the row level.

Sequential Prefetch Threshold (SPTH): 90%

When DB2 is performing sequential prefetching, I/O and CP processing can overlap each other. The ability to request prefetching is a result of a **BIND** and can be seen in your **PLAN_TABLE**.

When the sequential prefetch threshold is reached, no sequential prefetching occurs until more buffer pool pages become available. As a result, large table scans are affected adversely.

DB2 checks this fixed threshold before scheduling a prefetch operation and during buffer pool allocation for a prefetch operation that has already been scheduled. If the threshold has been exceeded, the prefetch either is not scheduled or is canceled. Of course, if the page is in the buffer pool, no I/O is scheduled.

Variable Thresholds

In addition to the fixed buffer pool thresholds, DB2 provides several variable thresholds, whose values you can change:

- Deferred write threshold (**DWQT**)

- Vertical deferred write threshold (**VDWQT**)

- Sequential steal threshold (**VPSEQT**)

- Virtual buffer pool parallel sequential threshold (**VPPSEQT**)

- Virtual buffer pool assisting parallel sequential threshold (**VPXPSEQT**)

Updated pages are queued by data set until either a checkpoint or the **DWQT** or **VDWQT** is reached. Keep in mind that if increased, **DWQT** and **VDWQT** permit more page updates to collect in the buffer pool.

Buffer pool attributes are set initially in the installation process. You can use the **ALTER BUFFERPOOL** command to change the variable thresholds. When you use this command, DB2 stores the changes to the buffer pool attributes in the bootstrap data set. Changing one buffer pool does not affect the other buffer pools in the system.

To see the current thresholds for a specific buffer pool, use the **DISPLAY BUFFERPOOL** command. Look for message DSNB404I to determine the current thresholds.

Keep in mind that synchronous I/O means one I/O for one page, while asynchronous I/O means multiple pages per I/O. Having said that, let's take a closer look at the variable thresholds that govern the use of buffer pools.

Deferred Write Threshold

The **DWQT** threshold deals with the unavailable pages in a buffer pool; these pages can be updated pages or in-use pages. If you reach this threshold, it means that the percentage of unavailable pages specified for the threshold has been met. When the **DWQT** threshold is reached, DB2 begins to schedule writes (I/Os) to externalize data.

Once the deferred write threshold percentage is reached, the data sets with the oldest updated pages are written asynchronously. DB2 continues writing pages until the ratio falls below the threshold. DB2 checks this threshold each time an update to a page is completed. If the unavailable pages percentage in the buffer pool exceeds **DWQT**, DB2 schedules write operations for enough data sets (at up to 128 pages per data set) to decrease the number of unavailable buffers to 10 percent below the threshold value.

You have the option of setting the **DWQT** threshold value as an absolute number or as a percentage. If you want to avoid writing a large number of pages at once by writing a small number of pages on a steady basis, you should lower the **DWQT** setting. Review the performance of DB2 deferred write processing by looking at the **DWQT** and **VDWQT** parameters.

When considering **DWQT** and **VDWQT**, you might think that keeping these numbers low will help avoid spikes in page writing activity. Of course, this conclusion is wrong for the sorting buffer pools that DB2 uses in support of the sort database (**DSNDB07**); for these buffer pools, you should assign a high value for these two thresholds. Obviously, if you decrease the buffer pool size, you will reach **DWQT** and **VDWQT** more often.

Vertical Write Threshold

The **VDWQT** threshold applies to the number of updated pages for a single page set or data set in the buffer pool. Each time **VDWQT** is reached, it is related to the number of asynchronous writes. You can use the **VDWQT** threshold to reduce the number of pages that are forced out synchronously and to increase the pages written before the transaction commits by writing pages asynchronously.

If the updated pages for a data set exceed the threshold, as many as 128 pages for each data set can be scheduled to be written. DB2 schedules I/Os to externalize the data set pages to DASD and begins writing these pages asynchronously.

You can specify the **VDWQT** threshold as a percent value ranging from **0** to **90**, or you can indicate a number of buffers from **0** to **9999**. If you use a number of buffers as your threshold, you must set the percentage to **0**. The default value for the percentage is **5**.

To set the **VDWQT** values, you use the **ALTER BUFFERPOOL** command:

```
-ALTER BUFFERPOOL(xxx) VDWQT(integer1, integer2)
```

The command's syntax does not let you set the **VDWQT** percentage to a value greater than **DWQT**. You can specify a number of buffers for **VDWQT** that is higher than **DWQT**, but this setting will have no effect.

Some DB2 utilities override the **VDWQT** threshold and use a constant limit of 64 pages rather than a percentage of the buffer pool size. The **LOAD, RECOVER**, and **REORG** utilities use a constant limit of 128 pages.

The **VDWQT** setting controls asynchronous write operations, so your goal is to set this threshold to a small value so that you have more "regular" asynchronous writes to DASD. If you run out of write engines, lower the **VDWQT** write threshold to keep the writes more constant.

If you are working with large buffer pools, be mindful that using even a small number as a percent could cause an I/O spike. If you raise the **DWQT** and **VDWQT** or even the size of the buffer pool, you invite the possibility that page updates will accumulate, with the chance that more updates per page are captured.

Set **VDWQT** to **0** (zero) when the average pages per write is a low single digit (this does not include pools dedicated to sort/work files). Setting **VDWQT** to zero causes DB2 to use an internal threshold of 40 pages as the trigger point for the asynchronous write process.

What you want to watch for in your monitoring of the buffer pools is the tendency for a particular page set to monopolize the buffer pool with a lot of changed pages, causing asynchronous writes to hit your system all at once. You want these writes to occur over time, not in spikes. Adjusting the size of the buffer pool and this threshold will achieve this goal.

Sequential Steal Threshold

The **VPSEQT** threshold specifies the percentage of the buffer pool that can be occupied by sequentially accessed pages, which can be in any state, including updated, in-use, or available. In a non–data-sharing environment, you can increase **VPSEQT** to reduce prefetching from becoming disabled.

If the **VPSEQT** threshold is exceeded, DB2 tries to steal a buffer that holds a sequentially accessed page rather than one that holds a randomly accessed page. You have two basic types of processing, one for transactions and one for queries, and the value you choose for **VPSEQT** should reflect the processing type in the particular buffer pool. The higher the number, the more you are tuning toward query performance versus transaction processing performance. The default for **VPSEQT** is 80 percent; with this setting, you would have 80 percent of **VPSIZE** (the number of buffers in the buffer pool).

You can use the **ALTER BUFFERPOOL** command to specify any percentage from **0** to **100**. Setting the threshold to 0 percent prevents any sequential pages from taking up space in the buffer pool. As a result, prefetch is disabled, and any sequentially accessed pages are discarded as soon as they are released. Setting the threshold to 100 percent lets sequential pages take over the entire buffer pool. If you use your buffer pool only for sequential processing, set it to 100 percent.

Virtual Buffer Pool Parallel Sequential Threshold

The **VPPSEQT** parallel sequential threshold is a percent of **VPSEQT**'s buffer and is used in support of parallel operations. Setting **VPPSEQT** to **0** (zero) disables parallel operations in the buffer pool.

The virtual buffer pool parallel sequential threshold is measured as a percentage of the sequential steal threshold (**VPSEQT**). The default value is 50 percent of

VPSEQT. The **ALTER BUFFERPOOL(*xxx*) VPPSEQT** option allows a value from 0 percent to 100 percent.

Remember that if you set **VPPSEQT** to **0**, you are disabling parallel processing operations in the buffer pool. You also need to think about:

- The impact on work files for parallel query execution: A lack of work files or work files of differing size will affect parallelism by reducing the degree.

- A lack of buffer pool resources: This condition can cause a reduced degree of parallelism or cause a query to run sequentially. This situation requires an increase in **VPSIZE**.

- The impact on sequential prefetching: Sequential prefetching may be reduced if the buffer is busy with parallel operations.

Virtual Buffer Pool Assisting Parallel Sequential Threshold

The **VPXPSEQT** threshold is used only for Sysplex query parallelism. A **0** (zero) setting for this threshold disallows DB2 from assisting with Sysplex query parallelism at run time for queries that use the buffer pool.

VPXPSEQT specifies the portion of the buffer pool that might be used to assist with parallel operations initiated from another DB2 in the data-sharing group. It is measured as a percentage of the parallel sequential threshold (**VPPSEQT**); the default value is 0 percent of **VPPSEQT**. You can set **VPXPSEQT** to any value from **0** to **100** by using the **VPXPSEQT** option on the **ALTER BUFFERPOOL** command.

You can disable Sysplex query parallelism system-wide by specifying **COORDINATOR=NO** and **ASSISTANT=NO** on installation panel **DSTIPK**, the panel where you define a group or member for a data-sharing function.

General Guidelines for Setting Buffer Pool Thresholds

Setting buffer pools depends on your workload and on the type and size of data being cached. Think in terms of the entire system when making buffer pool tuning decisions. If you can afford larger buffer pools, you can achieve in a higher hit ratio, thereby reducing I/O.

Table 6.6 provides some general guidelines to keep in mind regarding buffer pool thresholds.

Table 6.6: Buffer pool threshold guidelines	
Condition	**Notes**
Pages frequently re-referenced and updated	Set a high value for **DWQT** and **VDWQT**.
Mixed workloads	Use the default setting for a mixed workload or if you are unsure about the type of workload.
Type of processing: query or transaction	Queries perform better when **VPSEQT** is set higher.
Buffer pools containing large objects (LOBs)	Only LOBs should be stored in the buffer pool(s). Set **DWQT** to **0** for both **LOG YES** and **LOG NO** LOBs. For LOBs specified with **LOG NO**, changed pages are written at commit time.
Pages that are rarely referenced	Lower **DWQT** or **VDWQT** to avoid a flood of write I/Os; doing so should make your writes more even over time.
Query-only buffer pools	For exclusive query processing, set **VPSEQT** to 100 percent.
Parallel processing	Set **VPPSEQT** and **VPXPSEQT** high.

Buffer Pool Hit Ratios

In discussing buffer pool hit ratios, we need to address the two types of hit ratios, system and application, to get a better look at what is going on in the system. The goal is to have pages reused in the buffer pool to avoid I/O operations. This arrangement produces a better response time by lowering the resources used.

The buffer pool hit ratio is a measure of how often DB2 finds a page in the buffer pool without having to execute an I/O operation to retrieve the data — in other words, how often a page access (a *getpage*) is satisfied without requiring an I/O operation. The following formula calculates the buffer pool hit ratio:

Hit ratio = (Getpages – Pages read from disk) / Getpages * 100

(The number of getpages equals the number of randomly plus sequentially accessed pages.)

A low buffer pool hit ratio occurs when the requested page is not in the buffer pool. A low hit ratio is not necessarily bad. It could mean that you have pages in the buffer pool that were not referenced because the pages were stolen before they could be used. Or perhaps the query stopped before it got to the end of accessing the table space pages or was using table space scans and the pages were never reused. Another example would be index non-leaf pages, which are frequently re-referenced and have a high hit ratio from staying in the buffer pool.

To review, the buffer pool hit ratio measures how often a getpage needs to be performed in an I/O operation in order to be satisfied. Remember, we are talking about pages that are "repetitively" scanned for the same information. Just providing DB2 with more memory for buffer pools does not necessarily provide better performance. What you need is an understanding of the grouping of your objects based on how they are accessed and how large they might be before you assign a pool to them.

Next, let's look at a little more detail on the types of hit ratios.

System Hit Ratio

If you are looking for something to measure, the I/O rate is a great place to start. Ask these questions:

- Is the object accessed by random or sequential I/O?

- Which objects have the highest I/O rate?

This information guides you to which objects are the focus of activity.

The system hit ratio represents the percentage of pages that are found in the buffer pool without performing any type of I/O:

System hit ratio = (Getpages – Sum of all pages read) / Getpages

The system hit ratio is expressed as a percentage of all getpage requests. If dynamic prefetch is not used, you have no sequential prefetch, and all access to data is random. In that case, your system hit ratio and your application hit ratio (covered next) will match.

When DB2 does use prefetching I/O, the system hit ratio will be affected. The value usually is lower in an application that causes mostly sequential accesses.

A negative system hit ratio points out that the number of prefetched pages is greater than the number of getpages. This situation indicates that prefetch operations are bringing in pages that are not referenced later. In this case, to improve the ratio, consider increasing the buffer pool size, increasing the sequential steal threshold (**VPSEQT**), or revising the assignments of table spaces to buffer pools.

Application Hit Ratio

The application hit ratio reflects the number of getpage requests issued by applications and satisfied by the buffer pool. This ratio is expressed as a percentage of all getpage requests issued by applications:

Application hit ratio = (Getpages – Read I/Os) / Getpages

As an example, an application that retrieves one row at a time by virtue of using an index with a low cardinality or using a non-matching index scan could account for a high getpage-per-SQL ratio. A low hit ratio indicates the level of synchronous I/O because prefetched pages that are already in the buffer pool count as hits. An application that browses large amounts of data that is not contiguous may well have a buffer pool hit ratio of 0.

Buffer Pool Page Management

Let's turn our attention now to two parameters used for buffer pool page management: **PGFIX** and **PGSTEAL**.

PGFIX

When you specify **YES** for the **PGFIX** parameter, the buffer pool is fixed in real storage for the long term. This option is intended for buffer pools with high I/O rates for updated or read pages. Using **PGFIX** results in lower CPU usage in the **DBM1** address space for I/O-intensive buffer pools.

The **PGFIX** parameter is a keyword on the **ALTER BUFFERPOOL** command. To prevent buffer pools from exceeding real storage, DB2 uses an 80 percent threshold. By implementing **PGFIX(YES)**, you can reduce the excessive paging for these high I/O rates. Here is an example:

```
-ALTER BPOOL (xxxx) VPSIZE(xxxx) PGFIX(YES)
```

Remember, you need to have enough real storage available for the buffer pool.

PGSTEAL

Making room for a newer page in the buffer pool is called "stealing" the page. By default, DB2 uses a least-recently-used (LRU) algorithm to manage pages in storage. This method keeps the most frequently accessed pages in the buffer pool.

Buffer pools can use other page-stealing algorithms to manage pages, one of which is first-in, first-out (FIFO). This alternative removes the oldest pages regardless of how often they are used.

You must decide which algorithm is best for your DB2 subsystem and installation. You use the **ALTER BUFFERPOOL** command with the **PGSTEAL** option to specify the page-stealing method, either **LRU** or **FIFO**. Most installations use the default of **LRU**, but if you have table spaces or indexes that should always remain in memory, you should use **FIFO**. You can also use **FIFO** for buffer pools that have no I/O.

Buffer Pool Statistics

To gather statistics about a specific buffer pool, you can use the **DISPLAY BUFFERPOOL** command:

```
-DISPLAY BUFFERPOOL BPxx DETAIL
```

Figure 6.4 shows sample output produced by this command.

```
DB2 Admin ---DBW1 Browse DB2 Command Output ---Line 00000000 Col 001 080
  Command ===>                                              Scroll ===> PAGE

   -DISPLAY BPOOL(BP28) DETAIL(*) LIST(*) LSTATS

                          Top of Data
******************************************************************
DSNB401I  -DBW1 BUFFERPOOL NAME BP28, BUFFERPOOL ID 28, USE COUNT 2
DSNB402I  -DBW1 BUFFER POOL SIZE = 15000 BUFFERS
            ALLOCATED       =    15000    TO BE DELETED  =         0
            IN-USE/UPDATED  =        0    BUFFERS ACTIVE =     11528
DSNB406I  -DBW1 PGFIX ATTRIBUTE -
            CURRENT = NO
            PENDING = NO
          PAGE STEALING METHOD = LRU
DSNB404I  -DBW1 THRESHOLDS -
            VP SEQUENTIAL    = 50
            DEFERRED WRITE   = 30   VERTICAL DEFERRED WRT  =  5,  0
            PARALLEL SEQUENTIAL =50   ASSISTING PARALLEL SEQT=  0
DSNB410I  -DBW1 CUMULATIVE STATISTICS SINCE 08:35:53
DSNB411I  -DBW1 RANDOM GETPAGE    =    69202 SYNC READ I/O (R) =247
            SEQ.  GETPAGE     =    32366 SYNC READ I/O (S) =     272
            DMTH HIT          =        0 PAGE-INS REQUIRED =    7100
```

Figure 6.4: Sample DISPLAY BUFFERPOOL output

How Buffer Pools Affect Performance

Memory use in DB2 is one of the most important areas of tuning for performance. Buffer pools will give you better performance with careful planning in allocating memory.

The buffer pools store table spaces and index spaces whose pages are accessed and brought into memory. The following are some buffer pool best practices:

- Employ a multiple buffer pool strategy.

- Consider defining separate buffer pools for index and table space.

- Isolate the DB2 catalog in **BP0**, **BP8K0**, **BP16K0**, and **BP32K0**.

- Isolate heavy hit data in its own buffer pool.

- Use a separate buffer pool for work files in **DSNDB07**; **BP7** is usually designated for this purpose.

- Try to separate buffer pools that are accessed sequentially versus randomly.

- If your buffer pools are used heavily or exclusively for sorting, set the **DWQT**, **VDWQT**, and **VPSEQT** thresholds to very high values. Appropriate values for **DSNDB07** are a **DWQT** of **90**, a **VDWQT** of **90**, and a **VPSEQT** of **95**.

- The term "current buffers active" refers to the number of buffers that are *not* available.

- **IWTH** is a critical threshold, but if you find counts here but do not have counts in **SPTH** or **DMTH**, ignore this count.

Automatic Buffer Pool Management

In DB2 9 and z/OS 1.8, Workload Manager (WLM) assisted buffer pool management lets you enable or disable individual buffer pool sizes by using the **AUTOSIZE** parameter of the **ALTER BUFFERPOOL** command.

When you enable automatic buffer pool management, WLM drives a DB2 exit to adjust buffer pool size, increasing or decreasing the size of a given buffer pool by up to 25 percent of the originally allocated size. No other option but the size can be changed, and the changes are maintained across start-ups of DB2. When adjusting the buffer pool size, WLM takes into account the overall system storage usage and performance goals.

When WLM-assisted buffer pool management is activated, DB2 communicates to WLM each time an allied agent encounters delays due to read I/O and periodically reports buffer pool size and random hit ratios to WLM. To activate this feature, run this **ALTER BUFFERPOOL** command:

```
-ALTER BUFFERPOOL(bpname) AUTOSIZE(YES)
```

The specified buffer pool is now registered with WLM.

Once activated, automatic buffer pool management can be deactivated using this command:

```
-ALTER BUFFERPOOL(bpname) AUTOSIZE(NO)
```

AUTOSIZE(NO) is the default setting on the **ALTER BUFFERPOOL** command. This attribute is added to the **DISPLAY BUFFERPOOL** output as well. If you manually alter a buffer pool with the command **ALTER BUFFERPOOL VPSIZE**, DB2 deregisters the buffer pool and then registers it at the new size with WLM.

IFCID 201 records the **ALTER BUFFERPOOL** command information for the status of the buffer pool before and after the command is issued.

Two new messages are associated with the WLM sizing of buffer pools. Message DSNB544I is issued in response to an **ALTER BUFFERPOOL** command to indicate that the requested change to the **AUTOSIZE** attribute has been accepted:

```
DSNB544I AUTOSIZE FOR bpname HAS BEEN SET TO xxxxx
```

Message DSNB555I is issued when WLM notifies DB2 to adjust the size of a buffer pool:

```
DSNB555I WLM RECOMMENDATION TO ADJUST SIZE FOR BUFFER POOL bpname HAS
   COMPLETED
OLD SIZE = csize BUFFERS
NEW SIZE = nsize BUFFERS
```

Sort Pool

DB2 9 offers some new sort-avoidance techniques that help with performance. The **DISTINCT** class sort avoidance with a non-unique index is interesting. **DISTINCT** can now use a duplicate index to remove duplicates from the result without performing a sort.

Also available in DB2 9 is a group collapsing enhancement for **GROUP BY** queries without a column function and for **DISTINCT**, reducing both work file getpages and CPU time. Group collapsing removes duplicates from the sort tree in the input phase, eliminating the requirement for an additional pass in the sorting process.

In-memory sorts are now available for the **FETCH FIRST *n* ROWS** clause. For this type of sort, the row size must fit in a 32 KB page. Therefore, the number of rows times the size of the data, plus the key, must be equal to or less than 32,704. Only the final results will be written to a work file.

Sparse indexing (in-memory data cache) with nested loop join is an alternative for the optimizer when no index exists on the inner table. This situation can take place if the space is available in the local storage pool above the bar.

If sufficient space exists, your sorting will be done in the database address space. If there is not enough space, the sorting occurs in **DSNDB07** work files. Expect in-memory sorts to be the most beneficial when you have SQL statements that run for a short time and the number of rows is small. If small sorts fit into one 4 KB or 32 KB page, no work files are used.

DB2 uses local storage and buffer pool storage for sorting; you can find these sizes on the **DSNTIPC** installation panel. The calculated size for the sort pool could actually be 10 percent to 20 percent higher than indicated because of the type of disk and cylinder rounding. We generally set this size as large as possible to make the sort more efficient. The default is 2,000 KB; sizes up to 128,000 KB are supported.

In DB2 9, the sort pool has moved above the 2 GB bar. Each sort initially allocates 240 KB and then keeps adding storage until the limit is reached or until the 32 KB nodes at the sort tree bottom are reached.

DB2 uses a *tournament sort*. This technique employs an algorithm that produces logical work files called runs, which are intermediate sets of ordered data. If the sort area is large, fewer sort runs are produced.

Work Files and the DSNDB07 Database

The work file database is **DSNDB07**. In a data-sharing environment, each member has its own work file database.

You assign multiple data sets consisting typically of five to six work data sets without secondary extents. These are segmented table spaces whose **SEGSIZE** value is always set to 16. We try to avoid contention by using different volumes on different channels. DB2 assigns the space in a round-robin fashion over the volumes. To minimize I/O contention, you can also use disk with parallel access volume (PAV) support.

When assigning the buffer pools and setting the buffer pool thresholds to support your work files, do not make the access 100 percent sequential. You want to allow for a small amount of random page searches by setting **VPSEQT** to 95 percent to 98 percent. If the **DWQT** or **VDWQT** threshold is reached because of the writes that are scheduled, increase the buffer pool deferred write threshold (**DWQT**) or the data set deferred write threshold (**VDWQT**) value.

Work files are usually assigned to buffer pool **BP07**, but regardless of which buffer pool you assign, work files should always have their own buffer pool. DB2 uses this buffer pool when it writes to the logical work file. The buffer pool size will limit the number of work files used in a sorting process. DB2 uses these file work sets for sorting, temporary tables, and other events. DB2 assigns logical work files to a sort process, and these logical files reside in the work file table spaces in **DSNDB07** for non–data-sharing environments. Work files are assigned on an LRU basis.

There is a limit to the number of physical files that are assigned at installation time, and the number of both 4 KB and 32 KB work files cannot exceed 500. However, you can allocate physical work files in excess of this default and then put those in their own buffer pool.

For performance and tuning purposes, you need to monitor how the work files use space as well as the I/O response times. By keeping work files in a separate buffer pool, you can use IFCID 0311 in performance trace class 8 to distinguish global temporary tables from other uses of the work files. You can use IFCID 0199 statistics class 8 to monitor I/O activity of database data sets.

You can also obtain statistics relating to the average write I/O delay. This information is also available in the **DISPLAY BUFFERPOOL** command's **LSTATS** option. If you need more detail, use performance class 4, but remember that this method will cost you more overhead.

If your buffer pool statistics messages indicate that a work file request was rejected, you may need to increase the size of the work files. Make sure you allocate more 32 KB data sets for DB2 9.

Remember, any records that exceed 100 bytes are using 32 KB work files. No priorities apply to the uses of work file data sets in DB2, so one task can affect the performance of another task. Changing the data set size or increasing the number of data sets can be done by deleting and redefining them when DB2 is not running or when the work file database is stopped. You can find examples of how to do this in job **DSNTIJTM**. Another part of this job defines the initial buffer pool sizes as they relate to the values specified on installation panels **DSNTIP1** and **DSNTIP2**.

EDM Pool

The components that make up the EDM pool contain skeleton and active application plans and packages. Making sure that your EDM pool size is large enough so that it does not inhibit the loading of these objects is critical for performance.

You usually want a hit ratio of 80 percent for the EDM pool, which means 80 percent of requests are made in the EDM pool without executing any I/O. EDM pools that are too small can cause problems with increased I/O on the directory and can reduce the number of threads that can be used concurrently.

The storage needed for a package is the sum of the base size of the package and the size of the executed sections. The storage needed for a plan is the sum of the base plan size and the size of the executed sections.

Pages are allocated by allocating any available pages first. Then, if more space is needed, pages are stolen from inactive SKPTs, DBDs, SKCTs, or dynamic SQL skeletons. If all else fails and there is not enough space, an error is sent to the application. The OMEGAMON statistics report provides information about the efficiency of your EDM pool.

Dynamic Cache

A new subsystem parameter, **EDMSTMTC**, defines the amount of storage available to the dynamic statement cache, which is a pool that saves prepared SQL statements. This area is located above the 2 GB bar.

The field **CACHE DYNAMIC SQL** on panel **DSNTIP8** enables the dynamic cache. If you use Java Database Connectivity (JDBC) or Open Database Connectivity (ODBC) or you have a large amount of reusable dynamic SQL, you should increase the value for this pool.

You can decide whether to increase or decrease the size based on your monitoring statistics for the hit ratio. The EDM cache hit ratio is available in the OMEGAMON statistics report and is calculated as follows:

EDM cache hit ratio = (Prepare requests – Full prepares) / Prepare requests

The **EXPLAIN STATEMENT CACHE ALL** statement provides a snapshot of the dynamic statement cache by current authorization ID, storing it in the **DSN_STATEMENT_CACHE_TABLE**. Look at column **STAT_CPU** to indentify the queries that use the most CPU time. This column reports the accumulated CPU time used for a statement. Of course, you have to have the statement cache turned on for this technique to work.

Collecting dynamic statement cache statistics can increase the cost of statement execution. To keep this cost at a minimum, you can use IFCID 0318 as needed. You would start performance trace class 30 for IFCID 0318, enabling statistics collection for statements in the dynamic statement cache. If you are not actively monitoring the dynamic cache, you should turn off this trace. Know also that if you start or stop IFCID 0318, DB2 resets the statistic counters for IFCID 0316 to zero.

IFCID 0316 collects information about the contents of the dynamic statement cache. DB2 reports on the cached statement, the statement name, and the unique ID for the statement. If you have IFCID 0318 active as well, you will receive the performance statistics for all dynamic SQL statements and the first 60 bytes of the statement text. You can filter by authorization ID, SQL ID, bind options, or statistics information.

DBD Structures

The **EDMDBDC** subsystem parameter defines the storage space available for caching just the DBD structures above the 2 GB bar. The smallest this pool should be is four times the size of your largest DBD.

A DBD cannot occupy more than 25 percent of this DBD pool; DB2 will not let this happen. To determine the size of DBDs in a DB2 subsystem, you can use the following command:

```
-DISPLAY DATABASE(*) ONLY
```

The keyword **ONLY** will show each database name, status, and DBD length.

RID Pool

An area of local storage for sorting record identifiers (RIDs) is allocated, when needed, above the 2 GB bar in 32 KB blocks known as RID blocks. The default size is 8 MB, with a limit of 10,000 MB. You can set this number on panel **DSNTIPC**. The storage is allocated when it is needed to sort the RIDs for list prefetching, enforcing unique keys for multiple row update, and hybrid joins.

You can estimate the storage required for the RID pool using the following formula:

Number of concurrent RID processing activities * Average number of RIDs * 2 * 5 (bytes per RID)

If an SQL statement runs out of RID pool space for sorting the RIDs, the SQL statement will revert to sequential processing at the point of failure.

Workload Manager and Stored Procedures

DB2 9 for z/OS supports both external and native SQL stored procedures. Native SQL stored procedures and their management using Workload Manager are performance benefits in DB2 9.

One of these benefits is the DB2 workload enclave SRBs in WLM that can be dispatched to a zIIP engine. These include the rebuilding of an index with the option of **SHRLEVEL CHANGE** and native stored procedures that are called remotely over a TCP/IP connection.

Thread Management

Job **DSNTIJUZ** includes the parameter **URLGWTH** in **DSN6SYSP** that deals with long-running reader threshold. The default value for this parameter is **0** (zero), which means that long-running UR (uncommitted unit of recovery) checking is not activated by default. This feature provides notification about long-running URs. The parameter's value specifies the number of log records to be written by a UR before a message is issued to the console. IFCID 0313, if active, will be written when a long-running UR is detected.

Maximum Number of Data Sets

Subsystem parameter **DSMAX** specifies the maximum number of data sets that can remain open at one time. The value you select depends on available storage below the line. It also depends on how many partitioned or large object (LOB) table spaces you have as well as how many indexes are defined.

When you reach the maximum specified in **DSMAX**, DB2 closes either 3 percent of the value of **DSMAX** or 300 data sets, whichever is lower. The opening and closing of data sets requires resources and impacts performance, so you want to set **DSMAX** large enough so that frequently used data sets can remain open.

The sizing rule is to make **DSMAX** larger than the maximum number of data sets used at one time. Determining this value will require you to use statistic reports to see the open/close activity within your monitor. When the open/close activity is high at peak periods on your data sets and there is one event per second, you should increase your **DSMAX** value.

Your page sets are defined with the **OPEN/CLOSE** attribute to manage the opening and closing of the data set. There are physical closes and logical closes. A physical close is DB2 closing and deallocating the data set. A logical close occurs at either commit or deallocation time, depending on the **BIND** command's **RELEASE** parameter value (**COMMIT** or **DEALLOCATE**). When a data set it is logically closed, the page set use count is decreased. When the page set use count goes to zero, the page set is a candidate for a physical close.

Practice Questions

Question 1

Where in DB2 can you find all the descriptions of the IFCIDs that are shipped with DB2?

○ A. **SDSNMACS**

○ B. **SDSNSAMP**

○ C. Catalog tables

○ D. Directory tables

Question 2

What is the most common trace destination to which trace information is written for DB2?

○ A. GTF

○ B. RES

○ C. SMF

○ D. SRV

Question 3

Which trace is the most costly to run in DB2?

○ A. Accounting

○ B. Performance

○ C. Statistics

○ D. Monitor

Question 4

Audit trace reports in DB2 provide information about which *two* of the following?

○ A. **GRANTs**

○ B. Unsuccessful access attempts

○ C. Processor resources consumed

○ D. RID pool processing

Question 5

Accounting traces in DB2 are designed to:

○ A. Collect application program information

○ B. Collect data-sharing information

○ C. Document sensitive data uses

○ D. Report unsuccessful access

Question 6

Before you can send data to SMF (choose *two* answers):

○ A. SMF must be stopped.

○ B. No members must be updated.

○ C. SMF must be running.

○ D. Member **SMFPRM*xx*** must be updated.

Question 7

If you wanted to stop all the traces running in DB2, which of the following commands would you use?

○ A. **-STOP TRACE**

○ B. **-STOP TRACE (*)**

○ C. **-STOP TRACE ALL**

○ D. **-STOP TRACE CLASS ALL**

Question 8

When you install a new set of application programs, which *two* of the following areas would concern you most in regard to storage?

- ○ A. **EDMPOOL**
- ○ B. **EDM_SKELETON_POOL**
- ○ C. **SKPT**
- ○ D. **CT**

Question 9

On average, what percentage of free pages should you have in the EDM pool?

- ○ A. 80 to 90 percent
- ○ B. 50 to 60 percent
- ○ C. 0 percent
- ○ D. 10 to 20 percent

Question 10

Which fixed thresholds are associated with the buffer pools in DB2?

- ○ A. **VPSEQT, VPPSEQT, VDWQT**
- ○ B. **IWTH, DMTH, SPTH**
- ○ C. **DWQT, VDWQT, VPSEQT**
- ○ D. **IWTH, DWQT, VPSEQT**

CHAPTER 7

Systems Operations and Troubleshooting

Identifying and collecting information and solving system-level problems in DB2 9 for z/OS is the focus of this chapter. We look at how you go about identifying a problem and then resolving it by applying effective resolution methods. This background will help prepare you for Section 3 (System Operation and Maintenance) and Section 6 (Troubleshooting) of the DB2 9 System Administrator for z/OS certification exam. Together, these two parts of the exam make up 36.5 percent of the test.

Your DB2 system administration skill set requires a knowledge of DB2 and z/OS operator commands, when to execute those commands, and how to interpret the resulting information. Knowing how to use these tools to find solutions to the day-to-day problems you encounter in DB2 will help you keep DB2 running smoothly.

Managing DB2 Components and Processes

You know that multiple DB2 subsystems can run in z/OS. Each one of those DB2s has a DB2 command prefix consisting of characters that identify the subsystem to which the command should be directed. You define the command prefix at installation time on installation panel **DSNTIPM**. It can be from one to eight characters long. The default command prefix is **DSN1**.

The command structure syntax consists of the DB2 subsystem recognition character (i.e., the command prefix), the command, a primary keyword, other keywords, and values. Figure 7.1 illustrates this structure.

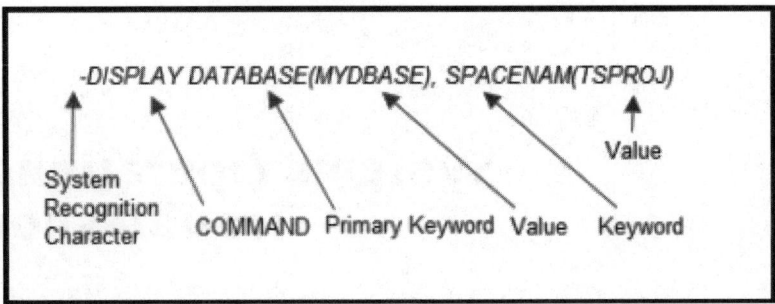

Figure 7.1: Command structure

In the figure, the hyphen (-) at the beginning of the command string serves as the prefix for the command. The examples in this chapter all follow this style.

Some characters have special meaning in the syntax of the DB2 commands. For example, commas and blank characters are separators. Multiple consecutive blanks are equivalent to a single blank (except in strings enclosed within apostrophes (')).

You can control most of the operational environment by using DB2 commands. Commands in DB2 are divided into several categories: DB2 commands, DSN command processor commands, IMS commands, CICS commands, TSO commands, Internal Resource Lock Manager (IRLM) commands, and administrative scheduler commands.

Commands can be entered from different sources, including a z/OS console or application program, a TSO terminal, a CICS terminal, an IMS program or terminal, an APF-authorized program, or an IFI application program. The **START DB2** command, however, can be entered only from a z/OS console (or from an APF-authorized program that passes the command to the z/OS console).

You can also enter DB2 commands from the DB2I primary options menu, using option 7, **DB2 Commands**. From the resulting display (Figure 7.2), you can execute saved commands by tabbing down to the desired command and pressing **Enter**.

```
DB2 COMMANDS                       SSID: DBPT
===>
Position cursor on the command line you want to execute and press ENTER
Cmd 1 ===> -DISPLAY THREAD(*) TYPE(*)
Cmd 2 ===> -DISPLAY UTILITY(*)
Cmd 3 ===> -DISPLAY BUFFERPOOL(ACTIVE)
      ...>
Cmd 4 ===> -DISPLAY DATABASE(*)
      ...>
Cmd 5 ===> -DISPLAY TRACE(*)
      ...>
Cmd 6 ===> -DISPLAY DDF
      ...>
Cmd 7 ===>
      ...>


PRESS:  ENTER to process    END to save and exit    HELP for more information
```

Figure 7.2: DB2 Commands panel

Command Scope

The scope of a DB2 command is the range of a data-sharing command. In a data-sharing environment, commands have either group scope or member (or local) scope.

A command with group scope is one that affects all members of the group. For example, the **STOP DATABASE** command issued from any member of a group stops the specified database for all members of that group.

Member or local commands affect only the DB2 subsystem in which you issue them. The **CANCEL THREAD** command, for example, cancels the specified threads for the member identified by the command prefix used with the command.

Command Output

Output from a DB2 command is returned to the entering terminal, to a printed listing (for batch jobs), or to another terminal (e.g., for CICS). The output from a command is always less than 256 KB.

The amount of storage available to your DB2 subsystem and the command itself determine the maximum amount of output returned. For example, the **DISPLAY**

THREAD command will not display more than 254 lines. For the **DISPLAY DATABASE** command, the value of the **LIMIT** parameter determines the amount of output. If you issue a DB2 command from an IMS console, the output is limited to 32 KB.

Remember that the z/OS console log is a source of information about DB2. You can look here for details about bind problems, DB2 startup messages, lock contention, log information, and object problems. The z/OS console log is also a good place to examine statistics. IBM's Screen Definition Facility (SDF) or a similar product can help you display the output list.

If you need to find the DB2 start-up information, check the MVS console for message DSNZ002I, which will show you the DSNZPARM name with which you started the system. You can also find the message in the JES **SYSLOG** and the JES log of the **MSTR** address space. The DSNZ messages deal with the system parameter manager.

The message contains the name of the DSNZPARM load module entered by the operator. If no name was entered for the start-up procedure, the default name of the DSNZPARM is used and displayed:

```
DSNZ002I - SUBSYS ssnm SYSTEM PARAMETERS
                    LOAD MODULE NAME IS dsnzparm-name
DSNY001I - SUBSYSTEM STARTING
```

Command Authorization

To issue any DB2 command, you must have the appropriate authorization or privilege. These can be granted to authorization IDs in many combinations.

You can restrict access to data using an option on the **START DB2** command. Specify **ACCESS(MAINT)** to limit access to only those users who have installation **SYSADM** or installation **SYSOPR** authority. To later restore access to all users, issue the **STOP DB2** command and then restart, omitting the **ACCESS** keyword or using **ACCESS(*)** to let all users connect to the DB2 subsystem.

Address Spaces

To start and stop DB2 subsystems, you use the **START DB2** and **STOP DB2** commands. The **START DB2** command starts the system services address space, the database services address space, the IRLM address space, and, depending on specifications in the load module for subsystem parameters (which is **DSNZPARM** by default), the distributed data facility address space.

DB2 Commands

Let's take a closer look now at some of the key DB2 commands used to operate and troubleshoot a DB2 9 for z/OS system.

STOP DB2

To stop the DB2 subsystem, you issue the **STOP DB2** command:

```
-STOP DB2 MODE(QUIESCE)
```

When specified with the **MODE(QUIESCE)** option, the command lets any currently active programs complete and prohibits any new programs from initiating. All connected address spaces must terminate their connections before DB2 is stopped.

Figure 7.3 shows the syntax of the **STOP DB2** command.

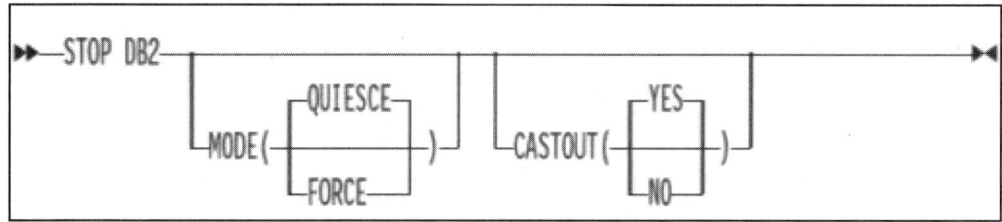

Figure 7.3: STOP DB2 command syntax

The **CASTOUT** option applies only in a data-sharing environment; it causes DB2 to cast out page sets for which the specified member was last updated. The **FORCE** option performs a termination that might leave some tasks in an abnormal status, causing dumps and messages.

START DB2

Figure 7.4 shows the syntax of the **START DB2** command.

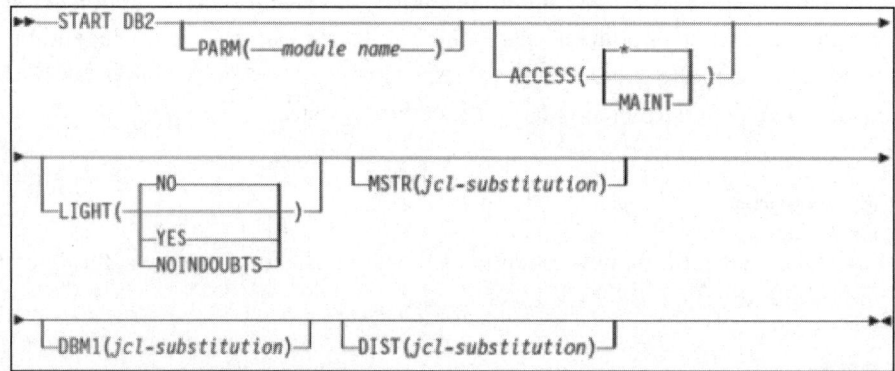

Figure 7.4: START DB2 command syntax

If you are experiencing problems with DB2 and need to evaluate the subsystem to ensure it is in a consistent state or to restrict access to data, you can stop DB2 using the **QUIESCE** option and then use the **START DB2** command to start DB2 in maintenance mode.

Maintenance mode permits only those users with installation **SYSADM** and installation **SYSOPR** authority to access DB2. In maintenance mode, **SYSOPR** can access DB2, run utilities on the catalog and directory, run the **REPAIR** utility, and issue dynamic SQL not controlled by the DB2 governor, to name a few actions. **SYSADM** can run **CATMAINT**, start the **DSNDB01** database, run the **DSNDB06** database when in restricted status or stopped, and run the **DIAGNOSIS** utility with the wait option. Stored procedures will receive message DSNX9444I while the system is in maintenance mode.

Use the following commands to assess whether the subsystem is in a consistent state:

```
-DISPLAY THREAD(*) TYPE(*)
-DISPLAY UTILITY (*)
-TERM UTILITY(*)
-DISPLAY DATABASE(*) RESTRICT
-DISPLAY DATABASE(*) SPACENAM(*) RESTRICT
-RECOVER INDOUBT
```

Figure 7.5 shows the messages that appear on the console to show the subsystems starting up DB2.

```
$HASP373 xxxxMSTR STARTED
DSNZ002I - SUBSYS ssnm SYSTEM PARAMETERS LOAD MODULE NAME IS
          dsnzparm-name
DSNY001I - SUBSYSTEM STARTING
DSNJ127I - SYSTEM TIMESTAMP FOR BSDS=87.267 14:24:30.6
DSNJ001I - csect CURRENT COPY n ACTIVE LOG DATA SET IS DSNAME=...,
          STARTRBA=...,ENDRBA=...
DSNJ099I - LOG RECORDING TO COMMENCE WITH STARTRBA = xxxxxxxxxxxx
          $HASP373 xxxxDBM1 STARTED
DSNR001I - RESTART INITIATED
DSNR003I - RESTART...PRIOR CHECKPOINT RBA=xxxxxxxxxxxx
DSNR004I - RESTART...UR STATUS COUNTS... IN COMMIT=nnnn, INDOUBT=nnnn,
          INFLIGHT=nnnn, IN ABORT=nnnn, POSTPONED ABORT=nnnn
DSNR005I - RESTART...COUNTS AFTER FORWARD RECOVERY IN COMMIT=nnnn,
          INDOUBT=nnnn
DSNR006I - RESTART...COUNTS AFTER BACKWARD RECOVERY INFLIGHT=nnnn,
          IN ABORT=nnnn, POSTPONED ABORT=nnnn
DSNR002I - RESTART COMPLETED
DSN9002I - DSNYASCP 'START DB2' NORMAL COMPLETION
DSNV434I - DSNVRP NO POSTPONED ABORT THREADS FOUND
DSN9022I - DSNVRP 'RECOVER POSTPONED' NORMAL COMPLETION
```

Figure 7.5: Subsystem start-up messages

SET SYSPARM

The **SET SYSPARM** command, whose syntax is shown in Figure 7.6, lets you change the DB2 subsystem parameters while DB2 is running.

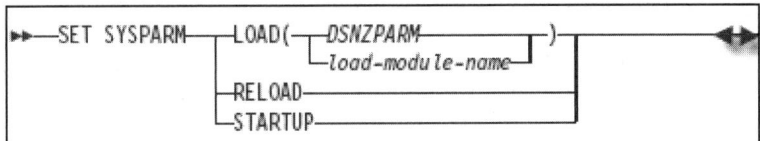

Figure 7.6: SET SYSPARM command syntax

Using the command's **LOAD** option, you supply the name of the load module to load into storage; the default value is **DSNZPARM**. The **RELOAD** option reloads the last named subsystem module. The **STARTUP** option resets the loaded parameters to their start-up values.

To change from the current load module to a new module named **CBIPARM**, you would run the following **SET SYSPARM** command:

```
-SET SYSPARM LOAD(CBIPARM)
```

To reload the parameters that were loaded at start-up:

```
-SET SYSPARM STARTUP
```

DISPLAY BUFFERPOOL

The **DISPLAY BUFFERPOOL** command reports the current status of one or more active or inactive buffer pools. Figure 7.7 shows the command's syntax.

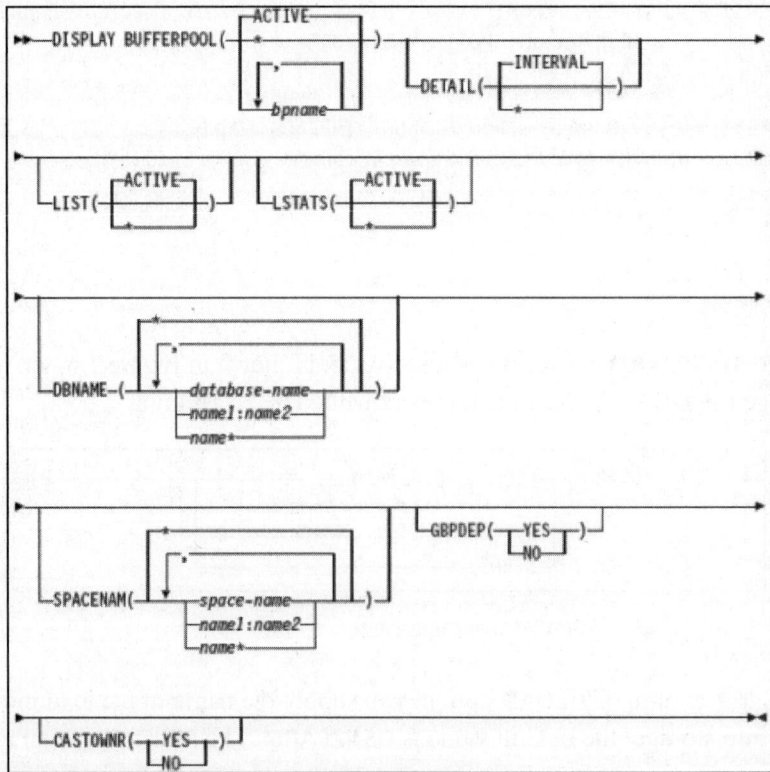

Figure 7.7: DISPLAY BUFFERPOOL command syntax

The **DISPLAY BUFFERPOOL DETAIL** output shows you how well parallel operations are satisfied in the specified buffer pool(s) and reports sequential prefetches, list prefetches, dynamic prefetches, read I/O, and whether prefetching has been disabled (an indicator of lack of buffer space). You can view the thresholds that have been set, the number of pages in the buffer, and more.

The command's **LIST** parameter lists the open index spaces and table spaces associated with the buffer pools included in the command output. This option provides basic information for non–data-sharing systems; more detail is provided if data sharing is active. To restrict the list of open index spaces and table spaces to those currently in use, you can use the **LIST** parameter's **ACTIVE** option. Specifying **ACTIVE(*)** lists all open index spaces and table spaces, whether in use or not.

Using **LIST** with the **LSTATS** option provides detail statistics about the open table spaces and index spaces for a buffer pool. If you are looking for the number of cached pages, the number of synchronous and asynchronous I/O operations against the objects using the buffer pool, and similar details, then **LSTATS** with **LIST** (**LIST ALL**, **LIST QUERIES**, or specific object names) is what you need.

The command's **GBPDEP** parameter gives you a way to see which buffers are group buffer pool (GBP) dependent.

DISPLAY THREAD

When used with the **ACTIVE** or **INACTIVE** parameter, DB2's **DISPLAY THREAD** command provides information that is quite useful in debugging. Messages DSNV403I and DSNV404I result when you run the command; check out the detail provided in DSNV404I. This message also appears when you use the command's **SYSTEM** option to display a subset of the system agents.

Figure 7.8 shows the syntax of the **DISPLAY THREAD** command.

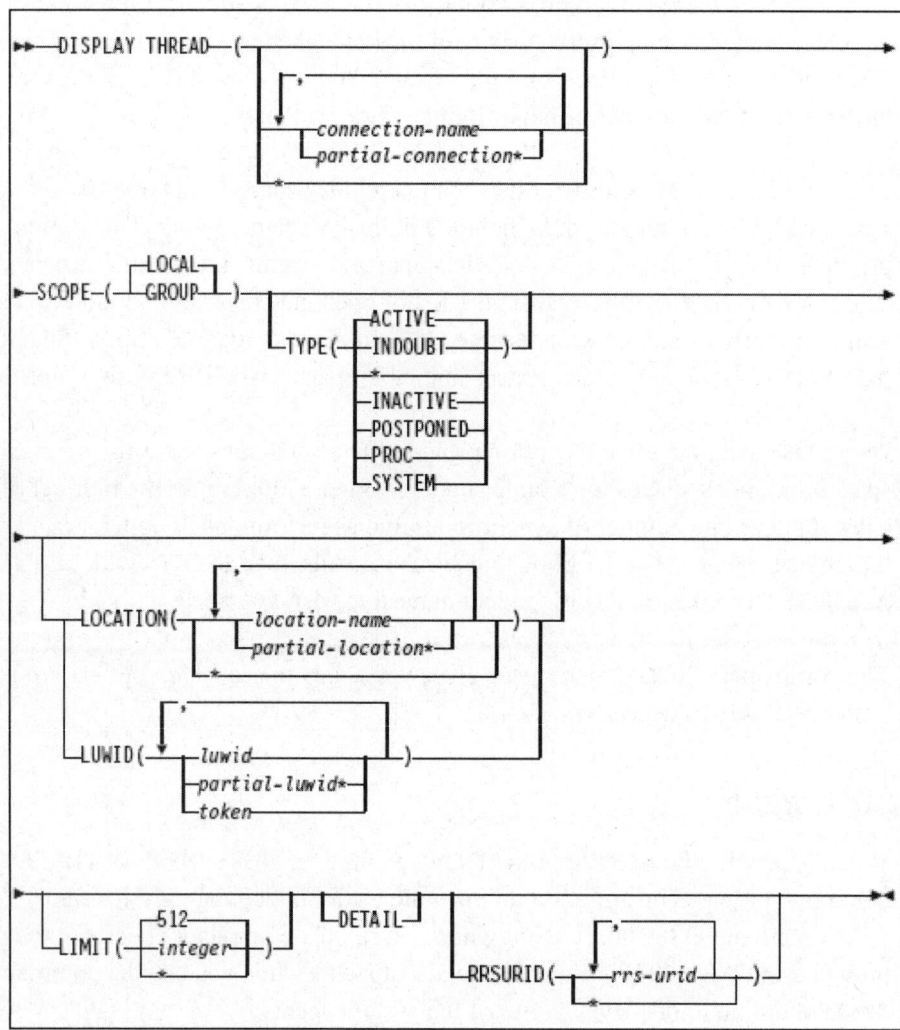

Figure 7.8: DISPLAY THREAD command syntax

Keep in mind that the status displayed by the **DISPLAY THREAD** command is dynamic; if you enter the same command again, the information may change. The abbreviation for this command is **DIS THD**.

In general, what you are looking for when you use the **DISPLAY THREAD** command is what is running, task-wise, in the system. Specifically, you are interested in tasks that have the potential to pose a problem or affect system performance. Note that the information returned by **DISPLAY THREAD** represents only one address space.

One way you can use this command is to display threads in order to see the active units of work (UOWs) that were suspended following execution of the **SET LOG SUSPEND** command. You will need to resolve these UOWs when restarting DB2 at the recovery site.

If you issue the **DISPLAY THREAD** command from the MVS console, the **LIMIT** keyword specifies the maximum number of lines displayed per member; the default is 512 lines of output per member.

To view the health of your system, issue the following **DISPLAY THREAD** command:

```
-DISPLAY THREAD(*) TYPE(SYSTEM)
```

You can use this next **DISPLAY THREAD** command to identify CPU stalls:

```
-DISPLAY THREAD(*) SERVICE(WAIT)
```

In DB2 9, a built-in monitor augments the **DISPLAY THREAD** command support to help automate problem identification and correction. The health monitor automation helps you identify CPU stalls for DBAT, system, and allied agents that are in latch contention. When storage below the 2 GB bar reaches thresholds of 88 percent, 92 percent, 96 percent, and 98 percent of available storage, messages DSNV508I, DSNV510I, DSNV511I, and DSNV512I report the storage consumption and identify the agents that are consuming the most storage. It used to be that you would use IFCID 225 and this display to detect CPU stalls and below-the-bar storage constraints.

In DB2 9, the **DISPLAY THREAD** command is extended with a new "serviceability option" (via APAR PK20800) to let you include storage as an option. Issue the command in the following form to look at storage:

```
-DISPLAY THREAD(*) SERVICE(STORAGE)
```

Use the **DETAIL** keyword on the **DISPLAY THREAD** command to see accounting information for active, inactive, and indoubt threads. Valid DB2 threads can include database access threads, allied threads, and parallel threads, and these threads can be in postponed, active, indoubt, or inactive state. The display command shows current status information about the threads. If you specify **TYPE(*)**, the command displays both **TYPE(ACTIVE)** and **TYPE(INDOUBT)** threads in one report.

The following **DISPLAY THREAD** command displays remote connections that happen to be idle and are waiting on a new UOW to begin from a remote system:

```
-DISPLAY THREAD(*) TYPE(INACTIVE)
```

CANCEL THREAD

The **CANCEL THREAD** command (Figure 7.9) cancels thread processing for local and distributed systems.

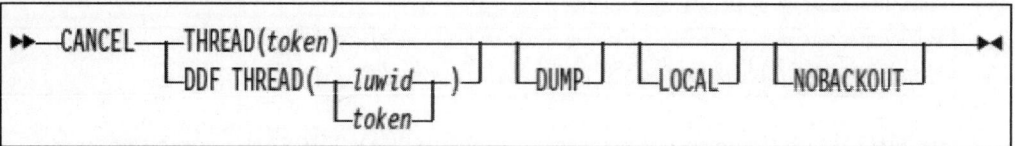

Figure 7.9: CANCEL THREAD command syntax

In the command syntax, notice the parameter value called *token*. Each thread is assigned a one- to six-digit number, or token, that is unique for a subsystem. (The specific number may be repeated across subsystems.) You can obtain the token for a particular thread using the **DISPLAY THREAD** command.

When you specify the **CANCEL THREAD** command's **NOBACKOUT** parameter, DB2 does not try to back out the data on a rollback; instead, the object is left in an inconsistent state, and it is up to you to resolve the data inconsistency.

Issuing a **CANCEL THREAD** on a table space that is **NOT LOGGED** may cause the table space to be placed in the logical page list (LPL, which applies to either data-sharing or non–data-sharing systems); you will then need to recover the table space.

RECOVER INDOUBT

Canceling a thread can cause the thread to be left in an indoubt state. DB2 releases the resources associated with this state when you resolve the state by performing an automatic resolution with the coordinator or by issuing the **RECOVER INDOUBT** command. Figure 7.10 shows this command's syntax diagram.

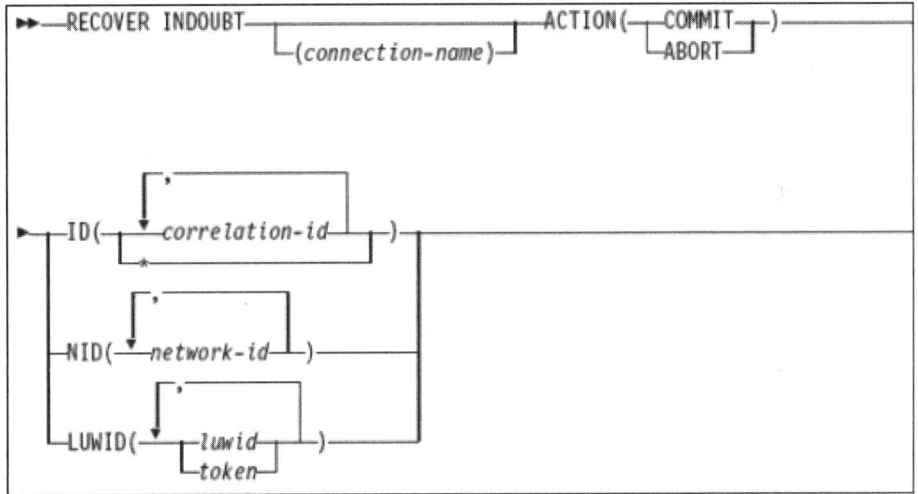

Figure 7.10: RECOVER INDOUBT command syntax

The **RECOVER INDOUBT** command's **ACTION** parameter defines whether to cancel or commit the indoubt thread. For example, if you have a non-executing thread (no longer active in DB2) that is holding resources, this situation causes –904 (resource unavailable) conditions on those unavailable resources when other applications try to access them. You must free up those resources by using the **RECOVER INDOUBT** command:

```
-RECOVER INDOUBT ACTION(ABORT) ID(*)
```

DISPLAY ARCHIVE

The **DISPLAY ARCHIVE** command displays information about the archive log data sets in use, including the availability status of allocated archive logs:

```
-DISPLAY ARCHIVE
```

ACCESS DATABASE

The **ACCESS DATABASE** command (Figure 7.11) forces a physical open of a table space, index space, or partition, or removes the GBP (global buffer pool in a data-sharing environment) dependent status of a table space, index space, or partition. The **MODE** parameter defines the state.

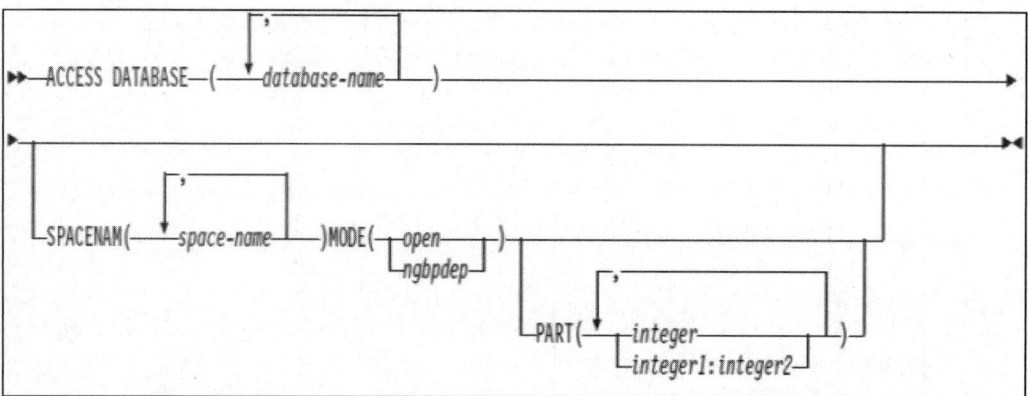

Figure 7.11: ACCESS DATABASE command syntax

To remove the intersystem read or write interest against a table space, you would issue the command as follows (the abbreviation **DB** here stands for **DATABASE**):

```
-ACCESS DB(DB1) SPACE(TS1) MODE(NGBPDEP)
```

This command converts the specified page set or partition to be non-GBP dependent. You should use this command before running large batch processes against a particular page set or partition to improve performance in a data-sharing environment. Note that if you are using an authorization that does not contain the **STARTDB** privilege for a specific database, DB2 will issue a message, and the **ACCESS MODE(NGBPDEP)** command will fail.

To force the physical opening of a partition or page set on a local member, specify the **MODE(OPEN)** option. This option gives you a new way to open data sets before SQL requests for them:

```
-ACCESS DATABASE(DSN4449) SPACENAM(DSN4450) MODE(OPEN)
```

START DATABASE

The **START DATABASE** command follows this basic syntax flow:

```
-START DATABASE(nnnnnnn) SPACENAM(nnnnn) ACCESS(xx)
```

The value of the **ACCESS** parameter can be **RW** (read/write), **RO** (read only), **UT** (utility), or **FORCE**. Note that use of the **FORCE** value can leave an index or table space in an inconsistent state.

Utility mode lets only DB2 online utilities and the SQL **DROP** statement access the objects in the specified database. You can start a database object with **ACCESS(UT)** to let the **REPAIR DBD** utility execute and then start the database object with **ACCESS(RW)**. This is a typical method for finding a problem.

You can start the **DSNDB06**, **DSNDB01**, and work file databases only by specifying them explicitly on the **START DATABASE** command.

STOP DATABASE

The **STOP DATABASE** command (Figure 7.12) makes the objects you specify unavailable and closes the data sets. In a data-sharing environment, this command applies to every member in the group. The objects you designate can be databases, table spaces, index spaces, or partitions.

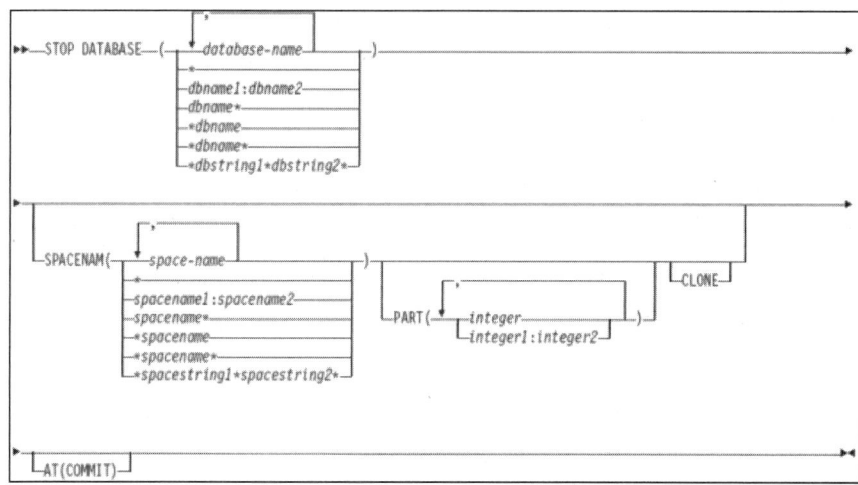

Figure 7.12: STOP DATABASE command syntax

Sometimes, you may stop a specific table space for some type of maintenance but forget to check whether the table space is currently in use (using the **DISPLAY DATABASE** command). If you stop a table space that is currently being used, DB2 places the page set in a **STOPP** restrictive state. You can make the page set "available" by using the **DISPLAY THREAD(*) TYPE(SYSTEM)** command to find the identifying token that issued the command. Then, issue the **STOP DATABASE** command followed by the **CANCEL THREAD(*token*)** command and, finally, the **START DATABASE** command.

DISPLAY DATABASE

The **DISPLAY DATABASE** command displays details about a variety of database objects and is an important tool in performance and problem resolution in DB2. Figures 7.13 and 7.14 show the **DISPLAY DATABASE** syntax.

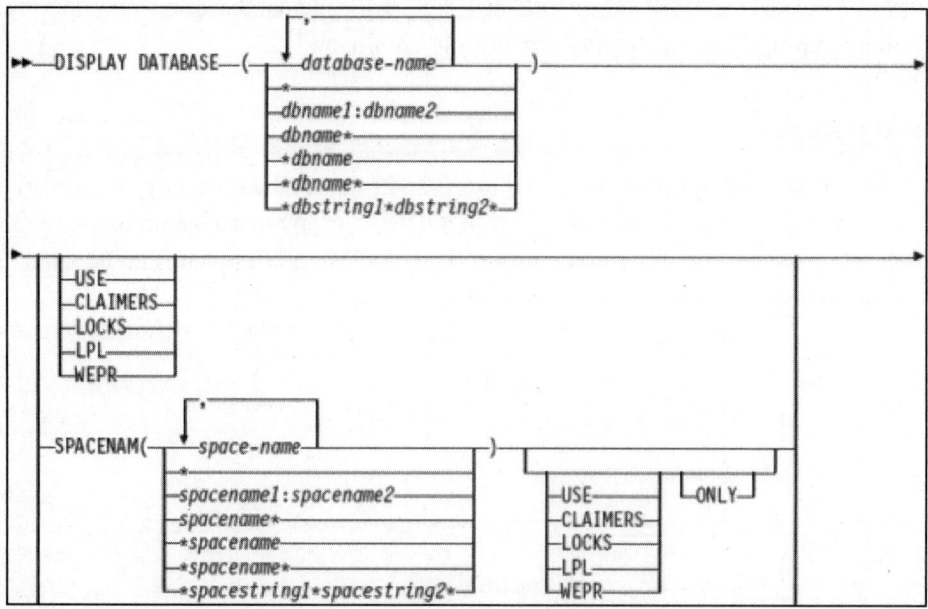

Figure 7.13: DISPLAY DATABASE command syntax (part 1 of 2)

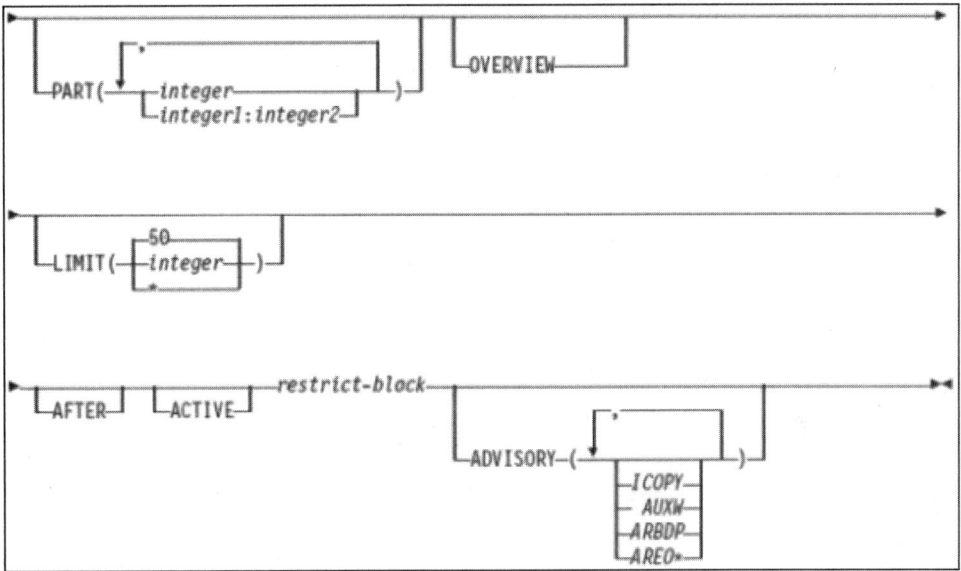

Figure 7.14: DISPLAY DATABASE command syntax (part 2 of 2)

You can limit the displayed objects to those in a specific "state" by using the
RESTRICT parameter with the following keywords:

- **ACHKP** (auxiliary advisory warning state)

- **CHKP** (**CHECK**-pending status)

- **COPY** (**COPY**-pending status)

- **GRECP** (group buffer pool **RECOVER**-pending status)

- **LPL** (logical page list entries)

- **RBDP** (**REBUILD**- or **RECOVER**-pending status)

- **RECP** (**RECOVER**-pending status)

- **REORP** (**REORG**-pending status)

- **RO** (read-only mode)

- **STOP** (stopped)

- **UT** (utility access mode)

- **UTRO** (utility access and read-only access mode)

- **UTRW** (utility access and read-write access mode)

- **UTUT** (utility access and unavailable)

- **UT*** (any utility access mode)

- **WEPR** (write error page range information)

To display objects for which read-write access is allowed but some action is recommended, use the command's **ADVISORY** option. If you use the **DISPLAY DATABASE ADVISORY** command without **RESTRICT**, you can specify one or more of the following keywords to limit the displayed objects:

- **ARBDP** (advisory **REBUILD**-pending status)

- **AREO*** (advisory **REORG**-pending status)

- **AUXW** (auxiliary warning advisory state)

- **ICOPY** (informational **COPY**-pending advisory state)

If you use **DISPLAY DATABASE** with the **PART** option to display a logical partition, the command output uses an **L** followed by a four-digit number to represent the logical partition number.

One of the things you will want do is limit the amount of output from the **DISPLAY DATABASE** command. When you use this command, you usually will be interested in a specific area, such as locks. To show the specific table spaces with locks but omit all the other table spaces from the output, you would use the command like this:

```
-DISPLAY DATABASE(*) SPACENAME(*) LOCKS ONLY
```

It is always a good idea to follow a daily ritual to stay on top of any potential problems, so using the display command in different formats can keep you informed. **RESTRICT(*xxx*)** shows the restricted states in the database, and **LIMIT(*)** says you want to see them all. The variety of options available on the **RESTRICT** parameter means you can be very specific about what you want to see:

```
-DIS DATABASE(*) SPACE(*) RESTRICT(STOP, CHKP) LIMIT(*)
```

When you issue the command **DISPLAY DATABASE SPACENAM(*)**, you may see pages in LPL status. This is the logical page list where DB2 inserts entries for pages in logical error. When the cause of a problem is undetermined, DB2 records the error in the LPL. You can restrict the display command to showing only those objects that have LPL pages. These LPL pages are listed in the output. If a program or SQL statement tries to read these pages, a –904 error will be issued, so you need to know about and recover these pages if necessary. You may encounter an error such as the following:

```
DSNB312I - csect-name DBNAME database SPACE NAME spacename PARTITION
part-number HAS PAGES IN THE LOGICAL PAGE LIST
```

To see such errors, issue this **DISPLAY DATABASE** command:

```
-DISPLAY DATABASE(DBFW8401) SPACENAM(*) LPL ONLY
```

DB2 always tries to recover the LPL pages, but you can also do this manually. To have DB2 recover the pages, issue the **START** command for the object with the **RW** or **RO** option (this works even if the object is already started). Then, issue a **START DATABASE** command to get DB2 to recover the LPL pages. You will see message DSNI021I when the process is completed.

To remove LPL pages manually, issue a **RECOVER**, **LOAD**, or **REBUILD INDEX** statement (which requires a **START DATABASE** first if you use the **PART** keyword). These are the only utilities that can run on an object that has pages in LPL. You can use **LOAD** with **MERGECOPY**, **REBUILD INDEX**, **RECOVER**, or **REPLACE** but not with **PAGE** or **ERROR RANGE**. You can use **REPAIR** with **REPORT** or **SET**.

DISPLAY UTILITY (*)

DB2's handy **DISPLAY UTILITY** command keeps you informed about how far along a utility has progressed. You can see the number of rows that might be loading to a table space. With this information, you can figure out where you are in the loading process time and estimate how much further you have to go. Figure 7.15 shows the **DISPLAY UTILITY** syntax.

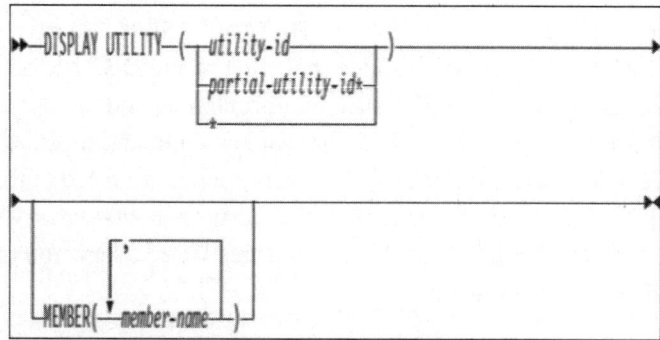

Figure 7.15: DISPLAY UTILITY command syntax

z/OS IRLM Commands

Several z/OS IRLM commands let you start, stop, and change services in the Internal Resource Lock Manager. Operands available on the **MODIFY** *irlmproc* command consist of **ABEND**, **DIAG**, **PURGE**, **SET**, and **STATUS**.

This **MODIFY** *irlmproc*,**STATUS** command, for example, displays information about one or more subsystems connected to the **IRAPROC** IRLM:

```
MODIFY IRAPROC,STATUS
```

IRLM manages locks in DB2, and a separate IRLM exists for each DB2 subsystem. You specify the module for IRLM in the subsystem parameters. It is also defined in member **IEFSSN***xx* in **SYS1.PARLIB**. IRLM must be available when you start DB2; if it is not started, DB2 will terminate. You can have IRLM start automatically. Once IRLM is started, you will see this IRLM message:

```
DXR117I irlmnm INITIALIZATION COMPLETE
```

You know that the size of a lock (whether at the row, page, table space, or index space level, for example), how long the lock is held, and the **BIND** method affect the amount of time a lock is "held" on an object. If locks are not released in a timely manner, performance problems can result. Applications must do periodic **COMMIT**s to release the locks they hold on objects.

The amount of storage available to support the locking in IRLM is also a performance issue. You can use the command **MODIFY** *irlmproc,*STATUS,STOR to monitor and view the amount of private storage that IRLM has available in DB2. In DB2 9, all locks reside in the IRLM private address space; they are no longer in the extended common service area (ECSA).

The operating system and the IPL parameters determine IRLM storage for locks and private control blocks. Ninety percent of the total space is given to the IRLM private address space during the start-up procedure. Ten percent is reserved for IRLM system services known as "must complete" processes and for z/OS system services to prevent the IRLM address space from abending and bringing down DB2. When the storage limit is reached, lock requests are rejected with an out-of-storage reason code.

You can abbreviate the **MODIFY** command to **F**, so you could use the following command to monitor the amount of storage available for locks:

```
F irlmproc,STATUS,STOR
```

Use the **MODIFY** *irlmproc,*SET command to dynamically change the maximum mount of IRLM private storage to use for locks.

The command **MODIFY irlmproc,STATUS,ALLD** displays the status of all subsystems in a data-sharing group. The command **MODIFY** *irlmproc,*ABEND terminates IRLM abnormally.

IRLM Startup Procedure Options and Locks

The **START irlmproc** command starts an IRLM procedure that is defined by the installation. The options **DEADLOCK**, **SCOPE**, **MAXCSA**, and **PC** are IRLM options relevant to DB2 locking. (Remember that **MAXCSA** is positional and is required but ignored by IRLM.) You use these options to control how DB2 uses locks.

One of the choices, **SCOPE**, has two options: **LOCAL** and **GLOBAL**. You use **SCOPE** with the data-sharing parameter **GLOBAL**; a **GLOBAL** lock provides locking serialization across the data-sharing groups. You use **LOCAL** within a single DB2 subsystem (this is the same as a non–data-sharing or single-system scope in DB2).

Be aware that data sharing increases the storage requirements in IRLM. In a data-sharing environment, IRLM handles global locking, and each DB2 member has its own IRLM.

DB2 Utilities

IBM's DB2 online utilities are available for purchase just like any other vendor products, so **COPY**, **REORG**, and other DB2 utilities are chargeable items from IBM. The IBM product code for the DB2 Utilities Suite is 5655-N97 (FMIDs JDB991K). Remember that DB2 does come with a core set of utilities at no extra charge.

Many other vendors also have products that support DB2. For example, Responsive Systems offers the Buffer Pool Tool, and HLS Technologies has tools to help you with **BIND** and migration strategies for plans and packages (including Access Path Comp, Avoid Bind, DBRM Check, Describe, Express Hints, and Path Check). BMC Software, Computer Associates, NEON Enterprise Software, and others provide a whole array of tools.

You can go to conferences, attend user group meetings and inquire around to other shops to see what tools they use. Do your research, and then contact the vendors for more information.

COPY

IBM's **COPY** utility enables the recovery of data. You can use the utility to create image copies of any of the following object types: table space, table space partition, data sets of a linear table space, index space, or index space partition. You do need to know whether the table space or index space you are copying has any restricted states.

One of the utility's major functions, besides making a backup copy of data, is setting off **COPY**-pending status once a full image copy of a table space is made. Note that if the table space is partitioned, copying one partition sets off only that partition's **COPY**-pending status. The same method applies when copying indexes. The **COPY** utility resets the informational **COPY**-pending status column of **ICOPY** for an index and resets the pending status for **NOT LOGGED** table spaces. It also places a row in **SYSIBM.SYSCOPY**. You can use the **DISPLAY DATABASE ADVISORY** command to display objects with the **ICOPY** status.

The utility's **CLONE** option lets you specify that **COPY** is to copy a particular cloned table. The **CHECKPAGE** option tells DB2 to check the validity of the pages and issue a message if it finds an error. This option is enabled by default for table spaces; it is not the default for indexes.

You must specify each of the following table spaces as a single object to be copied: **DSNDB01.SYSUTILX**, **DSNDB06.SYSCOPY**, and **DSNDB01.SYSLGRNX**.

Here are additional points of note about the operation of the **COPY** utility:

- If a **REORG** of a partition-by-growth table space leaves a partition empty, the **COPY** utility still copies the empty partition.

- If a table space contains new partitions as a result of **INSERT**s after the image copy, the newly added partitions will be recovered via the DB2 logs.

- Image copies of indexes that were created with the **COMPRESS YES** option are not compressed.

RECOVER

You use the **RECOVER** utility to recover data, from the table space level down to the page level. You have the option to recover a list of objects, system-level backups, or a single object. As input to the utility, you can use image copies or system-level backups. Use the output from the **REPORT RECOVERY** utility to determine your recovery strategy. If you recover a table space to a point in time, you will have to rebuild the indexes.

When recovering a list of objects, keep in mind that each object could have a different base: an image copy, a concurrent copy, or a system-level backup.

For system-level backups, you will need to determine where the data resides (on DASD or tape). To do so, issue the DFSMShsm **LIST COPY POOL** command with the **ALLVALS** option, and then run the stand-alone utility **DNSJU004** to obtain output that contains the DB2 system-level backup. By reviewing this information, you should be able to discover where the data resides.

Recovering a Page

Imagine that while using the **RECOVER** utility to recover a table space, you encounter a problem with a damaged page. At the end of the recovery, you receive a message that looks like this:

```
DSNI012I: PAGE LOGICALLY BROKEN TYPE type NAME name MODNAME modname
  ERQUAL erqual
```

The message identifies the damaged page by **TYPE** and **NAME**. An **ERQUAL** value of **x'0000'** indicates that the abend occurred during an online or recovery utility. The page is broken, and the recovery has failed; the system issues a 04E ABEND with reason code 00C90102, and a dump is taken. The **RECOVER** utility finishes running, but the damaged page is in a stopped state and is not recovered.

At this point, you could use the **REPAIR** utility to correct the broken page and then continue by issuing the following **RECOVER** utility job specification:

```
RECOVER TABLESPACE(xxxxx) PAGE(nnn) CONTINUE
```

Be extremely careful when using the REPAIR utility to replace data. Improper use of REPAIR can result in damaged data or, in some cases, system failure.

CAUTION

LOAD

The purpose of the **LOAD** utility is to load data to one or more tables of a table space. The syntax of the **LOAD** control statement is quite extensive. It takes time to understand the parameters and what works best in your day-to-day loading of data.

In DB2 9 for z/OS, the **KEEPDICTIONARY** keyword is ignored if the **REORG** utility changes the table space from basic row format (BRF) to reordered row format (RRF).

If you specified the **NOT LOGGED** attribute for the table space, the **LOAD** utility performs no logging (even though **LOG YES** is the default).

For partition-by-growth table spaces, you load data at the table space level, not the partition level.

You cannot run **LOAD** on the **DSNDB01** or **DSNDB06** database. However, you can add rows to the following tables in the catalog: **LOCATIONS**, **LULIST**, **LUMODES**, **LUNAMES**, **MODESELECT**, **SYSSTRINGS**, and **USERNAMES**.

For performance reasons, you should run concurrent loads against separate partitions of a partitioned table space. Preprocess the data (converting from integer to decimal, for example) so that no "conversion" is required within DB2. Sort the data before loading, doing so in the order specified by your cluster index.

The utility's **PREFORMAT** option can eliminate execution delays, but it adds setup time before the application's execution. This preformatting is recommended for high-volume inserting but is not recommended if the tables have a high ratio of reads to inserts, especially if the reads result in table space scans. **PREFORMAT** can cause empty preformatted pages to be read.

REORG

DB2's **REORG** online performance utility is designed to reclaim space and organize the data in a table space or index space in clustering order. Inserts and page splits can cause fragmentation in your data that is detrimental to overall SQL performance. Using **REORG**, you can address this issue.

The reorganization increases the effectiveness of prefetching operations in DB2. Note that you cannot run **REORG** on the **DSNDB07** database.

In DB2 9, **REORG** no longer has a **BUILD2** execution phase. This means that the building of non-partitioned indexes (NPIs) will require shadow data sets for each NPI. In addition, it is no longer possible to run **REORG**s of different partitions on the same table space in separate jobs in parallel.

In DB2 9, the **REORG** utility can reformat the row definitions in a table to the new reordered row format. Remember that the **KEEPDICTIONARY** keyword is ignored if **REORG** changes the table space from basic row format to reordered row format.

Running more than one **REORG SHRLEVEL CHANGE** job concurrently on separate tables is acceptable. You can run more than one job with **REORG SHRLEVEL CHANGE** on different partitions of the same table space, but only if no non-partitioned indexes exist on the table space. If you run jobs concurrently, each job must have its own mapping table. A failure will occur if multiple **REORG** jobs try to access the same mapping table. To keep things in order, just assign the same name to the mapping table as your utility ID.

You can run **REORG** with inline statistics gathering. Using the **REPORTONLY** option, you can produce a report that shows recommendations for reorganization without actually performing the **REORG**.

If DB2 holds a lock on an object or a long-running application is not committing, do not run **REORG** on the object. Use the **DISPLAY GROUP** command to check out the member status and see whether it has failed. By using the **DISPLAY DATABASE** command with the **LOCKS** option, you can determine whether locks are being held on the object.

If the **REORG** utility is not completing in a reasonable amount of time, you may want to change the current settings with which it is running. You can use the **ALTER UTILITY** command to change the settings of a currently running **REORG**, provided the **REORG** specifies **SHRLEVEL REFERENCE** or **SHRLEVEL CHANGE**. The settings you can alter are **DEADLINE**, **DELAY**, **LONGLOG**, and **MAXRO**.

You cannot reorganize a single table space partition (or range of partitions) if the table space is in recover-pending (**RECP**) status. This is the only recover-pending restrictive state. The **REBUILD**-pending restrictive states are:

- **RBDP** on an index that is inaccessible

- **PSRBD** on a non-partitioning index

- **RBDP*** on logical partitions of a non-partitioning index

If any of these states apply, you need to rebuild the index using the **REBUILD INDEX** utility.

You cannot reorganize a table space until the **CHECK**-pending status is removed. If both the **REORG**-pending status and the **CHECK**-pending status are in force, run **REORG** first. Then you can run the **CHECK DATA** utility to clear the **CHECK**-pending status.

It is not uncommon for a **REORG** to fail because the size of the unload work data set or the sort work data set is inadequate. The unload data set must be large enough to hold all the unloaded records in the tables from the table space. Sort work data sets can be used for collecting statistics and sorting the input. The recommendation is to make the sort work data set twice the size of the table.

If you restart the **REORG TABLESPACE** utility, by default it is restarted with either **RESTART(CURRENT)** or **RESTART(PHASE)**. There are exceptions for restarting that involve the **SHRLEVEL**, the phase you were in when the **REORG** abended, and the data set statuses used. You need to pay special attention to the phase the utility was in at the time of the failure to assess the correct procedure to use in starting the utility again.

REPAIR

The **REPAIR** utility repairs data. You can use this utility to test and repair database descriptors (DBDs), manage version numbers, reset a pending status on an index or table space, verify the contents of data areas in indexes and table spaces, delete a single row from a table space, produce a hex dump of an area within an index or table space, and perform large object (LOB) maintenance.

The **REPAIR** utility supports repairing clone table spaces with the **CLONE** parameter. This keyword tells DB2 to process only the table spaces that contain clone tables or indexes on clone tables.

The utility requires **DBADM**, **DBCTRL**, **SYSADM**, or **SYSCTRL** authority for the database authorization. You can execute the command using the **TEST** parameter to compare the DBD in the directory with a DBD built from the catalog; if the result is not zero, there is a problem:

```
REPAIR DBD TEST
```

A word of caution: You can make a bad thing worse by misusing the **REPAIR** utility. Be careful, and always have a backup. You can use **REPAIR** to reset a page set level ID, **CHECK**-pending status, **COPY**-pending status, **REBUILD**-pending status, or **RECOVER**-pending status.

REPORT

The **REPORT** utility provides information about table spaces and is usually used for planning recovery. Figure 7.16 shows the first part of the command syntax.

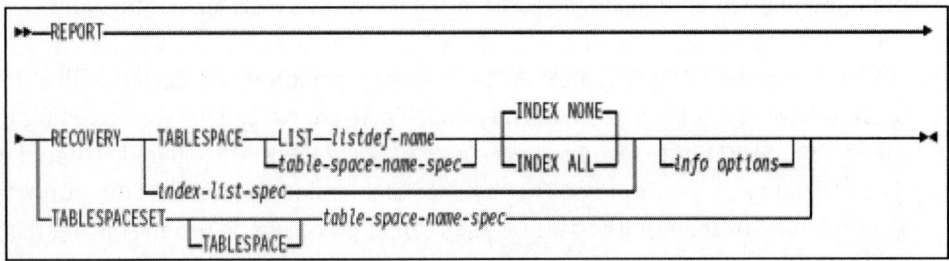

Figure 7.16: Partial syntax of the REPORT utility control statement

A nice feature of the **REPORT** utility is that you can use **REPORT TABLESPACESET** to find the names of all the tables and table spaces, including LOB table spaces, in a referential structure. The utility also provides information if an object is cloned; the output will include both the base and the clone.

If you need to find information necessary for recovering a table space, an index, or a table space and all its indexes, you use the **REPORT RECOVERY** option. The output consists of the names of all table spaces in the specified table space set.

Parameter **SHOWDSNS** (not shown in the figure) specifies that the VSAM data set names are to be included in the report for the table space set. A separate area of the report shows the data set names for **CLONE** tables. The report also lists all tables in the table spaces and the tables that are dependent on those tables. **SYSIBM.SYSCOPY** entries are marked with an asterisk if they are not **COPY** entries (e.g., a **QUIESCE**).

Another feature of the **REPORT** utility shows image copies of the table spaces **DSNDB01.DBD01**, **DSNDB01.SYSUTILX**, and **DSNDB06.SYSCOPY** that are not included in **SYSIBM.SYSCOPY**. Run the utility on the DB2 catalog and directory if you need recovery information. You will see log ranges from **SYSIBM.SYSLGRNX**, volume serial numbers, archive log locations, and information about **COPY**-pending status for data sets.

DB2 Subsystem Recommendation

To properly detect CPU stalls, run the started task for the DB2 **MSTR** address space with the **SYSSTC** dispatching priority. This is the default service class for VTAM, TCP/IP address spaces, and IRLM.

The highest priority should go to the DB2 system monitoring task. Just to be clear, the address spaces of IRLM, TCP/IP, and **ssnmMSTR** should all be assigned to service class **SYSSTC**. VTAM, IRLM, and TCP/IP must always have a higher dispatching priority than all database management system (DBMS) address spaces, attached address spaces, and subordinate address spaces. WLM should not be allowed to reduce these priorities.

MVS Commands

You can use the **D A,*jobname*** MVS command to display information about target address spaces. For example, the command **D A,OAA*** displays information about all address spaces whose associated job name begins with the string "OAA".

The **DA** (Display Active Users) command, part of the z/OS System Display and Search Facility (SDSF), gives you the ability to monitor the current system workload. You can view active tasks and see information about each task, including CPU usage, the amount of CPU time a task has used, and I/O-related **EXCP** statistics. Useful forms of the **DA** command include:

- **DA OTSU**: Displays only TSO users

- **DA OJOB**: Shows only the JES jobs running

- **DA OSTC**: Shows only the active started tasks

Stand-Alone Utilities

In this section, we look at the stand-alone utilities and discuss some of their purposes in problem solving. These utilities run as batch jobs. Table 7.1 lists the DB2 stand-alone utilities.

Table 7.1: DB2 stand-alone utilities	
Utility	**Description**
DSN1CHKR	Verifies the integrity of DB2 directory and catalog table spaces. This diagnostic tool requires detailed knowledge to use this service aid properly.
DSN1COMP	Estimates the space savings possible using compression in table spaces.
DSN1COPY	The stand-alone copy utility.
DSN1LOGP	Formats the contents of the recovery log for display.
DSN1PRNT	Prints DB2 VSAM data sets that contain tables spaces or index spaces, image copy data sets, and sequential data sets that contain DB2 table spaces or index spaces.
DSN1SDMP	Forces dumps when selected DB2 trace events occur. Writes DB2 trace records to a user-defined z/OS data set. Use under the direction of IBM Support.
DSNJCNVB	Converts the bootstrap data set (BSDS) so that it can support up to 10,000 archive log volumes and 93 active log data sets per log copy.
DSNJLOGF	The preformat active log utility; avoids delay by preformatting the active log data sets before bringing them online to DB2.
DSNJU003	The change log inventory utility; changes the BSDS, such as adding or deleting active or archive data sets.
DSNJU004	The print log map utility; can execute with DB2 running or not running.

DSNJU003

Utility **DSNJU003** (change log inventory) changes the bootstrap data sets. You can create a conditional restart control record for the next start of DB2, alter the VSAM catalog name in the BSDS, modify the communications record, delete or add archive data sets or checkpoint records, or change the highest written or offloaded RBA value.

The utility supports these statement options:

- **NEWLOG**: Used for active logs and archive logs. A new log truncation timestamp is supported in the **SYSPITRT** parameter in the BSDS.

- **DELETE**: Used to delete log sets with errors out of the BSDS. This operation does not change the log sets in any way.

- **CRESTART**: Creates or cancels a conditional restart control record for the next restart of DB2.

- **NEWCAT**: Changes the BSDS VSAM catalog name.

- **DDF**: Updates **LOCATION**, **LUNAME**, and other DDF information in the BSDS.

- **CHECKPT**: The **STARTRBA** value indicates the start checkpoint log record. *Caution:* if you do not understand conditional restarting, do not use this statement.

- **HIGHRBA**: Used to update the highest-written log RBA, in either active or archive logs.

DSNJU004

The **DSNJU004** (Print Log Map) utility lists a number of different items:

- The log and BSDS data set name, log RBA association, and log LRSN for both copies of all active and archive log data sets

- New log data sets for active logs

- Conditional restart control records and their status in the BSDS

- Checkpoint queue contents

- Command history for the archive log

- Checkpoint records queue contents in the BSDS

- The communications record (if present) in the BSDS

- **QUIESCE** history record contents

- System and utility timestamps and CCSID information

- History information for the **BACKUP SYSTEM** utility

- System-level backup information

DSN1COPY

The purpose of the **DSN1COPY** stand-alone utility is to copy VSAM data sets. The utility runs when DB2 is active or inactive.

You can use **DSN1COPY** with the **CHECK** option to perform validity checking on a page or pages in your table space, one page at a time. You can also use it to make copies of data sets. Of course, these are not registered in **SYSCOPY**. Also the row formats between the data sets must match.

The utility can also print hexadecimal dumps of data sets and databases and translate OBIDs to allow the moving of data sets between different DB2 systems. You can use this unformatted dump to find a specific page that might have an integrity problem.

IFCEREP1

To obtain a listing of the **SYS1.LOGREC** data set information, you would execute the **IFCEREP1** stand-alone utility.

DSN1CHKR

Use the **DSN1CHKR** utility when you need to verify the integrity of objects in the directory (**DSNDB01**). Using this utility, you can check the catalog and directory for broken links.

You probably **REORG** your catalog once a year to ensure integrity; you could use the sample job **DSNTIJCX** for this purpose. If you ran the health checks before migrating to DB2 9, you should be in pretty good shape starting into the migration.

DSN1LOGP

Utility **DSN1LOGP** reports RBAs and LRSNs. When working with log records, you can use this utility to analyze the entries.

Log Formats

With the reordered row format available in DB2 9, you specify the order of columns when you use the **CREATE TABLE** statement. DB2 writes the row with the variable-length columns at the end of the physical row within the data page, which can reduce the amount of logging. Because the variable-length columns are at the end of the row, DB2 can use offsets to find the column values. All the rows are formatted in RRF when you do a **REORG** or a **LOAD REPLACE**. Be fully aware of this fact if you use replication and the **DSN1COPY** utility. This formatting usually requires fewer writes to the log for updates.

Log Performance

Here are some guidelines to help with log write performance:

- Reduce the number of wait conditions associated with writing the data from the **OUTPUT BUFFER** in the system services address space to the logs. On panel **DSNTIPL**, if you make the **OUTPUT BUFFER** size used for writing active log data sets as large as you can, you will reduce the forced I/O operation when no more buffers are available. The maximum size of this buffer (**OUTBUFF**) is 400,000 KB.

- When you allocate any new active log data sets, you must preformat them using the **DSNJLOGF** utility.

- To avoid contention, place the bootstrap data set and, if you are using dual active logging, the active log data sets, on different paths/volumes from that of their primary counterparts.

- In environments with high levels of write activity, use high-capacity storage systems, such as the IBM TotalStorage DS8000, to avoid logging bottlenecks.

- Striping is most effective when many changes to log records occur between commits, and it can improve the throughput of the log.

Problem Resolution Methods

The console log is an enormous source of information about what is going on in the system. Your tool bag should include a well-structured set of SQL statements to **SELECT** against the catalog tables to collect information for performance tuning.

Data to Collect for DB2 Problems

It is useful to have a tool bag with a list of commands and utilities that you know and have ready to run when problems arise. It is always good to be prepared. There is no perfect list of commands, but a few are definitely worth the time to put in your tool bag.

Issue the following commands to assist in problem diagnosis before taking a dump of the DB2 address space:

- -DISPLAY THREAD(*) DETAIL

- -D GRS,CONTENTION

- -D A,ALL (or **D A,ssid*** or **D A,IRL***)

- -DISPLAY DATABASE(*) USE/LOCKS LIMIT(*)

- -D OPDATA

- -DISPLAY UTILITY (*)

Keep the MVS **SYSLOG** that is the **DISPLAY** command output. This log is also stored in the master trace table, which, if it is large enough, will contain the results of the commands listed here as well.

If your installation is experiencing problems in data-sharing environments, collect additional useful data with these two **MODIFY** commands (**F** is the abbreviation for **MODIFY**):

- -F irlmproc,STATUS,ALLD

- -F irlmproc,STATUS,ALLI

Run the DB2 **DIAGNOSE** utility with the **MEPL** option to produce a Module Entry Point Listing. This report shows the PTF level of the DB2 modules. The DB2 **MSTR** dump also contains this data.

It is very possible that if the DB2 subsystem or the **MSTR** address space is hung, you will get no response from the **DISPLAY** commands. In this case, a dump of the related DB2 address spaces is the only option. You do your best!

Space Issues

As you operate and troubleshoot your DB2 for z/OS system, you may encounter situations, such as those described here, where space is a concern. Knowing how to respond to these situations is part of your role as a system administrator.

Work File Database

Your work file database, **DSNDB07**, is used for sorting, specifically for SQL processing with sort, for materializing views, for handling triggers, and for storing DB2 global temporary tables. In DB2 9, the **TEMP** database has merged with the work file database. The default buffer pool assigned to the work file database is **BP0**, which is the 4 KB default for sorting operations. Changing this to another buffer pool for your work file table spaces is recommended. Remember that you have 4 KB page sizes and 32 KB page sizes for your work file database.

If you experience an out-of-disk-space or extent-limit problem with the work file database, you need to add space to the data set. To do so, you can use the SQL **CREATE TABLESPACE** command to add more table spaces in the database. Or, to enlarge a fully extended data set for the work file database, you would add space to the DB2 storage group by issuing **STOP DATABASE(DSNDB07)**, using the **ALTER**

TABLESPACE command to add volumes if necessary, and then issuing **START DATABASE(DSNDB07)** to allow access to **DSNDB07**.

Space Problems Related to DASD I/O

Accounting reports are useful in determining DASD problems. You can use the accounting report to determine DASD I/O by dividing the synchronous I/O wait time by the number of synchronous I/O operations. The report can show class 3 wait time, and you can find the amount of service task switch time for an application. This type of contention is open or close data set time.

Catalog Tables

A number of problems and conditions can occur for the DB2 catalog and directory. The most common issue is probably one or more of the system table spaces running out of space. For your transactions, these crucial spaces and indexes in the catalog are critical to watch: **DSNDB06.SYSPKAGE**, **DSNDB06.SYSPLAN**, and indexes on **DSNDB06.SYSPLANAUTH**. For queries, you should also be concerned about **DSNDB06.SYSDBASE**, **DSNDB06.SYSVIEWS**, and **DSNDB06.SYSVTREE**.

You know you can reorganize table spaces in **DSNDB06** and **DSNDB01** to reclaim space, but in general you do not run **REORG** on catalog tables very often. You also know that there are dependencies and orders to doing this **REORG** correctly.

But if you run out of space for a catalog table, what is the proper sequence of events to handle this incident? You know that table spaces in both the directory and the catalog are linear VSAM data sets. And you know you do not want users trying to use this data while you are trying to update. You want to make sure that if you fail, you can get back to the point where you started. So, to get things started, you need the name of the data set.

Data set names have the following format:

```
aaaaaaaa.DSNDBb.cccccccc.dddddddd.y0001.znnn
```

where:

- *aaaaaaaa* is the high-level qualifier

- *b* is either **C** (for VSAM clusters) or **D** (for VSAM data components)

- *cccccccc* is the database name

- *dddddddd* is the table space or index space name

- *y*0001 is the instance qualifier for the data set, with the *y* value being either **I** or **J** (i.e., **I0001** or **J0001**)

- *zccc* corresponds to the data set number, with the data set's first character being a letter (**A–E**) that represents the first digit (**0–4**) of the partition number:

  o If the partition number is less than 1000, the data set number is **A***nnn*; for example, **A999** is partition 999.

  o For partitions 1000 to 1999, the data set number is **B***nnn*; for example, **B000** is partition 1000.

  o For partitions 2000 to 2999, the data set number is **C***nnn*.

  o For partitions 3000 to 3999, the data set number is **D***nnn*.

  o For partitions 4000 through 4096 (the maximum), the data set number is **E***nnn*.

For example:

```
DSNCAT.DSNDBD.DSNDB06.SYSPLAN.I0001.A001
```

So, the method would be:

1. **COPY** the **DSNDB06.SYSPLAN** table space (you always need a backup).

2. Stop **SYSPLAN**.

3. Delete the VSAM data set for **DSNDB06.SYSPLAN**.

4. Define the preceding data set with more space.

5. Start **SYSPLAN**.

6. Recover **SYSPLAN**.

7. Check the status with a display command to make sure things look good.

You can find the VSAM definitions of the catalog tables in the installation in job **DSNTIJIN**, which defines VSAM and non-VSAM data sets for DB2.

WLM and Stored Procedures

DB2 9 for z/OS provides support for native stored procedures. These native procedures run entirely in DB2, provide the ability to define multiple versions, and are eligible for zIIP processing (if invoked via a DDF request using DRDA).

DB2 stored procedures can execute in the Workload Manager stored procedure address space and the database services address space.

Multiple stored procedures can run concurrently, each under its own task control block (TCB). The value in field **NUMBER OF TCBS** on installation panel **DSNTIPX** defines the number of concurrently executing stored procedures in an address space. You can override this value in the JCL that starts the stored procedure address space by changing the **NUMTCB** parameter. You can also change the value on the create panel for an application environment when setting up a Workload Manager application environment. There are special cases (including REXX stored procedures, where the **NUMTCB** value must be set to 1). In addition, a stored procedure can invoke only one utility at a time, so the value of **NUMTCB** is forced to 1 for the utility.

When working with stored procedures, you can use the **DISPLAY PROCEDURE** command to see the status of each named stored procedure. A stored procedure's status can be **STARTED**, **STOPABN**, **STOPPREJ**, or **STOPQUE**. The **STOPABN** status can result from an abnormal termination of the stored procedure application. You can use the **START PROCEDURE** command to place such a stored procedure in **STARTED** status.

When you implement a new version of a stored procedure, you typically want the executing version to finish before you invoke the new version. To accomplish this, use the following command:

```
VARY WLM, APPLENV=name, REFRESH
```

You may want to stop all stored procedure address spaces associated with a particular application environment once the current requests are completed. To do so, use this command:

```
VARY WLM, APPLENV=name, QUIESCE
```

When you are ready to restart all stored procedure address spaces associated with the application environment, use:

```
VARY WLM, APPLENV=name, RESUME
```

Your stored procedure environment can have many types of stored procedures (e.g., COBOL, native, REXX). These different types of stored procedures can run in separate WLM stored procedure address spaces to provide multiple isolated environments for the procedures.

Changing VCAT Names

At installation time, you entered the integrated catalog facility catalog (VCAT) names for the DB2 system data sets (this is for the directory and the catalog). By using utility **DSNJU004** or running the stored procedure **DSN8ED7**, which is part of job **DSNTEJ6Z**, you can retrieve the VCAT information.

Changing the high-level qualifier of these system data sets can be done only if you alter the bootstrap data set using utility **DSNJU003** and the corresponding DSNZPARM entries. This task would involve changing each group member in a data-sharing environment. You can find other VCAT names in the following DB2 catalog tables (column name **VCATNAME**): SYSIBM.SYSINDEXPART, SYSIBM. SYSSTOGROUP, SYSIBM.SYSTABLEPART.

CATMAINT

You run the **CATMAINT** utility when migrating to a new release of DB2 or if IBM support asks you to do so. **DSNTIJTC** is the job that runs the **CATMAINT UPDATE** function to update the catalog. This function changes the catalog name used by storage groups, user indexes, and table spaces, but only in the catalog tables.

The **CATMAINT** utility's **VCAT SWITCH(***name***, *new-name***)** option changes the catalog name used by storage groups, table spaces, and user indexes.

You can also use the **CATMAINT** utility with the **SCHEMA SWITCH** option to rename the owner, creator, and schema of database objects, plans, and packages. All the grants made are changed to the new owner.

Uncompressed Log Records

Imagine that you have a table space that is compressed, and you want to see the compressed log records in decompressed form. The **DSNJSLR** macro or any external routine cannot interpret compressed data without the associated compression dictionary. To have the log record data in decompressed format, you could use IFCID 306. You could retrieve this information using the IFI **READS** function.

EDM Pool

EDM storage pools that are too small will cause the following problems. You will see increased I/O activity against the directory tables **DSNDB01.DBD01**, **DSNDB01. SCT02**, and **DSNDB01.SPT01**. This activity can cause increased response times due to the time required to load the DBDs, SKCTs, and SKPTs versus them being in the EDM pool. Because of the lack of storage, fewer threads can be supported, potentially causing waits for your threads.

DBD Size

You should always be aware of the size of your database descriptors for large databases. The best practice is to monitor and manage these DBDs to prevent them from becoming too large.

The problem is that very large DBDs can reduce concurrency. But because of increased logging and I/O, they can also degrade the performance of SQL operations that create or alter objects.

You do not need contiguous storage for DBDs, but you do need chunks of 32 KB to load the sections. (Older DBDs do require contiguous storage.)

When you **CREATE**, **ALTER**, or **DROP** objects in a database, the storage is not automatically reclaimed in the DBD. Use the **MODIFY** utility to reclaim storage in a DBD.

Data Sharing

The data-sharing function of DB2 for z/OS enables multiple applications to read from, and write to, the same DB2 data concurrently. The applications can run on different DB2 subsystems that reside on multiple central processor complexes (CPCs) in a Parallel Sysplex.

The DB2 subsystems that access shared DB2 data are known as a data-sharing group. Each subsystem that belongs to a data-sharing group is a "member" of that group.

A Sysplex is a group of z/OS systems that are connected through a Sysplex Timer and enterprise system connection channels. These systems cooperate with each other using special hardware and software. A Parallel Sysplex is a Sysplex that uses one or more coupling facilities to provide list processing, lock processing, and high-speed caching for the applications on the Sysplex.

To enable data sharing, you must define the coupling facility structures. You must have one list structure, one lock structure, and at least four cache structures (group buffer pools). The list and lock structures do not have to be in the same coupling facility. You define these structures to the Parallel Sysplex by using a coupling facility resource management (CFRM) policy, which determines where and how the structure resources are allocated.

If you experience a power failure to the CPC and no automatic resource manager (ARM) policy is active, the members of the data-sharing group will terminate abnormally and will be unable to process any work until they are restarted.

To implement a data-sharing system, you could set up "two-way" data sharing in a DB2 subsystem. The two members of the data-sharing group reside on different systems, and each can have its own coupling facility to support the lock and shared communications area (SCA) structures. This is a simple example of how to establish a data-sharing environment. Note that duplexing enables you to use internal coupling facilities, which typically represent a cost savings over stand-alone coupling facilities.

Working with WLM, the incoming requests are balanced across the members of the data-sharing group. The group members share the data and have read/write access to it. If one DB2 subsystem is being brought down, the other DB2s pick up the workload. The DB2 subsystems share the same DB2 catalog and directory. You can stop and start members in the data-sharing group, and the other members continue to run.

All members must reside in the same Parallel Sysplex. The maximum number of members in a data-sharing group is 32. When you add a new DB2 subsystem onto another CPC in a data-sharing environment, applications can access the same data through the new member (subsystem) just as easily as through any of the existing members.

You can have batch jobs connected randomly to members of a data-sharing group on the same z/OS by using the DSN command **DSN SYSTEM(*xxx*)**, where the **SYSTEM** parameter defines the group attachment name of the data-sharing group. Because of the separate logs that exist for each member, DB2 uses the SCA in a coupling facility to coordinate recovery.

If a data-sharing group member is running a utility (UID) and the member fails, DB2 retains the lock on the UID until the member is restarted; at that point, the lock is converted to an active lock. To recover (release) the locks held by the member as quickly as possible and minimize the storage required to restart the member, you can restart the member in "light" mode. DB2 will restart in light mode only if you have defined an ARM policy for the group. The automatic restart manager will not restart the member again after a light restart is performed.

You use one of the following clauses on the **START DB2** command to restart the member in light mode:

- **LIGHT (YES)**

- **LIGHT(NOINDOUBTS)**

If you use **LIGHT(YES)** to restart a member and indoubt units of recovery (URs) exist, DB2 issues message DSNR052I at the end of the restart, and the member continues to run in light mode to allow the indoubt URs to be recovered. If you use **LIGHT(NOINDOUBTS)**, the member terminates without waiting for resolution of any indoubt URs.

DISPLAY GROUPBUFFERPOOL

With DB2 data sharing, group buffer pools are a key component of cache coherency. You can use the **DISPLAY GROUPBUFFERPOOL** (abbreviated **DIS GBPOOL**) command to monitor the size of group buffer pools in addition to write failures, reclaims, and other statistical information. Specify the **GDETAIL** parameter to produce a detailed statistics report for the specified group buffer pool:

```
-DISPLAY GROUPBUFFERPOOL GDETAIL
```

The **GDETAIL** output includes information about whether the group buffer pool has enough data entries; if it does not, castout to disk will occur more frequently. If you see "failed due to lack of storage" statistics, the data page resources of the coupling facility are being consumed more quickly than the castout processes can free them. By increasing the total size of the group buffer pool or adjusting the ratio of directory entries to data pages in favor of data entries (using the **ALTER GROUPBUFFERPOOL** command), you can increase the number of data entries in the group buffer pool.

Checkpointing can cause surges in the coupling facility. Check your requests per checkpoint to see if this is a possibility. You may need to decrease the checkpoint interval (parameter **GBPCHKPT** on the **ALTER GROUPBUFFERPOOL** command). The following monitoring IFCIDs can help with determining your problems:

- IFCID 0261 provides summary statistics for each group buffer pool checkpoint.

- IFCID 0263 provides summary statistics for the castouts.

You can monitor group buffer pools with the z/OS **DISPLAY XCF,STR** command. This command retrieves information about the coupling facility structures, including the coupling facility name, connections, duplexing status, preference list, and CFRM policy definition. If the group buffer pool is duplexed, you will see information about both allocations of the structure.

```
D XCF,STR,STRNAME=DSNDBAA_GBP1
```

Command Scope

In data sharing, some commands affect only the member on which they are issued. Other commands have group scope because they affect all member of the group. The following commands have group scope:

- **ALTER GROUPBUFFERPOOL** (DB2)

- **BIND PACKAGE** (DSN)

- **BIND PLAN** (DSN)

- **DCLGEN** (DSN)

- **DISPLAY DATABASE** (DB2)

- **DISPLAY GROUP** (DB2)

- **DISPLAY GROUPBUFFERPOOL** (DB2)

- **FREE PACKAGE** (DSN)

- **FREE PLAN** (DSN)

- **MODIFY *irlmproc*,DIAG** (z/OS IRLM)

- **REBIND PACKAGE** (DSN)

- **REBIND PLAN** (DSN)

- **REBIND TRIGGER PACKAGE** (DSN)

- **START DATABASE** (DB2)

- **STOP DATABASE** (DB2)

The following commands have group or member scope (the syntax determines the scope):

- **ARCHIVE LOG** (DB2)

- **DISPLAY FUNCTION SPECIFIC** (DB2)

- **DISPLAY PROCEDURE** (DB2)

- **DISPLAY THREAD** (DB2)

- **DISPLAY TRACE** (DB2)

- **DISPLAY UTILITY** (DB2)

- **MODIFY** *irlmproc*,**SET** (z/OS IRLM)

- **MODIFY** *irlmproc*,**STATUS** (z/OS IRLM)

- **START FUNCTION SPECIFIC** (DB2)

- **START PROCEDURE** (DB2)

- **START TRACE** (DB2)

- **STOP FUNCTION SPECIFIC** (DB2)

- **STOP PROCEDURE** (DB2)

- **STOP TRACE** (DB2)

- **TERM UTILITY** (DB2)

All other commands have member scope.

Group Buffer Pools

A group buffer pool failure restricts access to the data assigned to that group buffer pool; it does not cause all members of the group to fail. If a loss of connectivity to the group buffer pools occurs, your applications may receive –904 return codes.

You can use the **AUTOREC(YES)** option of the **ALTER GROUPBUFFERPOOL** command to enable automatic recovery should a structure failure or loss of connectivity to the group buffer pool occur. When you enable this option, DB2 automatically recovers the page sets and partitions that are in group buffer pool **RECOVER**-pending (**GRECP**) status or in LPL pages. Group buffer pools are placed in **RECOVER**-pending or **GRECP** status if the coupling facility failed with pages that were not externalized.

The way around the issue is to use either the **RECOVER** utility or the **START DATABASE** command to recover the object and clear the condition. To see this condition, you can use the **DISPLAY DATABASE** command with the **RESTRICT** option to find the exception statuses for the object.

You should have at least two coupling facilities. This strategy lets the secondary coupling facility take over for the primary if the primary facility is damaged. Configure at least one of the two facilities as non-volatile, which typically means you use power backup. If the backup fails, the coupling facility enters a volatile state; you will receive a warning message if this occurs. When a coupling facility is in a volatile state, the data in that facility is not saved in the event of a power failure.

Duplexing the SCA, lock, and group buffer pool structures is also a good backup strategy. The coupling facility contains a lock structure that data sharing uses. This lock structure contains two parts: a lock entry table and a list of update locks.

If a non-duplexed group buffer is unavailable and you receive a –904 error code (loss of connectivity) for a pool specified with **AUTOREC(NO)**, the first and quickest action to resolve this issue is to issue a **START DATABASE** command, specifying the table space that is in the **GRECP** status.

If you see a very high page p-lock contention, you should think about how to alleviate the situation. One option is to reduce row-level locking for objects that might be used in high-volume transactions. Another is to **ALTER** the heavily used table spaces to use **TRACKMOD NO**.

DB2 Administration Tool

We conclude this chapter (and the book) with a quick look at some of the system administration functions you can perform with IBM's DB2 Administration Tool for z/OS (program number 5697-L90):

- Displaying and managing traces
- Displaying and updating resource limits (RLIMITs), including the predictive governing limits in DB2
- Displaying and altering buffer pools
- Displaying threads
- Displaying and terminating utilities
- Displaying and setting archive log parameters and archiving the log
- Displaying DB2 system parameters and updating dynamic parameters
- Dynamically managing system parameters

For the distributed data facility (DDF):

- Starting and stopping DDF
- Displaying and updating the communications database (CDB)
- Displaying and canceling distributed threads
- Displaying active locations

Practice Questions

Question 1

How do you restrict or limit user access to data with the **START DB2** command?

○ A. -**START DB2 ACCESS(MAINT)**

○ B. -**START DB2**, with no parameters

○ C. -**START DB2 LIGHT(NO)**

○ D. -**START DB2 ACCESS(NO)**

Question 2

Which command changes to the **CBIPARM** member for restarting DB2?

○ A. –**SET SYSPARM STARTUP**

○ B. –**SET SYSPARM RELOAD(CBIPARM)**

○ C. –**SET SYSPARM LOAD(CBIPARM)**

○ D. –**SET SYSPARM STARTUP**

Question 3

What is the abbreviation for the IRLM command **MODIFY**?

○ A. **O**

○ B. **Y**

○ C. **M**

○ D. **F**

Question 4

Which of the following commands produces thread accounting information to show inactive, active, and indoubt threads?

○ A. **–DISPLAY THREAD(*) SERVICE(STORAGE)**

○ B. **–DISPLAY THREAD(*) SERVICE(WAIT)**

○ C. **–DISPLAY THREAD(*) DETAIL**

○ D. **–DISPLAY THREAD(*) TYPE(SYSTEM)**

Question 5

Which command could leave the database in an inconsistent state?

○ A. **–START DATABASE(name) SPACENAME(name) ACCESS(RW)**

○ B. **–START DATABASE(name) SPACENAME(name) ACCESS(FORCE)**

○ C. **–START DATABASE(name) SPACENAME(name) ACCESS(UT)**

○ D. **–START DATABASE(name) SPACENAME(name) ACCESS(RO)**

Question 6

What does the **CLONE** parameter on the **COPY** utility do?

○ A. Makes another copy of the table

○ B. Checks for clones and then stops

○ C. Does not copy clone table spaces

○ D. Copies cloned tables

Question 7

How can you set off logging on the **LOAD** utility even if the default is **LOG YES**?

○ A. Specify **NOT LOGGED**

○ B. Specify **DEFAULT**

○ C. Specify **LOG YES ONLY**

○ D. Specify **NOT LOGGED ONLY**

Question 8

Which dispatching priorities order is recommended?

○ A. IRLM, TCP/IP, DBMS address spaces, VTAM

○ B. DBMS address spaces, VTAM, IRLM, TCP/IP

○ C. DBMS address spaces, IRLM, VTAM, TCP/IP

○ D. VTAM, IRLM, TCP/IP, DBMS address spaces

Question 9

When you are deciding whether or not to use compression, which utility can provide compression estimates?

○ A. **DSN1COPY**

○ B. **DSNJU004**

○ C. **DSN1CHKR**

○ D. **DSN1COMP**

Question 10

If you wanted to obtain a listing of the **SYS1.LOGREC** data set, which of the following would you execute?

○ A. **DSN1CHKR**

○ B. **IFCEREP1**

○ C. **DSNJLOGF**

○ D. **REPAIR**

DB2 Message Numbers

DB2 messages have unique message numbers. Messages are ordered by subcomponent identifier and numeric identifier within groups in the message manual. The message number can be from eight to 10 characters long and follows the format DSN*XnnnY*, where:

- "DSN" is the DB2 component prefix.

- *X* is the subcomponent identifier, which is a hexadecimal identifier. Table A.1 lists the subcomponents or functional areas and the associated IDs.

- *nnn* is a numeric identifier three to five characters in length.

- *Y* is the message type code. The codes are:

  » A = Action required immediately, task does not continue until action taken

  » D = Action or decision required immediately, task does not continue until action taken

  » E = Action required at some point, task continues

  » I = Informational only, no action is required

Table A.1: Subcomponent key		
Subcomponent/functional area	Identifier for messages	Identifier for reason codes
Call attach facility	A	x'C1'
Buffer manager	B	x'C2'
TSO attachment	E	x'C5'
Message generator	F	x'C6'
Database descriptor manager	G	n/a
Precompiler, DSNH CLIST	H	x'C8'
Data manager	I	x'C9'
Recovery log manager	J	x'D1'
Distributed data facility	L	x'D3'
IMS attachment facility	M	x'D4'
XML manager	n/a	x'D5'
Data space manager	P	x'D7'
MQListener	Q	n/a
Recovery manager	R	x'D9'
Storage manager	S	x'E2'
Service controller, install	T	x'E3'
Utilities	U	x'E4'
Agent service manager	V	x'E5'
Instrumentation facility	W	x'E6'
Relational data system	X	x'E7'
Initialization procedures	Y	x'E8'
System parameter manager	Z	x'E9'
Services facilities	1	x'F1'
Subsystem support	3	x'F3'
Group manager	7	x'F7'
Sample applications	8	x'F8'
General command processor	9	x'F9'

References

Useful Web Sites

Computer Business International, Inc. (CBI)
http://www.cbi4you.com

DB2 for z/OS
http://www-01.ibm.com/software/data/db2/zos

DB2 for z/OS – Technical Resources
http://www-01.ibm.com/support/docview.wss?rs=64&uid=swg27011656

IBM Information Management Books
http://www-01.ibm.com/software/data/education/bookstore

IBM Redbooks
http://www.redbooks.ibm.com

DB2 9 for z/OS Manuals

These manuals are available in HTML and PDF format at *http://www-01.ibm.com/ support/docview.wss?uid=swg27011656#manuals.*

Administration Guide (SC18-9840)

Application Programming and SQL Guide (SC18-9841)

Application Programming Guide and Reference for Java (SC18-9842)

Codes (GC18-9843)

Command Reference (SC18-9844)

Data Sharing: Planning and Administration (SC18-9845)

Diagnosis Guide and Reference (LY37-3218)

Installation Guide (GC18-9846)

Internationalization Guide (SC19-1161)

Introduction to DB2 for z/OS (SC18-9847)

IRLM Messages and Codes for IMS and DB2 for z/OS (GC19-2666)

Licensed Program Specifications (GC18-9848)

Messages (GC18-9849)

ODBC Guide and Reference (SC18-9850)

Performance Monitoring and Tuning Guide (SC18-9851)

RACF Access Control Module Guide (SC18-9852)

Reference for Remote DRDA Requesters and Servers (SC18-9853)

Reference Summary (SX26-3854)

SQL Reference (SC18-9854)

SQL Reference for Cross-Platform Development (Version 3.1)

Utility Guide and Reference (SC18-9855)

What's New? (GC18-9856)

XML Extender Administration and Programming (SC18-9857)

XML Guide (SC18-9858)

Program Directories for DB2 9 for z/OS

These program directories are available in PDF format at *http://www-01.ibm.com/ support/docview.wss?uid=swg27011656#db29-pd*.

DB2 9 for z/OS Program Directory (GI10-8737)

DB2 Accessories Suite for z/OS Program Directory (GI10-8749)

Data Studio Workbench Program Directory (GI10-8773)

DB2 Utilities Suite for z/OS, V9R1, Program Directory (GI10-8746)

DB2 Management Clients Package Program Directory (GI10-8738)

z/OS Application Connectivity to DB2 for z/OS (GI10-8739)

Program Directories for DB2 9 for z/OS VUE

These program directories are available in PDF format at *http://www-01.ibm.com/support/docview.wss?uid=swg27011656#db29-vue*.

DB2 9 for z/OS VUE Program Directory (GI10-8779)

DB2 Management Clients Package VUE Program Directory (GI10-8780)

z/OS Application Connectivity to DB2 for z/OS VUE Program Directory (GI10-8781)

Program Directories for DB2 Accessories Suite for z/OS

These program directories are available in PDF format at *http://www-01.ibm.com/support/docview.wss?uid=swg27011656#accessories*.

OmniFind Text Search Server for z/OS Installation, Administration, and Reference (GC19-1146)

Optimization Service Center for DB2 for z/OS Getting Started (GC19-1143)

Spatial Support for DB2 for z/OS User's Guide and Reference (GC19-1145)

C

Answers to the Practice Questions

Chapter 2

Question 1

> Name the three major groups of subcomponent code structure in DB2.
>
> ○ A. *SSAS, DBAS, DDF*
>
> ○ B. SSAS, DBAS, IRLM
>
> ○ C. SSAS, DBAS, SPAS
>
> ○ D. SSAS, DBAS, WLM

☑ *The answer is **A**. These three are the major subcomponents of DB2 as they relate to the code.*

Question 2

> At DB2 address space termination, what happens to the DB2 shared memory object area?
>
> ○ A. It continues to run, but the VSO is deleted.
>
> ○ B. *It is freed, and interest in the VSO is deleted.*
>
> ○ C. It will continue to be available on the next start-up of DB2.
>
> ○ D. It will not be affected.

☑ *The answer is **B**. Each address space, when it is terminated during shutdown, requests that its interest in the virtual shared object (VSO) be deleted.*

Question 3

An inactive connection in DB2 was previously called:

○ A. *Type 2 inactive thread*

○ B. Inactive DBAT

○ C. Active DBAT

○ D. Type 2 active thread

☑ *The answer is A, Type 2 inactive thread. The terminology has changed in describing threads in a distributed environment. Just remember, not all threads can be inactive connections.*

Question 4

When trying to establish the total number of threads that can access data in DB2, what should you do?

○ A. Add **MAXDBAT** and **CTHREAD**

○ B. Subtract **CTHREAD** from **MAXDBAT**

○ C. Divide **MAXDBAT** by **CTHREAD**

○ D. Check **MAXDBAT** only

☑ *The answer is A. Here, you want to think about which parameters are associated with threads and how they work together. **MAXDBAT** is the maximum number of concurrently active database access threads (DBATs). **CTHREAD** defines the number of concurrently allocated threads for local connections. To find the total, you add the two together.*

Question 5

> Native stored procedures, if invoked from DRDA TCP/IP connections to DB2, may:
>
> ○ A. Be eligible for zap processing
>
> ○ B. *Be eligible for zIIP processing*
>
> ○ C. Be eligible for zIIP and zap processing
>
> ○ D. Are not eligible for either zIIP or zap processing

☑ *The answer is **B**, they may be eligible for zIIP processing. This is one of the important points of using native stored procedures. It helps offload some of the work and helps relieve storage constraints in DB2.*

Question 6

> What are the associated pools in the EDM pool (RDS)?
>
> ○ A. *EDMDBDC, EDMSTMTC, EDM_SKELETON_POOL*
>
> ○ B. **EDMDBDC, EDMSTMTC**
>
> ○ C. **EDMDBDC, EDM_SKELETON_POOL**
>
> ○ D. **EDMDBDC**

☑ *The answer is **A**. A new area in the pool helps with skeletons, and the others are areas we have had in previous releases. The **EDM_SKELETON_POOL** parameter is available on the **DSNTIPC** installation panel (field **EDM SKELTON POOL SIZE**). Keep in mind that the size of this pool is not automatically increased or decreased.*

Question 7

> The DSNZPARM parameter **MAXKEEPD** is used to:
>
> ○ A. Limit the number of threads
>
> ○ B. *Limit the number of dynamic statements held in the cache*
>
> ○ C. Limit the number of statistics kept on dynamic cache
>
> ○ D. Limit the number of threads to keep

☑ *The answer is **B**. **MAXKEEPD** controls the maximum number of prepared statements.*

Question 8

> Which DSNZPARM defines the number of RID blocks in the RID pool storage?
>
> ○ A. **CONDBAT**
> ○ B. **URLGWTH**
> ○ C. **NUMTCB**
> ○ D. *MAXRBLK*

☑ *The answer is **D**. The **MAXRBLK** value is stored internally, and DB2 then allocates row identifier (RID) blocks in 32 KB chunks.*

Question 9

> What buffer sizes are supported for the **DSNDB07** database?
>
> ○ A. 4 KB, 8 KB, 16 KB, 32 KB
> ○ B. *4 KB, 32 KB*
> ○ C. 4 KB, 16 KB
> ○ D. 4 KB, 8 KB

☑ *The answer is **B**. The sizes have not changed, but we know that our requirements for more 32 KB space will increase in DB2 9.*

Question 10

> What are the types of dumps in z/OS?
>
> ○ A. Transaction, abend, stand-alone
> ○ B. *SVC, transaction, abend, stand-alone, snap*
> ○ C. Stand-alone and snap
> ○ D. Stand-alone, abend, snap, dump

☑ *The answer is **B**. All the dump types in z/OS are listed in this answer.*

Chapter 3

Question 1

In the migration/installation process, which is the logical sequence of events if you need to fall back from ENFM?

- ○ A. ENFM to CM* to CM
- ○ B. ENFM to CM to CM*
- ○ C. *ENFM to CM**
- ○ D. ENFM to CM

☑ *The answer is **C**. Remember that you cannot fall back to CM from ENFM or to DB2 8 NFM.*

Question 2

What is the FMID for the base code for DB2 9 for z/OS (not VUE)?

- ○ A. JDB991Z
- ○ B. *HDB9910*
- ○ C. HDRE9910
- ○ D. JDB991K

☑ *The answer is **B**. All others are different components. A is VUE, C is RACF, and D is the DB2 Utilities Suite.*

Question 3

Which target library contains the DB2 early code?

- ○ A. ***prefix.SDSNLINK***
- ○ B. ***prefix*.SDSNLOAD**
- ○ C. ***prefix*.SDSNEXIT**
- ○ D. ***prefix*.SDSNIVPD**

☑ *The answer is **A**. Answer B contains load modules. C is empty at first and then later contains DSNZPARMs. D is the installation verification programs.*

Question 4

> Which mode converts the DB2 catalog?
>
> ○ A. CM
> ○ B. *ENFM*
> ○ C. NFM
> ○ D. CM*

☑   *The answer is **B**. CM is step 1 using the DB2 9 code. NFM is not the conversion of the catalog. CM* indicates a fallback mode only.*

Question 5

> Which job assembles DSNZPARMs?
>
> ○ A. *DSNTIJUZ*
> ○ B. **DSNTIJEN**
> ○ C. **DSNTIJMS**
> ○ D. **DSNTIJTC**

☑   *The answer is **A**. **DSNTIJEN** is the job to go from CM to ENFM, **DSNTIJMS** is an SMP/E job, and **DSNTIJTC** is the job that takes you to CM.*

Question 6

> Which job is used to check DB2 release incompatibilities in DB2 9?
>
> ○ A. **DSNTIJTC**
> ○ B. **DSNTIJIC**
> ○ C. **DSNTIJP9**
> ○ D. *DSNTIJPM*

☑   *The answer is **D**, **DSNTIJPM**. This job is shipped with DB2 9. Job **DSNTIJTC** tailors the catalog, **DSNTIJIC** takes copies of the catalog, and **DSNTIJP9** is the DB2 8 version of the job.*

Question 7

> Which job is used to convert the BSDS to the new format for DB2 9?
>
> ○ A. **DSN1COPY**
> ○ B. **DSNJU003**
> ○ C. *DSNJCNVB*
> ○ D. **DSNJU004**

☑ *The answer is **C**; job **DSNJCNVB** performs the conversion to the new format for the BSDS. **DSN1COPY** does let you copy DB2 VSAM data sets, but it does not reformat the BSDS. **DSNJU003** does the format only. D is the print log map job.*

Question 8

> Which command reloads a previous DSNZPARM load module?
>
> ○ A. *-SET SYSPARM RELOAD*
> ○ B. **-SET SYSPARM LOAD**
> ○ C. **-SET SYSPARM STARTUP**
> ○ D. **-SET SYSPARM AGAIN**

☑ *The answer is **A**. B (**SET SYSPARM LOAD**) loads a new system parameter load module, and C (**SET SYSPARM STARTUP**) reloads a load module used at startup. Answer D (**SET SYSPARM AGAIN**) is a good idea but does not exist.*

Question 9

> What is the size or sizes of the work files in DB2 9?
>
> ○ A. 4 KB, 8 KB, 16 KB
> ○ B. *4 KB, 32 KB*
> ○ C. 4 KB, 8 KB, 16 KB, 32 KB
> ○ D. 4 KB

☑ *The answer is **B**. Remember that DB2 9 eliminates other work files and now has only two sizes for these. **MAXTEMPS** is the parameter discussed in Chapter 3 for setting the work file size for each agent. It specifies the maximum amount of temporary space an agent can use. If this size is too small, failures will occur. For example, you may have a declared global temporary table fail from lack of work file space. The other answers are nice, but incorrect.*

Question 10

From panel **DSNTIPA1**, what are the four types of changes you can make through CLIST generation?

○ A. **INSTALL, MIGRATE, UPDATE, NFM**

○ B. **INSTALL, MIGRATE, ENFM, DELETE**

○ C. **INSTALL, MIGRATE, UPDATE, CM**

○ D. **INSTALL, MIGRATE, ENFM, UPDATE**

☑ *The answer is **D**; the panel allows the install types **INSTALL, MIGRATE, ENFM**, and **UPDATE**.*

Chapter 4

Question 1

> Name the two encryption options available for DB2 for z/OS:
>
> ○ A. FIELDPROC and SSAS encryption
>
> ○ B. Built-in encryption and FIELDPROC
>
> ○ C. *Built-in encryption at the column level and EDITPROC*
>
> ○ D. FIELDPROC and EDITPROC

☑ *The answer is **C**. These two options provide data encryption in DB2.*

Question 2

> When creating a column for data encryption, you must define the column as:
>
> ○ A. **CHAR**
>
> ○ B. ***VARCHAR FOR BIT DATA***
>
> ○ C. **DECIMAL**
>
> ○ D. **INTEGER**

☑ *The answer is **B**. The length of your **VARCHAR** depends on the password and the password hint to compute the final length.*

Question 3

> Why is trusted security context important to establishing connections? Identify *two* reasons:
>
> ○ A. *User identity can be passed to the database server.*
>
> ○ B. *Trusted security is an object that give users a specific set of privileges.*
>
> ○ C. Trusted security context is only for DDF.
>
> ○ D. Trusted security context does not require an RACF ID.

☑ *The answers are **A** and **B**. These answers bring up the fact that trusted security context deals with the user identity and provides a way to use that as an object with a specific set of privileges.*

Question 4

> Which *two* of the following statements are true of role-based security:
>
> ○ A. *A role is a database entity.*
> ○ B. *One role can be associated with one thread at any point in time.*
> ○ C. More than one role can be associated with a thread.
> ○ D. You cannot use **GRANT** and **REVOKE** with **ROLE**.

☑ *The answers are **A** and **B**. Role-based security can grant privileges on an object to a role. A role is a database entity to which or from which one or more DB2 privileges can be granted or revoked.*

Question 5

> **SYSCTRL** authority is designed:
>
> ○ A. *To be an administrator in a system that contains sensitive data*
> ○ B. To allow access to all data directly in DB2
> ○ C. Not to be a part of the administrative authorizations
> ○ D. So that group privileges cannot be granted to **SYSCTRL**

☑ *The answer is **A**. This answer also relates to the previous question because to create a role, you must have either **SYSADM** or **SYSCTRL** authority.*

Question 6

> What is the sample exit code routine that supports RACF in DB2?
>
> ○ A. **DSNX@XAC**
> ○ B. **IRR@XACS**
> ○ C. **DSNTIJEX**
> ○ D. *DSNXRXAC*

☑ *The answer is **D**. This is the sample code exit and can be found in library* prefix. *SDSNSAMP.*

Question 7

> What is the RACF resource class for DB2?
>
> ○ A. **RADB**
>
> ○ B. *DSNR*
>
> ○ C. **RSNR**
>
> ○ D. **DADB**

☑ *The answer is **B**. **DSNR** is the resource class for DB2. The list of classes and descriptions are listed in the material.*

Question 8

> What are the default exit routines for authorization and connection and for a sign-on process in DB2? Choose *two* answers:
>
> ○ A. *DSN3@ATH*
>
> ○ B. **DSNAUTH**
>
> ○ C. *DSN3@SGN*
>
> ○ D. **DSNSGON**

☑ *The answers are **A** and **C**. **DSN3@SGN** is the sign-on routine, and **DSN3@ATH** is the default exit routine for connections.*

Question 9

> Which SMF type are the audit trace records?
>
> ○ A. 101
>
> ○ B. *102*
>
> ○ C. 103
>
> ○ D. 104

☑ *The answer is **B**. Type 102 is the SMF type for the audit trace records you collect.*

Question 10

> If you are using an audit trace in DB2, how much overhead is typical?
>
> ○ A. More than 5 percent
>
> ○ B. *Less than 5 percent*
>
> ○ C. More than 20 percent
>
> ○ D. Less than 20 percent

☑ *The answer is **B**. It is sometimes surprising to note that the impact of audit tracing can be very minimal.*

Chapter 5

Question 1

> What resources does the **REPORT** utility use to give you the recovery history of a table space?
>
> ○ A. *SYSCOPY, SYSLGRNX, BSDS*
>
> ○ B. **SYSTABLESPACE, SYSCOPY, BSDS**
>
> ○ C. **SYSTABLE, SYSCOPY, BSDS**
>
> ○ D. **SYSUTILX, SYSCOPY, BSDS**

☑ *The answer is **A**. **SYSCOPY, SYSLGRNX**, and **BSDS** are the table spaces from which the **REPORT** utility extracts information for printing.*

Question 2

> What is the first table space in the system that you recover using the **RECOVER** utility?
>
> ○ A. *DSNDB01.SYSUTILX*
>
> ○ B. **DSNDB01.DBD01**
>
> ○ C. **DSNDB01.SYSDBASE**
>
> ○ D. **DSNDB06.SYSCOPY**

☑ *The answer is **A**. **DSNDB01.SYSUTILX** is always the first table space to copy. **SYSCOPY** is the last.*

Question 3

> What are the two new phases in the **RECOVER** utility in DB2 9?
>
> ○ A. **TOLOGPOINT** and **TORBA**
>
> ○ B. *LOGCSR* and *LOGUNDO*
>
> ○ C. **COMLOG** and **COMRBA**
>
> ○ D. **UNDO** and **REDO**

☑ *The answer is **B**. **LOGCSR** and **LOGUNDO** are new phases within the **RECOVER** utility.*

Question 4

> If you lose one of the archive logs during the offload process — for example, due to an out-of-space condition — what will DB2 do? Choose *two* answers:
>
> ○ A. Stop processing until the log is restored and then resume
>
> ○ B. *Record only one copy in the BSDS if offload is successful*
>
> ○ C. *Continue to process without the log*
>
> ○ D. Does not record in the BSDS

☑ *The answers are **B** and **C**. When the archive is lost, DB2 continues to process. If the archiving to one log is successful, DB2 records that log in the bootstrap data set.*

Question 5

> Which offline utility do you use to create a conditional restart record?
>
> ○ A. **DSNLOG1P**
>
> ○ B. *DSNJU003*
>
> ○ C. **DSNJU004**
>
> ○ D. **DSN1COPY**

☑ *The answer is **B**. The other utilities print the log or copy data sets.*

Question 6

> If you perform a conditional restart of DB2, what type of mode is the system in?
>
> ○ A. Ready mode
>
> ○ B. *System recover pending mode*
>
> ○ C. System recover mode
>
> ○ D. Stopped mode

☑ *The answer is **B**. The system goes into system recover pending mode after you use a conditional restart control record (CRCR).*

Question 7

> The new advisory pending state of **DBETE**:
>
> O A. *Reduces DBET abends*
>
> O B. Increases start-up time
>
> O C. Causes the system to restart
>
> O D. Automatically removes pending states

☑ *The answer is **A**. This new advisory pending state requires the user to take further action to reset the error status on the object with the DBET error. The **DBETE** state is designed to reduce DBET abends.*

Question 8

> What is the purpose of **DSN1LOGP**?
>
> O A. Updates the active logs
>
> O B. *Formats and displays the active logs*
>
> O C. Truncates the active logs
>
> O D. Switches the active logs

☑ *The answer is **B**. The **DSN1LOGP** utility prints the active log segments you choose and formats the display.*

Question 9

> Which command displays a list of currently running utilities and the **RECOVER LOGAPPLY** phase progress?
>
> O A. *-DIS UTIL(*)*
>
> O B. -DISPLAY DATABASE
>
> O C. -DISPLAY THREAD(*) TYPE(SYSTEM)
>
> O D. -DISPLAY THREAD(*) SERVICE(STORAGE)

☑ *The answer is **A**. In DB2 9, when you use the display utility statement, a new piece of the display shows the phases of the recover phase progress.*

Question 10

How many disk copy pools can you have when using the **BACKUP SYSTEM** utility?

- ○ A. Four copy pools: two for data, two for logs.
- ○ B. *Two copy pools: one for data, one for logs.*
- ○ C. You can assign as many as you need.
- ○ D. You are allowed only one for the utility.

☑   *The answer is **B**. There are two disk copy pools: one for data and one for logs.*

Chapter 6

Question 1

Where in DB2 can you find all the descriptions of the IFCIDs that are shipped with DB2?

○ A. *SDSNMACS*

○ B. **SDSNSAMP**

○ C. Catalog tables

○ D. Directory tables

☑   *The answer is **A**. The data set **yourprefix.SDSNMACS** that is shipped with DB2 contains the IFCID descriptions.*

Question 2

What is the most common trace destination to which trace information is written for DB2?

○ A. GTF

○ B. RES

○ C. *SMF*

○ D. SRV

☑   *The answer is **C**. The System Management Facility (SMF) is the most common destination for traces in DB2.*

Question 3

Which trace is the most costly to run in DB2?

○ A. Accounting

○ B. *Performance*

○ C. Statistics

○ D. Monitor

☑   *The answer is **B**. To avoid high system overhead with performance traces, you should turn on only those performance trace classes that are required to address a specific performance problem.*

Question 4

> Audit trace reports in DB2 provide information about which *two* of the
> following?
>
> O A. *GRANTs*
> O B. *Unsuccessful access attempts*
> O C. Processor resources consumed
> O D. RID pool processing

☑ *The answers are **A** and **B**. Processor resources consumed and RID pool processing information are reported by the accounting trace.*

Question 5

> Accounting traces in DB2 are designed to:
>
> O A. *Collect application program information*
> O B. Collect data-sharing information
> O C. Document sensitive data uses
> O D. Report unsuccessful access

☑ *The answer is **A**. Accounting traces collect application program information and are key to determining a task's activity and whether you are experiencing a DB2 performance problem.*

Question 6

> Before you can send data to SMF (choose *two* answers):
>
> O A. SMF must be stopped.
> O B. No members must be updated.
> O C. *SMF must be running.*
> O D. Member **SMFPRM**xx *must be updated.*

☑ *The answers are **C** and **D**. SMF must be running before you send data to it. To make the facility operational, you must update member **SMFPRMxx** to indicate which types of SMF records it will accept and whether SMF is active.*

Question 7

If you wanted to stop all the traces running in DB2, which of the following commands would you use?

○ A. **-STOP TRACE**

○ B. *-STOP TRACE (*)*

○ C. **-STOP TRACE ALL**

○ D. **-STOP TRACE CLASS ALL**

☑ *The answer is **B**. **STOP TRACE** is not a valid form of the command.*

Question 8

When you install a new set of application programs, which *two* of the following areas would concern you most in regard to storage?

○ A. *EDMPOOL*

○ B. *EDM_SKELETON_POOL*

○ C. **SKPT**

○ D. **CT**

☑ *The answers are **A** and **B**. You want to effectively use the storage but not over-allocate it.*

Question 9

On average, what percentage of free pages should you have in the EDM pool?

○ A. 80 to 90 percent

○ B. 50 to 60 percent

○ C. 0 percent

○ D. *10 to 20 percent*

☑ *The answer is **D**. The percentage of free pages in the EDM pool should be low.*

Question 10

Which fixed thresholds are associated with the buffer pools in DB2?

○ A. **VPSEQT, VPPSEQT, VDWQT**

○ B. *IWTH, DMTH, SPTH*

○ C. **DWQT, VDWQT, VPSEQT**

○ D. **IWTH, DWQT, VPSEQT**

☑ *The answer is **B**. These are the three fixed thresholds in DB2. The other thresholds listed are variable thresholds, whose values you can change.*

Chapter 7

Question 1

> How do you restrict or limit user access to data with the **START DB2** command?
>
> ○ A. *-START DB2 ACCESS(MAINT)*
> ○ B. -**START DB2**, with no parameters
> ○ C. -START DB2 LIGHT(NO)
> ○ D. -START DB2 ACCESS(NO)

☑ *The answer is **A**. The* **ACCESS(MAINT)** *parameter limits access to users who have installation* **SYSADM** *or installation* **SYSOPR** *authority.*

Question 2

> Which command changes to the **CBIPARM** member for restarting DB2?
>
> ○ A. –**SET SYSPARM STARTUP**
> ○ B. –**SET SYSPARM RELOAD(CBIPARM)**
> ○ C. *–SET SYSPARM LOAD(CBIPARM)*
> ○ D. –**SET SYSPARM STARTUP**

☑ *The answer is **C**. This command changes from the current load module to a new module named* **CBIPARM**.

Question 3

> What is the abbreviation for the IRLM command **MODIFY**?
>
> ○ A. **O**
> ○ B. **Y**
> ○ C. **M**
> ○ D. *F*

☑ *The answer is **D**. **F** is the abbreviation for the IRLM* **MODIFY** *command.*

Question 4

Which of the following commands produces thread accounting information to show inactive, active, and indoubt threads?

○ A. –DISPLAY THREAD(*) SERVICE(STORAGE)

○ B. –DISPLAY THREAD(*) SERVICE(WAIT)

○ C. *–DISPLAY THREAD(*) DETAIL*

○ D.– DISPLAY THREAD(*) TYPE(SYSTEM)

☑ *The answer is **C**. Use the **DETAIL** keyword on the **DISPLAY THREAD** command to see accounting information for active, inactive, and indoubt threads.*

Question 5

Which command could leave the database in an inconsistent state?

○ A. –START DATABASE(name) SPACENAME(name) ACCESS(RW)

○ B. *–START DATABASE(name) SPACENAME(name) ACCESS(FORCE)*

○ C. –START DATABASE(name) SPACENAME(name) ACCESS(UT)

○ D. –START DATABASE(name) SPACENAME(name) ACCESS(RO)

☑ *The answer is **B**. Use of the **FORCE** value on the **ACCESS** parameter could leave an index or table space in an inconsistent state.*

Question 6

What does the **CLONE** parameter on the **COPY** utility do?

○ A. Makes another copy of the table

○ B. Checks for clones and then stops

○ C. Does not copy clone table spaces

○ D. *Copies cloned tables*

☑ *The answer is **D**. The **CLONE** option instructs the **COPY** utility to copy a particular cloned table.*

Question 7

> How can you set off logging on the **LOAD** utility even if the default is **LOG YES**?
>
> ○ A. Specify *NOT LOGGED*
>
> ○ B. Specify **DEFAULT**
>
> ○ C. Specify **LOG YES ONLY**
>
> ○ D. Specify **NOT LOGGED ONLY**

☑ *The answer is **A**. If the **NOT LOGGED** attribute is specified for the table space, the **LOAD** utility performs no logging (even though **LOG YES** is the default).*

Question 8

> Which dispatching priorities order is recommended?
>
> ○ A. IRLM, TCP/IP, DBMS address spaces, VTAM
>
> ○ B. DBMS address spaces, VTAM, IRLM, TCP/IP
>
> ○ C. DBMS address spaces, IRLM, VTAM, TCP/IP
>
> ○ D. *VTAM, IRLM, TCP/IP, DBMS address spaces*

☑ *The answer is **D**. VTAM, IRLM, and TCP/IP must always have a higher dispatching priority than all database management system (DBMS) address spaces, attached address spaces, and subordinate address spaces.*

Question 9

> When you are deciding whether or not to use compression, which utility can provide compression estimates?
>
> ○ A. **DSN1COPY**
>
> ○ B. **DSNJU004**
>
> ○ C. **DSN1CHKR**
>
> ○ D. *DSN1COMP*

☑ *The answer is **D**. The **DSN1COMP** stand-alone utility estimates space savings that can be achieved through compression on table spaces.*

Question 10

If you wanted to obtain a listing of the **SYS1.LOGREC** data set, which of the following would you execute?

○ A. **DSN1CHKR**

○ B. *IFCEREP1*

○ C. **DSNJLOGF**

○ D. **REPAIR**

☑ *The answer is **B**. To obtain a listing of the **SYS1.LOGREC** data set information, you would execute the **IFCEREP1** stand-alone utility.*

Index

NOTE: Boldface indicates illustrations and code; t indicates a table.

NOTE: Boldface indicates illustrations and code; t indicates a table.

NOTE: Boldface indicates illustrations and code; t indicates a table.

NOTE: Boldface indicates illustrations and code; t indicates a table.

397

NOTE: Boldface indicates illustrations and code; t indicates a table.
